D1154276

Biography Today

**Profiles
of People
of Interest
to Young
Readers**

Volume 12 — 2003
Annual Cumulation

Cherie D. Abbey
Managing Editor

Kevin Hillstrom
Editor

615 Griswold Street
Detroit, Michigan 48226

Cherie D. Abbey, *Managing Editor*
Kevin Hillstrom, *Editor*

Sheila Fitzgerald, Leif Gruenberg, Laurie Lanzen Harris, Kevin Hile,
Laurie Hillstrom, Sarah Lorenz, and Sue Ellen Thompson, *Staff Writers*

Barry Puckett, *Research Associate*

Allison A. Beckett and Linda Strand, *Research Assistants*

Omnigraphics, Inc.

* * *

Matthew P. Barbour, *Senior Vice President*
Kay Gill, *Vice President — Directories*
Kevin Hayes, *Operations Manager*
Leif Gruenberg, *Development Manager*
David P. Bianco, *Marketing Consultant*

* * *

Peter E. Ruffner, *Publisher*
Frederick G. Ruffner, Jr., *Chairman*

This book is printed on acid-free paper meeting the ANSI Z39.48 Standard. The infinity symbol that appears above indicates that the paper in this book meets that standard.

Printed in the United States

Contents

Preface

Biography Today is a magazine designed and written for the young reader—ages 9 and above—and covers individuals that librarians and teachers tell us that young people want to know about most: entertainers, athletes, writers, illustrators, cartoonists, and political leaders.

The Plan of the Work

The publication was especially created to appeal to young readers in a format they can enjoy reading and readily understand. Each issue contains approximately 10 sketches arranged alphabetically. Each entry provides at least one picture of the individual profiled, and bold-faced rubrics lead the reader to information on birth, youth, early memories, education, first jobs, marriage and family, career highlights, memorable experiences, hobbies, and honors and awards. Each of the entries ends with a list of easily accessible sources designed to lead the student to further reading on the individual and a current address. Obituary entries are also included, written to provide a perspective on the individual's entire career. Obituaries are clearly marked in both the table of contents and at the beginning of the entry.

Biographies are prepared by Omnigraphics editors after extensive research, utilizing the most current materials available. Those sources that are generally available to students appear in the list of further reading at the end of the sketch.

Indexes

A new index now appears in all *Biography Today* publications. In an effort to make the index easier to use, we have combined the **Name** and **General Index** into one, called the **Cumulative Index**. This new index contains the names of all individuals who have appeared in *Biography Today* since the series began. The names appear in bold faced type, followed by the issue in which they appeared. The General Index also contains the occupations, nationalities, and ethnic and minority origins of individuals profiled. The General Index is cumulative, including references to all individuals who have appeared in the *Biography Today* General Series and the *Biography Today* Special Subject volumes since the series began in 1992.

In a further effort to consolidate and save space, the Birthday and Places of Birth Indexes will be appearing only in the September issue and in the Annual Cumulation.

Our Advisors

This series was reviewed by an Advisory Board comprised of librarians, children's literature specialists, and reading instructors to ensure that the concept of this publication—to provide a readable and accessible biographical magazine for young readers—was on target. They evaluated the title as it developed, and their suggestions have proved invaluable. Any errors, however, are ours alone. We'd like to list the Advisory Board members, and to thank them for their efforts.

Sandra Arden, *Retired*
Assistant Director
Troy Public Library, Troy, MI

Gail Beaver
University of Michigan School of Information
Ann Arbor, MI

Marilyn Bethel, *Retired*
Broward County Public Library System
Fort Lauderdale, FL

Nancy Bryant
Brookside School Library,
Cranbrook Educational Community
Bloomfield Hills, MI

Cindy Cares
Southfield Public Library
Southfield, MI

Linda Carpino
Detroit Public Library
Detroit, MI

Carol Doll
Wayne State University Library and Information Science Program
Detroit, MI

Helen Gregory
Grosse Pointe Public Library
Grosse Pointe, MI

Jane Klasing, *Retired*
School Board of Broward County
Fort Lauderdale, FL

Marlene Lee
Broward County Public Library System
Fort Lauderdale, FL

Sylvia Mavrogenes
Miami-Dade Public Library System
Miami, FL

Carole J. McCollough
Detroit, MI

Rosemary Orlando
St. Clair Shores Public Library
St. Clair Shores, MI

Renee Schwartz
Broward County Public Library System
Fort Lauderdale, FL

Lee Sprince
Broward West Regional Library
Fort Lauderdale, FL

Susan Stewart, *Retired*
Birney Middle School Reading Laboratory, Southfield, MI

Ethel Stoloff, *Retired*
Birney Middle School Library
Southfield, MI

Our Advisory Board stressed to us that we should not shy away from controversial or unconventional people in our profiles, and we have tried to follow their advice. The Advisory Board also mentioned that the sketches might be useful in reluctant reader and adult literacy programs, and we would value any comments librarians might have about the suitability of our magazine for those purposes.

Your Comments Are Welcome

Our goal is to be accurate and up-to-date, to give young readers information they can learn from and enjoy. Now we want to know what you think. Take a look at this issue of *Biography Today*, on approval. Write or call me with your comments. We want to provide an excellent source of biographical information for young people. Let us know how you think we're doing.

Cherie Abbey
Managing Editor, *Biography Today*
Omnigraphics, Inc.
615 Griswold Street
Detroit, MI 48226

editor@biographytoday.com
www.biographytoday.com

Congratulations!

Congratulations to the following individuals and libraries, who received a free copy of *Biography Today* for suggesting people who appeared in 2003:

Carol Arnold, Hoopeston Public
   Library, Hoopeston, IL
Vondell Ashton, Washington, DC
Karina Avina, Northhighlands, CA
S. Backus, Brooklyn, NY
Ayanna Black, Southfield, MI
Crystal Brown, Wheatland, OK
Susan Caldwell, Evansville, IN
Lauren Darrow, Alpharetta, GA
Jasmine Dillard, Chicago, IL
Bridget E. Doughtery,
   Wyomissing, PA
Nichole Eason, Laconia, IN
Ashlee Glastetter, Chaffee, MO
Susan Hales, Wimberley, TX
Catherine Harris,
   Pleasant Ridge, MI
Helen Ideno, Chicago, IL
Marti Ingvarsson, Grayling, MI
Leigh Jordan, Lancaster, SC
Lucille M. Koors, Clarence
   Farrington Middle School,
   Indianapolis, IN
Ricza Lopez, Bronx, NY

Miranda Louis, Cambridge, MA
Jasmine McKinney, Stockton, CA
Johnny Missakian, Fresno, CA
Howard Norris, Toledo, OH
Rosemary Orlando,
   St. Clair Shores Public Library,
   St. Clair Shores, MI
Katey Peck, Vienna, VA
   Erica Perez, Chicago, IL
Mimy Poon, San Lorenzo, CA
Tiffany Robertson, Melbourne, FL
Kierra Robinson, Toledo, OH
Janice P. Saulsby, Dr. Phillips High
   School, Orlando, FL
Sherry Shaheen, Oregon, OH
Janet A. Speziale, Hilltop
   Elementary School Library, Lodi,
   NJ
Donna Szatko, Chicago, IL
Autumn Tompkins, Allegan, MI
Miranda Trimm, Allegan, MI
Rose Walker, Brownsburg, IN
Tina Watson, Philadelphia, PA
Hana Yoshimoto, San Rafael, CA

Yolanda Adams 1961-

American Gospel Singer
Creator of the Award-Winning Albums *Mountain
High . . . Valley Low*, *The Experience*, and *Believe*

BIRTH

Yolanda Adams was born on August 27, 1961, in Houston,
Texas. Her mother, Carolyn Adams, was a schoolteacher who
gave piano lessons on the side and was the gospel pianist for
their local church. Her father, Major Adams, was also a teacher

who coached sports at a middle school. Yolanda was the oldest of the Adamses' six children. She has three younger brothers and two younger sisters.

———— " ————

After her father's death, Yolanda joined a youth gospel group. "My brother's godmother knew how close [my dad and I] were, and she thought it would be a good outlet for me, so she convinced my mom to let me try out for the choir, and I made the audition." Although she had lots of experience performing with her church's choir, Yolanda says she started out "singing with my head down, looking at my shoes, just all nervous."

———— " ————

YOUTH

Life in the Adams family revolved around religion and music. Yolanda's mother had been a music major in college, and she exposed her children to all kinds of music. They listened to "everything from Stevie Wonder to Beethoven," Yolanda says — including classical symphonies, rhythm-and-blues, jazz, and modern gospel. At age three, Yolanda sang her first solo, "Jesus Loves the Little Children," in the Baptist church where her mother played the piano and her father sang in the choir. "Our family was always in church," Yolanda recalls. Their involvement in church activities kept the Adams children close to their parents and away from what she calls "the negative elements" in Houston society.

When Yolanda was just a young teenager, her father, Major Adams, taught her how to write checks, pay bills, and invest her money, just in case anything ever happened to him. Four months later, he died from complications following a car accident. Yolanda was only 13 at the time. Her mother was so overwhelmed by grief that Yolanda had to make all the funeral arrangements and take care of her five younger siblings. She says that without her faith in God, she never could have gotten through this difficult period in her life.

Not long after her father's death, Yolanda joined the Southeast Inspirational Choir, a youth gospel group made up of young singers from Houston-area churches. "My brother's godmother knew how close [my dad and I] were, and she thought it would be a good outlet for me," Yolanda explains, "so she convinced my mom to let me try out for the choir, and I made the audition." Although she had lots of experience performing with her church's

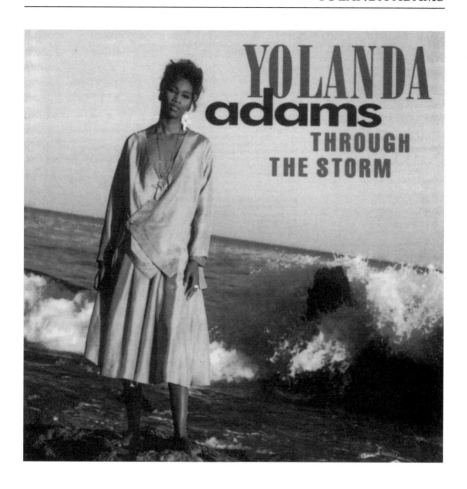

choir, Yolanda says she started out "singing with my head down, looking at my shoes, just all nervous." Despite her shyness, she soon became a lead singer for the Choir. In 1980 their first big hit, "My Liberty," featured a solo by Adams.

EDUCATION

As a student at Sterling High School in Houston, Yolanda dreamed of becoming a model. With her good looks and height of more than six feet, that dream seemed well within her reach. But her grandfather told her that as the oldest of her family's six children, she should set a good example for her siblings by going to college. So after graduating from high school in 1979, she went to her father's alma mater, Texas Southern University. She majored in radio and television communications there, planning to be-

13

come a television news anchor. After serving as an intern at a local television station during her senior year, she was confident of getting a full-time job there when she graduated. But the job fell through, so she decided to follow in her parents' footsteps and become a teacher. She went back to school and got her teaching certificate. She graduated from Texas Southern University in 1983.

Some years later, in 1997, Adams enrolled in Howard University's divinity program to earn her master's degree. But by then her singing career was taking up so much of her time that she had to discontinue her studies.

"I got a chance to see kids on all levels: suburbanite, upper middle class, [and] poor, inner-city kids," Adams says about her years teaching elementary school. "I was teaching school during the week and singing on the weekends. So I had the best of everything."

BECOMING A GOSPEL SINGER

After graduating from Texas Southern, Adams taught second and third grade at Patterson Elementary School for seven years. "I got a chance to see kids on all levels: suburbanite, upper middle class, [and] poor, inner-city kids," she recalls. At the same time, she continued to sing with the Southeast Inspirational Choir. "I was teaching school during the week and singing on the weekends," she says. "So I had the best of everything."

In 1986 Thomas Whitfield, a well-known gospel producer and composer, heard Adams sing with the Choir and offered to help her produce an album. The result was *Just As I Am,* released by Sound of Gospel Records the following year. The album stayed on the Billboard gospel chart for two years and was in the Top Ten for eight months. This caught the attention of Tribute Records, a gospel label that signed Adams to a five-record deal. They produced her second album, *Through the Storm,* in 1991. Adams had written or co-written most of the songs on this album, which won two Dove Awards from the Gospel Music Association and was nominated for a Grammy Award.

By 1992 Adams was earning more from her singing career than from her teaching job, so she decided to leave her job and focus on singing. "It took all the courage I had," she says of her decision. "I never dreamed of leaving the school system, and when I did it was a huge step, but I'm so glad I took that step on faith."

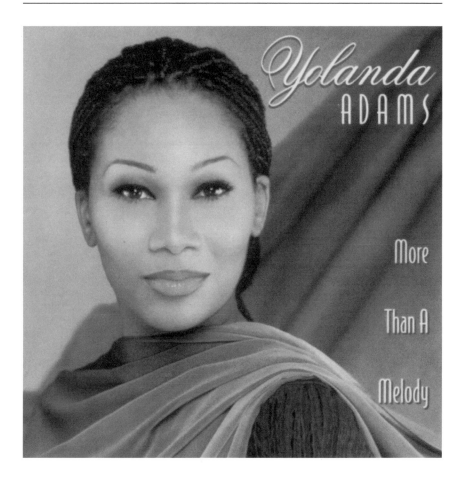

CAREER HIGHLIGHTS

Since that time, Adams has built a successful career as a top gospel singer. Her next release, *Save the World* (1993), showcased her powerful voice and unique way of combining traditional gospel music with contemporary pop and salsa rhythms. She wrote or collaborated on most of its songs, which dealt not only with faith and spirituality but with the problems that confront Christians in today's world. One of the songs, for example, was inspired by a teenage girl in Adams's church who committed suicide, while others dealt with loneliness and depression. Rather than limiting herself to the subject matter of traditional gospel music, she pointed out, "I like to deal with issues that people are facing." *Save the World* was even more successful than her earlier releases, winning three Stellar Gospel Music Awards. It became a top-selling album, spending more than a year on Billboard's gospel chart.

More Than a Melody

Although she had already made three albums, it wasn't until *More Than a Melody* was released in 1995 that people began to think of Adams as more than a gospel singer. This album showed the influence of such pop singers as Anita Baker and Whitney Houston. It also included a re-make of the 1970 Steve Miller hit "Fly Like an Eagle," as well as the rap-inspired "Gotta Have Love." The basic message was still a Christian one. But it was also clear that Adams was trying to reach a broader audience by interspersing jazz and R&B songs with more traditional gospel tunes. When accused of making a "secular" (non-religious) album, Adams replied, "In order to get kids listening to gospel you've got to give them what they're used to listening to." Kids want to hear music with rhythms they recognize, she explained, "so I have to have something in there with a beat."

> ❝
>
> *"In ordered to get kids listening to gospel you've got to give them what they're used to listening to," Adams says. Kids want to hear music with rhythms they recognize, "so I have to have something in there with a beat."*
>
> ❞

More Than a Melody sold more that 100,000 copies and marked a turning point in Adams's career. It led to invitations to perform on the 1996 Soul Train Music Awards, the 1997 Essence Awards, and *The Tonight Show.* President Bill Clinton invited her to sing at a White House Christmas celebration, where she was given a standing ovation, and contemporary gospel singer Kirk Franklin invited her to join his "Tour of Life" stage review. Franklin had made history in 1993 when he became the first singer since Aretha Franklin to sell a million copies of a gospel album. Touring with Kirk Franklin gave Adams a chance to observe an artist who had "crossed over" to a more contemporary, mainstream style without abandoning his roots in traditional gospel music.

In 1996 Adams made what was supposed to be a concert video in front of a live congregation at a church in Washington, D.C. People who had heard her sing began calling the recording company to say that they wanted to listen to her music in their cars, and it soon became clear that she had another album in the works. *Yolanda . . . Live in Washington* sold more than 150,000 copies and brought Adams a second Grammy nomination and a Stellar Award. It was followed two years later by *Songs From the Heart,* a collection of standard gospel songs and hymns interpreted in Adams's own unique

way. This was the last of the five albums she was under contract to record with Tribute/Diadem Records, so Adams began looking around for a recording company that would bring her music to a wider audience.

Joining the Mainstream

One such company was Elektra Records, which had produced albums for such well-known artists as Tracy Chapman, Natalie Cole, and Missy Elliott. Sylvia Rhone, an executive for Elektra, had heard Adams perform with the "Tour of Life" in New York. When Rhone signed her to a five-record contract, Adams became the label's first gospel artist. Rhone compared her to such legendary female vocalists as Dinah Washington, Nancy Wilson, Sarah Vaughan, and Whitney Houston, predicting that Yolanda Adams would be just as famous some day. Elektra was definitely a "mainstream"

Adams performs at the Soul Train Music Awards, March 2002.

label. But unlike other recording companies that had approached Adams in the past, Elektra was not interested in forcing her to change her style or her message to increase her appeal to secular audiences.

Mountain High . . . Valley Low, Adams's first album with Elektra, was released in 1999. It gave her an opportunity to team up with top R&B and pop producers like Keith Thomas, who had worked with Vanessa Williams and Wynonna Judd, and Jimmy Jam & Terry Lewis, who had produced Janet Jackson and Mary J. Blige. With Jam and Lewis she sang the contemporary soul ballad "Open My Heart," in which she asks God for spiritual guidance. The song was picked up by a number of pop and R&B radio stations and became her first big crossover hit, winning a Soul Train Lady of Soul Award for Best R&B/Soul Song. "What surprised me was how many people needed to hear that song," Adams told *Essence* magazine. "It spoke to so many people, so many ages, so many hearts." Also on the album were hip-hop-influenced songs like "Time to Change" and "Yeah," along with others in which jazz and R&B elements could clearly be heard.

Mountain High . . . Valley Low became Adams's "coming out" album, selling more than a million copies and winning a Grammy Award. It was praised for being "both uplifting and inspirational," and it helped disprove the myth that women gospel singers couldn't sell as many albums as men. "Few vocalists can match the range, power, and control of this 38-year-old singer, and these new pop-funk beats give that voice the showcase it deserves," observed the reviewer for the *Washington Post*. The wide exposure the album received on television and mainstream radio stations reassured Adams that she had made the right decision in signing with Elektra. "I need to be in a place where my message can be heard by everyone," she said. At the same time, she made it clear that she had no intention of becoming another Whitney Houston. "As a Christian," she explained, "I'm not supposed to be like everybody else or follow what's going on. I am supposed to tread new ground. I'm out to give God his just due, and my goal is to show people how really cool God is."

—— **"** ——

"What surprised me was how many people needed to hear that song," Adams said about her ballad *"Open My Heart,"* in which she asks God for spiritual guidance. *"It spoke to so many people, so many ages, so many hearts."*

—— **"** ——

Recent Releases

Adams released *Christmas with Yolanda Adams* in 2000, a compilation that featured both gospel hymns and traditional Christmas songs, often with a contemporary R&B sound. After that, she made another live recording in 2001. She had been traveling with the first all-female gospel tour, "Sisters in the Spirit," and her performance at Constitution Hall in Washington D.C became her next live album, *The Experience*. Although Adams was criticized for releasing another album so soon after *Mountain High . . . Valley Low*—especially one that contained seven of the same songs—it won a Grammy Award for Best Contemporary Soul Gospel Album.

Later that same year, Adams released her tenth album, *Believe*. This, too, included some of the same songs that were originally heard on *Mountain High . . . Valley Low*, but it also featured R&B-flavored pop, ballads, and gospel tunes with a gospel choir singing backup. Adams co-wrote four of the songs, including one called "Darling Girl," written as a tribute to motherhood and the birth of her first child. The album as a whole received mixed reviews, but it still debuted at No. 1 on the Billboard gospel charts and won the Soul Train "Lady of Soul" Award for Best Gospel Album.

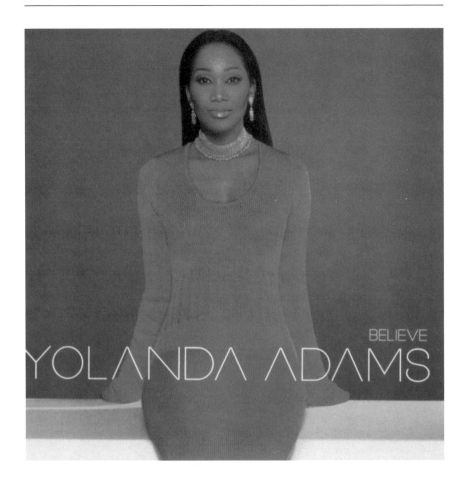

BELIEVE

YOLANDA ADAMS

Reaching Out to Young People

Like the schoolteacher she used to be, Adams has put just as much energy into helping young people as she has into her music career. She is very involved with the FILA athletic wear company's youth outreach program, Operation Rebound. With this program, she visits inner-city schools and speaks to the students about the dangers of substance abuse and the importance of staying in school and getting an education.

Adams has also formed her own management company, Mahogany Entertainment, to help young people who are just starting out as gospel performers. "Our goal is to bring mentorship to young people in gospel music," she explains. She tries to bring their talents to the attention of record companies so that they are well represented and don't have to struggle as hard to get noticed or worry about being taken advantage of.

Some day Adams would like to open an all-girls Christian school with an emphasis on the performing arts. She would also like to build a children's art center in Houston. "I'm hoping my success in the music field can make that happen," she says.

Devoted to Gospel

Despite frequent complaints from fans who accuse her of abandoning gospel for pop, Adams remains devoted to gospel music. She says she will remain true to it for two reasons: "The first reason is that I've never had a desire to sing anything other than gospel music. The second is that I believe we can make gospel just as popular as country music is now." To achieve this, she knows that she will have to show that there is more to gospel music than "choir robes and folks shouting."

"You can't sell beyond the gospel community without alienating that gospel audience," Adams admits. "You just have to have the right song. For artists who are involved in gospel, the whole point is to encourage people to make their lives better, to lift them up. How better to do that than to sing to someone?" She believes that since the terrorist attacks of September 11, 2001, more people have turned to gospel music for comfort and inspiration, and that its popularity will continue to grow during these troubled times.

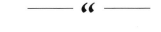

"For artists who are involved in gospel, the whole point is to encourage people to make their lives better, to lift them up. How better to do that than to sing to someone?"

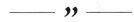

MARRIAGE AND FAMILY

Adams was first married in 1988. But she felt that she was making a mistake almost from the start, and they divorced after only two years. In 1997 she married former New York Jets football player Tim Crawford, Jr., whom she had known since she was 16. They never really lost touch, and when both of them ended up divorced in their 30s, their relationship changed from friendship to romance. Crawford, who now works as a financial advisor, has a teenage daughter from a previous marriage named Ashley, and in January 2001 he and Yolanda had their first child, a girl named Taylor Ayanna. They still live in the Houston area, within a 20-mile radius of Yolanda's mother and five siblings.

*Adams at the Soul Train Awards with
her daughter Taylor, February 2001.*

MAJOR INFLUENCES

Adams says that one of her greatest influences was Rosa Parks, the now-famous African-American civil rights heroine. Adams was only seven years old when Parks refused to give up her seat to a white passenger and move to the back of a public bus in Montgomery, Alabama. Her action helped to spark the civil rights movement. "I think Rosa touched my life in a very strong way," she says, "because I knew that I didn't have to bend or bow down. . . . I could be a strong person, especially a strong black woman."

As far as her music is concerned, Adams says that she has been influenced by a wide range of singers. "I take my jazz from Nancy Wilson, my gospel and R&B from people like Aretha [Franklin], my pop from Celine Dion, and my country from Reba McEntire." Her favorite singers also include Stevie Wonder and Donny Hathaway.

FAVORITE ALBUMS

Adams's favorite album is gospel singer Tramaine Hawkins's *Highway to Heaven*, which she describes as "the first album I got as a youngster that made me say, 'Whoa!'" She also loves Aretha Franklin's two-album set, *Amazing Grace,* and Nancy Wilson's *All My Heart.* "I think they are the epitome of artists," she comments. "They can still belt out a song and make you cry or belt out a song and make you laugh and shout."

HOBBIES AND OTHER INTERESTS

When she has some free time, Adams heads to the golf course. In addition to playing golf with her husband, she enjoys running.

RECORDINGS

Just As I Am, 1987
Through the Storm, 1991

Save the World, 1993
More Than a Melody, 1995
Yolanda . . . Live in Washington, 1996
Songs from the Heart, 1998
*Mountain High . . . Valley Low,*1999
Christmas With Yolanda Adams, 2000
The Experience, 2001
Believe, 2001

SELECTED HONORS AND AWARDS

Stellar Awards (Stellar Awards Gospel Music Academy): 1992, Best Female
Contemporary Gospel Artist, for *Through the Storm;* 1994 (three awards),
Song of the Year, for "The Battle is the Lord's", Contemporary Album of
the Year, for *Save the World*, Best Traditional Female Solo Performance,
for "The Battle is the Lord's"; 1996, Female Vocalist of the Year, for
Yolanda . . . Live in Washington; 2001 (five awards), Artist of the Year,
Female Vocalist of the Year, CD of the Year, Contemporary Female
Vocalist of the Year (all for *Mountain High . . . Valley Low*), Music Video of
the Year, for "Open My Heart"
Dove Awards (Gospel Music Association): 1992 (two awards), Best
Traditional Gospel Album, for *Through the Storm*, Best Traditional Gospel
Song, for "Through the Storm"; 1999, Traditional Gospel Recorded Song
of the Year, for "Is Your All on the Altar?"
Soul Train Music Awards: 1995, Best Gospel Album, for *More Than a
Melody;* 2001, Best Female R&B/Soul Single, for "Open My Heart"
Image Awards (NAACP): 2000, Best Contemporary Gospel Artist, for
Mountain High . . . Valley Low; 2001 (four awards), Outstanding
Performance in a Variety Series/Special, for "Soul Train Lady of Soul
Awards," Outstanding Song, Outstanding Female Artist, Outstanding
Contemporary Gospel Artist (all for "Open My Heart"); 2002,
Outstanding Contemporary Gospel Artist, for *Believe*
Grammy Awards: 2000, Best Contemporary Soul Gospel Album, for
Mountain High . . . Valley Low; 2002, Best Contemporary Soul Gospel
Album, for *The Experience*
American Music Award: 2002, for Favorite Contemporary Inspirational
Artist
Lady of Soul Award (Soul Train): 2002, Best Gospel Album, for *Believe*
Gospel Music Excellence Award (Gospel Music Workshop of America):
2002, Female Vocalist of the Year, Urban Contemporary, for "Never Give
Up"
Best Gospel Artist (Black Entertainment Television): 2002

FURTHER READING

Books

Contemporary Black Biography, Vol. 17, 1998
Contemporary Musicians, Vol. 23, 1999
Who's Who among African Americans, 2002

Periodicals

Chicago Tribune, Dec. 24, 1995, p.2
Current Biography Yearbook, 2002
Detroit Free Press, Dec. 10, 1999, p.D1
Ebony, Aug. 2000, p.42; May 2001, p.58
Essence, July. 2001, p.106
Jet, June 12, 2000, p.55; Feb. 5, 2001, p.61
Today's Christian Woman, Sep.-Oct. 2002, p.94
Washington Post, Feb. 11, 2000, p.NO8

Online Database

Biography Resource Center Online, 2003, articles from *Contemporary Black Biography,* 1998, and *Contemporary Musicians,* 1999

ADDRESS

Yolanda Adams
Elektra Entertainment Group
75 Rockefeller Plaza
New York, NY 10019

E-mail: yolanda@yolandaadams.org

WORLD WIDE WEB SITES

http://www.yolandaadams.org
http://www.elektra.com/elektra/yolandaadams/index.jhtml

BRIEF ENTRY

Olivia Bennett 1989-

American Artist Known for Her Floral Watercolor
Paintings
Raised $33,000 to Aid Afghan Children through Sales
of Her Painting "Let Freedom Bloom"

BIRTH

Olivia Bennett was born in Salt Lake City, Utah, on August 16,
1989. Her father, Matt, is a grocery company executive, and her

mother, Michele, is a homemaker. She has a younger brother, Michael, and a younger sister, Sarah. In 1999, the Bennett family moved to Southlake, Texas, a booming community northeast of Fort Worth.

YOUTH

The first indications of Olivia Bennett's artistic talent appeared when she was in kindergarten. While other children her age tried to master coloring inside the lines, she already showed advanced drawing abilities. It was also around this time that the young girl was diagnosed with leukemia — a type of cancer in which the bone marrow produces abnormal numbers of white blood cells. Doctors treated her disease with chemotherapy, which involved injecting her with toxic chemicals to kill the cancer. Chemotherapy often causes side effects, such as nausea, weakness, and hair loss.

"I think I definitely appreciate life in a different way than I would if I hadn't had cancer," Bennett said.

Bennett underwent chemotherapy for two years. Her mother recalled that the treatments made her very sick: "She was just out, on the couch violently ill." To make matters worse, one medication caused temporary nerve damage that made her hands curl up and become stiff, like claws. "I couldn't even hold a pencil," Bennett remembered. As she recovered from leukemia and chemotherapy, she turned to painting to occupy her time. She eventually overcame the disease and has been in remission (cancer-free) for several years. "I think I definitely appreciate life in a different way than I would if I hadn't had cancer," she stated.

Meanwhile, Bennett's artistic talent attracted considerable attention. When she was in third grade, she won first place in the Utah division of a national competition to design a postage stamp featuring a duck. Her winning painting was eventually turned into a stamp. She sold her first painting at the age of eight, when a visitor noticed it hanging on the wall in her home and insisted on giving her $50 for it. By the time Bennett was 11, a Fort Worth art gallery had asked to exhibit her work and represent her. "I think there is a reason why she is here [on earth]," her mother noted. "She went through so much and then to come out and have this gift . . . it's amazing."

Many of Bennett's watercolor compositions are of flowers.
"Roses and magnolias are my favorites," she says.

EDUCATION

Bennett attended Rockenbaugh Elementary in Southlake. A middle school student, she currently attends Eubanks Intermediate School in Southlake, where she is a straight-A student. "School is always my first priority, so homework comes before anything else," she explained.

Olivia Bennett's painting "Let Freedom Bloom"
raised $33,000 to aid Afghan children.

MAJOR ACCOMPLISHMENT

Despite her young age, Olivia's work has attracted the attention of art lovers across the country. Many people are drawn to the youthful energy in her paintings. In addition, some people find her work to be inspirational and feel that her paintings reflect her triumph over leukemia.

Olivia is best known for her large, vibrant watercolor paintings of flowers. "I don't know why [I paint] flowers," she noted. "I've just always been drawn towards them. Roses and magnolias are my favorites." She often visits flower gardens and takes pictures of the colorful blooms. "Mostly, I paint them from pictures, but when I do paint them live, I try to examine them and look at them, see how they grow," she explained. Her floral paintings have been compared to the works of such famous artists as Georgia O'Keeffe and Claude Monet.

During the summer of 2001 Olivia began experimenting with oil paints. She also expanded the subject matter of her work to include portraits and abstracts. Nearly all of her paintings feature bright colors, which have become a sort of trademark for her. "She loves color, and she's sick of me saying, 'Let's get subtle with some shades,'" said her art teacher, Mary Kay Krell. "We'll get halfway through something, and it's very muted, and she can't stand it any longer. That's her youth."

The first major showing of Olivia's work took place in 2001 at Art in the Square, an annual art festival in Southlake that raises money for charity. The event attracts many fine artists from surrounding states, along with thousands of visitors. Olivia sold dozens of paintings at the festival for between $25 and $350 each. A few months later the 11-year-old was a featured artist at the Thurburn Gallery in Fort Worth, where her work sold for up to $1,000 per painting.

Raising Money to Aid the Children of Afghanistan

The terrorist attacks of September 11, 2001, affected Olivia as they did many other American children. She was stunned by the tragic events and longed to find some way to help the families of those killed in the attack. At the same time, she felt a surge of patriotism and wanted to express it. She soon found an outlet for her feelings. On October 11, 2001, President George W. Bush made a radio address in which he asked the children of the United States to donate money

"My mom and I were driving to Wal-Mart, and President Bush was on the radio asking everyone to donate a dollar to America's fund for Afghan Children. I was very excited. I said, 'Oh my gosh. I want to do my part,'" Bennett remembered. "When I thought about how much freedom we have in this country, I really wanted to do something to help those children. I wanted to paint something big and powerful that would be my tribute to the victims and the heroes from September 11."

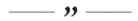

to help the children of Afghanistan, which the U.S. invaded because of its terrorist ties. "My mom and I were driving to Wal-Mart, and President Bush was on the radio asking everyone to donate a dollar to America's Fund for Afghan Children. I was very excited. I said, 'Oh my gosh. I want to do my part,'" Olivia remembered. "When I thought about how much freedom we have in this country, I really wanted to do something to help those children. I wanted to paint something big and powerful that would be my tribute to the victims and the heroes from September 11."

Olivia created a special painting called "Let Freedom Bloom," which shows a rose interwoven with the American flag. She made 199 limited-edition, signed prints and put them up for sale at $495 each. Within about six months, her efforts raised $33,000 for America's Fund for Afghan Children. Her goal was to raise $100,000 by the end of 2002. Thousands of other American children were also inspired to respond to President Bush's message. The fund ended up raising more than $4 million to buy winter clothing and medical supplies for the children of Afghanistan.

In recognition of her charitable contributions, Olivia was invited to meet President Bush in March 2002. She attended a speech at an elementary school in Virginia, during which the president publicly thanked her. "I wanted to single her out as someone who has done a little extra—not a little extra, a lot extra—for the fund to help Afghan boys and girls," Bush stated. Olivia had a chance to speak with the president afterward. "President Bush told me several times how beautiful he thinks the painting is, and that made me feel really good. He told me he thought it was a great way to help the charity and encouraged me to keep it going," she recalled. "It still hasn't sunk in that I actually met the president. It is just so cool. I have always said I wanted to meet the president, but I never thought I would be able to this soon."

> "President Bush told me several times how beautiful he thinks the painting is, and that made me feel really good," Bennett recalled. "It still hasn't sunk in that I actually met the president. It is just so cool."

In September 2002, Olivia was invited to New York City for ceremonies honoring the anniversary of September 11. She donated 3,000 prints of "Let Freedom Bloom" to the families of the victims of the terrorist attacks. It seems likely that her original painting will hang in the September 11 memorial when it is built.

A Promising Future

In 2002 Olivia began working with an agent, Ben Valenty of International Art and Entertainment, who represents other child art prodigies (young people with exceptional talents). "I've probably seen the portfolios of at least 5,000 kids, and many of them were extremely talented," Valenty stated. "But I have only seen what I consider to be a gift three times, and in Olivia's case, I think it is the most profound gift I've ever seen."

A Life In Full Bloom

The Story and Paintings of

Olivia Bennett

In July 2002 Olivia was invited to appear on a special edition of the "Oprah Winfrey Show" dedicated to child prodigies. She ended up selling several paintings to members of Winfrey's staff, and one of her works now hangs in the show's offices. In the fall of 2002 Olivia published a book called *A Life in Full Bloom: The Story and Paintings of Olivia Bennett*. The book tells about her battle with leukemia and her development as an artist, and it also features color reproductions of 40 of her works. "To say I'm going to have a book coming out is a great accomplishment," she noted. "To go to a store and see it on the shelf is going to be a great feeling."

Olivia says that an average painting takes between five and seven hours to complete, although some take over 20 hours. She usually paints late at night in an art studio above the garage in her family's home. Sometimes

———— 〝 ————

"I see things—a flower or a frog or a violin—and it's like they're saying, 'Paint me. Paint me.' Because they're just so beautiful, and I feel as though I'm just driven to paint them. It's like a bolt of lightning. I just have to do it. . . . I think no matter what, I would have become an artist. Being sick just kind of helped me discover my passion sooner rather than later. And it helped me really focus in a way that just a typical life without cancer might not have. And it made me really appreciate that every moment is a unique and rare opportunity, and I should just take advantage of that."

———— 〞 ————

her mother reads aloud to her while she works. Although prints of her paintings now sell for $500, and original canvases sell for $10,000 to $15,000, Olivia claims that the money is not important to her. "I love to paint," she stated. "I see things—a flower or a frog or a violin—and it's like they're saying, 'Paint me. Paint me.' Because they're just so beautiful, and I feel as though I'm just driven to paint them. It's like a bolt of lightning. I just have to do it. . . . I think no matter what, I would have become an artist. Being sick just kind of helped me discover my passion sooner rather than later. And it helped me really focus in a way that just a typical life without cancer might not have. And it made me really appreciate that every moment is a unique and rare opportunity, and I should just take advantage of that."

HOME AND FAMILY

Olivia Bennett continues to live in Southlake with her family. Her parents—neither of whom are artists—are continually amazed by her talent. "Just the other day I was watching her paint, and I was thinking to myself, 'Who is this person?'" her mother noted. "Just within a few paintings she had evolved so much it just blew me away." As Olivia's art gets more and more attention, her parents try to keep her grounded. They never push her to paint and instead encourage her to go to the mall and live the life of a normal teenager.

WRITINGS

A Life in Full Bloom: The Story and Paintings of Olivia Bennett, 2002 (with Derek Partridge)

FURTHER READING

Books

Bennett, Olivia, and Derek Partridge. *A Life in Full Bloom: The Story and Paintings of Olivia Bennett,* 2002

Periodicals

Dallas Morning News, Feb. 21, 2002, p.A21; Mar. 22, 2002, p.N1; Apr. 21, 2002, p.S1
Fort Worth Star-Telegram, Feb. 12, 2002, Metro sec., p.3; July 22, 2002, Metro sec., p.10
Houston Chronicle, Mar. 23, 2002, p.1
Teen People, Apr. 2003, p.145

Online Articles

http://www.mothernaturesparadise.com/
   (*Mother Nature's Menagerie,* "Olivia Bennett," 2002)
http://www.boeing.com/
   (*Boeing Global Advertising,* "Olivia Bennett: Painter" and "Olivia Bennett Radio Essay Transcript," 2003)

Further information for this profile was gathered from interviews with Bennett that aired on the *Today Show,* Mar. 21, 2002, and on the *Oprah Winfrey Show,* July 11, 2002.

ADDRESS

Olivia Bennett
International Art and Entertainment
23121 Antonio Parkway
Suite 140
Rancho Santa Margarita, CA 92688

WORLD WIDE WEB SITE

http://oliviabennett.com/

Mildred Benson 1905-2002

American Novelist and Journalist
Creator of the "Nancy Drew" Mystery Series

BIRTH

Mildred Augustine Wirt Benson—known as Millie to her friends—was born on July 10, 1905, in Ladora, Iowa. Her father, J.L. Augustine, was a doctor, and her mother, Lillian (Mattison) Augustine, was a homemaker.

YOUTH

Throughout her youth, Benson always dreamed of becoming a writer. "I always wanted to be a writer from the time I could walk," she recalled. "'When I grow up I'm going to be a GREAT writer,' I proclaimed to anyone who would listen." Benson published her first story, "The Courtesy," in the *St. Nicholas* children's magazine in 1919. She won a silver badge for her efforts and went on to publish dozens more stories in magazines during her school years.

Benson loved to read as a girl. But her book options were limited because her rural Iowa community was too small to support a public library. She had to satisfy her urge to read by borrowing books from friends and neighbors. "Families had their own libraries and traded with each other. I read constantly and quickly exhausted the stpply of children's books available," she remembered. "As far as I can tell I read every book that they had in the town, regardless of what it was about."

> **"I think that everything I did in my childhood had a terrific impact on what I did [later in life]. I was given quite a bit of freedom. Although my mother tried to make me into a traditional person I resisted that. I was just born wanting to be myself and I couldn't see why girls couldn't do the same thing that boys were allowed to do."**

Benson grew up at a time when activities for girls were often restricted. But she was an independent-minded girl who refused to allow her gender to determine the types of activities she enjoyed. "I detested dolls, but played with hundreds of tiny wooden spools, moving them as actors on a stage," she noted. Benson also participated in sports — which was somewhat unusual for girls in those days — and became an accomplished swimmer and diver. "I think that everything I did in my childhood had a terrific impact on what I did [later in life]," she stated. "I was given quite a bit of freedom. Although my mother tried to make me into a traditional person I resisted that. I was just born wanting to be myself and I couldn't see why girls couldn't do the same thing that boys were allowed to do."

EDUCATION

Benson attended the University of Iowa, where she worked on the student newspaper and became a champion diver. She also wrote and sold numer-

Benson recalled reading constantly when she was young, quickly exhausting the supply of books for children.

ous short stories during her college years to help pay for her education. After earning her bachelor's degree in English in 1925, Benson spent a year working as a reporter and society editor for the *Clinton Herald,* a newspaper based in Clinton, Iowa. Then she returned to the university to study journalism. "Journalism was just what I was interested in," she explained. "It was opening up for the first time for women back then." In 1927 Benson became first person — male or female — to earn a master's degree from the school of journalism at the University of Iowa.

CAREER HIGHLIGHTS

Benson wrote more than 130 books between 1927 and 1959. Most of her books were published as part of various popular series aimed at juvenile audiences. She wrote some books under her own name (she was known as Mildred A. Wirt during her career as a novelist), but most of her books were published under pseudonyms (false names used by writers). Benson is best known for creating the enormously popular teenage detective Nancy Drew. Under the pseudonym Carolyn Keene, she wrote 23 of the first 30 books in the "Nancy Drew Mystery" series between 1930 and 1953.

Although several other authors wrote "Nancy Drew" books over the years, Benson is widely acknowledged as the original creator of the character.

In addition to the "Nancy Drew" series, Benson wrote a number of "Dana Girls" mysteries under the pseudonym Carolyn Keene. She also published books in the "Ruth Fielding" series under the pseudonym Alice B. Emerson; the "Kay Tracey" series under the pen name Frances K. Judd; the "Honey Bunch" series as Helen Louise Thorndyke; and the "Dot and Dash" series as Dorothy West. Among the series published under her own name were the "Ruth Darrow Flying Stories" and "Penny Parker Mystery Stories." Benson worked as a journalist throughout the years that she wrote juvenile novels. In 1959 she decided to stop writing novels and concentrate on her career in journalism. She published thousands of newspaper articles and columns during her years as a reporter.

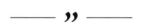

"All the books that were handled as series in those days were written under pen names. The reason they did that was so that if an author ceased to write the book, it could be turned over to another author and you do not change the name [on the cover]."

Writing for the Stratemeyer Syndicate

After earning her master's degree in journalism, Benson went to work as a reporter for the *Iowa City Press-Citizen*. It was there that she met her first husband, Asa Wirt, who was a correspondent for the Associated Press. In the late 1920s Benson traveled to New York City to look for free-lance writing jobs. She met with Edward Stratemeyer, the head of a publishing company that produced several popular series of juvenile fiction, including the "Bobbsey Twins" and "Hardy Boys" books. Stratemeyer's company, known as the Stratemeyer Syndicate, hired lots of unknown writers to produce the frequent installments in its many series of books. All of these series were published under pseudonyms. "All the books that were handled as series in those days were written under pen names," Benson explained. "The reason they did that was so that if an author ceased to write the book, it could be turned over to another author and you do not change the name [on the cover]."

The people who actually wrote the books for the Stratemeyer Syndicate were bound by the terms of a strict contract. They received a flat fee for their manuscripts, and they gave up all rights to receive royalty payments on future sales of the books. They were not allowed to take credit for the books they wrote for Stratemeyer under pseudonyms. As far as readers knew, "Carolyn Keene" and the other Syndicate pseudonyms were real people. The authors were also forbidden to use the pseudonyms for work published outside of the Syndicate.

Creating Nancy Drew

Stratemeyer contacted Benson shortly after she returned to Iowa. The publisher asked her to write several books in his established "Ruth Fielding" series under the pseudonym Alice B. Emerson. Pleased with this early work, Stratemeyer invited Benson to write the first few volumes of a new series called "Nancy Drew Mysteries." This series, which would feature a teenage girl detective, was intended as a counterpart to the Syndicate's popular "Hardy Boys" books.

Stratemeyer provided Benson with a one-page outline that included the names of the main characters and the general story line. The writer then expanded upon this information to produce full-length novels featuring a heroine who became one of the most beloved characters in young adult literature. "The plots provided me were brief, yet certain hackneyed [unoriginal] names and situations could not be bypassed," she recalled. "Therefore I concentrated upon Nancy, trying to make her a departure from the stereotyped heroine commonly encountered in series books of the day."

Benson intentionally made Nancy Drew into an idealized character. Nancy was attractive and popular, bold and intelligent, independent and athletic. "I wanted to do something different," Benson explained. "The heroines of girls' books back then were all namby-pamby. I was expressing a sort of tomboy spirit." At first it appeared as if the author had gone too far in creating her heroine. The publisher did not like her version of the character and initially threatened to reject the book. "Mr. Stratemeyer expressed bitter disappointment when he received the first manuscript, *The Secret of the Old Clock,* saying the heroine was much too flip and would never be well received," Benson remembered. But he reluctantly agreed to publish Benson's stories. "When the first three volumes hit the market they were an immediate cash-register success for the syndicate," she recalled triumphantly.

The "Nancy Drew" Series Becomes a Blockbuster

Benson's character attracted the attention of girls across the country, who scrambled to buy the early volumes in the "Nancy Drew" series. "America's blond-haired, blue-eyed, lock-picking dynamo instantly captured

A modern cover of The Secret of the Old Clock,
the first book in the "Nancy Drew" series.

readers' hearts when the first title in the series, *The Secret of the Old Clock,* was released in 1930," wrote Karen Plunkett-Powell, author of *The Nancy Drew Scrapbook.* "And why not? Unlike the majority of her rather prim, Victorian predecessors, Nancy burst onto the scene early in the Great Depression as a courageous, intelligent, and inspiring heroine."

By 1933 the "Nancy Drew" books were outselling the most popular series of boys' books by a two to one margin. The girl detective became a publishing phenomenon that continues to draw readers 70 years later. The books have sold 100 million volumes and been translated into 17 languages. They have also inspired a television series, several movies, and a variety of products. Benson wrote the first seven volumes of the "Nancy Drew" series, which were published between 1930 and 1932. Then the Stratemeyer Syndicate notified her that, due to financial problems, it wanted to cut her usual payment of $125 in half. Benson refused to accept the lower amount, and another writer (war historian and novelist Walter Karig) produced the next three volumes in the series. But Benson eventually came back to write 16 more "Nancy Drew" books (numbers 11 through 25, and 30). Her last contribution to the series, *The Clue of the Velvet Mask,* was published in 1953.

> "
>
> *Benson intentionally made Nancy Drew into an idealized character who was attractive and popular, bold and intelligent, independent and athletic. "I wanted to do something different. The heroines of girls' books back then were all namby-pamby. I was expressing a sort of tomboy spirit."*
>
> "

Through the years, the basic facts of the series have remained unchanged. Nancy Drew lives with her doting father, the handsome and wealthy lawyer Carson Drew, in the fictional town of River Heights. Her mother died when she was three, so 16-year-old Nancy is cared for by their German housekeeper, Hannah Gruen. Nancy's best friends are tomboy George (short for Georgina) Fayne and timid Bess Marvin. Her steady boyfriend, Ned Nickerson, is a star athlete at Emerson College. Nancy drives around in her blue roadster, encountering mysteries and solving crimes. She considers herself the equal of any boy and most adults, and insists upon being taken seriously by everyone she meets.

Many fans claim that the key to the series' success is the main character that Benson created in 1930, when Nancy Drew seemed to be ahead of her time. "Before those books came out, literature for girls were entirely a different style," Benson noted. "The most exciting things they put in stories for girls were going to camp or making a trip somewhere. They didn't promote the idea at all that girls could have careers or experiences on an equal level with boys. Girls were ready for that theme. . . . Now that kind of woman is common, but then it was a new concept, though not to me. I just naturally thought that girls could do the things boys did."

"Before those books came out, literature for girls was entirely a different style. The most exciting things they put in stories for girls were going to camp or making a trip somewhere. They didn't promote the idea at all that girls could have careers or experiences on an equal level with boys. Girls were ready for that theme. . . . Now that kind of woman is common, but then it was a new concept, though not to me. I just naturally thought that girls could do the things boys did."

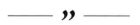

Continuing as a Journalist

During the years when she produced the "Nancy Drew" books, Benson also wrote a number of other books and continued working as a journalist. For the most part, she considered writing novels to be a good way to earn extra money. "It was just a job to do," she admitted. "Some things I liked and some things I did not like. It was a day's work. I did it just like I did my newspaper work. I wrote from early morning to late night for a good many years." In fact, Benson once wrote 13 novels in a single year while also working as a journalist, raising her young daughter, and caring for her husband, who had suffered a stroke. She claimed that she never read any of her books once she had finished them. "Because the minute I do I'm going into the past, and I never dwell on the past," she explained. "I think about what I'm doing today and what I'm going to do tomorrow."

In addition to writing for the "Nancy Drew" series, Benson produced volumes for several other series in the Stratemeyer Syndicate. For example, she wrote 12 books for the "Dana Girls" mystery series under the pseudonym Carolyn Keene. The Dana Girls were younger versions of Nancy Drew who solved mysteries between classes at the Starhurst Boarding School. The popularity of Benson's work for the Syndicate led to opportunities to publish her own stories independently, under her own name. Her favorite was her "Penny Parker" mystery series, which followed the daring adventures of the daughter of a newspaper editor. Benson's novels under her own name were successful enough that in 1936 publisher Cupples and Leon asked her to create her own series. Known as "Mildred A. Wirt Mystery Stories," the series eventually included eight titles.

Benson and her first husband moved from Iowa to Ohio during these years, settling first in Cleveland and then in Toledo. In 1944, during World War II, she began working as a reporter at the *Toledo Times*. She reported on events at city hall and on significant local court cases. She worked hard to prove herself, even though she was certain that she would lose her job at the end of the war, when large numbers of American men started returning from military duty. "I was told after [World War II] ended there would be layoffs and I would be the first one to go," she remembered. "I took the warning seriously and for years I worked with a shadow over my head, never knowing when the last week would come." But the pink slip that she feared never arrived. Instead, she continued working at the paper and its successor, the *Toledo Blade,* for a grand total of 58 years.

Benson's first husband died in 1947. Three years later she married George Benson, who was the editor of the *Toledo Times*. He died in 1959, the same year she published her last novel, *Quarry Ghost*. At this point Benson decided to quit writing novels and concentrate on her career as a journalist. In the late 1960s a publisher approached her about starting a new series of juvenile novels. But Benson realized that she no longer felt connected with the problems of modern teens. "For a moment I was tempted. Plots began to percolate," she remembered. "Then fog settled over my typewriter. The teenagers for whom I wrote lived in a world far removed from drugs, abortion, divorce, and racial clash. Regretfully, I turned down the offer. Any character I might create would never be attuned to today's social problems."

The Mystery of Nancy Drew's Creator

For 50 years after she wrote the first book in the "Nancy Drew" series, Benson honored the terms of her contract with the Stratemeyer Syndicate and never publicly took credit for her work. As the popularity of the series grew, however, fans began searching for information about Carolyn Keene. As it became clear that Carolyn Keene was a pseudonym, the true identity of the series' author became a big mystery. Some sources claimed that Edward Stratemeyer had written the first three "Nancy Drew" books himself. After Stratemeyer's death in 1930, his daughter Harriet Stratemeyer Adams took charge of the publishing company. Many people assumed

Benson visited with her alter-ego, Nancy Drew, in the children's department of the Main Library in Toledo, Ohio, 2001.

that Adams had also taken over writing the Syndicate's most popular series at this time.

In fact, Adams did become more involved with the "Nancy Drew" books over the years. In the late 1940s Benson started noticing differences between her original manuscripts and the published versions of the books. It started out with minor changes of wording, then gradually expanded to include rewriting or deleting whole sections of the text. She suspected that Adams was behind the changes, which were a major factor in Benson's decision to stop writing "Nancy Drew" books in 1953.

Revealing the Truth

In 1959 Adams began rewriting the early volumes of the series. The publisher claimed that she was reworking the original stories in order to bring them up to date and eliminate racial stereotypes and other objectionable material. But Benson, along with many "Nancy Drew" fans, felt that Adams also weakened the main character. "She made her into a traditional sort of a heroine," Benson noted. "More of a house type."

During the 1960s Adams became the primary author of new volumes in the "Nancy Drew" series. Around this time, Adams also began claiming in interviews that she had written all of the "Nancy Drew" books from the beginning of the series. Benson, of course, knew that this claim was false. But she continued to honor her contract and did not contradict the publisher's statements. Still, some fans remained curious about the origins of the series. A librarian named Geoffrey S. Lapin conducted research over several years and finally tracked down Benson in 1969. He called her at the *Toledo Blade* offices and asked whether she was the original creator of Nancy Drew. Benson admitted that she had written the early books in the series, but explained that she was sworn to secrecy by the terms of her contract.

The truth behind the mystery of Nancy Drew's creator finally came out in 1980, when the Stratemeyer Syndicate became involved in a highly publicized lawsuit. Adams wanted to change the publisher of the Syndicate's many series of books from Grosset and Dunlap to Simon and Schuster. But Grosset and Dunlap sued to maintain control over the "Nancy Drew" series, arguing that it had contributed to the books' success by providing original illustrations. Benson was called to testify in court to help establish the ownership of the series. She informed the court that she had written many of the early volumes featuring Nancy Drew. Her lawyer produced a number of

"Years ago, when I tapped out the opening lines of the first Nancy Drew mystery ever written, I never dreamed that I would spend most of my life defending it," Benson once wrote. *"Does authorship really matter? Probably not, but loyal Nancy Drew fans, especially the earliest readers, deserve true information, rather than slanted or incorrect publicity statements."*

documents, including letters from Adams, to prove her claim. "Even if I didn't get it across to the court," she stated, "I know who wrote those books, and I set up the form which made Nancy Drew top sellers." Grosset and Dunlap ended up maintaining hardcover print rights to the first 56 titles in the "Nancy Drew" series, while Simon and Schuster received rights to publish all later volumes.

Despite the fact that Benson's authorship had been proven in court, Adams continued to claim that she had written the entire "Nancy Drew" series until her death in 1982. Some periodicals and reference books repeated this false claim through the early 1990s. Adams undoubtedly had an enormous influence on the series. She was an outstanding business-woman whose career was closely linked with the books' success, and she wrote many of the later volumes. But Benson was the person who created the popular main character. "Years ago, when I tapped out the opening lines of the first Nancy Drew mystery ever written, I never dreamed that I would spend most of my life defending it," Benson once wrote. "Does authorship really matter? Probably not, but loyal Nancy Drew fans, especially the earliest readers, deserve true information, rather than slanted or incorrect publicity statements."

——— " ———

"All of [Benson's] tales display a certain crafts-manship, a clear narrative line, and the suspense that Edward Stratemeyer said was essential in books for young readers," wrote Anita Susan Grossman in the **San Francisco Chronicle.** *"Many of her stories — long out of print — hold up surprisingly well, with an appeal that is not entirely due to their period charm. Adult collectors of children's books overwhelmingly prefer the old Nancy Drews to the updated, rewritten versions that have come along since 1959."*

——— " ———

Celebrating Nancy Drew

Benson finally started receiving public recognition for her role in creating Nancy Drew in the 1990s. In 1993 fans and scholars held an academic conference about the series at the University of Iowa. Benson — now in her late 80s — was invited to take part as a special guest. "All of [Benson's] tales display a certain craftsmanship, a clear narrative line, and the suspense that Edward Stratemeyer said was essential in books for young readers," wrote Anita Susan Grossman in the *San Francisco Chronicle*. "Many of her stories — long out of print — hold up surprisingly well, with an appeal that is not entirely due to their period charm. Adult collectors of children's books overwhelmingly prefer the old Nancy Drews to the updated, rewritten versions that have come along since 1959."

The Iowa conference received a great deal of media attention. Benson was interviewed for a number of sources, including *Good Morning America* and *People* magazine. "I always knew the series would be successful," she said. "I just never expected it to be the blockbuster that it has been. I'm glad that I had that much influence on people." Many experts at the conference

Nancy Drew has been popular in many different forms for the past 70 years. Here she is shown in a scene from Nancy Drew, *an original TV movie starring Maggie Lawson as the teenage sleuth. This contemporary version of the mystery series was shown on ABC-TV in December 2002.*

praised the "Nancy Drew" series for providing young women with a role model who gave them the confidence and independence to pursue careers. Others commended the books for helping children learn to enjoy reading.

The conference brought Benson a great deal of public attention. She soon started receiving a huge amount of fan mail at her *Toledo Blade* office. "Most of them identified with [the character of Nancy Drew]. In my fan mail that I receive, they say that they were inspired to go do things for themselves, to go build themselves careers. I think it was incentive to go out in to the world and to become someone as a woman," she noted. "Most of them say, 'Nancy influenced me greatly,' and, you know, 'Today I am a lawyer,' 'I'm a doctor,' 'I'm a judge.' And I get some from boys, too, but mostly from girls." Until her eyesight began to fail, Benson made an effort to write back to all her fans. "I answer each letter, probably because of a throwback to my own kid days when I wrote to movie stars and then hung around the village post office, hoping for a reply," she admitted.

The Final Chapter

Benson continued working at the *Toledo Blade* during the 1990s, although she gradually scaled back her activities as a reporter. In 1990 she began writing a weekly column called "On the Go with Millie Benson." The column was aimed at active senior citizens, "people who are willing to go out and do things," she explained. "It's slanted toward elderly people, but it covers a wide scope of people, too." In 1997 Benson was diagnosed with lung cancer, but she came back to work the next day. Whenever someone had the nerve to suggest that she retire, she always responded, "Talk to my lawyer."

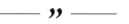

"I always knew the series would be successful," Benson said. *"I just never expected it to be the blockbuster that it has been. I'm glad that I had that much influence on people."*

In 2001 Benson became the subject of a 30-minute documentary film, *The Storied Life of Millie Benson,* that aired on Toledo's public television station, WGTE-TV. Health issues forced her reluctantly to enter semi-retirement in January 2002, though she continued to prepare a monthly column for the paper called "Millie Benson's Notebook."

On May 28, 2002, Benson became ill at work and was taken to a Toledo hospital. She died later that evening at the age of 96. She managed to finish her last column, which was about her love of books and libraries, before her death. Her colleagues rushed to honor her contributions to the field of journalism. "Millie Benson was one of the greatest women writers and journalists of the 20th century," said John Robinson Block, editor-in-chief of the *Toledo Blade*. "She was gutsy and daring, a living embodiment of her Nancy Drew heroine. She influenced generations of *Blade* reporters."

The Underwood typewriter Benson used to write the first "Nancy Drew" books now resides in the Smithsonian Institution in Washington, D.C. Her papers, including a personal scrapbook she kept during her youth, form an exhibit at the Iowa Women's Archives in the University of Iowa Library System. "So now it is time for the final chapter, seemingly one destined from the beginning," Benson once wrote. "A fadeout becomes the most difficult of all, for though the story is finished, the reader must be led to believe that the very best lies directly ahead. New worlds to conquer! New horizons to explore!"

Benson working at her desk at the Toledo Blade *in the mid-1990s. She continued to work as a journalist until just before her death in 2002.*

MARRIAGE AND FAMILY

Benson was married twice. In 1928 she married Asa Alvin Wirt, an Associated Press correspondent. They had one daughter, Margaret (known as Peggy), before he died in 1947. Three years later Millie married George A. Benson, a newspaper editor. Her second husband died in 1959. Benson lived in the Old Orchard neighborhood of Toledo until her death in 2002.

HOBBIES AND OTHER INTERESTS

Benson remained active well into her 90s. She enjoyed swimming and golf for much of her life. She also had a strong interest in archaeology and made several trips to Mexico and Central America to study pre-Columbian cultures. On one trip during the 1960s, she traveled through the remote jungles of Guatemala in a dugout canoe.

Of all her hobbies, flying was Benson's favorite. She first took flying lessons in 1959, following the death of her second husband. "Learning to fly was sort of accidental," she recalled. "I was sent to the airport for a story and they had this $5 promotion going. That $5 promotion cost me hundreds and hundreds of dollars." Benson eventually earned private, commercial, instrument, and seaplane pilot's licenses. She also owned her own plane for many years and logged thousands of hours in the sky.

SELECTED WRITINGS

Note: Mildred Wirt Benson published more than 130 juvenile novels during her career. Many of these works were contributions to series written under various pseudonyms that were also used by other writers. The following list of selected writings focuses on the novels written under her own name and those written under her best-known pseudonym, Carolyn Keene.

"Nancy Drew Mystery Stories," Under Pseudonym Carolyn Keene

The Secret of the Old Clock, 1930
The Hidden Staircase, 1930
The Bungalow Mystery, 1930
The Mystery at Lilac Inn, 1930
The Secret at Shadow Ranch, 1930
The Secret of Red Gate Farm, 1931
The Clue in the Diary, 1932
The Clue of the Broken Locket, 1934
The Message in the Hollow Oak, 1935
The Mystery of the Ivory Charm, 1936
The Whispering Statue, 1937
The Haunted Bridge, 1937
The Clue of the Tapping Heels, 1939
The Mystery of the Brass Bound Trunk, 1940
The Mystery at the Moss-Covered Mansion, 1941
The Quest of the Missing Map, 1942
The Clue in the Jewel Box, 1943
The Secret in the Old Attic, 1944
The Clue in the Crumbling Wall, 1945
The Mystery of the Tolling Bell, 1946
The Clue in the Old Album, 1947
The Ghost of Blackwood Hall, 1948
The Clue of the Velvet Mask, 1953

"Dana Girls Mystery Stories," Under Pseudonym Carolyn Keene

The Secret at the Hermitage, 1936
The Circle of Footprints, 1937

The Mystery of the Locked Room, 1938
The Clue in the Cobweb, 1939
The Secret at the Gatehouse, 1940
The Mysterious Fireplace, 1941
The Clue of the Rusty Key, 1942
The Portrait in the Sand, 1943
The Secret in the Old Well, 1944
The Clue in the Ivy, 1952
The Secret of the Jade Ring, 1953
Mystery at the Crossroads, 1954

"Penny Parker Mystery Stories," Under Name Mildred A. Wirt

The Tale of the Witch Doll, 1939
The Vanishing Houseboat, 1939
Danger at the Drawbridge, 1940
Behind the Green Door, 1940
The Clue of the Silken Ladder, 1941
The Secret Pact, 1941
The Clock Strikes Thirteen, 1942
The Wishing Well, 1942
Ghost Beyond the Gate, 1943
Saboteurs on the River, 1943
Hoofbeats on the Turnpike, 1944
Voice from the Cave, 1944
The Guilt of the Brass Thieves, 1945
Signal in the Dark, 1946
Whispering Walls, 1946
Swamp Island, 1947
The Cry at Midnight, 1947

"Mildred A. Wirt Mystery Stories," Under Name Mildred A. Wirt

The Clue at Crooked Lane, 1936
The Hollow Wall Mystery, 1936
The Shadow Stone, 1937
The Wooden Shoe Mystery, 1938
Through the Moon-Gate Door, 1938
Ghost Gables, 1939
The Painted Shield, 1939
The Mystery of the Laughing Mask, 1940

Other Novels, Under Name Mildred A. Wirt

The Sky Racers, 1935
The Twin Ring Mystery, 1935
Carolina Castle, 1936
Courageous Wings, 937
Linda, 1940
Pirate Brig, 1950
Dangerous Deadline, 1957 (under name Mildred Wirt Benson)
Quarry Ghost, 1959 (under name Mildred Wirt Benson)

HONORS AND AWARDS

Boys' Life-Dodd Mead Prize: 1957, for *Dangerous Deadline*
Ohio Women's Hall of Fame: 1993
Iowa Women's Hall of Fame: 1994
Lifetime Achievement Award (Ohio Newspaper Women's Association): 1997
Lifetime Achievement Award for Outstanding Journalism (*Toledo Blade*): 1998
Edgar Allan Poe Special Award (Mystery Writers of America): 2001

FURTHER READING

Books

Dyer, Carolyn Stewart, and Nancy Tillman Romalov, eds. *Rediscovering Nancy Drew,* 1995
Kismaric, Carole, and Marvin Heiferman. *The Mysterious Case of Nancy Drew and the Hardy Boys,* 1998
The 100 Most Popular Young Adult Authors, 1997
Plunkett-Powell, Karen. *The Nancy Drew Scrapbook,* 1993
Something about the Author, Vol. 65, 1991; Vol. 100, 1999
Writers' Directory, 1999

Periodicals

Detroit News, Aug. 13, 1971, p.B9
Editor and Publisher, June 3, 2002, p.9
The Lion and the Unicorn, Vol. 18, No. 1, 1994 (special Nancy Drew edition)
Los Angeles Times, May 30, 2002, p.B12; May 31, 2002, p.E1
Milwaukee Journal Sentinel, June 9, 2002, p.3

New York Times, Apr. 19, 1993, p.A1; May 9, 1993, p.D7; July 11, 1998, p.B7;
   May 30, 2002, p.A23; June 2, 2002, p.6
Newsday, Nov. 18, 1998, p.B6
People, Dec. 21, 1998, p.143
Publishers Weekly, May 30, 1986, p.30; Sep. 26, 1986, p.12
USA Today, Apr. 14, 1993, p.D6
Washington Post, May 30, 2002, pp. B7, C1

Online Articles

http://www.lib.uiowa.edu/spec-coll/Bai/benson.htm
   (*University of Iowa Libraries,* "The Ghost of Ladora," Nov. 1973)
http://www.lib.uiowa.edu/spec-coll/Bai/lapin.htm
   (*University of Iowa Libraries,* "The Ghost of Nancy Drew," Apr. 1989)

Online Database

Biography Resource Center Online, 2002, article from *Contemporary Authors Online,* 2002

WORLD WIDE WEB SITES

http://www.lib.uiowa.edu/spec-coll/Bai/lapin.htm
http://sdrc.lib.uiowa.edu/iwa/findingaids/html/BensonMildred.htm

Alexis Bledel 1981-

American Actress
Star of the TV Series "Gilmore Girls" and the Movie
Tuck Everlasting

BIRTH

Alexis Bledel was born in Houston, Texas, on September 16, 1981. Both of her parents are multimedia artists (artists who use audio and video components in their work). Her father, Martin, was born in Argentina, while her mother, Nanette, was born in Mexico. Alexis and her younger brother, Eric, grew up speaking Spanish at home. "It's my first language," she said. "I learned English in school."

YOUTH

As a young girl, Bledel was terribly shy and never felt as if she fit in. To help her overcome these feelings, her parents encouraged her to become involved in community theater in Houston when she was eight. "My parents felt that theater would help me adjust better," she recalled. Bledel went on to perform in productions of *Our Town, The Wizard of Oz,* and *Aladdin.*

When Bledel was 14, she stopped by a booth at a local mall that was staffed by talent scouts from a modeling agency. The talent scouts liked her look, and she soon began training to work as a model. Part of the training involved reading commercials in front of a video camera. The shy teenager found this part of the process very painful. "It's horrifying to see yourself on video," she explained. "It's unnatural, like having mirrors around you all day."

> "It's horrifying to see yourself on video. It's unnatural, like having mirrors around you all day."

Bledel worked as a catalog model throughout high school, although she admits that she disliked some aspects of modeling. "I hated it because they were constantly telling me to lose weight and to change my appearance," she remembered. "But it was a good way to make money." Her modeling career also gave her the opportunity to travel to some of the world's major cities, like New York, Los Angeles, Tokyo, and Milan. It also brought her closer to her mother, who took time off from her own career to travel with her daughter. "I realized how dedicated she was," Bledel stated. "My mom had put her life on hold to be with me."

EDUCATION

Bledel graduated from an all-girls Catholic high school in Houston in 1998. "It was my choice to go there because it was a good school," she noted. "And I like being challenged. It was really good for girls to be separated from boys in subjects like math, because statistically they're more apt to raise their hands and speak up." Bledel was an excellent student, except when it came to gym class. She was not athletic and would go to great lengths to avoid participating in gym. "It's not something I'm proud of, but my friend and I would write excuse notes and sign each other's parents' signatures," she admitted.

After graduating from high school, Bledel attended New York University's Tisch School of the Arts for a year. She enjoyed her studies as a film major. "The first year's an overview where you learn about editing, the camera, and writing," she recalled. "I loved it. There are a lot of really creative people, there is a constant exchange of ideas. We talk about what's been done and all the rules for filmmaking and then we talk about how to break them." By the end of her freshman year, Bledel felt certain that her life would revolve around writing or directing films. But a few months later, she left college to pursue an unexpected opportunity as an actress.

> "The whole process of going on auditions and getting cast [for "Gilmore Girls"] took less than a month. It all happened so fast that I didn't really get time to weigh my alternatives. I had really wanted to get a university education. This acting thing had happened accidentally, but still it was one of those opportunities you just can't ignore."

CAREER HIGHLIGHTS

Winning a Role in a New TV Series

During her freshman year in college, Bledel had continued modeling and had begun working with a manager. In the fall of 1999, her manager arranged for her to audition for a role in a new television series called "Gilmore Girls." Bledel went to the audition, though she never really expected to land the part. After all, she had very little acting experience. Her career plan at that time was to finish college and then begin working as a director or screenwriter. "I always thought that I would work behind the camera, because it's a more comfortable place for me to be, really," she explained.

To her surprise, Bledel aced her audition and was asked to join the cast of the "Gilmore Girls" in the role of Rory Gilmore, the sweet and intelligent 16-year-old daughter of a single mother. "The whole process of going on auditions and getting cast took less than a month," she recalled. "It all happened so fast that I didn't really get time to weigh my alternatives. I had really wanted to get a university education. This acting thing had happened accidentally, but still it was one of those opportunities you just can't ignore."

Bledel and Graham from "Gilmore Girls."

Bledel made the difficult decision to put college on hold and move to Los Angeles, California, to pursue a career as an actress. "I was just worried about leaving school, because I know it's important to have a degree, and I just wanted to make the right decision," she stated. "When you do a pilot for a TV show, you don't know if it's going to work out or not. So I took a little leap of faith that the material was good and that people would like it."

Bledel was initially attracted to "Gilmore Girls" because of the high quality of the script written by series creator Amy Sherman-Palladino. "I thought it was funny. I was laughing out loud when I read it," she remembered. "And there are so many great dramatic elements in the writing, as well as the comedy. You get to see both sides of [Rory's] personality, which is a plus. She's not crying all the time. And it's also not, like, all silly jokes. It's got more of an edge and it's more real, so she seems more realistic."

Sherman-Palladino had auditioned thousands of girls for the part of Rory. She explained that Bledel's lack of acting experience actually helped her land the role. "She's got this angel face. She's just so beautiful," Sherman-Palladino said. "And despite how beautiful she is, Alexis is truly an amazing kid. She's just a good soul. She's got a good heart, and she just doesn't know how good or smart she is. She's just a kid. She's so real. There's nothing false that comes out of her. And she is innocent. I was looking for innocence, and that's something that's really hard to find in kids who work [in show business]. When kids work, they're not so innocent anymore."

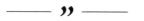

"She's got this angel face. She's just so beautiful," said "Gilmore Girls" creator Amy Sherman-Palladino. "And despite how beautiful she is, Alexis is truly an amazing kid. She's just a good soul. She's got a good heart, and she just doesn't know how good or smart she is. She's just a kid. She's so real. There's nothing false that comes out of her. And she is innocent. I was looking for innocence, and that's something that's really hard to find in kids who work [in show business]. When kids work, they're not so innocent anymore."

But Bledel's lack of experience — as well as her sudden move across the country from New York to Los Angeles — caused her some problems at first. "It's been really crazy," she acknowledged. "I had to get a car and learn to be a better driver so I can get around LA. Just the basic process of moving has been overwhelming. Then there's all the press and starting shooting and wanting to be good — it's a lot. I'm a mix of emotions — I'm very excited, but at the same time, it's all a lot to take in."

Starring on "Gilmore Girls"

The first episode of "Gilmore Girls" aired on the WB television network on October 5, 2000. The series centers on the relationship between a single mother, Lorelai Gilmore (played by Lauren Graham), and her daughter, Rory (played by Bledel). They live in the fictional small town of Stars Hollow, Connecticut, where Lorelai works as the manager of an inn. Lorelai became pregnant with Rory when she was 16 years old. She defied her proper, wealthy parents by deciding to have the baby and raise her alone. Mother and daughter have grown up together and share many interests, an addiction to coffee, and even their wardrobes. In fact, the innocent, bookish Rory sometimes seems more mature than her mother.

In the early episodes of the series, Lorelai must go to her parents for money in order to send Rory to an expensive, private high school. Her par-

The cast of "Gilmore Girls."

ents agree to pay the tuition, under the condition that Lorelai and Rory come to dinner once a week at their elegant Hartford mansion. The series follows Lorelai's struggle to relate to her parents as well as her own trials as a parent.

During its first season, "Gilmore Girls" aired at 8:00 p.m. on Thursdays, placing it in direct competition with the popular series "Friends" and "Survivor." But the show received rave reviews from critics and soon found a dedicated audience among young women. "'Gilmore Girls' is nothing short of a TV miracle: a family show that's sweet, but not too syrupy, bitingly funny, but not mean-spirited, and fun for viewers of all ages, without appealing to the blandest common denominator," wrote Alan Sepinwall in the *Newark Star-Ledger*. "'Gilmore Girls' seduces viewers with its own fantasy world—well-scrubbed New England town, elegant and happily hip young mom, a general sense of equilibrium—but the cast's chemistry bubbles and the script is exceptional," said John Carman in the *San Francisco Chronicle*.

"Gilmore Girls" went on to be named Outstanding New Series by the TV Critics Association and receive a Viewers for Quality Television Award.

Bledel earned Best Actress honors from the Family Television Awards and the Family Friendly Forum Awards. The show moved to 8:00 p.m. on Tuesday nights during its second season, where its main competition came from "Buffy the Vampire Slayer." It drew an enthusiastic audience of 5.2 million weekly viewers in 2001.

As "Gilmore Girls" began its third season in the fall of 2002, Bledel's character was applying to Harvard University and struggling to decide between her steady boyfriend and the dangerous new boy in town. "It's nice to play a character for so long that I like so much, because it's interesting to see her branch out," she noted. "It's nice to be part of something that you're really proud of. Everyone jokes that I'm too lucky, that the show just kind of caught on, and I haven't had the painful experience of being on something I'm not proud of. But that doesn't mean I appreciate 'Gilmore Girls' any less."

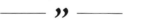

> "[Tuck Everlasting] *is just a great story with a lot of moral dilemmas. It's the kind of great storytelling that's been lost on our generation. It's not showy, in your face, or special effects. It's classic."*

Appearing in the Film *Tuck Everlasting*

Bledel's strong performance on "Gilmore Girls" led to several offers of roles in movies. "The show has definitely given me opportunities," she noted. "I guess I was sort of surprised but I hadn't had any prior experience with television, so I didn't really know what to expect." Still, the demands of shooting a TV series left Bledel with little time for anything else. She worked on "Gilmore Girls" 14 hours per day, five days per week, for nine months each year. The remaining three months, when the show was on hiatus, was her only chance to pursue film roles.

Bledel's first role on the big screen came in the live-action Walt Disney film *Tuck Everlasting*, which was released in October 2002. The movie was adapted from a best-selling 1975 young adult novel by Natalie Babbitt. (An entry on Babbitt will appear in *Biography Today* in 2003). The book was named one the most important children's books of the 20th century by *School Library Journal*, and it is required reading for many American schoolchildren. "It's just a great story with a lot of moral dilemmas," Bledel explained. "It's the kind of great storytelling that's been lost on our generation. It's not showy, in your face, or special effects. It's classic."

Scenes from Tuck Everlasting.
Above: Bledel and Jesse Tuck, played by Jonathan Jackson.
Right: Bledel as Winnie Foster.
Below: Bledel with Amy Irving as her controlling mother and Ben Kingsley as The Man in the Yellow Suit.

In the film version, the story takes place in 1914. Bledel plays Winnie Foster, an independent-minded 15-year-old girl from a wealthy family. "Her parents want her to be a refined young lady," Bledel noted. "And she's not. She's kind of rebellious. She just wants to do her own thing, but she's stifled at every turn by her mother." Bledel was the first person to audition for the role of Winnie. Director Jay Russell claimed that he knew immediately that she was the right person for the part. "When I set out to cast Winnie, I had a feeling that I might never find her. She is in practically every scene. It is her movie," Russell stated. "Alexis Bledel was the very first person I met for the role, and I knew instantly when she walked in the door that she was Winnie. Alexis has a timelessness about her. She doesn't belong to any particular century or any particular year."

In *Tuck Everlasting*, Bledel's character faces a life-changing dilemma. When Winnie learns that her domineering mother is planning to send her away to boarding school, she runs away from home and becomes lost in the woods. She eventually stumbles upon a handsome young man drinking from a beautiful, hidden spring. Jesse Tuck (played by Jonathan Jackson) is the youngest member of a very unusual family, which also includes his father, Angus (played by William Hurt), his mother, Mae (played by Sissy Spacek), and his older brother, Miles (played by Scott Bairstow). The Tucks welcome Winnie into their home and let her in on a secret. By drinking from the magical spring, they have become immortal (they live forever and never die).

Each member of the Tuck family views their immortality differently. The parents see it as a mixed blessing, while the sons' feelings run to opposite extremes. "The different characters react to it differently," Bledel related. "Jesse's character finds so much joy in being able to experience things over and over again, and take trips and see the world, with all the time he has. And then you have Miles' character, who is just tortured by the fact that he's around forever because he's lost his [wife and child]." As Winnie falls in love with Jesse, she must decide whether to drink from the spring and remain with him forever, or return to her normal life. For her part, Bledel claims that she would not choose to drink from the spring. "The film raises a lot of issues regarding the ability to live forever and the darker side of that," she noted. "I just don't think I'd want to see all my friends and family die while I live on."

Response to the Film

Tuck Everlasting received mixed reviews from film critics. Some reviewers praised its sensitive handling of deep issues and claimed that it would appeal to a wide audience. "*Tuck Everlasting*, a sweeping romantic fable about love and mortality, targets an audience of girls in their early teens, but has been made with such skill and sensitivity that its appeal spans generations," said Kevin Thomas in the *Los Angeles Times*. But other reviewers felt that the movie did a poor job of capturing the magic of the novel. "*Tuck Everlasting* is the softest, sorriest excuse for so-called 'inspirational cinema' that Hollywood has produced this year," wrote Craig Outhier in the *Orange County Register*. "It's overnarrated and underwritten, unimaginatively filmed and inflated with gaseous platitudes that rise, helium-like, into a vast and featureless sky of strained morality."

Bledel enjoyed her first film acting experience, although she admitted feeling out of place among big-name actors like Hurt and Spacek. "When I started working on *Tuck* I was this ball of nerves, because here I was with these real actors who had won Academy Awards and everything," she said. "They're all very accomplished and I'm . . . not. But making the movie made me feel like more of an actress, and I can't wait to make another." Bledel also felt a little strange while shooting her early romantic scenes with Jackson. "I had never met Jonathan before the day we filmed our first scene," she noted. "But there I was, dancing around a campfire in a Victorian undergarment in front of a crew I'd just met and kissing an actor I'd just met. That's just one of the absurdities of making movies."

> "I had never met Jonathan Jackson before the day we filmed our first scene. But there I was, dancing around a campfire in a Victorian undergarment in front of a crew I'd just met and kissing an actor I'd just met. That's just one of the absurdities of making movies."

Despite her success as an actress, Bledel remains uncertain about the future direction of her career. She says that she plans on "making a couple of good movies with good people I can learn from, just to make sure this is what I really want to do for the rest of my life." Starring in a popular TV series and movie has earned Bledel many fans, especially among young women. But she resists the idea of being a role model for teenagers. "There's all this emphasis on actors and entertainers, and there's so much more we could all be paying attention to," she stated. "There are teens volunteering, inventing things, making a difference. Plenty of people do things that are so much more redeeming than what I do, which is pretend to be someone else on a daily basis for entertainment value. Television and movies are a distraction and release for people, which I think is healthy, but there are so many girls out there who are so much more important than entertainers."

HOME AND FAMILY

Bledel, who is not married, lives in Los Angeles. But she loves her home state and takes every opportunity to visit friends and family in Houston. "It's so refreshing to go home because it puts everything in perspective. When I drive around town, so many buildings I pass are where something happened in my life. Certain neighborhoods are like different phases in my life," she explained. "Texas is like it's own country in a way. Everyone is so friendly. Plus, it has the best barbeque!"

Bledel remains close to her parents, whom she admires. "My parents are role models because they're strong people," she noted. "They've been very supportive of me my whole life." She claims that her relationship with her mother is different than the relationship between Rory and Lorelai Gilmore, but just as close. "We have much more of a traditional mother-daughter relationship," she stated. "But we can talk about almost anything."

> "There's all this emphasis on actors and entertainers, and there's so much more we could all be paying attention to. There are teens volunteering, inventing things, making a difference. Plenty of people do things that are so much more redeeming than what I do, which is pretend to be someone else on a daily basis for entertainment value. Television and movies are a distraction and release for people, which I think is healthy, but there are so many girls out there who are so much more important than entertainers."

HOBBIES AND OTHER INTERESTS

Bledel spends her spare time pursuing such relaxing hobbies as reading, writing, hiking, photography, and going to the movies. "Sometimes I feel like I am an old person trapped in a young person's body," she admitted. "I'm boring. I go to movies. I read. That's about it." She also enjoys playing the piano, and she keeps a keyboard in her trailer on the "Gilmore Girls" set. Another of her favorite pastimes is shopping, particularly at Target. "I love Target," she said. "How can anyone not love Target? When I'm bored, I go to Target. When I'm upset, I go to Target. I don't know what it is about Target. If you need something, it turns into 10 things."

HONORS AND AWARDS

Best Actress (Family Television Awards): 2000, for "Gilmore Girls"
Best Actress in a Drama (Family Friendly Forum): 2002, for "Gilmore Girls"

FURTHER READING

Periodicals

Dayton Daily News, Oct. 11, 2002, p.C3
Detroit Free Press, Oct. 9, 2002, p.F1
Entertainment Weekly, Apr. 6, 2001, p.99
Girls' Life, Aug./Sep. 2002, p.42
Houston Chronicle, Oct. 4, 2000, p.1
Los Angeles Daily News, Oct. 9, 2002, p.U4
Los Angeles Times, Oct. 11, 2002, p.F12
Newark (N.J.) Star-Ledger, Oct. 5, 2000, p.37
Seventeen, May 2002, p.144
Teen People, June 1, 2002, p.99
Toronto Sun, Oct. 9, 2002, p.56
USA Today, June 14, 2001, p.D4
Variety, Oct. 2, 2000, p.32; Sep. 9, 2002, p.27
YM, Mar. 2002, p.94

Online Articles

http://www.filmmonthly.com/Profiles/Articles/ABledel/ABledel.html
   (*Filmmonthly,* "Life and Love Everlasting for Alexis," Oct. 2, 2002)
http://filmforce.ign.com/articles/373/373676p1.html
   (*Filmforce,* "An Interview with Alexis Bledel," Oct. 8, 2002)

ADDRESS

Alexis Bledel
"The Gilmore Girls"
4000 Warner Boulevard
Burbank, CA 91522

E-mail: gilmoregirls@talk.thewb.com

WORLD WIDE WEB SITE

http://www.thewb.com/

Barry Bonds 1964-

American Professional Baseball Player with the
San Francisco Giants
Holds the Record for Hitting the Most Home Runs
(73) in a Single Season
Five-Time Winner of the National League Most
Valuable Player Award

BIRTH

Barry Lamar Bonds was born on July 24, 1964, in Riverside,
California. His father, Bobby Bonds, was a professional baseball player. His mother, Patricia (Howard) Bonds, stayed at

home to take care of Barry and his two younger brothers, Bobby Jr. and Ricky.

YOUTH

A few years after Barry was born, his father signed a contract to play professional baseball for the San Francisco Giants. Bobby Bonds was a very good ballplayer who possessed an unusual combination of speed and power. In fact, he hit 30 home runs and stole 30 bases in five different seasons during his career—more than any other player in baseball history.

One of Bobby Bonds's teammates on the Giants was the great Willie Mays, a member of the Hall of Fame who ranks among the all-time leaders in home runs, hits, runs, and runs batted in (RBIs). The elder Bonds and Mays became close friends, and Mays became young Barry's godfather.

> *"He definitely took to baseball at an early age,"* his mother remembered. *"He could hit the ball from the first day he lifted the bat. You'd walk in the door and he'd get a bat and ball and make you pitch to him."*

Barry and his brothers were raised in an upper-class neighborhood in San Carlos, California, a short distance from the Giants' home field, Candlestick Park. Barry's baseball skills became apparent when he was just a boy. "He definitely took to baseball at an early age," his mother remembered. "He could hit the ball from the first day he lifted the bat. You'd walk in the door and he'd get a bat and ball and make you pitch to him." By the time he was two years old, Barry could hit a whiffle ball hard enough to break a window.

When Barry was four, he began accompanying his father to the ballpark. He enjoyed playing in the Giants' clubhouse. Sometimes he would steal sticks of gum from the players' lockers and stuff them into his mouth to make a big wad, like the pros chewed. By the time he was five, Barry was allowed to wear a miniature Giants uniform and shag fly balls in the outfield alongside his father and Mays. He and his brother even signed autographs for their father's young fans. "The cutest thing I remember about Barry in those days was him signing autographs," his mother said. "Barry and Ricky would wait behind the fence outside the clubhouse with all the other youngsters. When kids couldn't get Bobby's autograph, they'd settle for Barry's or Ricky's."

Barry cherished the time he spent with his father at Candlestick Park, because Giants' road games often kept Bobby Bonds away from home. "I really remember more about my mom," Barry noted. "She did everything for me. She always took me to football or baseball practice. She always wrote 'from Dad' on the Christmas presents. My mom was at all the school events. My dad never went. He was playing baseball." Being the son of a professional baseball player created other problems for Barry as well. For example, he had trouble connecting with other kids his age. "You don't know who your friends are at times," he explained. "You don't know if they want to be your friend because you're the son of Bobby Bonds."

Bonds had trouble connecting with other kids his age. "You don't know who your friends are at times. You don't know if they want to be your friends because you're the son of Bobby Bonds."

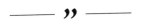

EDUCATION

Bonds attended Serra High School, an all-boys Catholic school in San Mateo, California. He was an outstanding athlete who played running back on the football team, guard on the basketball team, and centerfield on the baseball team. But baseball was always his best sport. He led his team to the Central Coast sectional championship three straight years. During his senior year, his batting average was a remarkable .467.

News about Bonds's exploits eventually reached the pros. Before long, professional baseball scouts were coming to see him play. In one game, a scout asked Bonds's coach to let his star player use a wooden bat like the pros used (high school players were allowed to use either wood or aluminum bats, but most chose aluminum because it allowed them to hit the ball farther). Bonds picked out a wooden bat and hit the next pitch over the rightfield wall.

Bonds had a difficult decision to make when he graduated from high school in 1982. He had always planned to go to college, but he was selected by the San Francisco Giants in the major league baseball draft. The team offered him a $70,000 contract to play in their minor league system. Bonds was tempted, but he turned down the money and instead went to Arizona State University on a baseball scholarship.

Bonds was an outstanding player for the Arizona State baseball team. He hit .347 over his three-year career and led the Sun Devils to the College World Series twice, though they were defeated in the championship both

The Bonds family in the 1970s.
From left: Barry, Bobby Jr., Bobby, Patricia, Rick.

times. During his sophomore year, he tied a National Collegiate Athletic Association (NCAA) record by getting seven straight hits in the College World Series. In his junior year, he hit 23 home runs and was named to the *Sporting News* All-America team.

Although Bonds was one of the best players on the Sun Devils baseball squad, he had trouble getting along with his teammates. He tried kidding around with the guys, but the other players generally viewed him as arrogant and boastful. "I liked the hell out of Barry Bonds," said Arizona State Coach Jim Brock. "Unfortunately, I never saw a teammate care about him. Part of it would be his being rude, inconsiderate, and self-centered. He bragged about the money he turned down, and he popped off about his dad. I don't think he ever figured out what to do to get people to like him." After completing his junior season at Arizona State, Bonds declared himself eligible for the pro baseball draft. He left college in 1985 without completing his bachelor's degree.

CAREER HIGHLIGHTS

Major League Baseball — The Pittsburgh Pirates

Bonds was selected sixth overall in the 1985 Major League Baseball draft by the Pittsburgh Pirates. He started out playing for the Pirates' Class A minor league team in Virginia. In professional baseball, most players start in the minor leagues, where they get the training they need to become good enough for a major league team. The Rookie League is the lowest, then Class A, Class AA, up to Class AAA. Bonds started out in Class A, where he hit .299 with 13 home runs. One of his teammates was Bobby Bonilla, who would become one of Bonds's best friends. In 1986 Bonds moved up to the Pirates' Class AAA farm team in Hawaii, where his batting average was .311. But the talented young player did not remain in the minor leagues for long.

One day, Pirates general manager Syd Thrift came to see the Class AAA club take batting practice before a game in Phoenix. Thrift watched as the lefthanded Bonds hit six balls in a row over the rightfield fence. "Any good hitter can do that," the general manager told him. "I'd like to see you hit a few over the leftfield fence." (It is generally considered easier for a left-handed hitter to pull the ball to rightfield. Hitting for power to the opposite field demonstrates true strength.) Bonds proceeded to hit five balls in a row over the leftfield fence. He then turned to Thrift and said, "Is that good enough for you?" Thrift took Bonds back to Pittsburgh with him that night, and the young player remained in the big leagues from that time on.

Bonds made an immediate impact as a rookie with the Pirates. Wearing number 24 like his godfather, Willie Mays, he got a base hit in his first game with the team and logged his first home run within a week. Even though he joined the team two months into the 1986 season, he still managed to lead all rookies in the league with 16 home runs, 36 stolen bases, and 48 RBIs. Unfortunately, the Pirates finished in last place in their division with a 64-98 record. "We may have lost, but we're not losers," Bonds stated. "We're young. We're getting better. In a year, two years, somewhere down the line, we are going to tip the city of Pittsburgh right on its ear."

During the 1987 season, Bonds batted leadoff and switched from center-field to leftfield. He had another solid season, batting .261 with 25 home runs and 32 stolen bases. The Pirates missed the playoffs again, but the team improved to post a .500 record. In 1988 Bonds raised his batting average to .283 while hitting 24 home runs and stealing 17 bases. Although his numbers were respectable, some people compared him unfavorably to his father and claimed that he was not playing to his full potential. In 1989

Bonds in 1991, while playing for the Pittsburgh Pirates.

Bonds hit 19 home runs, one of which broke the major league record of 407 career homers by a father-son combination. His stolen base total remained constant at 32, while his batting average dropped to .248. Once again, the Pirates failed to make the playoffs.

Bonds's contract expired between the 1989 and the 1990 seasons. The Pirates offered him a new contract worth $850,000 per year, while Bonds asked for a salary of $1.6 million per year. When the two sides could not reach an agreement, they took the matter to an arbitrator (an objective third party who listens to arguments on both sides and then makes a binding decision). After the arbitrator sided with the Pirates, Bonds grew determined to prove his worth. "I think Barry is one of those people who has to be challenged—whether it's by his dad, the media, fans, or whoever," said Pirates Manager Jim Leyland. "He's zeroed in and focused more now than any time since he's been here. He's a talented guy. Now he's coming of age."

National League MVP

Bonds was a solid, dependable player during his first four years with the Pirates, but he was not exceptional. Beginning in 1990, however, he transformed himself into the most productive player in the major leagues and

71

led the Pirates to three straight National League East titles. Bonds's career turnaround came about in an unusual way. "I went to get a haircut," he recalled, "at Fred Tate's barbershop in Pittsburgh. I'm getting my hair cut, and they have the radio on. A guy on the radio says what a great *athlete* Randall Cunningham is, but what a great *quarterback* Joe Montana is. I weighed the two and thought, I'm so bored with having great ability. I want to be a great *player* like Joe Montana. So that haircut was my inspiration. I realized that what I'd been doing—cutting myself short—was wrong. Wrong to me, my team, and even the game. That's when I thought, I'm going to work my tail end off before it becomes too late."

———— " ————

"I'm getting my hair cut, and they have the radio on. A guy on the radio says what a great **athlete** *Randall Cunningham is, but what a great* **quarterback** *Joe Montana is. I weighed the two and thought, I'm so bored with having great ability. I want to be a great player like Joe Montana. So that haircut was my inspiration. I realized that what I'd been doing—cutting myself short—was wrong. Wrong to me, my team, and even the game. That's when I thought, I'm going to work my tail end off before it becomes too late."*

———— " ————

Before the 1990 season, Bonds started a weight training program and spent hours running sprints and practicing in the batting cage. He showed up at spring training in the best shape of his life. Recognizing his new strength and power, his coach moved him from leadoff hitter to the fifth spot in the batting order. Bonds felt more comfortable in this key power position in the lineup. He responded by hitting a career-best .301 with 33 home runs and 52 stolen bases. In addition, he improved his slugging average—a measure of a hitter's effectiveness calculated by dividing the total number of bases reached on all hits by the total number of at bats. His slugging average of .565 was the best in the league. He also won a Gold Glove Award for his fielding. At the end of the 1990 season, Bonds was selected as the National League Most Valuable Player and the *Sporting News* Major League Player of the Year. The Pirates finally made the playoffs, but they lost to the Cincinnati Reds in the National League Championship Series (NLCS). The only disappointing aspect of Bonds's phenomenal season was that he hit only .190 in the playoffs.

The 1991 season started off on a bad note for Bonds. Frustrated by losing another contract arbitration hearing during the offseason, he had a highly publicized shouting match with Manager Jim Leyland in spring training. But Bonds overcame the controversy to hit .292 with 25 homers and 43 steals, narrowly missing a second consecutive MVP award. The Pirates made the playoffs again with a 98-64 record, but they lost to the Atlanta Braves in the NLCS. The media began criticizing Bonds for his poor playoff performance, as he hit just .148 over the seven-game series against the Braves.

Bonds was disappointed when his best friend on the Pirates, Bobby Bonilla, was traded before the 1992 season. Bonds signed a one-year contract worth $4.6 million, but he made it clear that he intended to become a free agent at the end of the season. Although Bonds had turned into the biggest star on the Pirates, few people expressed regret that he intended to leave the team. He was not close to any of his teammates besides Bonilla, and many of the players found him to be a negative presence in the clubhouse. In fact, one of his Pirates teammates said that "I'd rather lose without Barry Bonds than win with him."

Over the course of his career with the Pirates, Bonds also developed a terrible relationship with the Pittsburgh media. Reporters criticized him as rude and arrogant. Bonds admitted that he disliked dealing with the press, but claimed that it was only because he was a private person. He expressed anger that reporters characterized him as a bad person, and asked that they judge him instead by his performance on the field. "I'm not a media person. I don't like to answer the same questions. I just like to play baseball. I'm not into the other stuff. I turn down a lot of interviews. It's the United States of America. I have freedom of choice," he stated. "I feel the press puts a stamp on certain players and once they stamp you as a 'bad person' then that's what they feed on and there's nothing you can do about it. I know in my heart the type of ballplayer I am and the type of person I am."

Bonds had another outstanding year in 1992, hitting .311 with 34 home runs and 39 stolen bases and winning another Gold Glove Award. He claimed his second National League MVP honor and was named Associated Press Player of the Year. But disappointment awaited him once again in the playoffs. The Pirates led the Braves in the last inning of the deciding game of the NLCS. Bonds fielded a single to left and threw the ball to home plate. But the throw was too late and the Braves scored the winning run.

Bonds catches a ball during this World Series game, October 19, 2002.

The San Francisco Giants

Following his impressive 1992 season, Bonds attracted a lot of attention in the free agent market. To the star player's delight, the best offer came from his father's old team, the San Francisco Giants. The owner of the Giants, Peter Magowan, offered Bonds a six-year contract worth $44 million, making him the highest-paid player in baseball at that time. In fact, his average salary of $7.3 million per year was more than his father and god-father had earned in their entire careers. "My head blew up like a bal-loon," he recalled. "I wanted to go to the Empire State building and jump, since I could fly at that point."

Bonds was thrilled to have an opportunity to play for his hometown team. "I have never been more excited to play in a city in my entire life than I am now," he stated. He hoped that joining the Giants would give him a chance to make a fresh start. He even changed his uniform number to 25, his father's old number, since the club had retired Mays's 24. "My [new] teammates really took to me differently," he noted. "It wasn't about how you dressed or what you said—it was about how you play the game. They saw this guy play hard and work out every day. They said, 'This kid doesn't play for the money. He plays to be better than everybody.'" To make the deal even sweeter for Bonds, the Giants also hired his father as the team's batting coach.

Although the Giants had finished 26 games out of first place the previous year, they entered the 1993 season with a crop of good young players and a new manager, Dusty Baker. Bonds showed his determination to contribute by smacking a home run in his first at-bat in a Giants uniform. He went on to post the best season of his career. He became one of the most feared hitters in baseball, posting a .336 average with a league-leading 46 home runs, 123 RBIs, and .677 slugging percentage. At the end of the season, he received his third MVP award. Bonds thus became only the tenth player to win back-to-back MVPs, and the first player to do so with two different teams. Although the Giants improved significantly and won 103 games, they missed the playoffs by one game.

"I'm not a media person. I don't like to answer the same questions. I just like to play baseball. I'm not into the other stuff. I turn down a lot of interviews. It's the United States of America. I have freedom of choice. I feel the press puts a stamp on certain players and once they stamp you as a 'bad person' then that's what they feed on and there's nothing you can do about it. I know in my heart the type of ballplayer I am and the type of person I am."

The Giants Continue to Struggle

The 1994 season ended two months early when a labor dispute between team owners and players led to a strike. Bonds was hitting .312 with 37 home runs and 29 steals when the season concluded. In 1995, some opposing teams decided that the best way to deal with Bonds's impressive skills at the plate was to avoid giving him any good pitches to hit. He ended up leading the league in walks with 120 that year, though he still managed to hit .294. His 33 home runs and 31 stolen bases gave him his third career 30-30 season in those categories. Despite his personal accomplishments, however, the Giants finished in last place in their division.

The Giants remained in the NL West cellar during the 1996 season, but Bonds posted another impressive year. In addition to setting a new league record with 151 walks, he batted .308 with 42 home runs and 40 stolen bases. He thus became only the second player in major league history to post a 40-40 season, and he joined his father, Willie Mays, and Andre

Dawson as the only players to achieve 300 home runs and 300 stolen bases in a career. "It doesn't seem real right now," he said of joining the 300-300 club. "I've still got a lot of years left and it doesn't seem like it should be here that fast."

Prior to the 1997 season, the Giants gave Bonds a two-year contract extension worth $11.5 million per year. The team also made a few roster changes that helped the Giants cruise to a division title and a spot in the playoffs. Unfortunately, they lost to the Florida Marlins in the NLCS. "We're all down, and all losses are tough," Bonds said afterward. "It was very frustrating. We went out there and played hard. They went out there and played hard. They won." Bonds had another good year in 1997, hitting .291 with 40 home runs and 37 stolen bases. This was the fifth 30-30 season of his career, tying the record held by his father. Once again, however, the star player disappeared during the postseason, knocking out only three hits.

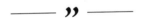

"Everything is perfect in that one particular second," Bonds said of his home-run swing. *"It's in slow motion. You don't hear anything, you don't even feel it hit your bat. That's the zone."*

In 1998 Bonds hit .303 with 37 home runs and 28 stolen bases as the Giants barely missed the playoffs. The following year Bonds missed some games due to injuries, and his numbers dropped to .262 with 32 home runs and 16 stolen bases. In 2000 the Giants moved to a new home field, Pacific Bell Park. Bonds liked the shorter fences and responded by hitting a career-high 49 home runs. He improved his average to .306 and finished second in MVP voting. The Giants won their division in 2000 for the second time in four years, but once again they lost in the NLCS.

Setting the Home Run Record

The 2001 season was a very special one for Bonds. On April 17 he hit his 500th career home run. "I never dreamed of hitting 500 home runs," he stated. "Everything after that is like icing on the cake." Bonds continued hitting home runs at a remarkable rate over the next few months. As the season progressed, it became clear that he would have a chance to beat the single-season home run record of 70 that had been set by St. Louis Cardinals slugger Mark McGwire three years earlier.

As Bonds made his bid to become baseball's new home run king, some people noticed a slight improvement in the star player's attitude toward

*Bonds hits his record-
setting 73rd home run,
October 7, 2001.*

*Bonds reacts to his
record-setting home run.*

*Bonds runs the bases
with a smile, after his
73rd home run.*

teammates, fans, and reporters. He seemed more willing to sign auto-graphs and more patient with the media. "He's made an effort," said Giants Manager Dusty Baker. "Sometimes Barry is tough to deal with, but most of the time he's a gentleman." "I'm just making myself a little bit more accessible to the public, as well as the media," Bonds noted. "I haven't in the past, and it has affected me."

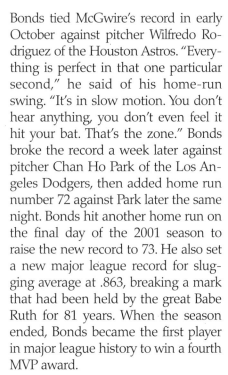

"There wasn't an amount of money that was going to make me leave San Francisco, to be honest with you," Bonds said after signing a new contract with the Giants. "To retire in a San Francisco Giant uniform . . . that's what I've always wanted to do my whole, entire life. Everyone knows my childhood idol is Willie Mays, and this is the greatest honor and perfect dream for me."

Bonds tied McGwire's record in early October against pitcher Wilfredo Rodriguez of the Houston Astros. "Everything is perfect in that one particular second," he said of his home-run swing. "It's in slow motion. You don't hear anything, you don't even feel it hit your bat. That's the zone." Bonds broke the record a week later against pitcher Chan Ho Park of the Los Angeles Dodgers, then added home run number 72 against Park later the same night. Bonds hit another home run on the final day of the 2001 season to raise the new record to 73. He also set a new major league record for slugging average at .863, breaking a mark that had been held by the great Babe Ruth for 81 years. When the season ended, Bonds became the first player in major league history to win a fourth MVP award.

Following his amazing 2001 season, Bonds signed a five-year, $90 million contract to play out the remainder of his career with the Giants. "There wasn't an amount of money that was going to make me leave San Francisco, to be honest with you," he said afterward. "To retire in a San Francisco Giant uniform . . . that's what I've always wanted to do my whole, entire life. Everyone knows my childhood idol is Willie Mays, and this is the greatest honor and perfect dream for me."

Making It to the World Series

Many people doubted that Bonds could ever top his outstanding achievements of the 2001 season. Yet the 38-year-old superstar managed to do so the following year. He claimed his first National League batting title with an amazing .370 average. He also set new league records with 198 walks and a .582 on-base percentage. In addition, Bonds hit 46 home runs and tallied 110 RBIs. In August he hit his 600th career home run, placing him fourth on the all-time list for career homers, behind only Hank Aaron, Babe Ruth, and Willie Mays. At the end of the season, Bonds was the unanimous choice as the 2002 National League MVP. He thus became the first five-time MVP, as well as the first player to win the award consecutively two different times.

Making the 2002 season even more special for Bonds was the fact that the Giants reached the World Series by defeating the St. Louis Cardinals in the NLCS. For a while it appeared as if Bonds would finally achieve his dream of a World Series championship. The Giants took a 3-2 lead over the Anaheim Angels in the seven-game series. As Game 6 got underway, they jumped out to a 5-0 lead. They held the lead through the seventh inning and found themselves just seven outs away from the world title. Champagne was placed on ice in the Giants' clubhouse in anticipation of a team celebration. But then the Angels started a rally that led to one of the most remarkable comebacks in World Series history. They chipped away at the Giants' lead and ended up winning the game 6-5 and tying the series 3-3. The Angels then won the deciding game by a score of 4-1.

Unlike his previous playoff performances, Bonds had an outstanding series. He batted an amazing .471 with 4 home runs and 6 RBIs. He also drew a record 13 walks—7 of them intentional—which helped him to reach base an incredible 21 out of 30 times he was at the plate. Unfortunately, the rest of the Giants only managed to hit a combined .266 for the series. "I don't think it's my last chance," Bonds said after the disappointing World Series loss. "You want the end to be different. What can you do about it? They outplayed us and they deserve it."

When the 2002 season ended, Bonds had 613 career home runs. Some observers predict that he will break Hank Aaron's all-time record of 755 career homers by the time he retires. In addition, Bonds needs only 7 more stolen bases to become the only player ever to achieve over 500 home runs and 500 steals in his career. Despite his individual accomplishments, however, Bonds says that his career will not be complete without a World Series championship. "You hear them say that Barry Bonds is one of the best players in the game today, but I'll never be in the elite category until I win [the World Series]. I have the God-given ability to be a contender, to be a big piece of the puzzle, but so far that's all I have," he noted. "Every year I go through a long season and I get close to a championship, and

Bonds hits a home run against the Anaheim Angels during game one of the World Series, October 19, 2002.

every year I go home disappointed. . . . I like putting up good numbers. But if I never reach another milestone, and the Giants finally win a World Series, that's all I could ask for. I'd be complete."

A Future Member of the Hall of Fame

Bonds is widely considered to be the best all-around player in professional baseball today. His name is often mentioned among the all-time greats, and he will certainly go into the Hall of Fame. He has posted a career batting average of .295 and a career slugging average of .595. His career statistics also include 1,652 RBIs, 1,830 runs scored, and 1,922 walks. Some experts have attributed Bonds's success to his unusual batting style, in which he chokes up on the handle of the bat farther than most professional players. "I started choking up when I was a kid. My dad gave me bats that were too big for me," he recalled. "We had to choke up so we wouldn't fall down [when we swung]." Bonds also possesses some of the quickest hands in the game. The speed of his swing allows him to wait a split second longer than other hitters before swinging at a pitch.

Bonds is known as a keen observer of the game of baseball. He often notices small quirks that clue him into a pitcher's intentions. But he annoys some of his teammates by refusing to share his observations with them. "If you're the star, you're supposed to go out of your way for everybody else," he said. "But I could tell a guy things that I know, and the following year he might be on a team I was talking about, and now he's telling his guys what my tendencies are or what I might do. How smart would that be? Hey man, I've gotta keep my edge."

Despite the slight improvement in his attitude that has taken place in recent years, Bonds still has a reputation as a moody, arrogant, and sometimes difficult player. He remains relatively unpopular among his teammates, who tend to resent some of the special treatment he receives. For example, Bonds never shows up for the annual team picture, refuses to stretch on the field with the team before games, has his own staff to handle his publicity and prepare his meals, and gets his own hotel suite on road trips while the other players share rooms. In the Giants' clubhouse, Bonds sits alone on one side with a fancy leather massage chair and big-screen TV, while his teammates hang out together and play cards on the other side. Bonds claims that he does not need to be popular among his teammates in order to contribute to the team. "The only criticism that really bothers me is when they say I'm not a team player," he stated. "Excuse me? I'm sorry, but that's the one that's not true. Because let me tell you something: You hit .300 every season, knock in a hundred runs, score a hundred runs, hit 30 home runs, you're every inch a team player."

———— " ————

"If you're the star, you're supposed to go out of your way for everybody else. But I could tell a guy things that I know, and the following year he might be on a team I was talking about, and now he's telling his guys what my tendencies are or what I might do. How smart would that be? Hey man, I've gotta keep my edge."

———— " ————

Bonds also continues to have a prickly relationship with the media. He does not like to analyze his game and wishes that reporters would let his on-field performance speak for itself. "Why talk about things?" he asked. "When you talk about stuff too much, you overkill it. You get your glory when the people are happy. That's the glory of it all—when your team wins, you got that big hit, made that big play. That says enough. Why talk about it?"

Finally, Bonds can be less than accommodating with fans. He thinks that people should be satisfied by watching the game of baseball being played at a high level. He does not understand why fans feel entitled to get players' autographs after a game. "Why can't people just enjoy the show? And then let the entertainer go home and get his rest, so he can put on another show?" he stated. "But in baseball, you get to see us, touch us, trade our cards, buy and sell jerseys. To me, that dilutes the excitement. Autograph seekers! When I go to a movie, after the final credits roll, I get up and leave. It's the end! But I'm supposed to stand out there for three hours and then sign autographs? If fans pay $10 to see Batman, they don't expect to get Jack Nicholson's autograph."

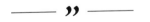

> *Bonds does not understand why fans feel entitled to get players' autographs after a game. "Why can't people just enjoy the show? And then let the entertainer go home and get his rest, so he can put on another show? But in baseball, you get to see us, touch us, trade our cards, buy and sell jerseys. To me, that dilutes the excitement. Autograph seekers! When I go to a movie, after the final credits roll, I get up and leave. It's the end! But I'm supposed to stand out there for three hours and then sign autographs? If fans pay $10 to see Batman, they don't expect to get Jack Nicholson's autograph."*

HOME AND FAMILY

Bonds has been married twice. He married Susann (known as Sun) Branco on February 6, 1988. They had a son, Nikolai, and a daughter, Shikari, before they divorced in 1994. Bonds married his longtime friend Elizabeth Watson on January 10, 1998. They have a daughter, Aisha Lynn. Bonds lives with his second wife and his three children in a three-story, 12,500-square-foot mansion in Los Altos Hills, California.

Since he remarried, Bonds has made an effort to become more involved in his children's lives. "Before, I just wanted to get to the field. That was my life," he admitted. "Now, I'm like a human carpool. I get up in the morning and take my kids to school and pick them up when I'm not at the ballpark. My kids are doing so many things. And I want to be there for them." His son, Nikolai, is a batboy for the Giants and hopes to become a professional baseball player someday.

HOBBIES AND OTHER INTERESTS

In his spare time, Bonds likes to watch basketball and hockey on television, play golf, practice martial arts, and ride motorcycles. He has worked on behalf of a wide range of charitable causes over the years, including the Adopt-A-Special-Kid program and the Cardiac Arrhythmias Research and Education Foundation. He also urges African-Americans to register as bone marrow donors.

Helping underprivileged children is one of Bonds's favorite causes, and he has given generously to many youth groups. During his many seasons with the Giants, he has purchased 50 tickets to each home game and given them away to children's organizations.

Bonds kisses his son Nikolai after hitting a home run in game six of the World Series, October 26, 2002.

The children sit in the leftfield bleachers, and Bonds always tips his hat to them before the game. Bonds also established a scholarship fund for his high school to help disadvantaged kids attend college.

Bonds is also an entrepreneur. He co-founded a company called Digital Interiors that installs high-tech electronic gadgets in people's homes. His own home features several such devices, which allow him to remotely adjust the temperature or fire up the hot tub. Bonds has also recently started doing endorsements for Armour hot dogs, Sega Dreamcast games, Kentucky Fried Chicken, Charles Schwab investments, MasterCard, and Fila.

HONORS AND AWARDS

College All-America Team (*Sporting News*): 1985
National League Most Valuable Player (Baseball Writers' Association):
    1990, 1992, 1993, 2001, 2002
Major League Player of the Year (*Sporting News*): 1990
National League Player of the Year (*Sporting News*): 1990, 1991
Major League Baseball All-Star Team: 1990, 1992-96
Gold Glove Award: 1990-94, 1996-98

Major League Player of the Year (Associated Press): 1992
Major League Player of the 1990s (*Sporting News*): 2000
Male Athlete of the Year (Associated Press): 2001
Athlete of the Year (*Sports Illustrated for Kids*): 2002

FURTHER READING

Books

Contemporary Black Biography, Vol. 6, 1994
Harvey, Miles. *Barry Bonds: Baseball's Complete Player,* 1994 (juvenile)
Muskat, Carrie. *Baseball Legends: Barry Bonds,* 1997 (juvenile)
Savage, Jeff. *Barry Bonds: Record Breaker,* 2002 (juvenile)
Sports Stars, Series 1-4, 1994-98
Travers, Steven. *Barry Bonds: Baseball's Superman,* 2002
Who's Who in America, 2002
World Book Encyclopedia, 2002

Periodicals

Baseball Digest, Dec. 2000, p.52
Current Biography Yearbook, 1994
Ebony, Sep. 1993, p.118; July 2002, p.116
Esquire, Aug. 1996, p.46
Los Angeles Times, Oct. 7, 2001, Sports sec., p.1
New York Times, Oct. 5, 2001, p.D13; Nov. 20, 2001, p.S4; Oct. 24, 2002, p.A1
New York Times Magazine, Sep. 1, 2002, p.36
People, Oct. 4, 1993, p.101; July 9, 2001, p.63; Oct. 22, 2001, p.73
San Francisco Chronicle, Feb. 17, 1997, p.D1; Oct. 6, 2001, p.F1
Sport, Apr. 1993, p.60; Oct. 1996, p.16
Sporting News, July 12, 1999, p.12
Sports Illustrated, June 25, 1990, p.59; May 24, 1993, p.12; June 5, 2000, p.48;
    Aug. 27, 2001, p.102; Oct. 8, 2001, p.38; Oct. 15, 2001, p.46; Aug. 19,
    2002, p.42; Nov. 4, 2002, p.32, 96
Sports Illustrated for Kids, Sep. 1, 2001, p.50; Jan. 2002
Time, July 2, 2001, p.62; Oct. 28, 2002, p.59
USA Today, Aug. 9, 2000, p.C1

Online Databases

Biography Resource Center Online, 2002, articles from *Contemporary Black Biography,* 1994, and *Sports Stars,* 1994-98

ADDRESS

Barry Bonds
San Francisco Giants
Pacific Bell Park
24 Willie Mays Plaza
San Francisco, CA 94107

WORLD WIDE WEB SITE

http://sanfrancisco.giants.mlb.com

Vincent Brooks 1959?-

U.S. Army Brigadier General
Deputy Director of Operations for U.S. Central
Command during the 2003 War in Iraq

BIRTH

Vincent Brooks was born in about 1959 in Anchorage, Alaska.
His parents are Leo A. Brooks, who was a major general in the
U.S. Army, and Naomi (Lewis) Brooks, a teacher. Vincent has
two siblings. His brother, Leo, Jr., is a year older and, like his
brother, is a brigadier general in the Army. He currently serves
as commandant of cadets at the U.S. Military Academy at
West Point. Vincent's younger sister, Marquita, is a lawyer.

After retiring from the military, Vincent's father, Leo Brooks, became managing director for the city of Philadelphia. In May 1985 he found himself in the national media spotlight due to a violent confrontation between city authorities and a radical anti-government group called MOVE. At that time, MOVE members lived in a row house in Philadelphia. On May 13, 1985, MOVE members opened fire on police from their rooftop. After a long gun battle, the police dropped a bomb on the building. The bomb missed its target and sparked a fire that soon raged out of control. The blaze eventually burned an entire city block, leaving 250 people homeless and killing 11 people. Brooks and other city authorities were blamed by some people for the disaster. He left the job soon afterward, but was later cleared of any legal responsibility for the bombing.

YOUTH AND EDUCATION

The Brooks family is very private, so little information about Vincent's early years has been made public. It is known, however, that during his childhood, his father received military assignments that took him all across the country. With each new assignment, his family left friends and familiar surroundings behind in order to accompany him. As a result, all of the Brooks children attended several different schools during their childhood years. But Leo and Naomi Brooks did not permit their children to use the relocations as an excuse for poor school work. Instead, they set very high standards for their children. If one of them brought home a report card with all As and a B, their father would encourage the child to pull that B up to an A.

> *"We were all very, very close," recalled Marquita Brooks. "My parents always did things with us."*

The family eventually settled in Sacramento, California, where both Brooks and his brother attended Jesuit High School. The school had very high academic standards and emphasized values that were similar to those the brothers had been taught at home, particularly hard work and self-discipline. "That high school," Leo Brooks later said, "was fundamentally a big part of helping prepare us to do what we were able to do." Besides Brooks and his older brother, only two other black students were enrolled at the school. But Vincent Brooks thrived at the school, posting outstanding grades and emerging as a leader of the school's basketball and track teams. He graduated from St. Jesuit in 1976.

During his high school years, Brooks had pondered a future career as a doctor. He also received a basketball scholarship offer from North Carolina State University. But during Christmas break of his senior year, his older brother arrived home for the holidays from the U.S. Military Academy in New York. This military college, usually called West Point after the city where it is located, trains students to be officers in the U.S. Army. Brooks was tremendously impressed by the changes he saw in his older brother after only a few months at West Point. Leo was in top physical condition and looked "sharp" in his uniform, as Brooks later recalled. He also noted that Leo and his roommate, who had been invited to join the Brooks family for Christmas, carried themselves with confidence and pride. Later that evening, Brooks tried on his brother's West Point uniform for himself. "That night, when we went to bed," his father recalls, "I said I thought he was hooked [on going to West Point]."

> *Vincent Brooks was tremendously impressed by the changes he saw in his older brother Leo after only a few months at West Point. When Leo came home at Christmas, Vincent tried on his brother's West Point uniform for himself. "That night, when we went to bed," his father recalls, "I said I thought he was hooked [on going to West Point]."*

Over the next few days, Brooks admitted to his brother that the idea of attending West Point had become more attractive to him than the idea of studying medicine. The application deadline for enrolling at West Point had already passed, but Leo spoke to the basketball coach at the military academy and showed him a video of his younger brother playing basketball for Jesuit High. Brooks's basketball abilities and his fine academic record convinced academy administrators to admit him without delay.

Brooks made an immediate impact at West Point. He made the varsity basketball team as a freshman and excelled in his studies. In addition, he became known among the other cadets for his easygoing manner and good sense of humor During his senior year, he was selected as First Captain, a position similar to that of class president. The selection process to fill this position of honor was quite rigorous. Brooks and other candidates for the post underwent a series of interviews, and each candidate was evaluated on their leadership qualities and their military, academic, and physical performance. Brooks's selection

Brooks and General Tommy Franks (left) update news reporters on the progress of the war in Iraq in a March 2003 press conference.

made him the first African-American cadet to assume the prestigious post in the 177-year history of the academy.

As soon as the news of his appointment appeared in the papers, Brooks learned that being in the spotlight has its drawbacks. He received hate mail from racists — both inside and outside of the academy — who were angered at West Point's decision to appoint a black cadet to such an important position. Brooks initially was shocked by the negative reaction. After all, he had grown up in integrated military neighborhoods, where families of different ethnic backgrounds lived, worked, and played together. He also was amazed that some people would dismiss his many accomplishments simply because of the color of his skin. But Brooks did not wilt under these hateful statements. Instead, the publicity surrounding the issue taught him how to handle media attention and pressure in a calm and graceful manner.

In 1980 Brooks graduated from West Point first in his class with a Bachelor of Science (B.S.) degree. He went on to earn a Master's Degree in Military Art and Science from the School of Advanced Military Studies at the U.S. Army's Command and General Staff College in Fort Leavenworth, Kansas. He later was awarded a National Security Fellowship to study at Harvard University's John F. Kennedy School of Government. While serving in the military, he returned to school to attend the U.S. Army War College in Pennsylvania, graduating in 1999.

Brooks holds up a 55-card deck of cards featuring members of Iraq's leadership to reporters covering the war. The top card on the deck is of Iraqi President Saddam Hussein — the Ace of Spades.

CAREER HIGHLIGHTS

A Career in the Infantry

Brooks began his military career as a second lieutenant in the infantry (the division of the Army to which foot soldiers belong), but rose quickly through the ranks. Unlike his brother Leo, who had trained in light infantry, Brooks pursued a career in heavy artillery, the maintenance and operation of large-caliber guns.

Brooks's duties took him to a number of places in the world where the U.S. Army maintains a strong military presence, including Panama, Europe, South Korea, and the Middle East. In many of these assignments during the 1980s and 1990s, his responsibilities included commanding troops as well as helping shape U.S. military policy. Although no detailed information is available about these postings, it is known that Brooks served with the 82nd Airborne Division, the 1st Infantry Division, and the 3rd Army in Kuwait, where the first Gulf War took place in 1991. He reached the rank of major with the 1st Cavalry Division in the early 1990s. As the decade unfolded, he received new assignments at military bases across North, South, and Central America. At every stop, he impressed his superiors with his intelligence and dedication to duty. "He is a no-nonsense leader who has studied his profession carefully, works hard, and delivers," recalled retired general Wesley Clark.

Brooks interrupted his military service to attend the U.S. Army War College in Pennsylvania. After graduating in 1999, he reported to Fort Stewart, Georgia, where he served as 1st Brigade commander in the 3rd Infantry Division. During his time at Fort Stewart, Brooks led 3,000 soldiers on a peacekeeping mission in the former Yugoslav province of Kosovo, which had been torn apart by ethnic conflicts in the late 1990s. His work brought him in contact with General Tommy Franks, who later became the top military commander of U.S. forces during the 2003 invasion of Iraq.

Brooks points to a map of Iraq during an April 2003 news conference on the U.S.-led invasion of Iraq.

After completing his assignment in Kosovo, Brooks was promoted to a job at the Pentagon in Washington, D.C., the headquarters of the U.S. Department of Defense. He held a number of positions there, including deputy director for political-military affairs at the Joint Chiefs of Staff. In June 2002 Brooks was nominated for a promotion to the rank of brigadier general. At 43, he was the youngest of that year's 38 nominees to achieve this honor. His nomination was later confirmed by the U.S. Senate. With his promotion, the Brooks family became the first African-American family in U.S. military history with three generals from two different generations.

Briefing the World on the War in Iraq

In January 2003 Brooks learned that he would be leaving the Pentagon. General Franks had selected him to work as deputy director of operations for the U.S. Central Command (known as CENTCOM) headquarters in Doha, Qatar. CENTCOM, which usually operates out of Tampa, Florida, is a group that represents all of the U.S. armed services. It is responsible for overseeing military, political, and economic events in various parts of the world.

This assignment came at a time when the United States was preparing for war in Iraq. According to U.S. political and military leaders, Iraq and its president, Saddam Hussein, posed a great threat to the United States and other nations. They claimed that Iraq supported terrorism, and that it possessed weapons of mass destruction.

Brooks knew that as deputy director of operations, he would be responsible for explaining the progress of the war to journalists. At times, this can be a tremendously challenging task. After all, military spokesmen are responsible for informing the public about the military's actions. But they also need to keep silent about some aspects of military operations to ensure the safety of soldiers. In addition, spokesmen must keep in mind that public support for wars and other military actions often depends on the tone and content of the news they read and watch on television. Reporters, on the other hand, have a professional duty to investigate stories and confirm the claims that government spokesmen make. In fact, they play a vital role in ensuring that the American public receives accurate information about issues and events around the world. At times, the differing goals of spokespersons and reporters can create tensions and conflict between the two parties.

> **"My son is not a hero,"
> said Brooks's father.
> "Those kids getting shot at
> and killed are. I will not
> exploit the hunger for
> knowledge, nor slip into a
> gloat for my son or my
> family, while other
> families weep."**

In March 2003, U.S. troops invaded Iraq. As the war unfolded, Brooks emerged as one of the military's most visible spokespersons. General Franks was uncomfortable in front of television cameras and did not enjoy answering reporters' questions. Brooks, on the other hand, seemed born to the task. His imposing physical appearance and ability to express himself clearly made him the perfect spokesperson for the military. For example, he explained the significance of battlefield slides and videos that were shown at the U.S. military's daily press briefings with great ease. Everyone who watched the daily briefings on television, which were broadcast live every weekday morning and then repeated throughout the day, was impressed by his intelligence and composure.

What's more, Brooks actually seemed to enjoy fielding questions from reporters, even when they were critical of military actions and decisions. Observers noted that he handled these comments with patience and good humor. For example, during a briefing early in the war one of the reporters complained that General Franks himself should be telling them what was going on. Brooks responded, "He's fighting a war now. And he has me to

Brooks fielded questions from dozens of reporters during his sessions with the media.

do this for him." Some of the journalists who attended Brooks's daily briefings were frustrated because his answers to specific questions about casualties and troop movements were often vague. One reporter described his manner as "robotic" because he tended to use standard phrases that sounded as though they had been "scripted" by his superiors. But he also showed a flair for expressing himself in a way that was almost poetic. At one point, for example, he compared America's military might to a "dagger" that was "clearly pointed at the heart of the Baghdad regime."

Brooks quickly became one of the war's most visible African-American faces, along with Secretary of State Colin Powell and National Security Advisor Condoleeza Rice. Brooks also served as a reminder that the forces fighting in Iraq reflected the diversity of the American population. Soon after he began appearing on television, he and his family members were bombarded with requests for interviews, most of which they turned down. Brooks's father summed up the family's feelings when he said that "My son is not a hero. Those kids getting shot at and killed are. I will not exploit the hunger for knowledge, nor slip into a gloat for my son or my family, while other families weep. When the war is over, I will speak."

Brooks is aware that he has become a role model for young African-Americans who are thinking about a career in the military. But he has never thought of himself as a celebrity. Raised by his parents to believe that he could accomplish anything if he gave his best effort, he suggests that discipline and sacrifice are the keys to success for others as well. In this regard, Brooks agrees that his life can be an example to others, especially young people. "People can see the achievement and how hard work leads to it," he said.

On April 24, 2003, Brooks concluded his duties as CENTCOM's spokesman. He returned to the United States, where he was assigned to the Pentagon.

> *Brooks agrees that his life can be an example for young people. "People can see the achievement and how hard work leads to it," he said.*

MARRIAGE AND FAMILY

When he is not serving overseas with the military, Brooks lives in northern Virginia with his wife, Carol, who is a physical therapist, and their four daughters.

HOBBIES AND OTHER INTERESTS

Brooks routinely works long days, so he says that his favorite way of relaxing is to "hang out with my wife." He describes himself as a "hopeless romantic" who loves nothing better than spending an evening on the sofa with his wife watching "Def Comedy Jam" or a movie. "Anything she's interested in," he says, "is good enough for me."

FURTHER READING

Periodicals

Chicago Sun-Times, Mar. 27, 2003, p.8
Current Biography Yearbook, 2003
Financial Times (London), Apr. 26, 2003, p.25
Jet, Apr. 21, 2003, p.8
New York Times, Apr. 4, 2003, p.B11
Philadelphia Inquirer, Apr. 10, 2003, p.D1
Sacramento Bee, Apr. 1, 2003, p.A10
Washington Post, May 22, 2003, p.T14

Online Articles

http://www.africana.com
   (*Africana.com*, "Who is Brigadier General Vincent Brooks?"
   Apr. 9, 2003)
http://www.cnn.com
   (*CNN.com*, "Military Man Brooks Steps Up to the Mike,"
   April 8, 2003)
http://www.sacobserver.com
   (*Sacramento Observer Online*, "General Brooks: Why Be Discredited for
   Excelling?" Apr. 28, 2003)
http://www.usma.edu
   (*USMA In The News*, "One Black Family, Three Generals: Brooks
   Brothers Reared in Military Tradition," Apr. 1, 2003)
http://dynamic.washtimes.com
   (*The Washington Times*, "Honorably Speaking," Apr. 11, 2003)

ADDRESS

Vincent Brooks
Room 2-E949
The Pentagon
Arlington, VA 20301

Laura Bush 1946-

American Librarian and Literacy Activist
First Lady of the United States

BIRTH

Laura Bush was born Laura Welch on November 4, 1946, in Midland, Texas. Her father, Harold, was a homebuilder who owned his own contracting business, and her mother, Jenna, was the company's bookkeeper. Laura is an only child.

YOUTH

Jenna Welch remembers that her daughter "was just born a nice quiet little kiddo." She started reading to Laura "from the time she could open her eyes." To this day, reading with her mother is one of Laura Bush's fondest childhood memories. Her favorite books included the "Little House" series by Laura Ingalls Wilder, in part because she and the heroine shared the same first name, "but what I loved even more was sitting with my mother, listening to her read." She also loved "Nancy Drew" mysteries by Carolyn Keene and *Little Women* by Louisa May Alcott.

Laura and her mother made frequent trips to the local public library, which was housed in the Midland County Courthouse. She still remembers the effect it had on her. "These trips to the library were a defining part of my childhood. Even at three and four years of age, I remember thinking how special the library must be. Here were so many books with people of all ages enjoying them, located in the most important building in our town."

In addition to reading, Bush enjoyed church and church activities, Brownies and Girl Scouts, and playing with friends. She particularly liked playing school. She'd line up her dolls as if they were in a classroom and "teach" them to read. "In a lot of ways, I had a perfect childhood," she told a reporter in 2000. "We felt very free to do whatever we wanted. You could ride your bike downtown, go to the Rexall Drug and get a ham sandwich for lunch. But at the same time, we were sheltered."

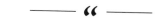

"These trips to the library were a defining part of my childhood. Even at three and four years of age, I remember thinking how special the library must be. Here were so many books with people of all ages enjoying them, located in the most important building in our town."

Midland is a middle-class town in west Texas, where many families made their living in the oil business. One of those was the family of George W. Bush. Yet even though they grew up in the same town, and even went to the same junior high, Laura Welch and George W. Bush didn't meet growing up or in school. They weren't officially introduced until they were adults.

EDUCATION

Laura Welch went to James Bowie Elementary School in Midland, where she was an excellent student. She especially loved her second grade teacher and credits her with the inspiration to become a teacher herself. Laura went on to Midland Junior High and Midland High School. An otherwise

First Lady Laura Bush with her mother, Jenna Welch

happy high school career was marred by tragedy in her junior year when she was involved in a fatal traffic accident. She was driving a car and ran a stop sign, hitting a car driven by a high school friend. The young man died in the accident. The boy's family never blamed her or brought charges against her, but it remains a difficult and painful memory.

After graduating from Midland High in 1964, Bush went to Southern Methodist University in Dallas, Texas. She studied education, receiving her bachelor's degree in 1968.

CAREER HIGHLIGHTS

Over the next ten years, Bush worked in elementary schools, first as a teacher and then as a librarian. She devoted herself to causes that she continues to champion today as First Lady: early childhood education and the importance of reading to learning.

Bush's first teaching job was at Longfellow Elementary School in Dallas, Texas. After a year of teaching at Longfellow, she took a job at John F. Kennedy Elementary in Houston, Texas. One of her former students remembers that "the kids really did love her. She'd go outside and play with us. If you had problems on reading and spelling, she'd take a little more time with you." She taught at Kennedy for several years, then decided she wanted to become a librarian. She went back to school, this time to the University of Texas at Austin, where she studied for a library science degree. She graduated in 1973 with her M.L.S. — Master's of Library Science.

Bush's first job as a librarian was in Houston, where she worked at a branch of the Houston Public Library. The next year, she returned to Austin, where she worked as the librarian at Dawson Elementary School, a job she held for three years.

MARRIAGE AND FAMILY

In the summer of 1977, Laura Welch met George W. Bush at the home of mutual friends in Midland, Texas. (Because of the confusion of names, the

A family portrait on the rocks in Kennebunkport, Maine.
Left to right: Jenna, George W., Laura, and Barbara.

son is usually referred to as George W. Bush, while his father is called George Herbert Walker Bush, or just George Bush. For more information on Laura's husband, George W. Bush, see *Biography Today*, Sep. 2000, and Updates in the Annual Cumulations for 2000, 2001, and 2002; for more information on his father, George Bush, see *Biography Today*, Jan. 1992.)

Laura's friends had been trying to get the two together for years, but she was a bit reluctant. She knew his background, with a father who was a prominent Republican politician. In 1977, George W. Bush was running for office, too, for a spot on the Texas legislature. She thought he sounded "too political," she laughingly recalls. George W. Bush remembers their meeting well, claiming it was "love at first sight." For her part, Laura remembers he was a lot of fun and had a great sense of humor. But the future President was also persistent, and they quickly hit it off. They dated for just three months before marrying in November 1977. Their twin daughters, Jenna and Barbara, were born in 1981.

George W. Bush campaigning for a seat in the Texas legislature with his wife, Laura Bush, 1978.

EARLY POLITICAL CAMPAIGNS

When Laura and George W. Bush married, she made him promise she would never have to make a political speech for him. But just months after their wedding, she was up on a stage, speaking at a political rally for her husband. With sly humor, she told the audience about his pledge and explained her appearance on his behalf: "So much for political promises." Bush didn't win that first election, but he learned a lot about politics that he put to use in later races.

Over the next several years George W. Bush headed an oil company, while Laura Bush devoted herself to raising her daughters and volunteering at the girls' school and at the local library. She also helped her husband quit drinking. George W. Bush has acknowledged that he had a problem with alcohol. He has said that he decided to quit drinking because he was "a high-energy person, and alcohol began competing with my ability to keep up my energy level." Some people have claimed that Laura greatly influenced his decision, but she won't take the credit. She says he's a disciplined man who did it on his own.

In 1987, the family moved to Washington, D.C. Bush's father, George Herbert Walker Bush, had served as Ronald Reagan's vice president from

1980 to 1988, and was running for President. George W. became one of his father's closest advisers. In 1988, George Bush was elected President, and George W. and his family moved back to Texas. From 1988 to 1994, Bush was a managing partner of the Texas Rangers baseball team, headquartered outside of Dallas. Laura and the girls attended many baseball games, and as Jenna and Barbara got older, Laura became more involved in library and literacy programs.

In 1994, George W. Bush announced his re-entry into politics. He decided to take on popular Texas governor Ann Richards. Laura Bush wasn't pleased. She was concerned about the effect on her family of the close press scrutiny that goes along with politics. She wanted to protect their privacy, particularly for her daughters, who were just 13 years old. She'd also lived through the tough times the press had given her father-in-law, George Bush, when he'd lost his re-election bid in 1992.

Despite her reservations, Laura Bush proved to be an able and intuitive campaigner. She has often been described as quiet and reserved, but she's also candid with her husband. On the campaign trail, George asked her what she thought of a speech he'd just given. "Well, it wasn't that good," she told him, after which he drove into the garage wall. He has often called her his "rock," a source of strength, but also someone who can rein him in when he gets a little too volatile.

> *As First Lady of Texas, Laura Bush had a statewide forum for the causes she believed in so deeply. She began a literacy campaign aimed at whole families, so that not just children, but parents and grandparents too, could learn to read together. She started organizations to help parents help children get ready for school.*

FIRST LADY OF TEXAS

George W. Bush won the Texas governor's race in 1994, and the family moved to the state capital in Austin. As First Lady of Texas, Laura Bush had a statewide forum for the causes she believed in so deeply. She began a literacy campaign aimed at whole families, so that not just children, but parents and grandparents too, could learn to read together. She started organizations to help parents help children get ready for school. One of the main themes of Bush's career has been that reading readiness is perhaps the most important indicator of a child's success in school. She believes that children need to be read to from infancy. The more they are read to, the more they'll be able to recognize words, word patterns, and all aspects that go into reading.

In 1998, Laura Bush helped write and promote a bill that provided $17 million for early childhood development programs, with increased funding going to established programs like Head Start. She worked with other governors' wives on women's health initiatives. She helped to create "Rainbow Rooms" for Texas children, which provide clothing and other important necessities to children who have been abused and neglected. She also helped raise money for breast cancer research and for art preservation.

———— **"** ————

"I've never been that interested in clothes," Bush said in response to media criticism of the way she dressed. She was really comfortable in "jeans, pants, T-shirts," and wasn't embarrassed about buying her makeup at the drug store. "I can take scrutiny or criticism of how I look with a grain of salt because I think there are things more important than how I look or wear my hair."

———— **"** ————

In 1996, Bush started the Texas Book Fair, an annual celebration of books, authors, and reading that has raised more than $1 million for Texas libraries. Among people from both political parties, Laura Bush became known as one of the finest First Ladies in Texas history. She continued to pursue her interests in her typical low-key way. At the same time, she did her best to guard her children's privacy and assure them a normal adolescence. She was firm with the press in how they were to treat her daughters. She asked that they not be photographed or interviewed, and that they be left alone by the media. The media generally did as they were asked, but some were not above criticizing the way Laura Bush looked or the way she dressed. That really didn't bother her. "I've never been that interested in clothes," she says. She was really comfortable in "jeans, pants, T-shirts," and wasn't embarrassed about buying her makeup at the drug store. "I can take scrutiny or criticism of how I look with a grain of salt because I think there are things more important than how I look or wear my hair."

*First Lady Laura Bush with her daughters, Barbara and Jenna,
at the inauguration of President George W. Bush, January 2001.*

THE ROAD TO THE WHITE HOUSE

In 1999, George W. Bush announced that he would seek the nomination to become the Republican candidate for President. Laura Bush traveled around the United States, campaigning for her husband. She attended and gave speeches at political rallies all around the country. She spoke at the 2000 Republican Convention, giving many Americans their first glimpse of the woman who would later become First Lady. The election of 2000 turned out to be one of the most hotly contested in years, and for over a month after the vote it was unclear who had actually won. It wasn't until December that the results were finally determined, and George W. Bush became the 43rd President of the United States. The day the election results were announced, Laura Bush was still busy with her work as the First Lady of Texas, chairing a meeting on that year's Texas Book Fair even as her husband got ready to give his acceptance speech.

FIRST LADY OF THE UNITED STATES

In January 2001, Laura Bush moved to Washington, D.C., and into the White House. Once again, she used her position as First Lady to promote the causes she believes in so passionately: reading initiatives and early childhood education. She launched new programs, including one to recruit teachers and to make sure children start school ready to learn.

THE TRAGEDY OF SEPTEMBER 11TH

Then, on September 11, 2001, the world of Laura Bush, and of all U.S. citizens, changed dramatically. On that day, terrorists attacked the United States. Hijackers forced two commercial airplanes to crash into the twin towers of the World Trade Center in New York City. Less than an hour later, hijackers forced a plane to crash into the Pentagon, the home of the Department of Defense in Washington, D.C. The damage to the World Trade Center was devastating. An hour after the attack, the twin towers collapsed. Almost 3,000 people died in New York. At the Pentagon, the death toll reached 184.

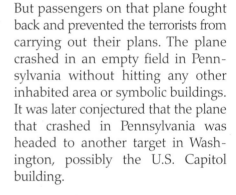

"The most comforting people I've been with since September 11 are the second graders I've read to. Children who are seven and eight years old have a wonderful outlook on life. They know what's important."

Later, it was learned that there were also terrorists on board a fourth plane. But passengers on that plane fought back and prevented the terrorists from carrying out their plans. The plane crashed in an empty field in Pennsylvania without hitting any other inhabited area or symbolic buildings. It was later conjectured that the plane that crashed in Pennsylvania was headed to another target in Washington, possibly the U.S. Capitol building.

Laura Bush was in the U.S. Capitol building that morning, about to give a speech to Congress on early childhood development. When news of the attack came, she was taken back to the White House, where she waited for news from her husband, who was out of town. When he finally landed in Washington several hours later, they both made an important decision. Against the recommendations of their advisers, they decided to stay in the White House, and not to move to a secret location.

Within hours of the attack, federal officials stated that they thought the terrorists were acting under the direction of Osama bin Laden. (For more information on bin Laden, see *Biography Today*, April 2002.) Bin Laden is a Saudi Arabian extremist who has been linked to other terrorist attacks against the U.S. He is reported to have financed and planned the 1993 attack on the World Trade Center. That attack killed six and injured several hundred. He is also considered to be behind the bombing of U.S. embassies in Kenya and Tanzania in 1998. And he is linked to the attack on the U.S.S. Cole, a Navy ship that was bombed in 2000 while in Yemen. Whether bin Laden is still alive is unknown, but the U.S. continues to pursue him and the worldwide terrorist network Al Qaeda. The U.S. is focusing its military actions on finding and destroying Al-Qaeda terrorist cells throughout the Middle East, Asia, and all over the world.

In the days after the terrorist attacks, Laura Bush became a constant and calming presence in the country. She appeared at the disaster sites, where she comforted the families who had lost loved ones and thanked the many rescue workers. She went to schools all over the country to meet with children and talk to them. She wanted to assure them that they were safe, and that their parents and teachers cared for them. They made her feel better, too. "The most comforting people I've been with since September 11 are the second graders I've read to," she said. "Children who are seven and eight years old have a wonderful outlook on life. They know what's important." In November 2001, Laura Bush became the only First Lady to give the weekly presidential radio broadcast. She spoke out against the oppression of women and children under the Taliban regime in Afghanistan.

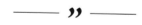

> "Children and teachers need library resources — especially books — and the expertise of a librarian to succeed. Books, information technology, and school librarians who are part of the schools' professional team are basic ingredients for student achievement."

Laura Bush's new, more visible role as what has been called "Caretaker in Chief" was warmly embraced by a grieving nation. And she returned to her role as an enthusiastic champion of education. She appeared before Congress again in January 2002, outlining her concern that preschool children get the help they need to get ready for reading and learning in school. She also encouraged more adults to get involved in their communities as mentors.

PROMOTING LIBRARIES AND LITERACY

In June 2002, Bush held a White House conference on school libraries, unveiling a $5 million federal funding initiative. "School libraries help teachers teach and children learn," she said. "Children and teachers need library resources — especially books — and the expertise of a librarian to succeed.

*First Lady Laura Bush reads a book to Big Bird, Elmo, and friends
on "Sesame Street."*

Books, information technology, and school librarians who are part of the schools' professional team are basic ingredients for student achievement."

In July 2002, she started the Laura Bush Foundation for America's Libraries. Its purpose is to enhance the collections in school libraries by providing grants to allow libraries to buy additional books. "My lifelong passion for books began when I was a little girl. This new Foundation provides yet another opportunity to share with America's children the magical world of books and reading," Bush said. "A love of books, of holding a book, turning its pages, looking at its pictures, and living its fascinating stories goes hand-in-hand with a love of learning. Every child in America should have access to a well-stocked school or community library. . . . An investment in libraries is an investment in our children's future."

BOOK FESTIVALS IN WASHINGTON

Bush had actually started a new reading initiative in Washington on the eve of September 11. On September 8, 2001, she launched the first annual National Book Festival at the Library of Congress. She invited more than 50 famous authors to read their works to people in a weekend celebration of books and authors. Inspired by the Texas Book Fair, the National Book Festival drew more than 30,000 people in its first year, and even more in 2002.

Bush also started another series of book-related events. She invited authors from all over the country to come to the White House for symposiums on American literature. So far, writers have attended series devoted to Mark Twain, the Harlem Renaissance, and American women writers of the West. Bush invited people from across the political spectrum, including several who disagreed strongly with the President's political stand on various issues. Some of these writers were surprised to be invited to the White House, because their political beliefs were so different from those of the Bush administration. But Laura Bush claimed that "There's nothing political about American literature," and the discussions inspired by the series were lively and far-reaching.

———— " ————

"A love of books, of holding a book, turning its pages, looking at its pictures, and living its fascinating stories goes hand-in-hand with a love of learning. Every child in America should have access to a well-stocked school or community library. . . . An investment in libraries is an investment in our children's future."

———— " ————

But the series came to a temporary halt in January 2003 when the First Lady postponed a planned symposium on the poetry of Emily Dickinson, Langston Hughes, and Walt Whitman. She had invited several poets who were disturbed at the Bush administration's proposed military action in Iraq. These poets planned to use the conference to protest President Bush's stance and to express their own political views. At this point the series is on hold, and a new date has not been set. Regardless of the future of the poetry symposium, Laura Bush will surely continue to promote reading and literacy through her role as First Lady.

HOBBIES AND OTHER INTERESTS

In her spare time, Bush still loves to read. She also likes to garden at the Bush's ranch in Crawford, Texas. She enjoys taking the family dogs, Barney and Spot, for walks on the ranch and at Camp David, a presidential retreat in the Maryland countryside.

FURTHER READING

Books

Anderson, Christopher. *George and Laura: Portrait of an American Marriage*, 2002
Watson, Robert P. *American First Ladies*, 2002

Periodicals

American Libraries, Feb. 2001, p.50; Oct. 2001, p.16
Austin-American, Sep. 29, 1996, p.E1
Current Biography Yearbook, 2001
Good Housekeeping, Jan. 2002, p.100
Library Journal, Oct. 2001, p.11
New York Times, Oct. 7, 2002, p.A1; Oct. 10, 2002, p.A34; Jan. 31, 2003
New York Times Magazine, Sep. 9, 2001, p.61
Newsday, Jan. 3, 2001, p.B6
Newsweek, Nov. 22, 1999, p.42; Sep. 27, 2001, p.69; Oct. 8, 2001, p.33
People, Oct. 9, 2000, p.64; May 14, 2001, p.159; Jan. 29, 2001, p.50; Jan. 21, 2002, p.84
Psychology Today, Dec. 2002, p.34
Publishers Weekly, Oct. 21, 2001, p.12
Texas Monthly, Nov. 1966, p.120; Apr. 2001, p.80
Time, Jan. 8, 2001, p.32
U.S. News and World Report, Sep. 10, 2001
Washington Post, June 15, 2001, p.C1

Other

"Morning Edition," National Public Radio Transcript, Sep. 4, 2001; Sep. 17, 2001
"Weekend Edition," National Public Radio Transcript, July 30, 2000

Online Database

Biography Resource Center Online, 2003

ADDRESS

Laura Bush
The Office of the First Lady
The White House
1600 Pennsylvania Ave.
Washington, D.C. 20500

WORLD WIDE WEB SITES

http://www.whitehouse.gov/firstlady
http://www.laurabushfoundation.org

Amanda Bynes 1986-

American Actress
Star of the TV Shows "All That," "The Amanda Show,"
and "What I Like about You," as Well as the Movies
Big Fat Liar and *What a Girl Wants*

BIRTH

Amanda Laura Bynes was born on April 3, 1986, in Thousand
Oaks, California. She lives with her father, Rick Bynes, who is
a dentist, and her mother, Lynn Bynes, who helps manage the
dental office. Bynes is the youngest of three children. She has
an older sister, Jillian, and an older brother, Tom.

YOUTH

Bynes displayed a natural talent and enthusiam for entertaining people from a very early age. Funny and uninhibited, she proved to be a natural crowd-pleaser at the dinner table and other family gatherings. "I guess I've always liked to make people laugh, ever since I was real little," Bynes said. Her father, meanwhile, often told friends that he wished that famous film director Steven Spielberg would drop by so that he could show off his precocious youngest daughter.

By age seven, Bynes had developed a deep interest in the theatre. She even learned to recite lines from plays in which her older sister was performing. At age seven she performed on stage herself for the first time, playing the role of the young orphan Molly in a local theatre production of *Annie*. As time passed, Bynes took part in other productions as well. For example, in 1995 she played Scout in a stage production of *To Kill a Mockingbird*. That same year, she took the role of Mary in the play *The Secret Garden*. Bynes admitted that her involvement in these productions required her to spend a lot of hours rehearsing and performing. But she claimed that she loved every moment. "Some kids like doing sports, and some kids like singing," she explained. "I just always liked to perform."

> "Some kids like doing sports, and some kids like singing," Bynes explained. "I just always liked to perform."

In 1996 Bynes's parents enrolled her in a children's "comedy camp" that was being held at a Los Angeles comedy club. At the end of the camp, all of the children performed for their teachers and parents. When Bynes's turn came to march out on the stage, she performed a skit about school that she had written with help from her dad. Unbeknownest to her, two television producers from the Nickelodeon television network were in the audience, scouting for new talent. Both of the producers, Dan Schneider and Brian Robbins, were bowled over by Bynes's performance. According to Robbins, Bynes was "a tiny little thing with a wonderful sense of irony and comic timing." Schneider was impressed as well. "When I saw her on stage, she was the size of an avocado," he said. "But she was hysterical, and just totally won over the audience. And we had her come in and audition."

If Bynes was nervous about auditioning for a spot on Nickelodeon, she did not show it. Instead, she skillfully delivered over four pages of dialogue in front of a camera and a live audience. Schneider and Robbins were delighted with the performance, which confirmed their belief that they had discovered a naturally funny, talented, and likable girl. They immediately offered her a role in the Nick sketch comedy show "All That," where she spent the next three years honing her skills as an actress and comedian.

EDUCATION

Bynes never let her love for performing interfere with her studies. On the contrary, she posted straight As not only in English—her favorite subject—but also in other classes. As Bynes's career in entertainment blossomed, however, she and her parents realized that it would be difficult for her to maintain a regular school schedule. With this in mind, they arranged for a private tutor for the young actress. Throughout Bynes's years at Nickelodeon, she began each morning with a long session with her tutor. She continued to use a private tutor after leaving Nick to pursue other television and film opportunities.

CAREER HIGHLIGHTS

One of Nickelodeon's Brightest Stars

Bynes joined the cast of the Nickelodeon television show "All That" in 1995. She spent the next several years working with other child actors on the variety show, which featured a group of young performers doing short comedy scenes. The series was aimed at young adolescents—"tweens" making the transition between childhood and the teen years. By the end of her first year on the show, Bynes had emerged as one of the show's most popular performers. Indeed, some of the roles she played—such as a starship commander named Captain Tantrum and Ashley the obnoxious advice columnist—ranked among the most popular characters on the show. In 1997 she even earned a Cable Ace Award nomination in recognition of her comic contributions to the show.

Bynes admitted that the demands of performing on a television series sometimes exhausted her. "Memorizing lines can be difficult," she noted. "It's hard when I have to go home and say to myself, 'Okay, Amanda, you've got to get the lines in your head!' Sometimes I try to write my lines down from memory. It's kind of like studying for a test."

Fortunately, Bynes's enthusiasm for her work always kept her in a positive frame of mind. In fact, she exhibited a strong determination to improve her skills as an actor. For example, during her years on "All That" she worked very hard to strengthen her comic timing and her delivery of lines. She did

Bynes relaxes with a book at her home in California.

not want to always rely on acting coaches or the director for guidance on her performance. Schneider and Robbins, meanwhile, expressed amazement at their young star's ability to handle anything they threw at her. "I've never written a part for her she couldn't pull off," declared Schneider.

In 1997 Bynes moved on to a new Nickelodeon game show called "Figure It Out," although she continued to make appearances on "All That" through 2000. On "Figure It Out," a panel of kids affiliated with the Nickelodeon network faced off against kid contestants with a secret talent or accomplishment. On each episode, the panelists quizzed the guest with questions in an effort to guess their secret—and avoid getting "slimed" with gallons of colorful goo. Bynes appeared regularly on "Figure It Out" from 1997 to 2000, showcasing a funny and exuberant personality that further boosted her popularity with Nickelodeon viewers.

"The Amanda Show"

In 1999 Nickelodeon decided to make Bynes the host and main attraction of a new comedy-variety television show patterned as a kids' version of "Saturday Night Live." This show, called "The Amanda Show" in honor of Bynes, featured comedy sketches and musical acts aimed at young audi-

Bynes poses for the camera on the set of "The Amanda Show,"
which broadcast on Nickelodeon from 1999 to 2002.

ences. "The first time I got the script, it said, 'The Amanda Show' on it," Bynes remembered. "I thought they were kidding. I'm still little Amanda, and to be getting my own show, it's like, oh, my gosh!"

When "The Amanda Show" premiered on Nickelodeon in October 1999, the 13-year-old Bynes became the youngest host of a weekly network show in television history. The program and its likable star immediately attracted big audiences. Each show began with Bynes delivering a stand-up monologue, then progressed with a series of comic skits and musical numbers. As the show progressed, Bynes developed a number of popular recurring characters, including Moody Fallon, part of a gang of teens based on the characters from the television series "Dawson's Creek." Other silly characters played by Bynes included the celebrity-obsessed Penolope Taynt and stern Judge Trudy.

Even as "The Amanda Show" brought Bynes legions of new Nick fans, however, she explored other career opportunities as well. In late 1999, for example, she appeared on the HBO program "Arli$$" as a star ice skater who discovers that her parents are stealing her earnings. This guest role marked Bynes's first appearance on a program for adults.

Balancing Fame and Normal Life

By 2000, Bynes had emerged as one of the country's most successful and popular young entertainers. That year she was honored at the Nickelodeon Kids Choice Awards as Favorite TV Actress (the first of four consecutive awards in this category). Soon, offers to appear on other television shows began to pile up. But she didn't let her rising popularity affect her. She claimed that she still preferred "jeans and a t-shirt" to any other type of clothing, and she made a special effort to maintain her friendships with people outside of the entertainment world. "When I'm at work, I'm 'Work Amanda,' but when I come home and talk to all my friends, I'm 'Regular Amanda,'" she explained. "My friends come to tapings of my show and hang out afterward. We never talk about show business. We talk about a lot more important things, like shopping and boys."

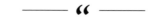

"When I'm at work, I'm 'Work Amanda,' but when I come home and talk to all my friends, I'm 'Regular Amanda,'" Bynes said. "My friends come to tapings of my show and hang out afterward. We never talk about show business. We talk about a lot more important things, like shopping and boys."

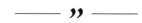

Bynes's family also has helped her stay grounded by treating her just like a normal teen-ager. "I think my parents are a big part of that because I'm still a normal kid," she said. "I can't do whatever I want! . . . Just like anyone else, [my parents] make important decisions for me. I'm a normal teen, and I have to listen to what they say." Bynes admitted, however, that she sometimes feels the normal teen resentment of parental authority. "Like there are times I get frustrated because I want to wear certain shoes and they don't want me to wear them. It's all good in the end because I realize that there will be a time and place for high shoes. . . . I wouldn't say I

115

was a different person at home, but I don't have a job at home and my parents make me do the exact same things like before I was on TV. I wake up and I'm the exact same lazy person who doesn't want to make her bed. That would be me!"

For their part, members of Bynes's family, who refer to her by the affectionate nickname "Chicky," have repeatedly expressed pride in the way their youngest member has handled the celebrity limelight. "The great thing about Amanda is that she doesn't have a Hollywood attitude," said her brother Tom. "She does her thing on camera, and when she's done she comes home and she's just an ordinary kid."

Breaking Into the Movies

In 2001, Bynes was approached to star in a feature film called *Big Fat Liar,* co-starring Frankie Muniz, the well-known star of the "Malcom in the Middle" television series. Bynes jumped at the opportunity, eager to accept the challenge of a role in a major motion picture. "People don't recognize I'm getting older," she said. "They see reruns of 'All That' so they assume I'm ten years old. I'm 16. I'm almost 5 [feet], 8 [inches]. I'm driving now."

Released in 2002, *Big Fat Liar* concerns a boy (played by Muniz) who constantly gets himself into trouble with his lies. When he writes a story about this terrible habit, a producer steals his idea to make a hit movie. Outraged, the boy tells everyone about the producer's actions, only to find that no one believes him. This leads him and his best friend, played by Bynes, to take off for Hollywood to

"Frankie [Muniz] and I had a lot of fun doing the movie," Bynes recalled. "We had golf carts in the movie, so sometimes we would steal them and drive around the Universal backlot. It was very fun."

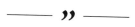

get revenge. The rest of the movie is about their adventures as they track the producer down. "Frankie and I had a lot of fun doing the movie," recalled Bynes. "We had golf carts in the movie, so sometimes we would steal them and drive around the Universal backlot. It was very fun—we had fun doing that, I must say."

Big Fat Liar proved to be a nice moneymaker for Universal Studios. It cost only $15 million to make, but earned over $50 million. The movie gathered only mixed reviews, but most critics agreed that Bynes's performance as the spunky, spirited sidekick was one of the film's highlights.

The year 2002 also marked Bynes's departure from Nickelodeon. She recognized that she owed her thriving career to shows such as "All That" and "The Amanda Show," but she knew that she needed to select more

The WB series "What I Like About You" features Wesley Jonathan (left),
Bynes (front left), Jennie Garth (front right), and Simon Rex (right).

grown-up roles. With this in mind, Bynes accepted a starring role in a new situation comedy (sitcom) called "What I Like About You" on the Warner Brothers (WB) television network.

In the show, which also features former "Beverly Hills 90210" star Jennie Garth, Bynes plays 16-year-old Holly, a spirited girl who has to move in with her uptight older sister (played by Garth) in Manhattan when her dad leaves for a job in Japan. Many of the show's early episodes highlighted Bynes's talent for slapstick comedy, while simultaneously exploring the deepening relationship between the two siblings. The show immediately proved popular with young viewers, and critics praised Bynes for her energetic performances. The *Los Angeles Times*, for example, declared that "Bynes handles the quick-tempo comic bantering [in the show] like the seasoned pro she already is."

What a Girl Wants

Bynes's hot streak continued in 2003 with her starring role in *What a Girl Wants*, a major motion picture that also featured Colin Firth and Kelly Preston. A remake of an older movie and play called *The Reluctant Debutante*, it featured Bynes as a girl named Daphne who has grown up in New York City with her free-spirited mother. She has never known her father, a haughty English lord played by Firth. In fact, Firth's character is not even aware that his brief marriage to Daphne's mother 17 years earlier produced a daughter. As the film unfolds, Daphne decides that she can't move on with life until she meets her father, so she flies off to London to introduce herself. The result is an amusing clash between Daphne's outgoing American ways and the stiff British manners of her father and his extended family.

> " *"We captured [Bynes] just at the moment she's becoming a woman, and of course, she has this amazingly huge following, so once we knew she was interested, it was a slam-dunk," said Dennie Gordon, director of* **What a Girl Wants.** *"This is the movie where she gets to show that she's a big, grown-up young lady who can both wear ball gowns [yet] look fabulous in T-shirt and jeans."* "

Director Dennie Gordon was thrilled that Bynes agreed to play the part of Daphne. "When I met Amanda, she was so clearly this girl," Gordon recalled. "She's worldly, yet still in awe of the world. We captured her just at the moment she's becoming a woman, and of course she has this amazingly huge following, so once we knew she was interested, it was a slam-dunk. This is the movie where she gets to show that she's a big, grown-up young lady who can both wear ball gowns (yet) look fabulous in T-shirt and jeans."

Bynes dances the night away in a scene from What a Girl Wants (2003).

Bynes and co-star Colin Firth in What a Girl Wants.

What a Girl Wants received a generally warm reception from critics, who saw it as an upbeat comedy especially well-suited to girls in their early to mid-teens. Most reviewers singled out Bynes's bubbly performance as the key to the movie's appeal. *Entertainment Weekly* observed that "in her sassy but scrubbed way, Bynes is a real charmer." The *Cincinnati Enquirer*, meanwhile, described her as "an appealing and energetic leading lady."

According to Bynes, her starring role in *What a Girl Wants* was a perfect match for her long-term career plans. "I want to be looked at as an adult actress," she said. "That's why I didn't want to do a big movie when I was 11. I was waiting till I was a little bit older." With this goal in mind, Bynes made numerous appearances on more adult-oriented programs in 2002 and 2003. In 2003 alone, for example, she appeared on "The Tonight Show with Jay Leno," cohosted MTV's "Total Request Live," and served as a presenter at the MTV Music Awards.

> ———— **"** ————
>
> *"You can watch the re-runs of 'I Love Lucy,' and it's just as good as the first time you saw it,"* Bynes said. *"[Lucille Ball is] kind of my idol — just go for the laughs, and don't worry about what you look like."*
>
> ———— **"** ————

MAJOR INFLUENCES

Bynes enjoys watching many actors and actresses, including Jim Carrey, Kirsten Dunst, Kevin Kline, Lisa Kudrow, Carol Burnett, Cameron Diaz, and Martin Short. But she claims that the actress who has inspired her the most in her own career is legendary comedian Lucille Ball. "You can watch the re-runs of 'I Love Lucy,' and it's just as good as the first time you saw it," Bynes declared. "She's kind of my idol — just go for the laughs, don't worry about what you look like."

HOBBIES AND OTHER INTERESTS

Bynes has many interests besides acting, including swimming, shopping, drawing, painting, writing, and reading. "I love the dictionary!" she has declared. "I love words and books. . . . I read right before bed mostly, and I feel like I have to know what every word means so I keep my dictionary next to me. I don't know why, I just have this fascination." She also likes word games like Scrabble and Jumble: "They're good for the mind," she says.

Another one of Bynes's passions is sketching fashion designs. "I've been drawing since kindergarten," she noted. "As I watch a fashion show or an

*Bynes and actor Jim Carrey laugh it up during a May 15, 2003,
appearance on the "Tonight Show."*

award show, I copy what I see. The Oscars have the newest fashions—
that's the show I look forward to the most." Bynes claims that she has
filled 50 sketch books with designs over the years. "My mom's artistic and
my dad's funny, so I guess that's where I get it from," she said.

Bynes's favorite foods include pizza, hamburgers, mint chocolate and
malt ball crunch ice cream, stir-fry vegetables, pasta, and chicken Caesar
salad. She also enjoys all types of music, from current bands like the
Dave Matthews Band, No Doubt, Blink 182, Britney Spears, Pink, and 'N
Sync to older performers such as James Taylor and Sting.

SELECTED CREDITS

Movies

Big Fat Liar, 2002
What a Girl Wants, 2003
Charlotte's Web 2, 2003 (voice of Nellie)

Television

"All That," 1996-2000
"Figure It Out," 1997-2000

"The Amanda Show," 1999-2002
"What I Like About You," 2002-
"Rugrats," 2002- (as voice of Taffy)

HONORS AND AWARDS

Nickelodeon Kid's Choice Award: 2000, 2001, 2002, and 2003, Favorite TV
   Actress
Nickelodeon Kid's Choice Award: 2003, Favorite Movie Actress

FURTHER READING

Periodicals

American Girl, Jan./Feb. 2000, p.12
Cincinnati Enquirer, Apr. 4, 2003, p.A5
Detroit News, Nov. 28, 2002, p.G5
Entertainment Weekly, Apr. 11, 2003, p.57
Los Angeles Times, Apr. 4, 2003, p.15; May 2, 2003, p.E30
McCalls, Dec. 2000, p.42
New York Daily News, Feb. 4, 2002, p.35
New York Times, Oct. 20, 2002, p.B27
Teen Magazine, Apr. 2002, p.48
Time, Apr. 14, 2003, p. 76
Washington Post, Nov. 17, 2000, p.C11

ADDRESS

Amanda Bynes
Warner Brothers
4000 Warner Blvd.
Burbank, CA 91522

WORLD WIDE WEB SITES

http://thewb.com
http://whatagirlwantsmovie.warnerbros.com
http://www.nick.com

Kelly Clarkson 1982-

American Singer
Winner of a Million-Dollar Recording Contract on the
2002 TV Series "American Idol"

BIRTH

Kelly Clarkson was born on April 24, 1982, in Burleson, Texas — a town with a population of 27,000 located about 10 miles south of Fort Worth. Her parents, Steve Clarkson and Jeanne Taylor, separated when she was six years old and eventually divorced. Kelly lived with her mother, a first-grade teacher, and her stepfather, Jimmy Taylor, a contractor. She has an older sister, Alyssa, an older brother, Jason, and five step-siblings.

YOUTH

Clarkson was an outgoing and fun-loving child who enjoyed performing from an early age. She often entertained her family by singing songs from Walt Disney musicals, like *Beauty and the Beast* and *The Little Mermaid*, in the living room of their middle-class home. Clarkson also had a kind heart and often tried to help others. As a teenager, she once gave the last five dollars in her wallet to a homeless person, then almost ran out of gas on her way home.

Jeanne Taylor recalled that her daughter had only one major fault growing up. "[Kelly] was easy to raise, except for having to get her up in the morning to go to school," she noted. "When they say she sometimes went [to school] in her pajamas, they mean it. The alarm clock would be blasting right beside her head, and she didn't hear a thing. The house could have fallen apart and she'd still be sleeping."

> **"**
>
> *"I was going to be in band, and Ms. Glenn, my seventh-grade choir teacher, heard me sing in the hallway and was like, 'Why aren't you in choir?' So I got in and realized I had a talent there."*
>
> **"**

EDUCATION

Clarkson attended the public schools in Burleson. She was a good student who impressed her teachers with her energy and willingness to work hard. One of her junior high teachers, Cindy Glenn, convinced her to join the school choir. "I was going to be in band, and Ms. Glenn, my seventh-grade choir teacher, heard me sing in the hallway and was like, 'Why aren't you in choir?'" Clarkson remembered. "So I got in and realized I had a talent there." Before long Clarkson began dreaming of making a career as a professional singer. "My first solo was 'Vision of Love' by Mariah Carey in seventh grade and afterward I told my mom that I thought I might do this for my career," she recalled.

As a student at Burleson High School, Clarkson played on the volleyball team and was a member of the school choir, which performed overseas. She also took part in several school musicals, playing the female lead in a production of *Brigadoon* during her senior year. "Already then Kelly could do any and all musical styles," said Burleson High choir director Philip Glenn. Clarkson graduated from high school in the spring of 2000.

CAREER HIGHLIGHTS

Trying to Launch a Singing Career

After graduating from high school, Clarkson recorded demo tapes in hopes of being discovered as a singer. In the meantime, she accepted a series of odd jobs in Burleson. She worked as a cocktail waitress at a comedy club, as a clerk at a bookstore and a pharmacy, as a ticket seller at a movie theater, and as a telemarketer. In 2001 she moved with a friend to Los Angeles, California, in hopes of breaking into show business. During her time in Los Angeles, she appeared as an extra on the TV series "Sabrina, the Teenage Witch" and recorded a few demo tapes for the well-known songwriter Gerry Goffin. But then Clarkson ran into a string of bad luck that made her question her decision to move to California. First Goffin became ill, then her apartment burned down, then her friend decided to leave Los Angeles. Clarkson took the series of events as a sign that she should return home to Texas.

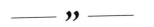

"Throughout the whole competition, I wasn't looking to win; I was looking for exposure. I'm just an 'average girl,' so I never expect the top. I never look that far in advance."

Although Clarkson was discouraged when she got back to Burleson, she remained determined to build a career as a singer. She told her mother, "I have to sing, I don't know what else to do." In the meantime, she got a job as a promotional worker for an energy drink. A few days after Clarkson returned from California, she went to visit one of her friends, Jessica Brake. Brake's mother showed the girls an Internet site about an upcoming TV series called "American Idol: The Search for a Superstar." The show—which was based on a popular British show called "Pop Idol"—was supposed to showcase young, unknown singers. On each episode, the singers would perform and then receive comments from a panel of judges. Once the episode ended, TV viewers would have two hours to call in and register their votes for the night's best performer. One singer would be eliminated from the show each week, and the final contestant would win a million-dollar recording contract.

Clarkson learned that auditions for "American Idol" would be held in seven U.S. cities, including nearby Dallas, Texas. Her friend immediately began trying to convince her to attend the Dallas audition. When Clarkson expressed doubts, Brake filled out the online application form for her.

Clarkson with Guarini.

Clarkson became more excited as the auditions approached. In fact, she was so worried about sleeping through her audition that she stayed up the whole night before. Across the country, more than 10,000 people between the ages of 16 and 24 tried out to appear on "American Idol." Judges held a series of callbacks to narrow the field to 30 contestants, who were invited to attend tryouts in Hollywood, California. These tryouts reduced the field to ten finalists who would compete on the air. Clarkson performed well at each stage and was selected to appear on "American Idol" as one of the ten finalists.

Appearing on "American Idol"

Clarkson and the other nine singers were asked to move to California for three months of filming. They all lived together in a 13-bedroom, 8-bathroom estate that featured a pool, hot tub, steam room, big-screen TV, workout equipment, and a chef. But the contestants had very little time to enjoy the luxurious house. Their days were packed with rehearsals, voice coaching, wardrobe selection, and promotional appearances. Clarkson claims that she often survived on three to four hours of sleep per night, and even admitted that "there are days I just don't shower." Despite the hectic schedule and the pressure of the show, however, all the contestants got along very well. "Of course, there are going to be ups and downs with people because of the stress, but nobody got in fights," Clarkson recalled. "We were all too busy. Nobody believes us, but we were literally too busy to have any kind of conflict."

> "I just try to be as real as I can be—the kind of person who doesn't really care if she is caught without makeup, not some ultra-professional musician who is only 'on' when in front of the camera."

"American Idol" made its premier on the Fox television network on June 11, 2002. Given the number of finalists, Clarkson did not perform in the first episode. The first time viewers got to hear her powerful voice was two weeks later, when she sang "Respect" by Aretha Franklin. "I wasn't on the first two shows and I thought I would have to come out with a big song," she remembered. "I had sung 'Respect' karaoke with friends. I feel that song and I love that song. It's upbeat, it's got soul, it shows your range. It's a show stopper, the song itself." Clarkson received mostly positive comments from the three judges—singer Paula Abdul, record producer Randy Jackson, and British music executive Simon Cowell. She also earned enough votes from viewers to remain on the show.

As the weeks passed, Clarkson turned in consistently strong performances that showcased the power and range of her voice. "I know my voice and what I can do," she explained. "I just rehearse and pray to God that He won't let me screw up on national television." Clarkson also appeared calm on stage and impressed both the judges and the viewers with her sweet, friendly nature. "I just try to be as real as I can be—the kind of person who doesn't really care if she is caught without makeup, not some ultra-professional musician who is only 'on' when in front of the camera,"

she noted. Clarkson also stood out from the other contestants because she wore sophisticated evening attire rather than sexy, belly-baring outfits when she performed. By mid-August, Clarkson had advanced to the final four contestants, along with Justin Guarini, Nikki McKibbin, and Tamyra Gray. She expressed nothing but fondness and admiration for her fellow contestants. "It's not a competition between the contestants," she stated. "It's me competing with myself."

Gray was voted off the show the following week, which shocked many viewers who believed she had the strongest voice in the competition. McKibbin was voted off next, leaving only Clarkson and Guarini to compete for the million-dollar prize. Although the judges and most viewers acknowledged that Clarkson was the better singer, the curly-haired Guarini had good stage presence and a huge fan base among young women, which placed the final vote in doubt. On the second-to-last episode of

Clarkson poses backstage after winning in the final episode of "American Idol," September 5, 2002.

"American Idol," Clarkson and Guarini performed the same songs back-to-back. Afterward the three judges, including the notoriously nasty Cowell, praised her performance and recommended that viewers select her as the winner.

Winning the Viewers' Hearts

Votes were tallied immediately after the show ended, and the winner was announced at the end of a two-hour special episode the following night, September 4. Shortly before the results were announced, Clarkson and Guarini sang a duet of "It Takes Two," which confirmed the fact that Clarkson's voice was much stronger than that of her rival. Finally, the show's hosts announced that Clarkson had defeated Guarini with 58 percent of the viewer vote to become the first American Idol and win the million-dollar recording contract. More than 15 million people had called in to express their opinions. Clarkson was surprised when she learned she had won. "Throughout the whole competition, I wasn't looking to win; I was looking for exposure," she explained. "I'm just an 'average girl,' so I never expect the top. I never look that far in advance."

Guarini was gracious in defeat, declaring that "No one deserves it more than this woman right here." "He is so sweet," Clarkson responded. "He is just the greatest. He didn't have to say what he said. He's a great guy inside and out. I know that he will probably outsell all of us. He's such a cutie and such a great writer." Several of the other finalists also expressed their agreement with the result of the final vote. "Kelly is phenomenal," said McKibbin. "Starting with that incredible voice. She has obviously been the crowd favorite and she just deserves every stitch of everything she is receiving." Shortly after learning that she had won, Clarkson was asked to sing "A Moment Like This," a song written especially for the "American Idol" winner. She struggled to get through the song while fighting back tears of happiness. The other finalists joined in to help her with the last few minutes of the finale.

Clarkson's life was a whirlwind in the weeks following the "American Idol" final vote. She appeared on countless TV talk shows and magazine covers, filmed music videos and a VH-1 documentary about her life, and launched a 28-city concert tour with the other finalists. Throughout all of the publicity, Clarkson was often asked whether the obviously close relationship between her and Guarini had turned romantic. She insisted that they were just friends and described her heartthrob fellow finalist as "like a brother." "Everyone always says there's something between me and Justin, but we get along so well because we are both so focused," she explained. "Neither of us wants to start a relationship knowing we don't have the time to sleep let alone have a boyfriend."

> "Being on stage in front of millions is the biggest rush for me. It's like I'm kind of nervous at first, but once I get out there I never want to leave the stage!"

Fans of "American Idol" also wanted to hear Clarkson's opinion of the show's acid-tongued judge, Simon Cowell. "He is a great guy off camera, funny as anything," she revealed. "But, I mean, on the show, and with his business in general, he's very serious and he doesn't want to work with people he doesn't think can handle the pressure or he doesn't think are good enough. I mean he's going to be honest with you business-wise but he's a great guy in general when you're not on camera or talking about business." Still, Clarkson admitted that her favorite judge was Randy Jackson. "He's the one who's been on every side of the whole equation for making an album," she noted. Clarkson added that the judges' comments were not difficult for her to take because "it's three people's opinion. There are a lot more people in the industry. Simon is not a fan of Britney Spears, and look how well she is doing."

Turning TV Success into a Recording Career

Although Clarkson received a great deal of attention as the winner of "American Idol," some people wondered whether she would be able to turn it into a successful recording career. She got off to a good start with her first single. "A Moment Like This"/ "Before Your Love" hit No. 1 on the *Billboard* Top 100 charts, selling 236,000 copies in a single week. Clarkson also contributed four songs, including "Respect" and "You Make Me Feel Like a Natural Woman" as well as the two songs from her single, to the *American Idol: Greatest Moments* collection. This album featured two songs from Guarini and one song from each of the other finalists. In addition, all ten finalists sang together on the song "California Dreamin.'"

> "The one thing I love about this show is our versatility, and I hope to do that on my album. I want to do a kind of rock meets soul, and I hope people are open to that since I've done that on the show. I'm all about my sound and my style. That's important for me to stand up to. I came out on the show being myself and doing what I like, and people voted for me. So I already have a fan base based on what I like and what I do."

Clarkson also began working on her solo album, which was scheduled for release in early 2003. Her record label recruited several well-known songwriters to provide material for it, and Clarkson hoped to add some of her own compositions. "The one thing I love about this show is our versatility, and I hope to do that on my album. I want to do a kind of rock meets soul, and I hope people are open to that since I've done that on the show," she noted. "I'm all about my sound and my style. That's important for me to stand up to. I came out on the show being myself and doing what I like, and people voted for me. So I already have a fan base based on what I like and what I do."

But some music industry insiders worried that Clarkson could become a "one-hit wonder" once the popularity of *American Idol* wore off. They criticized the songs that were included on her single and warned that she needed better material if her album was to be a success. "Celine Dion or

Mariah Carey wouldn't cross the street to spit on those songs. And that's who Kelly is competing against now—it's not just Justin anymore," said *Rolling Stone* music editor Joe Levy. "People voted for Kelly because she had a sweetness and a vulnerability in addition to astounding ability. They've got to give her songs that communicate something about her personality. Otherwise, she might as well be queen of the Thanksgiving Day parade rather than a pop star."

Clarkson experienced the downside of her newfound fame just a few days after her "American Idol" victory, when she was contacted by Champions of Hope, a national youth organization. The youth group invited her to sing the national anthem at the Lincoln Memorial in Washington, D.C., as part of a ceremony honoring the anniversary of the terrorist attacks of September 11, 2001. But many people criticized the group's choice. They claimed that Clarkson had only come to public attention through "reality

TV." They argued that allowing her to sing would be inappropriate because it would promote "American Idol" during a day of mourning. Upon learning of the controversy, Clarkson expressed some reservations about singing in Washington. "If I do it, I will get criticized, and if I don't do it and pull out of it, I'll also get criticized," she said. "It's a lose-lose situation." With the support of her management company, however, Clarkson did appear at the event.

Despite the hectic schedule and constant attention, Clarkson thoroughly enjoyed her experience on "American Idol." "Being on stage in front of millions is the biggest rush for me," she explained. "It's like I'm kind of nervous at first, but once I get out there I never want to leave the stage!" She also offered the following advice for future contestants: "Be confident. Do not show fear. That's the one thing Simon and Randy will get you for. They know a performer must be fearless. If you feel it, don't show it. Also take what's unique about you and go with it."

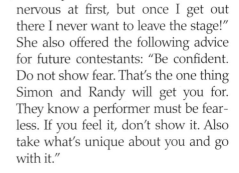

> *Clarkson offers the following advice for future contestants: "Be confident. Do not show fear. That's the one thing Simon and Randy will get you for. They know a performer must be fearless. If you feel it, don't show it. Also take what's unique about you and go with it."*

HOME AND FAMILY

Clarkson is not married and says she has no time for dating. She loves her home state and her fellow Texans, and she plans to remain there even if she becomes a pop star. "I'm living in Texas. I don't care how many times I have to fly," she stated. "I've been everywhere—New York and LA—and it's just a different feel when you go to Texas. . . . Everyone knows each other, so if you meet one person, you'll meet the whole town through them. We're just cool."

Clarkson remains close to her family. Her father, mother, stepfather, brother, and sister were all part of the studio audience for the final episodes of "American Idol." "My parents have been so supportive and kept me grounded," she noted. "I come from a Godly family and I know that helps."

HOBBIES AND OTHER INTERESTS

In her spare time, Clarkson loves watching movies. She has written a few film scripts and says she might try acting someday. She also wants to learn to play guitar. She plans to use some of her "American Idol" winnings to buy a 2003 Corvette for her friend Jessica Brake, who convinced her to audition for the show.

FURTHER READING

Periodicals

Austin American Statesman, Sep. 3, 2002, p.E1

Dallas Morning News, July 2, 2002, p.A19; Aug. 20, 2002, p.C1; Aug. 29, 2002, p.A33; Sep. 4, 2002, pp.A1, A25; Sep. 5, 2002, p.A15

Fort Worth Star-Telegram, July 24, 2002, Life and Arts sec., p.1; Sep. 5, 2002, News sec., p.1; Sep. 10, 2002, Metro sec., p.2; Sep. 28, 2002, Metro sec., p.1

Houston Chronicle, Sep. 9, 2002, p.3

Los Angeles Times, Sep. 5, 2002, p.A15; Sep. 23, 2002, p.F14

New York Post, Sep. 5, 2002, p.7; Sep. 6, 2002, p.111; Sep. 7, 2002, p.53

New York Times, Sep. 8, 2002, p.L1

People, Sep. 9, 2002, p.52

Tampa Tribune, Sep. 6, 2002, p.2

TV Guide, July 13, 2002, p.10; Sep. 21, 2002, p.40

Us, Sep. 23, 2002, p.44

USA Today, Aug. 29, 2002, p.D3; Sep. 5, 2002, p.D1; Sep. 26, 2002, p.D1

Washington Post, Sep. 5, 2002, p.C1

YM, Nov. 2002, p.86

ADDRESS

Kelly Clarkson
RCA Records
1540 Broadway
New York, NY 10036

WORLD WIDE WEB SITES

http://idolonfox.com
http://www.rcarecords.com
http://www.rollingstone.com/artists/bio.asp?oid=2044862&cf=2044862

Vin Diesel 1967-

American Actor
Star of the Hit Action Movies *The Fast and the Furious*
and *XXX*

BIRTH

Vin Diesel was born on July 18, 1967, in New York City. His
name was originally Mark Vincent, but he changed it when he
was in his late teens. Vin was raised by his mother, Delora, an
astrologer and psychologist, and his stepfather, Irving, an
actor and drama teacher. He never knew his biological father
and claims that he still has "no overwhelming desire to meet

him." Vin has a non-identical twin brother, film editor Paul Vincent, as well as two younger step-siblings.

YOUTH

Diesel grew up in the Manhattan section of New York City. His family lived in a small apartment in Westbeth, a government-funded housing complex in trendy Greenwich Village that was home to many actors, artists, and musicians. Diesel enjoyed exploring the city as a boy. "I had this magical childhood," he remembered. "In the winter, I remember my father pulling my brother and me around Washington Square Park in a cheap red plastic sled. In the summer, my mother would take us to the fountain at the park, and we'd swim in it."

Perhaps due to the influence of his stepfather, Diesel always wanted to be an actor. "Acting is the only thing I ever knew that I wanted to do. People are designed differently and I think I was designed in a way that I needed to perform and work out my things in front of the camera," he noted. "I was a huge fan of *Mad Max, The Terminator,* and *Conan the Barbarian* growing up. Whenever I was asked what I wanted to do when I grew up, I always said, 'Actor.' But if that was too implausible and I needed something to fall back on, my second choice would always be 'Superhero.'"

> "
>
> *"I had this magical childhood. In the winter, I remember my father pulling my brother and me around Washington Square Park in a cheap red plastic sled. In the summer, my mother would take us to the fountain at the park, and we'd swim in it."*
>
> "

Diesel's interest in performing was apparent from an early age. For example, he went to the circus with his family when he was three years old. Once the show ended and all the animals and clowns had left the ring, Diesel tried to climb in. When his mother grabbed him and asked what he was doing, the little boy replied, "Mommy, I'm ready to do *my* show." At the age of five, Diesel was cast in a Westbeth children's production of *Cinderella.* He played a horse, while his twin brother got the role of Prince Charming. But Paul suffered from stage fright and was too scared to go onstage. Diesel ended up covering for him and becoming the star of the show.

Diesel joined a local theater company at the age of seven, after he and some of his neighborhood friends broke into the building where the group performed. "We were terrorizing the neighborhood, a few of us, and we went into this theater," he recalled. "We went in and we were vandalizing the theater, playing around in the mezzanine, and this woman comes out in the spotlight, this heavyset woman who summons us. I thought she was going to get us in trouble and call the cops on us. She said, 'If you guys want to play here, come every day at four o'clock. Know your lines.' That was the first time I was ever able to make a whole audience laugh without getting sent to the dean's office."

———— **"** ————

"I am truly multicultural. I'm neither black nor white. People like to put each other in boxes because it allows them to categorize, create labels, and stereotype. In the neighborhood where I grew up, most of the kids I knew were multiracial. I had to deal with a lot of [stuff] growing up because I'm multicultural, and there were no multicultural icons or role models. It was a struggle to define myself as a person up against other people's expectations."

———— **"** ————

Diesel's racial heritage is a bit ambiguous. Many sources say his background includes African-American, Italian-American, and several other groups, although Diesel has avoided clarifying this. He does say that throughout his childhood, he struggled to come to terms with his heritage. The situation was difficult because he did not know his biological father, and his stepfather was black. As a result, Diesel always identified with many ethnic groups and resisted being linked with any one group. "I am truly multicultural. I'm neither black nor white," he stated. "People like to put each other in boxes because it allows them to categorize, create labels, and stereotype. In the neighborhood where I grew up, most of the kids I knew were multiracial. I had to deal with a lot of [stuff] growing up because I'm multicultural, and there were no multicultural icons or role models. It was a struggle to define myself as a person up against other people's expectations."

EDUCATION

Diesel's parents were educated people who emphasized the importance of learning. Diesel received his education at the prestigious Anglo-American International School in New York City. It was a private school in which half of the students came from foreign countries. After earning his high school diploma, Diesel studied acting at the Theater for the New City and English at Hunter College.

CAREER HIGHLIGHTS

Struggling to Make It as an Actor

Committed to building a career as an actor, Diesel performed in the repertory theater run by his father, then started appearing in off-off-Broadway plays. When he was 17, the muscular young man started working as a bouncer at some of New York City's trendiest nightclubs. Many of his fellow bouncers were known by nicknames, so he started calling himself Vin Diesel during this time. "I started bouncing because you need to have your days free to go and audition, rehearse, to be involved in theatrical productions," he explained. "The best job in the world was one that started at ten and ended at four in the morning. It was also a great job for someone at college. I don't think I was ever servile enough to be a waiter. I was always attracted to that nocturnal world."

Diesel ended up working as a bouncer for nine years while he struggled to make it as an actor. He eventually noticed that the tough-guy image he cultivated as a bouncer was hurting his chances at auditions. "What happened was I was going up for acting jobs and saying, 'Hi, my name is Vin Diesel,' and unwittingly reinforcing it with this giant monster standing behind me that I thought I'd left at work," he noted. "Even when I would go on auditions, and I had to be as amiable as possible, I still had this edge, this threatening physical presence. And I know that isn't who I really am."

In the early 1990s, Diesel took his life savings and some money borrowed from friends and moved to Hollywood, in California. He hoped that his experience on the New York stage would help him land roles in movies. After failing to find work for a year, however, he was forced to return to New York. At this point, he moved back in with his parents and spent his time watching classic movies on video. One day his mother gave him a book about filmmaking called *Feature Films at Used Car Prices*. Since Diesel was frustrated at his inability to find acting jobs, she suggested that he try making a movie of his own.

Diesel was captivated with the idea of shooting his own film. He wrote a screenplay about his own struggles to get discovered as an actor. Then he turned the screenplay into a short film, which he directed, produced, and starred in. The film, called *Multi-Facial,* was shot in two days for a budget of $3,000. It tells the story of a mixed-race aspiring actor who will play a character of any race in order to get a part. Diesel's film made its debut at the Anthology Film Archives in Manhattan in front of 200 people. In 1995 it was screened at the prestigious Cannes Film Festival in France, where it came to the attention of several high-profile filmmakers. "That night changed my life completely," Diesel remembered. "I still went through a few more years of sleeping on couches and struggling and taking odd jobs outside film. But I knew my life had changed."

The success of *Multi-Facial* gave Diesel the confidence to move back to Hollywood the following year. He took a job as a telemarketer in order to raise enough money to make a feature-length film. Once again acting as writer, director, producer, and star, Diesel created *Strays*, a film about a group of lowlife buddies living on New York's Lower East Side. Diesel's character, Rick, realizes that his friends are preventing him from reaching his goals when he meets Heather (played by Suzanne Lanza). Rick ends up feeling torn between his macho street image and the kind, sensitive side he shows to Heather. *Strays* was screened at the respected Sundance Film Festival in Utah in 1997, but it did not sell as well as Diesel had hoped.

> "I hated that I was the first to die," Diesel said about his role in **Saving Private Ryan**. "But, looking back, it made sense for [Spielberg] to kill the most formidable character first because you got a sense of the dangers that were present at war. The producer said afterwards that it was fortunate that I died first because everyone was now in restless anticipation of what I would do next as they didn't get enough of me the first time."

Being Discovered

Although Diesel's efforts as a film-maker did not earn much money, they did provide him with valuable exposure that led to important career opportunities. After seeing *Multi-Facial*, the famous director Steven Spielberg created a part for Diesel in his 1998 World War II movie *Saving Private Ryan*. Diesel played Private Adrian Caparzo, a tough-talking soldier with a soft heart. Caparzo ends up being the first member of the unit to be killed. He is shot by a German sniper as he tries to save the life of a French girl. "I hated that I was the first to die," Diesel admitted. "But, looking back, it made sense for [Spielberg] to kill the most formidable character first because you got a sense of the dangers that were present at war. The producer said afterwards that it was fortunate that I died first because everyone was now in restless anticipation of what I would do next as they didn't get enough of me the first time."

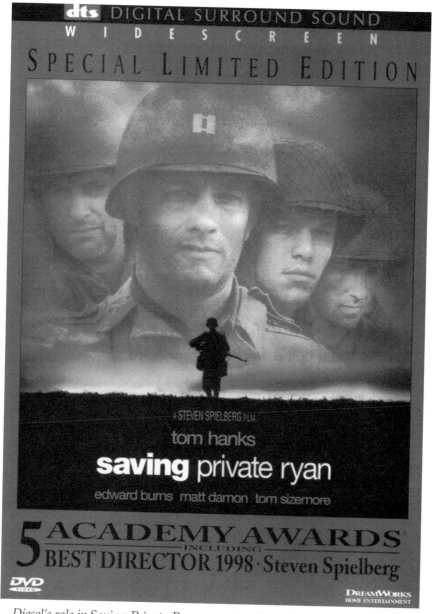

Diesel's role in Saving Private Ryan *was a turning point in his career, as the movie became a critical and audience hit.*

Saving Private Ryan went on to become a critical and audience hit, winning five Academy Awards. Thanks to his prominent role in Spielberg's picture, Diesel soon had his choice of acting roles. "That was a huge turning point because it introduced me, of course, to Hollywood," he recalled. "There's something about being *Saving Private Ryan's* Vin Diesel as opposed to the director of *Strays* and the director of *Multi-Facial,* an independent film-maker, that carries some validation, which is a huge blessing."

In 1999 Diesel provided his deep, gravelly voice to the title character in the animated film *The Iron Giant.* Based on a 1968 children's book by Ted Hughes, the movie tells the story of a young boy named Hogarth who meets a 50-foot-tall, metal-eating robot. At first Hogarth is frightened by the Iron Giant, but he still saves the creature when it becomes entangled in power lines. Hogarth takes the robot to live at a nearby scrap-metal yard, and the pair forge an unlikely friendship. But when local residents discover the Iron Giant, they call in government agents to deal with the creature, which they view as a threat. Diesel enjoyed giving voice to such a memo-rable animated character. "*Iron Giant* was one of the most amazing experi-ences," he noted. "It's such a positive film. We know that *Iron Giant* will be around forever, and it feels good to be associated with that, so loveable a character."

Getting His First Leading Roles

In 2000 Diesel played major roles in two very different movies that hap-pened to open at the same time. First he played Richard Riddick in the low-budget science-fiction thriller *Pitch Black.* Riddick has been convicted of murder and is being taken to prison on a space transport when the ship crash lands on a desolate planet. The crash allows Riddick to escape from the lawman who is responsible for him. At first the crew of the ship fear that Riddick will come after them. But in that hostile environment, the group comes together to fight the aliens and Riddick emerges as an un-likely leader and hero.

Diesel received positive reviews for his performance, and *Pitch Black* be-came a sort of cult classic. Marc Bernardin of *Entertainment Weekly* called the movie "intense and intelligent, unpredictable and inevitable." Diesel liked the Riddick character and the message that his transformation gave to the audience. "The film describes him as this convicted killer, but doesn't give any explanation or justification for it," he explained. "We find out later that maybe he was misrepresented. Maybe we prejudged him. Maybe we just critiqued him and measured him by what we heard. The Riddick character represents anybody who's been ruled out, given up on, or prejudged."

Although Diesel appreciated his character, he did not enjoy the experience of filming *Pitch Black* in the Australian desert. "I'm an ignorant guy from

New York. You say desert, I think hot. It was freezing," he remembered. "The crew were standing around with ear muffs on, and I was in a tank top with the wardrobe lady spraying water on me to look like sweat." Adding to his discomfort were the hard plastic contact lenses he had to wear to make his eyes look yellow. He compared wearing the lenses to putting hubcaps into his eyes. In fact, the lenses became stuck in his eyes during the first day of filming, and the director had to fly an eye doctor to the remote set to help Diesel remove them. "Between [the contacts] and the weather I needed absolutely no motivation to play homicidal," he admitted.

Diesel's second movie of 2000 was *Boiler Room,* a film about the pressure-filled world of stockbrokers that co-starred Ben Affleck and Giovanni Ribisi. Diesel played Chris Varick, a fast-talking, Italian-American stockbroker who makes a fortune by selling questionable investments to unsuspecting clients over the phone. Diesel enjoyed the fact that his character in *Boiler Room* was so different from his character in *Pitch Black*. The two movies opened at the same time, which allowed Diesel to demonstrate the range of his acting talents. "I picked this because it was a different kind of part," he said of *Boiler Room*. "I was in a suit and a tie the whole time, and there's something cool about that. There's something that adds to my filmography, the fact that this character in *Boiler Room* has nothing to do with this physically overbearing character in *Pitch Black*."

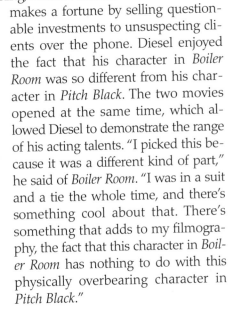

> "I picked this because it was a different kind of part," Diesel said of Boiler Room. "I was in a suit and a tie the whole time, and there's something cool about that. There's something that adds to my filmography, the fact that this character in Boiler Room has nothing to do with this physically overbearing character in Pitch Black."

Shortly after Diesel began landing major roles in movies, rumors began spreading around Hollywood that he was difficult to work with. These rumors started after he had a disagreement with director John Frankenheimer on the set of the action-thriller *Reindeer Games*. Diesel claims that upon reading the script, he was unhappy with his character. He says that Frankenheimer agreed to rewrite the role, but failed to follow through on his promise. When Diesel showed up on the set and found the script unchanged, he simply bowed out of the role. "I was inconsequential to the picture and thought I was leaving on good terms, that I did the right thing," he stated. "But Frankenheimer's ego was so bruised, he actually took the time to tell *Premiere* that he fired me. No director in the world would take time out to talk about firing a guy as insignificant as he thought I was."

Vin Diesel (black car) and Paul Walker (front car) in The Fast and the Furious.

The Fast and the Furious

With his unconventional looks and muscular build, Diesel was a natural to play leading roles in action movies. In 2001 he played outlaw street racer Dominic Toretto in the blockbuster *The Fast and the Furious*. In the film, Diesel's character is one of the best drivers in Los Angeles and the leader of a crew of rebels. When Toretto's crew is suspected of being involved in a series of high-profile carjackings, an undercover cop infiltrates the street-racing scene. The hot cars and fast action carried *The Fast and the Furious* to the top of the box office charts.

Although his character was a car nut and ace driver, Diesel admits that he did not know much about cars before making the movie. "I'm not that car-oriented, like I couldn't build an engine," he noted. "I grew up in New York City, so I guess I am more familiar with subways." Diesel tried to portray

———— " ————

"At first, this character doesn't care about the state of the world, like a large part of our youth," Diesel noted. *"And then he is recruited to save the world. The guy who is least likely to believe in anything learns to believe in something."*

———— " ————

Toretto as a complex character who has a tough side but is also very giving. "There's something very consistent about Dominic," he explained. "He lives outside of the law but he has his own moral code, which consists of many favorable and admirable attributes. He's honest, he's loyal, and he's a caretaker."

XXX

Diesel stayed with the action-movie genre in 2002, when he starred in the thriller *XXX*. He played Xander Cage, an underground athlete who sells videos of himself performing dangerous and often illegal stunts. Cage is finally arrested when he steals a politician's car, drives it off a bridge, and then parachutes to safety. But this stunt attracts the attention of the National Security Agency (NSA). The government agency decides that Cage's athletic ability—as well as the fact that they consider him expendable—would make him a good secret agent. He undergoes training and is then sent to Europe, where he tries to stop a terrorist group from using biological weapons against the United States. Using the code name XXX, or Triple X, Cage eventually comes to appreciate getting an opportunity to save the world. "At first, this character doesn't care about the state of the world, like a large part of our youth," Diesel noted. "And then he is recruited to save the world. The guy who is least likely to believe in anything learns to believe in something."

Diesel viewed his character as a sort of James Bond spy hero for a new generation. Xander Cage was intended to appeal to an audience that enjoyed the X-Games, body piercing, and industrial rock. "I mean, James Bond wears a suit. I don't know a kid today who wears a suit. So we've come up with a different kind of hero," Diesel explained. "A guy who's proficient at what he does because of all the time he wasted not doing his homework and learning how to do Superman grabs on a motocross instead. The kind of action hero people can relate to today."

Diesel went through a great deal of training in order to perform the complicated, dangerous stunts that appear in *XXX*. He trained with Navy SEALs, an elite group of highly trained naval officers. Diesel earned how to

Diesel in a scene from XXX.

speed-climb cliffs, ride a snowboard, and jump a motocross bike. Although he did many of his own stunts, the most harrowing feats—like snow-boarding down a mountain just ahead of an avalanche—were performed by professional stunt men. "I wanted to push the envelope as much as possible," Diesel said. "But I could not do it without my stunt team. The most amazing things were done by the professionals." The movie's non-stop action, along with its Generation X attitude and humor, helped propel *XXX* to the top of the box office charts in the weeks after its opening.

Following *XXX*, Diesel could be seen in theaters in *Knockaround Guys* (2002). This action film involves a mob family. One of the sons loses a bag of his father's money in a small Montana town, so several tough guys go to find it. But a crooked sheriff beats them to the bag and the cash, which leads to a lot of mayhem as they try to retrieve it. Following on the heels of Diesel's two blockbuster films, *Knockaround Guys* was less successful at the box office.

Living with Stardom

The success of Diesel's action films has led to a huge demand for his ser-vices. Some of his future projects include *Diablo*, in which he plays a drug enforcement agent who suffers from a mental breakdown; *Doorman*, based on his own script about his days as a bouncer; and sequels to *Pitch Black* (called *Riddick*) and *XXX*. Diesel has been careful to vary his roles so that he will not be pigeonholed as an action hero. "I don't want someone to think that's all I can do and then I can't have a career after 50, which is why I try to speckle my career with choices like *Boiler Room* and *Knockaround Guys*, less explosive-oriented films," he explained.

> **"**
>
> *Diesel viewed his character Xander Cage as a sort of James Bond spy hero for a new generation. "I mean, James Bond wears a suit. I don't know a kid today who wears a suit. So we've come up with a different kind of hero. A guy who's proficient at what he does because of all the time he wasted not doing his homework and learning how to do Superman grabs on a motocross instead. The kind of action hero people can relate to today."*
>
> **"**

Some critics claim that part of Diesel's appeal comes from his mixed racial background. They say that his unwillingness to reveal his ethnicity has allowed various audiences to adopt him as one of their own. Diesel is pleased that he can provide a role model for multicultural youths. "When I was younger there weren't any multicultural heroes. There was no such thing as a person who could list down 10 different nationalities. I feel I've overcome some stuff. What used to be the most restrictive aspect about me attaining my goals is now my ally," he stated. "In the early part of my career nobody knew what to do with me, but now I find I can do so many things because I come from origins that are a little ambiguous. I think I represent a certain future."

Although his imposing physical presence has led Diesel to play many tough characters, he is known for his ability to give those characters a gentler side. "Every character that I have, no matter how menacing he may appear to be, I try to layer it with colors," he noted. "And usually somewhere in that character, you'll find a door to his innocence." This combination of toughness and sensitivity has won Diesel huge numbers of female fans. "I never thought of myself as a sex symbol. It's always kind of weird and it's the one claim that kind of makes me blush," he admitted. "But it's very, very flattering."

Diesel claims that he would still be an actor even if he had never become a star. "The happiness that I derive from acting is a byproduct. It's a coincidence," he stated. "I act because I have to act. I've done it all my life, when

Diesel in a scene from Knockaround Guys.

the chips were down, I've done it because it's something that I have to do and that's the bottom line." He says that his 20-year struggle to make it as an actor "forced me to have huge respect for the craft. I'll give lines to other actors, I'll cast people who I know will steal scenes from me. It's really about the fact that I could die at any moment and if that's the last film I make, well, it had better be good."

HOME AND FAMILY

In 2000, Diesel purchased an 1,800-square-foot house with a pool in the Hollywood Hills, which he shares with his dog. "Getting a house was a huge, huge deal because my family always rented," he noted. Diesel, who is single, claims that he has little time for dating, though he has been linked romantically with several actresses and models. He says that he eventually wants to get married and have "a whole bunch of kids."

Diesel remains close to his parents, as well as many old friends from his neighborhood. Speaking about his stepfather, Diesel says that "My father taught me how to be a stand-up man, a man who fights for what he believes in. To me, my father is the pinnacle of what a real man is. In fact, it's hard to live up to him. I think I am fortunate that the people around me are very real. My friends are friends that I've had for many, many years and that's one way to keep your feet on the ground."

HOBBIES AND OTHER INTERESTS

In his spare time, Diesel enjoys yoga, Playstation, Dungeons and Dragons, classic movies, and Italian cooking.

FILMS

Multi-Facial, 1994
Strays, 1997
Saving Private Ryan, 1998
The Iron Giant, 1999
Pitch Black, 2000
Boiler Room, 2000
The Fast and the Furious, 2001
XXX, 2002
Knockaround Guys, 2002

FURTHER READING

Books

Contemporary Black Biography, Vol. 29, 2001

Periodicals

Boston Herald, Feb. 14, 2000, p.31; Aug. 6, 2002, p.37
Entertainment Weekly, Aug. 2, 2002, p.24; Aug. 16, 2002, p.43
GQ, Aug. 2002, p.109

Houston Chronicle, Aug. 4, 2002, p.10
Interview, Feb. 1999, p.40
Los Angeles Daily News, June 21, 2001, p.L3; Aug. 9, 2002, p.U6
Los Angeles Times, May 28, 2002, Calendar Sec., p.1
Minneapolis Star-Tribune, Feb. 19, 2000, p.E4
Newsweek, Aug. 5, 2002, p.56
People, Aug. 19, 2002, p.87
Seattle Times, Feb. 18, 2000, p.F7; Aug. 4, 2002, p.L3
Time, Aug. 5, 2002, p.61
USA Today, Aug. 7, 2002, p.D1

Online Articles

http://www.cnn.com/2000/SHOWBIZ/Movies/02/21/vin.diesel/index.html
(*CNN.com,* "The Drive of Vin Diesel," Feb. 21, 2000)
http://chat.msn.com/msnlive_feature.msnw?id=artist/vindiesel
(*MSN Celebrity Chats,* "Vin Diesel," June 2001 and Aug. 2002)
http://www.rollingstone.com/news/newsarticle.asp?nid=14127
(*RollingStone.com,* "Diesel Fuel," July 19, 2001)
http://actionadventure.about.com/library/weekly/2001/aa072801a.htm
(*About.com,* "You Vin Some, You Lose Some," July 28, 2001)
http://actionadventure.about.com/library/weekly/2002/aa072902.htm
(*About.com,* "XXX-Rated Interview with Vin Diesel," July 29, 2002)

Online Databases

Biography Resource Center Online, 2001, article from *Contemporary Black Biography,* 2001

ADDRESS

Vin Diesel
The Firm
9100 Wilshire Boulevard
Beverly Hills, CA 90212

WORLD WIDE WEB SITE

http://us.imdb.com/Bio?Diesel,+Vin

Eminem 1972 -

American Rap Artist and Songwriter
Creator of *The Slim Shady LP*, *The Marshall Mathers LP*, and *The Eminem Show*
Star of the Hit Film *8 Mile*

BIRTH

Eminem was born Marshall Bruce Mathers III on October 17, 1972, in Kansas City, Missouri. Although he is known professionally by the name Eminem, his friends call him Marshall or Em. His mother, Debbie Nelson, was 17 when he was born. She left his father less than a year later. She has worked off and on as a caregiver, cosmetologist, waitress, receptionist, and taxi-service operator. His father, Marshall Bruce Mathers II, a steelworker, has never been part of his son's life. Eminem said, "I never knew him. Never even seen a picture of him." Eminem has one younger half-brother, Nathan.

YOUTH

The anger that fuels Eminem's brilliant raps came straight from his tough childhood. He and his mother moved constantly and got by on a small, unsteady income. "I don't like to give the sob story: growing up in a single-parent home, never knew my father, my mother never worked, and when friends came over I'd hide the welfare cheese," he said. "It's like the real, stereotypical, trailer-park white trash."

Eminem spent his early life in South Dakota, his father's native state. When he was about two, his mother left him in the care of a great aunt in Missouri. His mother reclaimed him when he was five, and for the next seven years they bounced between Missouri and the Detroit area. He attended 15 to 20 schools during that time. "We just kept moving back and forth because my mother never had a job. We kept getting kicked out of every house we were in," Eminem said. "I believe six months was the longest we ever lived in a house."

"I don't like to give the sob story: growing up in a single-parent home, never knew my father, my mother never worked, and when friends came over I'd hide the welfare cheese," Eminem said. "It's like the real, stereotypical, trailer-park white trash."

From the time he was about 12, Eminem and his mother remained in the Detroit area. But they continued to move constantly. They drifted between run-down neighborhoods in the city of Detroit and the gritty, blue-collar suburbs just northeast of it. The city was mostly African-American, and the suburbs mostly white. A busy street called 8 Mile Road was the boundary between the two. According to Eminem, "It's the borderline of what separates suburbs from city. It's the color line. I grew up on both sides of it and saw everything," he said. "I had [white] friends who had racist redneck fathers and stepfathers. I had black friends. It's just American culture." When it was time to title his debut film about a white guy crossing the color divide into black rap music, *8 Mile* was a natural choice.

Whatever neighborhood he landed in, Eminem found it hard to fit in. He tried to lose himself in television and comic books. At one time he even wanted to be a comic-book artist. But he couldn't hide from the school bullies. Small for his age and forever the new kid, he got picked on a lot—he ticked people off with his smart-aleck attitude. In his song "Brain Damage" on *The Slim Shady LP*, he describes himself as "A kid who refused to respect adults/Wore spectacles with taped frames and a freckled nose/A corny lookin' white boy, scrawny and always ornery/'Cause I was always sick of brawny bullies pickin' on me." The song is based on the worst bullying he ever suffered, when he was nine. An older boy beat Eminem until he was unconscious. His hearing and vision were affected, and he spent 10 days in the hospital.

—————— *"* ——————

In his song "Brain Damage" on **The Slim Shady LP,** *he describes himself as "A kid who refused to respect adults/Wore spectacles with taped frames and a freckled nose/A corny lookin' white boy, scrawny and always ornery/'Cause I was always sick of brawny bullies pickin' on me."*

—————— *"* ——————

About the same time as the attack, Eminem first heard the music that would change his life. His mother's young brother Ronnie Polkingharn introduced him to hip-hop. (Polkingharn later committed suicide when Eminem was 19, which completely devastated him.) "My uncle put me on to the *Breakin'* soundtrack. The first rap song I ever heard was Ice-T, 'Reckless.' From L.L.[Cool J] to the Fat boys . . . I was fascinated," he said. "When L.L. first came out with 'I'm Bad,' I wanted to do it, to rhyme. Standing in front of the mirror, I wanted to be like L.L." Over time, Eminem and his uncle, who were close in age, moved on to more hardcore gangsta rappers like N.W.A. and 2-Live Crew. Gangsta rap sprang from urban African-American ghettoes. Full of graphic language and violent images, gangsta rap often denigrates women and portrays other men as rivals to be destroyed. Eminem found it irresistible. "Like about 14 years old . . . I first decided to become a hot rapper," he said.

Rap became an outlet for Eminem's frustrations. The family's financial troubles were constant. His mother was neglectful and manipulative. He had a hard time getting along with her, and their relationship got worse as he got older. "You couldn't even understand how crazy it was," said Proof, a close childhood friend. "He got kicked out of his house so much, I stayed there more than he did." School was another difficulty. Eminem was enrolled at Lincoln High School in Warren, a suburb of Detroit. But he skipped a lot of classes and failed ninth grade twice. A former high-school class-mate said Eminem stood out only for his skill at rapping and rhyme. He got attention rapping against others in the school lunchroom, and he also gave a rousing performance at a school talent show. In 1989, he dropped out for good. In 1999 he said, "I tried to go back to school five years ago, but I couldn't do it. I just wanted to rap and be a star."

FIRST JOBS

Like Jimmy "Rabbit" Smith in the movie *8 Mile,* Eminem pursued his dream of hip-hop stardom with seriousness and purpose. But he had to earn money in the meantime. He held a series of low-paying jobs while he practiced rapping. For several years in the mid-1990s, he worked as a cook and dishwasher at a family restaurant in an eastside suburb of Detroit. His co-workers remember him as a funny, friendly guy who rapped out the food orders. And they noticed how diligent he was about his music. "I had to tell him to turn down the radio occasionally, but overall he was one of the better cooks we had," said his former boss. "We're all very happy for [his success]. I know he worked hard for it."

CAREER HIGHLIGHTS

After he dropped out of school, Eminem threw himself into composing rhymes and rapping. He developed a habit he keeps to this day—filling sheets of paper with tiny, almost unreadable lines as he worked out the best rhymes. A notorious perfectionist, he works his material over and over again until he is satisfied. During this period, he began to call himself "M&M"—a play on his initials. (His manager later convinced him to re-spell it.) He also got up his nerve to enter rapping battles at Detroit night clubs. These contests, known as freestyle, pitted one rapper against anoth-er to see who could spew out the fastest, most outrageous insults in the cleverest rhymes. A skinny, blue-eyed white kid was an unlikely sight in these venues. The vast majority of the contestants and audiences were African-American, and Eminem had to be quick to win their respect. He developed a coping strategy that he still uses: he'd joke about his own flaws and weaknesses before his critics could. Not only was it hilarious, but it stymied his opponents.

Breaking In

In 1990, Eminem got his first break. A young Detroit-area music producer named Mark Bass heard him rap on an open-mike radio program in De-

troit. Bass called the station and invited Eminem to his FBT Productions studio for an impromptu audition. Eminem turned up at 4 a.m. Before long, Mark Bass and his brother Jeff began to record some cuts with Eminem. He was then a rough-edged teenager who was just developing his style, according to Mark Bass. His rhymes weren't out of the ordinary, "but his rhythm was fantastic. It always reminded me of a drum solo, suddenly going in a different direction in the middle of a lick. And you understood what he was saying — the enunciation was incredible."

In 1996, Mark and Jeff Bass borrowed $1,500 from their mother to produce 1,000 copies of Eminem's first recording, *Infinite*, under their Web Entertainment label. "*Infinite* was me trying to figure out how I wanted my rap style to be, how I wanted to sound on the mic [microphone] and present myself," Eminem said. "It was a growing stage." He placed high hopes on the record—and not just to satisfy his ego. He and his longtime girlfriend, Kim Scott, had had a daughter on Christmas Day 1995. (He and Kim later married and divorced). He needed money to support the baby, Hailie Jade. But the album sold only a handful of copies. And Eminem got little credit for his rapping. "I caught a lot of flak: 'You're trying to sound like AZ. You're trying to sound like Nas. You're trying to sound like somebody from New York. And you're white. You shouldn't rap. You should go into rock-and-roll.'. . . That started pissing me off. And I started releasing that anger in the songs." These songs became eight cuts on his next release, *The Slim Shady EP*.

Creating the Slim Shady Character

On *The Slim Shady EP* (1997), Eminem created a character who has become a fixture on all of his albums: his vile, outrageous alter-ego, Slim Shady. Shady is a drug-taking, law-breaking, woman-abusing, foul-mouthed rap monster. He rants about the real-life figures in Eminem's life—everyone from his girlfriend Kim, to his mother, to people on Detroit's music scene. He doesn't hesitate to blast them by name. Eminem described Slim Shady as "the evil side of me, the sarcastic, foul-mouthed side of me." According to Eminem, the character let him vent his anger—and pour more feeling and creativity into his rapping. "[The] more I started writing and the more I slipped into this Slim Shady character, the more it just started becoming me," he said. "My true feelings were coming out and I just needed an outlet to dump them in. I needed some type of persona. I needed an excuse to let go of all this rage, this dark humor, the pain, and the happiness." Unlike his earlier release, Eminem saw *The Slim Shady EP* as a record to please himself—and no one else. The material "brought more of my personality in," he said. "That's when I found myself."

> *When Eminem was starting out, says producer Mark Bass, his rhymes weren't out of the ordinary, "but his rhythm was fantastic. It always reminded me of a drum solo, suddenly going in a different direction in the middle of a lick. And you understood what he was saying—the enunciation was incredible."*

Eminem's creativity was flourishing. But real life still dogged him. He had been fired from the restaurant. He was completely broke and discouraged. But he was about to get the break that launched his career. With help from a magazine journalist who liked his Slim Shady cuts, he won a spot to compete at *Rap Sheet* magazine's 1997 "Rap Olympics." This major freestyle competition in Los Angeles was an important showcase for talent—and carried a first prize of $1,5000 that Eminem badly needed. He battled furiously for an hour, toppling every opponent. He rhymed brilliantly, hurling back every insult thrown at him about his race. Then in a slip-up, he missed first place. He was furious. But though he didn't win the competition, he grabbed the interest of an intern from Interscope Records. Eminem got noticed for his distinctive, nasal-sounding voice, his complex rhythms, and his clear enunciation. The outrageous content of his lyrics grabbed attention, too. And so did his race.

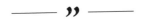

> Slim Shady is "the evil side of me, the sarcastic, foulmouthed side of me," according to Eminem. "[The] more I started writing and the more I slipped into this Slim Shady character, the more it just started becoming me. My true feelings were coming out and I just needed an outlet to dump them in. I needed some type of persona. I needed an excuse to let go of all this rage, this dark humor, the pain, and the happiness."

His Rap Olympics performance won him a slot on an influential Los Angeles radio program. "The Wake Up Show" with DJs Sway and Tech was a major rap showcase. "I felt like, 'It's my time to shine. I have to rip this,'" Eminem said. "At that time, I felt like it was a life-or-death situation." He unleashed a savage stream of lyrics that amazed the DJs and the audience. The feat won him the 1997 Wake Up Show Freestyle Performer of the Year. His underground record "5 Star Generals" caught notice in Japan, New York, and Los Angeles. He also won a place performing on a national rap tour.

At the same time, the intern from Interscope Records passed *The Slim Shady EP* to producer Jimmy Iovine. Iovine placed it in the hands of performer and producer Andre Young. Better known as Dr. Dre, he founded the rap groups N.W.A. and The Chronic. Dr. Dre is renowned and respected as a godfather of gangsta rap. And he wanted to sign Eminem to his label. "Growing up, I was one of the biggest fans of N.W.A., from putting on the sunglasses and looking in the mirror and lip-synching to wanting to be Dr. Dre, to be Ice Cube," Eminem said. "This is the biggest hip-hop producer ever." For Dr. Dre, race was no issue in signing Eminem. "You know, he's got blue eyes, he's a white kid," said Dr. Dre. "But I don't give a [care] if you're purple. If you can kick it, I'm working with you."

The Slim Shady LP

Taking to the recording studio, Dre and Eminem hit it off immediately. In the first six hours of working together they recorded four songs. "[Messin'] with the best producer in hip-hop music, I had to be more on point," Eminem said. "When I got in the studio with him, I had to show him something extra. . . . I had to be *extra.*" Three of their initial cuts made it to *The Slim Shady LP*: "Guilty Conscience," "Role Model," and the hit single "My Name Is." All three songs trashed the notion of celebrities and other adults as shining examples for youth. In "Role Model," Eminem attacked then-President Bill Clinton with the line, "If I said I never did drugs/that would mean I lie and get [sex] even more than the president does." Many of the songs contained irreverence for public figures and colleagues in the music business. In addition, he often used dark humor that targeted Eminem himself—making him what the *New York Times* called "hip-hop's first self-mocking anti-hero." He often played his race for laughs, using his Midwestern twang to emphasize his white-boy geekiness.

The lyrical content of *The Slim Shady LP* set the tone for the future. Eminem was apparently playing a character or a role—although it's impossible to tell when he's speaking as Slim Shady and when he's speaking as himself. From his recording, it's impossible to tell what Eminem really believes. *The Slim Shady LP* demonstrates his talent as a charismatic, gifted wordsmith. Many of the rhymes are clever and even funny. As Eminem said, "The kids listening to my music get the joke. They can tell when I'm serious and when I'm not. They can tell the entertainment of it." But others weren't so sure.

The songs on *The Slim Shady LP* are filled with hate, self-loathing, and violence. He expresses a lot of hate toward his ex-wife Kim, his mother, women in general, and homosexuals. He calls women bitches, sluts, and worse; he calls homosexuals faggots. His language offended many people, although Eminem claimed that wasn't his intent. For example, as he told Kurt Loder of MTV, "'Faggot' to me doesn't necessarily mean gay people. 'Faggot' to me just means . . . taking away your manhood. You're a sissy. You're a coward. . . . So, when I started saying 'faggot' on record, I started getting people going, 'You have something against gay people' and I thought it was funny, because I don't." Throughout the record, the songs are riddled with swear words and rants about drugs. The album also includes disturbing images about people close to Eminem. "My Name Is" rips into his mother for drug-taking and neglect. "97 Bonnie and Clyde," in which he fantasizes about killing his wife, includes the gurgling voice of his daughter, Hailie, then aged three. The rapper imagines a father-daughter outing to dump the body of the child's murdered mother in a lake: "There goes Mommy splashing in the water/ No more fighting with dad, no more restraining order." So while critics and audiences enjoyed his rhythm and dazzling, lightening-quick rhymes, many struggled to come to terms with the offensive nature of his lyrics.

The Slim Shady LP was released in 1998, and it debuted on the *Billboard* magazine album chart at No. 3. The record went on to sell more than four million copies. Eminem won two Grammy Awards, for Best Rap Solo Performance (for "My Name Is") and Best Rap Album. But as the acclaim rained down, so did criticism. Music executives and advocates for women and homosexuals attacked Eminem for his material [see the sidebar entitled "Eminem's Changing Reputation," pages 46–47]. He was also targeted during his tour in the spring of 1999. Many criticized his lackluster performances—some as brief as 25 minutes. Typically, Eminem shot back in songs, which he released on his second major album.

> "Rap, overall, is entertainment. I'm trying to bring it in an entertaining way that's clever—you never know what's going to come, what I'm going to say next. I try to catch people off guard with punch lines. I catch myself off guard a lot of times when I'm writing."

The Marshall Mathers LP

Eminem released *The Marshall Mathers LP* in 2000. He said his own favorite song from the album is "The Way I Am," which he called "a message to everybody to get off my back." The album is also a furious assault not only on his mother, his wife, and homosexuals, but also on a string of celebrities whom the rapper insults personally. He addresses the critics of his first album, including the hypocrites of middle America: in "Who Knew," he scorns parents who complain about his lyrics, but let their kids freely watch violent movies.

But *The Marshall Mathers LP* was more than a revenge rant. The beats are seductive, and the wordplay is as brilliant as ever. Beneath the rage and profanity, listeners found material that was intelligent and ironic. "After *The Marshall Mathers LP* I upgraded everything. Flow, rhyme, character, and the whole shebang," Eminem said. Many noted that Eminem had polished his skill as a storyteller. The hit "Stan" creates a vivid picture of a fan

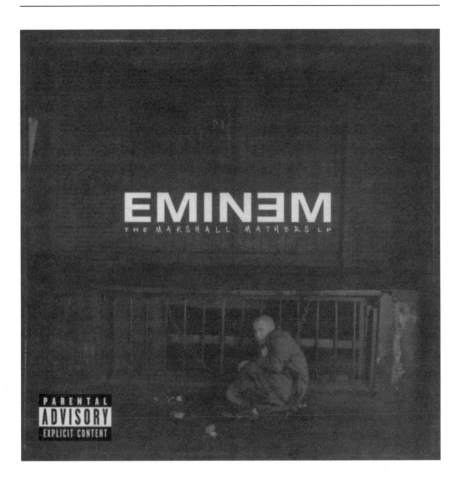

obsessed with Slim Shady. After Shady ignores his fan letters, Stan kills his pregnant girlfriend and commits suicide. Played against a song-sample by pop singer, Dido, the song tells a tale that is shocking, funny, and poignant, all at once. "Kim" recounts a murderous argument between Eminem and his wife as their then-five-year-old daughter looks on. Such songs often have Eminem acting out several characters' voices. And the stories are propelled by rapid-fire background remarks. These side comments are like sound balloons in a comic strip that comment on the main action of the story.

In his introduction to Eminem's book, *Angry Blonde*, Jonathan Schecter noted Eminem's skill for painting scenes: "Em's active imagination turns records into mini movies featuring multiple characters and cartoonish ad-lib tracks. Recurring figures such as Ken Kaniff, Kim, and now Stan create

Eminem's Changing Reputation

Beginning with the release of *The Slim Shady LP*, Eminem has come under a barrage of criticism for corrupting young audiences. *Billboard Magazine* editor Timothy White wrote an entire article denouncing his lyrics. They are "violent and inflammatory," White said, accusing Eminem of "exploiting the world's misery." Not long afterward, Lynne Cheney, the wife of the U.S. vice president, testified before Congress that Eminem promoted the worst forms of violence against women. Her comments were echoed by Kim Gandy, the executive vice president of the National Organization for Women. "Offensiveness is not the issue," she said. "I think [his music] is actually dangerous to girls and women." The authorities at the Gay and Lesbian Alliance Against Defamation (GLAAD) called his lyrics "the most hateful, homophobic, and violence-encouraging we have ever seen." Yet these charges didn't seem to affect his popularity, his record sales, or his appeal to young listeners.

Controversy about Eminem continued in June 2002, when he got in trouble with the law. He was accused of assaulting two different men in Michigan on two consecutive days. He was also charged with carrying a concealed weapon. He received three years probation for both incidents. That means he had to visit a government probation officer once a month. He also had to go to counseling sessions and undergo alcohol and drug testing. He could have been sentenced to a lengthy term in jail.

But for Eminem, nearly going to jail was a wake-up call; he has proclaimed it "almost a blessing in disguise." Since then he has reportedly given up drugs and drinking. His famous workaholic attitude and perfectionist standards are more intense than ever. "Something really bad could have hap-

a Simpsons-like world, occupied by misfits and ruled mercilessly by an unpredictable king." Eminem acknowledges that, bottom line, he wants to entertain listeners. "Rap, overall, is entertainment," he said. "I'm trying to bring it in an entertaining way that's clever—you never know what's going to come, what I'm going to say next. I try to catch people off guard with punch lines. I catch myself off guard a lot of times when I'm writing."

The Marshall Mathers LP debuted at No. 1 on U.S. album charts and became the fastest-selling rap album ever, eventually selling over eight mil-

pened to me. I could be in jail. I could have been shot. I could have been killed," Eminem said. "And I'm proud of myself now for not only my accomplishments but for pulling through all that."

Since the release of *8 Mile*, Eminem has reached a wider audience. The movie seemed to appeal to many people who wouldn't have normally been interested in the rap star. Director Curtis Hanson said, "So many people have come to me and said, 'I had this impression of Eminem and of hip-hop in general, and this movie completely turned me around.' I couldn't get a better compliment. And neither could Marshall."

While many are still offended by Eminem's lyrics and his content, they are for the most part keeping quiet these days. With his huge album sales— 30 million and counting—and his worldwide exposure in *8 Mile*, he seems to have achieved an almost mainstream acceptance. The *New York Times Magazine* put him on their cover labeled "American Idol." The *New York Times* is known as a staid and serious newspaper, but its columnist Maureen Dowd said she had a "yuppie love" for Eminem and called him "as cuddly as Beaver Cleaver." Eminem is distinctly uncomfortable with this turn of events. He responded to the Dowd column: "That's when it's getting bad. That's when it gets scary. When everyone loves you, who's left to hate you? The kids want something they can hold onto that their parents hate." At this point, much of the public condemnation of Eminem seems to have subsided.

lion copies. In addition, it was the first rap record ever to be nominated for the "Album of the Year" category in the Grammy Awards. Although it didn't win, it took home prizes in two other categories. The album won Eminem more fans than ever—but riled more critics, too. When Eminem was invited to perform at the MTV Video Music Awards in September 2000, he was widely denounced. Women's groups and other entertainers denounced him as a terrible influence on young listeners, and the Gay and Lesbian Alliance Against Defamation (GLAAD) staged a protest. A spokesperson from GLAAD said that "These are the words that kids hear in school hall-ways before they get beat up. For this kind of language to be put out there without any sense of responsibility on Eminem's part, or MTV's part, is simply not something that GLAAD can ignore. . . .We are very disappoint-ed that they continue to support him as heavily as they do." The U.S. Senate even heard testimony against him.

> "
>
> *A spokesperson from GLAAD said that "These are the words that kids hear in school hallways before they get beat up. For this kind of language to be put out there without any sense of responsibility on Eminem's part, or MTV's part, is simply not something that GLAAD can ignore. . . .We are very disappointed that they continue to support him as heavily as they do."*
>
> "

As for the anti-gay charges, Eminem has reacted with bewilderment. He said he is not homophobic (someone who hates homosexuals) but het-erophiliac (someone who loves the opposite sex). "If I said in one of my songs ["My Name Is"] that my Eng-lish teacher wanted to have sex with me in junior high, all I'm saying is that, I'm not gay you know?" he said. "People confuse the lyrics for me speaking my mind. I don't agree with that lifestyle, but if that lifestyle is for you, then it's your business." He made an apparent peace offering to the gay community at the Grammy Awards telecast in 2001. Eminem pointedly performed "Stan" with Elton John, the rock star who is openly gay. The two hugged at the end of the performance. (Ever the rebel, Eminem also made an obscene gesture. But that was edited out of the broadcast.) For his own part, Eminem says that his critics misunderstand him. "[At] the end of the day, it's all a joke," he said of his work. "Anybody with a sense of humor is going to put on my album and laugh from beginning to end."

The Eminem Show

During his rocket-ride to fame, Eminem stayed loyal to his old neighbor-hood and friends. He continued to live in the Detroit area. The Bass broth-ers still produced most of his tracks. And he kept working with five long-time friends in a rap crew called D12, or Dirty Dozen. In June 2001, the group released an album, *Devil's Night*. The effort produced a couple of top singles and eventually went to No. 1. It was also notable because it ap-peared on Eminem's own new record label, Shady Records.

But even sticking to familiar people and surroundings, Eminem couldn't sidestep the hassles of his newfound celebrity. His personal problems and run-ins with the law had been trumpeted in the media [see the sidebar entitled "Eminem's Changing Reputation," pages 46–47]. Long-lost friends and family members (including his father) were trying to get a piece of him. "Sometimes I don't know where my private life ends and my public life begins," he said. "It all seems to blend together a lot. I feel like there's nothing that I can do that is not wrote about, at least at this time in my life."

His next major album, *The Eminem Show* (2002), airs his gripes about life as a celebrity, a life that no longer feels like his own. As a reviewer for *Entertainment Weekly* observed, Eminem "plays to a culture obsessed with celebrity gossip and talk-show voyeurism at the same time it rails against that culture." He rants blisteringly about his mother in "Cleanin' Out My Closet." He delves into his divorce in "Superman." Beating his detractors at their own game, as always, he faces the charge that he peddles black music to white masses for his own profit: "I am the worst thing since Elvis Presley, To do black music so selfishly/and use it to get myself wealthy." Elsewhere he acknowledges, "Look at my sales/Let's do the math, If I was black I woulda sold half." His song "White America" scorns two vice presidents' wives, Lynne Cheney and Tipper Gore, and trashes the moral hypocrisy of middle America. He charges his critics with racism: he asserts that critics didn't object to rap music when it appealed to African-American kids, but that critics now complain because his rap music appeals to white kids. "See the problem is I speak to suburban kids who otherwise would of never knew these words exist/ . . . they connected with me too because I looked like them/that's why [critics] put my lyrics up under this microscope, searchin' with a fine tooth comb/ . . . All I hear is: lyrics, lyrics, constant controversy, sponsors working round the clock, to try to stop my concerts early/surely hip-hop was never a problem in Harlem only in Boston, after it bothered the fathers of daughters starting to blossom/so now I'm catchin' the flack from these activists."

But alongside the usual rage and profanity, critics note a softer tone to *The Eminem Show*. In "Sing for the Moment," he asks his critics to consider his tenderness to his daughter. He asks, "It's all political, if my music is literal and I'm a criminal/ How . . . can I raise a little girl? /I couldn't. I wouldn't be fit to." He also makes his singing debut with "Hailie's Song." He croons in a falsetto voice, "My baby girl keeps getting older, I watch her grow with pride/People make jokes 'cause they don't understand me, they just don't see my real side."

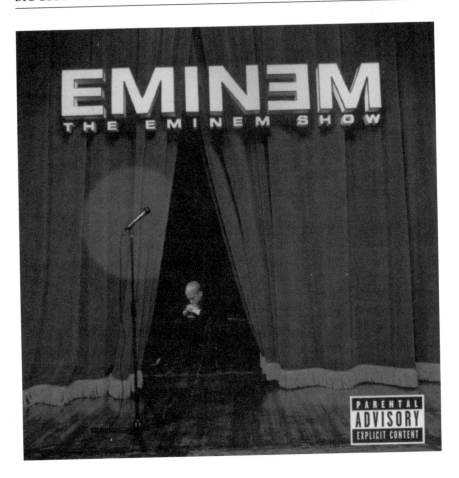

Rolling Stone noted that the song "Without Me" highlights the best and worst of Eminem: "It's his catchiest hit ever, the first one where the music behind him is every bit as extraordinary as his rhymes. . . . His brutal wit, his energy, his inventive rhyme-slinging are all at a peak. So, unfortunately, are the things that people can't stand about Em: his self-pity, his ego, his pomposity, his thin whine, his [cowardly] terror of women and gay people, and everyone else who doesn't fit into his [up-tight] little vision of the world." Several critics shared this general assessment. Eminem's verbal and creative gifts were gleaming as brightly as ever. But wasn't the subject matter wearing a little thin for a maturing artist? Shortly after his 30th birthday, Eminem told Frank Rich of the *New York Times* that he would always have a raw edge to draw on. "But as I grow as a person and as I get older I've got to mature," he said. "If you think that the only way I can make a record is by cussing, then I'll make a different record to outsmart you and prove you wrong."

The Eminem Show was a great success with critics and listeners alike. It won five Grammy nominations, including nominations for the coveted Album of the Year and Record of the Year awards. It eventually won two awards: Best Rap Album and Best Short Form Music Video, for "Without Me." In addition, it has sold over seven million copies.

8 Mile

In November 2002 Eminem surprised fans and critics with his charismatic film debut as a lead actor. In *8 Mile*, Eminem plays a fictional version of himself as struggling, would-be Detroit rapper Jimmy "Rabbit" Smith. When we meet him, he has just "choked" on stage at an important rap battle. He stands speechless and miserable while a rowdy crowd jeers him. We learn that his girlfriend has left him carless and homeless. He is forced to live in a beat-up trailer with his luckless mother (played by Kim Basinger) and neglected little sister, whom he adores. To make matters worse, his mom is sleeping with an obnoxious idiot whom Jimmy knew — and hated — in high school.

We follow Jimmy through a week of his life. He works at a dead-end factory job, hangs with his engaging, mostly African-American group of friends, and works doggedly toward the dream of a demo record and rap recognition. Along the way, romantic interest appears in the form of Alex (played by Brittany Murphy). She is an aspiring model who's out for herself, but she believes in his future. The film ends with an electrifying contest of rappers' wits. Though Jimmy triumphs in the battle, he hasn't won the war. We don't know what his future holds. But we get a sense that he has gained a better understanding of his own talent and where it can take him.

Eminem did no more than six weeks' intensive rehearsal as preparation for his lead role in the film, which he called a "grueling" process. But Curtis Hanson, the director of *8 Mile*, said Eminem's performance was not a re-

> **"**
>
> *["Without Me" is] his catchiest hit ever, the first one where the music behind him is every bit as extraordinary as his rhymes. . . . His brutal wit, his energy, his inventive rhyme-slinging are all at a peak. So, unfortunately, are the things that people can't stand about Em: his self-pity, his ego, his pomposity, his thin whine, his [cowardly] terror of women and gay people, and everyone else who doesn't fit into his [up-tight] little vision of the world."* — **Rolling Stone**
>
> **"**

sult of rehearsing. "This is a person who loves words, who loves rolling them around on his tongue, like most real actors do," Hanson said. "He's a great improviser, obviously, extremely quick on his feet. And while he can be extremely intense, he's also very funny. But most of all, whatever that magical thing is that draws us to people on the screen, he had it. All I had to do, really, was put a frame around it."

Eminem added to the movie's authenticity with steady input. He and his friends helped the screenwriter nail the language and concerns of their crowd. He provided the title. And Eminem apparently uses the film to answer his critics. It portrays his alter-ego rapper Jimmy as basically hard-working, purposeful, and devoted to his friends and sister. And the first time we see the character Rabbit really let go and rap, it's to defend a gay co-worker who was ridiculed by a rival rapper. Jimmy shoots him down with a clever, rapid-fire spree. "Paul's gay," he spits, "But you're a faggot." The scene demonstrates Eminem's contention that in the rap world, "faggot" can be an all-purpose put down, not an anti-gay slur.

> *When asked whether he wants to be a movie star, Eminem said, "I never intended that. I wanted to make a movie because I felt my story was unique, but at the same time not. If other roles [come up]? I don't know. I'll be too old to rap someday. Or when the music slows down. Then maybe, yeah, I'll take another role."*

The film boasts a top-flight Hollywood director, Curtis Hanson. And its producer, screenwriter, and cinematographer are also A-list talents. Even so, many were suspicious that this was merely a vehicle for exploiting Eminem's stardom, and the film industry was very cautious about the movie's potential. So the film's critical and commercial success were way beyond expectations. Critics praised the realistically gritty Detroit setting and the talented supporting cast. But many acknowledged that the force carrying the show was novice Eminem, who appears in nearly every scene. They responded to the authenticity of the story and to his powerful performance. "Compact, volatile, and burningly intense, he's got charisma to spare," noted David Ansen in *Newsweek*. Richard Schickel said in *Time* magazine that Eminem "understands the power of being still in front of the camera. He's a kid with the ability to put a sullen but seductive face on an open heart." But some critics found his performance too passive and understated. They would have liked to see him harness his famous humor

A scene from the movie 8 Mile. Jimmy (Eminem) and the Three One Three crew go for a ride in the Motor City. Left to right: Future (Mekhi Phifer), Cheddar Bob (Evan Jones), and DJ LZ (DeAngelo Wilson).

and anger. "A toned-down Eminem brings nothing special to the screen," said the reviewer for *People* magazine. Still, *8 Mile* proved to be a smash hit with fans. It was No. 1 after its first weekend in theaters, earning $54.5 million at the box office.

Viewers also enjoyed the great music, sending the *8 Mile* movie sound-track to No. 1 on the music charts when it debuted. On the movie sound-track, Eminem performs only five of the album's 16 songs — plus one with D12. In the title track "8 Mile," Eminem fires out 1,100 words in six minutes — and is credited with a masterful performance. The track "Lose Yourself" won acclaim as a great song of the year. In it, Eminem powerfully conveys the hunger for success and the importance of believing in your own talent, against all odds. In March 2003, "Lose Yourself" won an Academy Award for the best song in a film, becoming the first rap song ever to win an Academy Award.

Plans for the Future

Eminem has no immediate plans for future acting jobs. When asked whether he wants to be a movie star, he said, "I never intended that. I wanted to make a movie because I felt my story was unique, but at the same time not. If other roles [come up]? I don't know. I'll be too old to rap someday. Or when the music slows down. Then maybe, yeah, I'll take another role."

Since meeting Dr. Dre, Eminem has become more and more involved with producing music. He even helped Dr. Dre produce his own Chronic album, at Dr. Dre's request. With the launch of his label, Shady Records, producing consumes more of Eminem's time and interest. As of early 2003, he was producing his old crew D12, as well as acts like ObieTrice and 50 Cent, a New York rapper expected to hit it big. "I'm trying to build my clientele," he said, foreseeing a career one day as a record-label head and producer. "Eventually I want to branch off into being a producer and be able to one day sit back like Dre and kind of be behind the scenes and not always have to be the front man," he said.

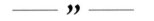

> "[Every] song that I make has to be better than the last one that I just made. Otherwise it gets scrapped. Because if you're not doing that, you're stagnant."

As for his own music, Eminem wants to keep growing. "[Every] song that I make has to be better than the last one that I just made," he said. "Otherwise it gets scrapped. Because if you're not doing that, you're stagnant."

MARRIAGE AND FAMILY

Eminem has called his longtime partner Kimberly Ann Scott "the first true girlfriend I ever had." The couple has been romantically linked since they were young teenagers—and have apparently spent the subsequent years breaking up and making up. They met when Eminem's mother took in the 12-year-old Kim. Eminem and Kim became romantically involved in the 1980s, had a daughter, Hailie Jade, in December 1995, and were married in June 1999. "Me and the missus, we go at it. It's no secret that we've had our problems," Eminem said. "Once you bring a child into this world, it makes it that much more complicated, especially when you don't get along with someone. You're trying to make it work, you want to make your family work, but [stuff] keeps happening that [screws] it up."

Their stormy relationship has inspired several notorious songs, including "97 Bonnie and Clyde" and "Kim," both violent revenge fantasies. "Kim has been the basis of a lot of his songs," said Eminem's longtime friend Jay Fields. "Pain, mystery, and drama—that's what motivates an artist, as much as love and affection." In July 2000, Kim Mathers attempted suicide while Eminem was performing at a nearby arena. A month later she sued him for "intentional infliction of emotional distress" for the lyrics of "Kim." She also threatened to deny him access to Hailie. They reached a settlement with an undisclosed cash award. They then attempted to reconcile. But it didn't work, and they divorced in 2001. Kim Mathers got physical custody of Hailie, while Eminem won legal custody and visitation rights.

Eminem acknowledged that his unexpected success and fame has been tough for the couple to handle. "Not to defend Kim, but I realize what has happened with me has probably been a strain on her too," Eminem said. "It's a crazy thing to deal with. You've really got to be in shape." After his divorce, Eminem was romantically linked for a short time with the singer Mariah Carey. There were also rumors that he was involved with his *8 Mile* co-stars, Brittany Murphy and Kim Basinger. There have also been media reports that he and his ex-wife have reunited.

If Eminem's relationship with his ex-wife has its ups and downs, his dealings with his mother are mostly down. Amid much publicity, Deborah Nelson sued her son in September 1999 for $10 million. She claimed that Eminem slandered her in press and radio interviews by suggesting that she was unstable and a drug user. A year later she filed another suit for $1 million. In total, she received settlements of $25,000. Eminem apparently doesn't communicate with her.

Amid his domestic problems, Eminem takes great joy in his relationship with his daughter. "I'm a father before anything," he said. A longtime friend called Eminem a big kid who loves to make his daughter laugh. He is said to do a great Kermit the Frog imitation. "He's a good daddy," the friend said. "He's trying to give Hailie more of a normal life than he had." They live in a large brown brick house in a gated neighborhood in the affluent northern suburbs of Detroit—much closer to 26 Mile Road than to 8 Mile Road. Eminem likes to feed Hailie breakfast and take her to school. She enjoys visiting him in the studio and has contributed to tracks on his records. When they play his music in the car, Eminem turns down the volume on the swear words. And cussing isn't allowed in front of Hailie. "She has a fairly normal life," Eminem said. "I love her so much."

RECORDINGS

Infinite, 1997
The Slim Shady EP, 1997
The Slim Shady LP, 1998
Just Don't Give a F——, 1998

The Marshall Mathers LP, 2000
Devil's Night, 2001 (with D12)
8 Mile: The Soundtrack, 2002
The Eminem Show, 2002

FILMS

8 Mile, 2002

BOOKS

Eminem: Angry Blonde, 2000

HONORS AND AWARDS

MTV Music Video Awards: 1999, for Best New Artist Award; 2000 (three awards), for Video of the Year, Best Male Video, and Best Rap Video, for "Forgot About Dre"; 2002 (four awards), for Video of the Year, Best Male Video, Best Rap Video, and Best Direction, all for "Without Me"

Grammy Awards: 2000 (two awards), Best Rap Album, for *The Slim Shady LP*, Best Rap Solo Performance, for "My Name Is"; 2001 (three awards), Best Rap Album, for *The Marshall Mathers LP*, Best Rap Solo Performance, for "The Real Slim Shady," Best Rap Performance by a Duo or Group, for "Forget about Dre" (with Dr. Dre); 2003 (two awards), for Best Rap Album, for *The Eminem Show*, Best Short Form Music Video, for "Without Me"

Billboard Music Awards: 2000 (two awards), for Maximum Vision Video and Best Rap/Hip-Hop Clip of the Year, for "The Real Slim Shady; 2002 (two awards), Album of the Year and R&B/Hip-Hop Album of the Year, both for *The Eminem Show*

Europe Music Awards: 2002 (three awards), for Best Male Artist, Best Hip-Hop Artist, and Best Album, all for *The Eminem Show*

American Music Awards: 2003 (four awards), Best Pop-Rock Male Artist, Best Soul/Rhythm & Blues Male Artist, Best Soul/Rhythm & Blues Album, and Best Pop-Rock Album, all for *The Eminem Show*

People's Choice Award: 2003, for Favorite Male Musical Performer

Academy Award (Oscar): 2003, for Best Song, for "Lose Yourself"

FURTHER READING

Books

Contemporary Musicians, Vol. 28, 2000
Eminem: Angry Blonde, 2000

Periodicals

Current Biography Yearbook, 2001
Detroit Free Press, Feb. 28, 1999, p.E1
Detroit News, Nov. 8, 2002, p.1
Entertainment Weekly, Nov. 8, 2002, p.20
Los Angeles Times, Feb. 7, 1999, p.3
New York Times, Nov. 17, 2002, p.L12
New York Times Magazine, Nov. 3, 2002, p.52
New Yorker, Nov. 11, 2002
Newsweek, May 29, 2000, p.62
People, Dec. 25, 2000, p. 64; July 24, 2000, p.139; July 8, 2002, p.111
Rolling Stone, May 23, 2002, p.23; July 4, 2002, pp.70 and 107
Teen, Feb. 2001, p.40
Teen People, May 15, 2001, p.34; Oct. 1, 2002, pp.104 and 110
Time, May 29, 2000, p. 73; Nov. 11, 2002, p.85
Vibe, Nov. 2002, p.91
Washington Post, July 27, 1999, p.C1

Online Database

Biography Resource Center Online, 2003, article from *Contemporary Musicians,* 2000

ADDRESS

Eminem
Interscope Records
10900 Wilshire Boulevard
Suite 1230
Los Angeles, CA 90024

WORLD WIDE WEB SITES

http://www.eminem.com
http://www.mtv.com/bands/az/eminem/artist.jhtml
http://www.rollingstone.com/artists/default.asp?oid=6395
http://www.vh1.com/artists/az/eminem/artist.jhtml

Michele Forman 1946-
American High School History Teacher
2001 National Teacher of the Year

BIRTH

Michele Forman was born in Biloxi, Mississippi, on April 7, 1946.

YOUTH AND EDUCATION

During Forman's childhood, her family moved from Mississippi to Atlanta, Georgia. She attended school in Atlanta, graduating from Sylvan Hills High School. She then went on to earn a bachelor's degree in history from Brandeis University in Massachusetts in 1967.

A few weeks after graduating from college, Forman joined the Peace Corps. Established in 1961 by President John F. Kennedy, the Peace Corps is a volunteer program run by the United States government that recruits and trains Americans to serve in nations around the world. Many Peace Corps volunteers work on projects that are designed to raise the living standards of people who live in villages, addressing such issues as agriculture, health standards, education, and business development. Forman served two years as a Peace Corps volunteer in Nepal, in south-central Asia. It's home to the Himalayas and to Mount Everest, the highest mountain in the world. In Nepal, Forman taught health classes to young people. "Everything was new — the country, culture, language, subject, and school system — not to mention teaching itself," she recalled. "I learned so much and found enormous rewards in teaching."

> "
>
> *Forman tries to remove any obstacles to learning for her students. "If they're not feeling well, I make them a cup of peppermint tea. If they're hungry, I feed them. It can be the simplest thing, but it sends an important message."*
>
> "

After leaving the Peace Corps, Forman returned to the United States. She settled in Vermont in 1970. Over the next decade she served as president of a nursery school, taught at the University of Vermont, and worked as an alcohol and drug education curriculum specialist for the Vermont Department of Education. In 1983 she earned a master's degree in teaching from the University of Vermont.

CAREER HIGHLIGHTS

Becoming a Respected High School Teacher

In 1986 Forman found her calling in the field of education. She accepted a position teaching social studies and history at Middlebury Union High School in Middlebury, Vermont. "Most of my career I have taught a range of world and U.S. history offerings and some social studies classes," she explained. "I especially enjoy teaching history because I find it fascinating and essential to all of us in understanding who we are." Forman decided that high school students were the ideal age group for her to teach. "I feel a special affinity for this age group and am fascinated by their intellectual development and creativity," she stated.

Forman developed a strong and supportive relationship with her students. She worked hard to create a classroom environment where her students would feel comfortable. "Making each student feel physically and psychologically safe and comfortable creates a sense of community and enables learning. Only in such an environment are students willing to take intellectual risks," she noted. "Whether it is big pillows in the resource area of the room, student artwork adorning every available space, or plants hanging from the ceiling, the room is above all my students' place much more than mine. In such an atmosphere, trust and respect, as well as collaboration, come naturally and learning is fun." Forman also tried to remove any obstacles to learning for her students. "If they're not feeling well, I make them a cup of peppermint tea," she said. "If they're hungry, I feed them. It can be the simplest thing, but it sends an important message."

Over the years, Forman expanded her role as a teacher to include serving as an advisor for several extracurricular classes and activities. For example, she started a non-credit Arabic language course that met three days per week for 45 minutes before school. To prepare to teach the course, Forman studied Arabic language and culture in a strict immersion program at Middlebury College. She spent two months living in the dormitories and speaking nothing but Arabic. "One of the reasons I chose to learn Arabic was that increasing my students' understanding of the Arab culture through that language could powerfully decrease the stereotypes many of them held of Arabs and Muslims," she explained. "My students' understanding of world history increased because of the new knowledge and resources I brought back to my classroom and, just as importantly, they gained a new understanding of and respect for the Arab world."

In 1990 Forman helped a group of students found a new student group, as she explains here. "The Student Coalition on Human Rights came about years ago when we decided that we wanted to celebrate Martin Luther King and his message," she recalled. "And students actually formed it and came together. And they decided that there were many human rights issues that they wanted to learn more about and that they wanted to educate their peers and others about." With Forman as their faculty advisor, the group brought a portion of the AIDS quilt to Middlebury and led local events during the statewide Holocaust Days of Remembrance.

In the past few years, Forman has been working with her students to form a model United Nations program. Model UN, as it's called, is a program in which students act as diplomats from around the world, assuming the roles of the delegates to the United Nations. The goal is to help students gain a broader perspective on contemporary international issues and to develop speech and debate skills. Forman feels that it is important to engage young people in world issues. "They have a lot to say. They have a lot to offer," she said of her students. "And I think we can learn a great deal from their idealism, because they know the world can be a better place and they have the energy and the idealism to work and make it that way. They're creative problem solvers. And they're wonderful to work with." Forman also became involved in professional activities outside of school. For example, she helped write the National World History Standards, headed the College Board History and Social Studies Academic Advisory Committee, helped design her school district's social studies curriculum, and trained numerous student teachers.

"There is little she wouldn't do for her students," said Forman's team-teaching partner, Richard Seubert. "Along with high expectations, she cares for them as human beings first, which helps kids appreciate their potential and set goals that push them to higher levels. She doesn't talk down to them but promotes a dialogue which honors their ideas and celebrates their uniqueness as human beings."

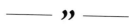

Named National Teacher of the Year for 2001

Throughout her career, Forman has earned the respect of her students, fellow teachers, and school administrators for her excellence in teaching. Her colleagues have praised her knowledge of the subjects she taught, her use of current materials in her classes, her passion for learning and personal improvement, and her effective communication skills. "There is little she wouldn't do for her students," said her team-teaching partner, Richard Seubert. "Along with high expectations, she cares for them as human beings first, which helps kids appreciate their potential and set goals that push them to higher levels. She doesn't talk down to them but promotes a dialogue which honors their ideas and celebrates their uniqueness as human beings."

In 2001, Forman received the highest honor in her profession when she was named National Teacher of the Year. The National Teacher of the Year Program is sponsored by a nonprofit group called the Council of Chief State School Officers (CCSSO) and the children's book publisher Scho-

President George W. Bush presents Forman with the 2001 Teacher of the Year award during a ceremony in the Rose Garden at the White House, April 23, 2001.

lastic, Inc. The process of selecting the National Teacher of the Year begins with the State Teachers of the Year. These teachers are chosen on the basis of nominations from students, teachers, principals, and school administrators. Each State Teacher of the Year must submit a written application to be considered for National Teacher of the Year. The application includes personal and career information, eight essays on topics ranging from teaching philosophy to issues facing education, and letters of endorsement. The winner is selected by a committee of representatives from 15 leading national education organizations.

The National Teacher of the Year is the oldest and most prestigious award for excellence in teaching in the United States. It has been presented annually for 50 years. Forman was the first Vermont educator to receive the honor. Her selection was announced by President George W. Bush at a special ceremony in Washington, D.C., on April 23, 2001. Forman recalled that accepting her award from the president "felt a little bit like an out-of-body experience."

The National Teacher of the Year is asked to take a year off from classroom activities in order to serve as a full-time national and international spokesperson on education. On June 1, 2001, Forman began a hectic schedule of traveling and lecturing. She looked forward to speaking out on a variety of issues that affect teachers and education. "There are a number of issues that concern me: vouchers, education funding, teacher accountability, high-stakes testing, and retaining new teachers," she stated. "Policymakers need to listen to [teachers] because we bring a perspective that no one else can."

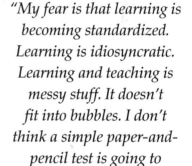

"My fear is that learning is becoming standardized. Learning is idiosyncratic. Learning and teaching is messy stuff. It doesn't fit into bubbles. I don't think a simple paper-and-pencil test is going to capture what students know and can do."

Speaking Out on Education Issues

During her travels as National Teacher of the Year, Forman tried to raise public awareness of a growing national shortage of qualified teachers. She pointed out that 30 percent of teachers nationwide have been teaching for 20 years or more, and that many of these teachers are expected to retire in the coming years. Yet fewer young people are training to become teachers, and 30 percent of new teachers leave the profession within three years. These factors, combined with increasing student enrollment, mean that the United States will need to recruit 2.5 million new teachers over the next 10 years.

Forman called upon the government and her fellow teachers to help address this problem by taking steps to retain good young teachers. "We know why teachers leave. They don't leave because of the money; surveys tell us they leave because of working conditions. What that usually means is an overwhelming amount of classes, or huge numbers of students in those classrooms—the lack of support and being given an impossible situation, many of our poorer schools especially," she explained. "We know how to hold teachers. We know that mentoring programs can be successful. We need to expand those. We need to demand that our schools and our communities increase those. Let's recognize that a license to teach is like a license to drive. When a new driver first gets a driver's license, it doesn't mean that he or she should set out to drive to New York City in a snowstorm, and we should not expect the equivalent from new teachers in the classroom. We are one of the few professions I know that eats its young. We fail to adequately support those joining us. We must change that."

Forman also spoke out about the need to maintain strict licensing requirements for teachers. "We must require high standards for all teachers if we want to raise the prestige of our profession and attract larger numbers of talented, dedicated people," she stated. Forman claimed that many teachers practice on waivers from basic licensing requirements, which has a strong negative effect on the quality of education they can provide. "In my state the man who gives care to my dogs cannot do so unless he is fully licensed. No waivers there. And the woman who cuts my hair cannot do so unless she is fully licensed, not on a waiver. We must educate others, you and I, to understand that teaching is just as important as engineering, medicine, veterinary medicine, and hairdressing," she said. "Can you see this now? You have an appointment with your doctor, you walk into your doctor's office, and this person comes to meet you and says, 'Hi, I'm the substitute physician. I have a high school diploma, a clean police record. I'm here to get hands-on experience.' We would not consider this in any field other than teaching, and it's time we stopped allowing it in our profession."

Forman also expressed her opinion about the current movement toward increased use of standardized testing of students as a way to evaluate schools and determine the level of government funding they receive. "I'm deeply concerned that the emphasis on high-stakes, multiple-choice testing is destructive," she stated. "It's gone too far. It's eating up too much of our resources. . . . It's of no value to teachers because it's not diagnostic. All it does is artificially spread out scores and rank kids. It doesn't tell me what my students can do and cannot do." Forman feels that such testing not only provides a poor assessment of student skills, but also limits teachers' creativity. "My fear is that learning is becoming standardized," she explained. "Learning is idiosyncratic. Learning and teaching is messy stuff. It doesn't fit into bubbles. I don't think a simple paper-and-pencil test is going to capture what students know and can do."

Forman thoroughly enjoyed her tenure as National Teacher of the Year. One of the things she learned from the experience was that many people have a deep appreciation for teachers. "People love teachers," she noted. "I've been on a 757 [airplane], packed with people at 39,000 feet, and when the flight attendant announced that the National Teacher of the Year is on board, the entire plane broke into applause, sustained applause. I couldn't get any work done after that, because everyone kept coming up to me and talking to me about their 'I-had-a-teacher' stories. No one on that plane knew me, but I can promise you that each person on that plane had in his or her mind a picture, a memory, of a teacher who meant a lot to him or her. I was overwhelmed by it, but I understand it. As the National Teacher of the Year, I'm a symbol for all of those wonderful teachers."

Among the many other memorable moments from her term, Forman received a special tour of the National Aeronautics and Space Administration (NASA) facilities and carried the Olympic torch as it passed through Vermont on its way to Salt Lake City, Utah, for the 2002 Winter Games. "It is bittersweet," she said at the end of her year of service. "It has been a magical year." At the same time, Forman was eager to return to school. "I feel that where I make the biggest difference is working in a classroom with kids," she noted.

"As a teacher, on a good day, when learning is happening, I'm a catalyst— something that allows a reaction to take place. The true power of learning is in the elements, the learners."

Learns from Her Students

Forman attributes part of her success as a teacher to her willingness to listen to her students. She has often discarded lesson plans and started over when her students made it clear that a different approach would create better opportunities for learning. In many cases, her flexibility has produced outstanding results. "Years ago I took students to Washington, D.C.," she recalled. "One named Holly had never been out of Vermont. We went to the Lincoln Memorial and the sun was setting. We're reading the words in the stone, and Holly looks up at Lincoln and says, 'Wow! I wish we had history where we live.' Now that's a voice I needed to listen to. We went back to Vermont and swept the plate for the next quarter, suspended regular classroom activities. With a supportive administrator and parents, we set out to become historians of our county. Students started with oral

Forman working with students.

histories and became fascinated by old farm buildings. They took pictures, read old diaries, newspapers, county fair programs. They produced an account of agricultural history, which is now part of a permanent collection in a museum."

On another occasion, Forman was leading a discussion of the European Renaissance in her World History class. She was pushing her students to understand the concept of a renaissance — building on past learning to create something new and exciting. Then the class took an unexpected turn. "A voice from the back of the classroom, Colin, said, 'Do you think there has been a renaissance in music in the past 50 years?' For about five seconds, nobody said anything," she remembered. "Then the deluge hit us. One after another, the students spilled out theories, evidence, arguments, counterarguments, displaying an astounding collective knowledge. I was amazed not only at what they knew about modern music, dwarfing my own knowledge to be sure, but at their excitement, and their deep understanding of what we mean by a renaissance. . . . They took control of the concept and constructed their learning. They owned it. It blew my lesson plan out of the water, but who needed it?"

As the end of class approached, Forman complimented her students for building on each other's ideas to develop unique insights. One of her students responded by giving credit to the teacher for allowing the discussion to flow. "That took me aback," Forman recalled. "In one light it was a bit flattering, but it was also very humbling. As a teacher, on a good day, when learning is happening, I'm a catalyst — something that allows a reaction to take place. The true power of learning is in the elements, the learners."

Despite the difficult issues facing education today, Forman finds her job tremendously rewarding. "The rewards I find in teaching are rooted in the joy of not only watching but also being part of my students' learning and development," she stated. "I love teaching. I wouldn't trade my job for anything in the world. Each day is different. Each day I learn something new. Each day I laugh. Some days I cry. But when I wake up each morning, I know that I have one of the most rewarding and important jobs in the world, for I am a teacher."

> *"The rewards I find in teaching are rooted in the joy of not only watching but also being part of my students' learning and development. I love teaching. I wouldn't trade my job for anything in the world. Each day is different. Each day I learn something new. Each day I laugh. Some days I cry. But when I wake up each morning, I know that I have one of the most rewarding and important jobs in the world, for I am a teacher."*

MARRIAGE AND FAMILY

Forman lives in a century-old former schoolhouse in Salisbury, Vermont. Her husband, Dick Forman, is a semi-retired professional musician who teaches jazz piano at Middlebury College. They have three grown children. Their daughter Elissa is a psychotherapist in Massachusetts, their daughter

Laura is attending medical school at the University of Vermont, and their son Tim is a student at Hampshire College in Massachusetts.

HOBBIES AND OTHER INTERESTS

In her spare time, Forman enjoys cross-country skiing, biking, hiking, jogging, gardening, and reading the poetry of Maya Angelou. She also likes to travel, and has shared stories with her students about her experiences in such places as West Africa, India, Korea, Greece, and Turkey. "Vermont is small, rural, and ethnically homogenous when compared with the rest of the nation," she noted. "Since I can't bring my students into the larger world on a regular basis, I bring diverse experiences and cultures to them."

HONORS AND AWARDS

State Teacher of the Year (Vermont): 2001
National Teacher of the Year: 2001

FURTHER READING

Periodicals

Burlington (Vt.) Free Press, Mar. 29, 2001, p.A1; Apr. 23, 2001, p.A1; Apr. 24, 2001, p.A8; May 30, 2002, p.A1
Columbus (Ga.) Ledger-Enquirer, Feb. 25, 2002, p.C1
NEA Today, May 2001, p.36; Oct. 2001, p.21
USA Today, Apr. 23, 2001, p.D7

Online Articles

http://www.ccsso.org/ntoy/2001/ntoy01.html
  (*National Teacher of the Year Program,* "Vermont Social Studies Teacher Named National Teacher of the Year," Apr. 23, 2001)
http://www.ccsso.org/ntoy/2001/01thoughts.html
  (*National Teacher of the Year Program,* "Thoughts on Teaching and Learning," Apr. 23, 2001)
http://www.nctr.org/content/indexpg/toy01.htm
  (*National Council on Teacher Retirement,* "National Teacher of the Year Address," Oct. 3, 2001)
http://www.uvm.edu/~uvmpr/vq/VQFALL01/teacher.html
  (*Vermont Quarterly,* "A Great Day to Be a Teacher," Fall 2001)
http://www.teachermagazine.org/tm/tm_printstory.cfm?slug=
  07inter view.h13 (*Teacher Magazine,* "Interview: Teacher for America," Apr. 2002)

Further information for this profile was gathered from interviews with Forman that aired on *The Early Show* and *CNN Live at Daybreak,* Apr. 23, 2001.

ADDRESS

Michele Forman
National Teacher of the Year Program
Council of Chief State School Officers
One Massachusetts Avenue, NW
Suite 700
Washington, DC 20001-1431

WORLD WIDE WEB SITES

http://www.ccsso.org/ntoy.html
http://www.vtnea.org/forman.htm
http://historymatters.gmu.edu/d/6830/

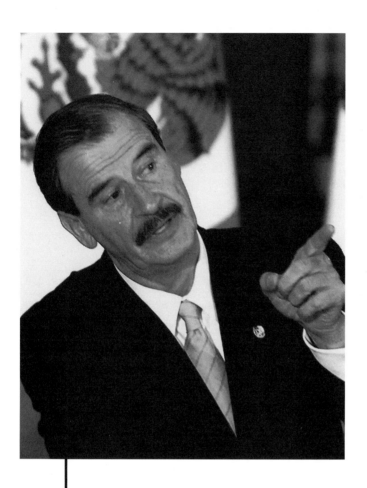

Vicente Fox 1942-
Mexican Political and Business Leader
President of Mexico

BIRTH

Vicente Fox was born Vicente Fox Quesada in Mexico City, Mexico, on July 2, 1942. In Mexico and other Spanish-speaking cultures, it is common for a child to be given the last name of both the father and the mother, the first being the father's and the second being the mother's. Vicente Fox's father, Jose Luis Fox, was a rancher in the Mexican state of Guanajuato who was born in Mexico. He was the son of an Irish immigrant who had first lived in Cincinnati, Ohio, and settled in

Mexico in 1913. Fox's mother, Mercedes Quesada, was born in Spain and moved to Mexico with her parents when she was still an infant. Vicente Fox is the second of nine children, with eight sisters and brothers.

YOUTH

Fox grew up on the family ranch in San Francisco del Rincon in the state of Guanajuato, Mexico. The ranch was large, 1,100 acres, and the family grew vegetables and raised animals. They also had family businesses in vegetable canning and boot manufacturing. Most Mexican families are poor, and very few families hold large pieces of property. So in that regard, Fox was born into a privileged family. But in his 1999 autobiography, *Vicente Fox a Los Pinos* (in Spanish), Fox said that he had close ties to poorer children as he grew up. "Something I'm proud of is that I became good friends with the children of the smallholders [owners of smaller farms] and peasants. With them I shared my infancy, my playthings, my house, and my food," he wrote. "From that time I began to understand our country's painful inequalities."

Not a lot has been written about Fox's life as a child. He often refers to his strong Catholic upbringing. His mother said he was an energetic, smart, and stubborn boy who would challenge friends to see who could withstand the most bee stings—and he would win. Fox has said that his interest in history and politics took form when he was a young man. One period in history that particularly fascinated him was the time of the Cristeros, who were militant Catholics who launched a rebellion shortly after the Mexican Revolution in 1910. The Cristeros fought the revolutionary government for three years before surrendering. In fact, in later years, as a campaigning politician, he would quote a Cristero battle cry: "If I advance, follow me! If I stop, push me! If I retreat, shoot me!"

For a time, Fox was interested in becoming a bullfighter, but his parents encouraged him to study business instead. His father once warned him about pursuing either farming or politics as a career. "My father only ever

> **"**
>
> *"Something I'm proud of is that I became good friends with the children of the smallholders [owners of smaller farms] and peasants. With them I shared my infancy, my playthings, my house, and my food. From that time I began to understand our country's painful inequalities."*
>
> **"**

gave me two pieces of advice," Fox said. "Study anything but agriculture because a farmer's life is too hard. And, please don't ever get into politics. It's dirty, it's rotten, it's corrupt." Fox joked, "So, I'm a politician and a farmer. I'm a very obedient son."

EDUCATION

Fox attended a Jesuit high school, which is a private, Catholic school run by an order of priests known for valuing knowledge and education. Part of his education included a year at a Jesuit high school in Prairie du Chien, Wisconsin, in the United States. Fellow students described him as a quiet student who did not fit in well.

Fox attended the Universidad Iberoamericana in Mexico City, which was a Jesuit college. He describes himself as a lackadaisical student, and has admitted to trying to cheat on exams. "I distinguished myself only because I was the only one who wore denims [blue jeans] while the great majority wore suits," he wrote in his autobiography. "I sat in the back of the classroom with my body slouched back and my feet stretched out."

Fox left the Universidad Iberoamericana without graduating in 1964, during what would have been his final semester. He later was awarded a degree, by Mexican President Ernesto Zedillo, in 1999.

CAREER HIGHLIGHTS

Climbing the Corporate Ladder

Fox decided to leave school in order to pursue a career opportunity with the Coca Cola Company. His work brought him a lot of business experience, and also expanded his knowledge of the Mexican people, especially in rural areas.

Fox started out as a route salesman. From there, he moved up to a position as route supervisor and eventually became marketing director for all of Coca Cola's Mexican business. He credits his time rising through the ranks at Coca Cola as the foundation of his later success. "At the university, they taught me to reflect and to analyze," he said. "But working at Coca Cola was my second university education. I learned that the heart of a business is out in the field, not in the office. I learned strategy, marketing, financial management, optimization of resources." But perhaps even more important, Fox said, "I learned not to accept anything but winning. I learned an iron discipline for getting results."

Fox's career gave him a close-up view of the Mexican government as well. He has spoken of his biggest frustration being bureaucracy—government that is slowed down by rigid rules and inefficiency. "What I hated most about those years at Coca Cola was the time I had to spend dithering with the government," Fox said. He mentions meetings at *Los Pinos* or "The Pines," the presidential residence in Mexico City, similar to the White House in the United States. The Mexican president would summon important business leaders there, including Fox, "so we could listen to a lot of foolishness."

While Fox was the marketing director for Coca Cola in Mexico, the soft drink passed Pepsi in sales, which had been No. 1 in the market for years. In 1979, Coca Cola offered Fox the opportunity to become the director of all its Latin American operations. Taking the position would have meant relocating to Miami, Florida, or Atlanta, Georgia, and leaving Mexico.

Running the Family Business

While the career move with Coca Cola might have offered Fox both prestige and money, he decided that living in Mexico was more important. After 15 years of success with the company, Fox resigned and moved back home to Guanajuato to work with his brothers in the family's business.

———— **"** ————

"At the university, they taught me to reflect and to analyze. But working at Coca Cola was my second university education. I learned that the heart of a business is out in the field, not in the office. I learned strategy, marketing, financial management, optimization of resources."But perhaps even more important, Fox said, "I learned not to accept anything but winning. I learned an iron discipline for getting results."

The family business, Grupo Fox, included primarily vegetable growing and boot and shoe manufacturing. The business grew as Fox added his marketing experience to the family's efforts. The 1980s brought a lot of difficulty to small- and medium-sized businesses in Mexico, however. The Mexican currency, the peso, went through a series of devaluations, and inflation was high. Because of the ability to sell their boots and shoes in markets other than Mexico, Grupo Fox stayed in business while many other businesses failed. "Every micro, small, and medium-sized entrepreneur in this country is a hero for surviving, growing, and exporting under these circumstances," Fox said of that period in Mexico's economic history.

Entering the Political Arena

In the late 1980s, Fox's business dealings brought him into increasing contact with the government—and reinforced his belief in the need for change. At the time a close friend, Manuel Clouthier, was running for president. Clouthier encouraged Fox to consider politics as a career change. He persuaded Fox to join the National Action Party (PAN), which opposed the Institutional Republican Party (PRI), the party that had dominated Mexican politics for more than 70 years. [For an explanation of the PRI and PAN, see the sidebar on "Mexico: Power and Turmoil," pages 65–67.]

Fox rides a horse on his ranch in San Cristobal, June 2000.

In 1988, Fox ran for Congress on the PAN ticket and won by a three-to-one margin. Part of his success in the election campaign was due to establishing his own fund-raising organization, called Friends of Fox. In this shrewd and forward-thinking move, he both distanced himself from the influence of PAN leadership and created a vehicle for funding future campaigns should he ever lose the support of PAN.

Making Waves

Fox immediately drew attention to himself in the Mexican Congress. In the same election year, 1988, PRI candidate Carlos Salinas was elected president in what many considered to be fraudulent circumstances. The race with the PRD candidate, Cuauhtemoc Cardenas, had been close; in fact, early returns indicated that Cardenas was in the lead. But PRI-controlled election officials suddenly announced that computers tabulating the election returns had crashed due to "atmospheric conditions." When the counting resumed, Salinas had taken the lead.

When the Mexican Congress met to confirm the election of Salinas, Fox ascended the podium with two charred ballots taped to the side of his head, representing Salinas's large ears. In a voice that mimicked Salinas, Fox said, "I've felt obligated to ask many of my friends to set aside moral scruples to help me achieve this victory, which I had to do because Mexico isn't ready for democracy." He summed up the comic satire of the president-elect by saying, "The truth is that the people did not vote for me; my friends had to stuff the ballot boxes."

Fox has created a political style that is open, brash, and very easy to understand by the average Mexican citizen. Throughout his political career, he's sported the *vaquero*—or cowboy—look of his native state of Guanajuato. Even in the legislative assembly, he'd sometimes wear jeans, cowboy boots, and an open shirt instead of the traditional suit and tie. His striking good looks and tall stature have also made him stand out from many of his counterparts.

And unlike other politicians, Fox has often used common Mexican slang in his speech-making, even to the point of occasionally using profanity. This common touch has served him well in his political career.

Battling the PRI

After serving two years in the Mexican legislature, Fox returned to Guanajuato to run for governor in the state's 1991 election. Hugely popular among Guanajuato's citizens and openly critical of the PRI and President Salinas, Fox invited the wrath of the PRI and all its resources. First, Salinas tried to dilute Fox's candidacy by reversing a court decision that would have prevented a second opposition candidate—in effect, taking support away from Fox.

Then, on election day, more votes were counted than there were registered voters, suggesting either ballot stuffing or manipulation of the numbers. The PRI candidate, of course, had "defeated" Fox. The PRI-controlled electoral commission certified that the ballots were correctly tabulated. But Fox publicly challenged the election results, backed by an angry group of thousands of supporters. Pressured by public opinion, the PRI admitted to the miscount. Instead of pronouncing either Fox or the PRI candidate the winner, they installed a PAN candidate in the governorship who was not even on the ballot.

After Fox failed in his bid for the governorship, however, key changes began to take place in the federal government that would eventually pave the way for his presidential election. President Salinas and his regime had been exposed for corruption and mismanagement of the economy. And there were indications of serious wrongdoing at the highest level. A number of key politicians had disappeared or been assassinated during the Salinas presidency. President Salinas's brother had been arrested and later found guilty of conspiracy to commit murder of a prominent PRI official. Salinas left office in 1994. The country was in an economic shambles, and public trust of the federal government was shaken. In the wake of his brother's arrest, Salinas left the country with millions of dollars in 1995.

Fox had long made clear his intention to run for Mexico's presidential office, even back in 1991 when running for governor. A law in the Mexican constitution, however, prevented him from running. The law stated that both of a candidate's parents had to have been born in Mexico; Fox's mother had been born in Spain. In 1993, the PRI-controlled legislature was publicly pressured to change the law. But they prevented Fox from running for president in 1994 by writing a provision that the new law would not take effect until the year 2000.

The new president in 1994 was Ernesto Zedillo. Despite his PRI affiliation, Zedillo instituted many reforms in Mexico's federal government [see the sidebar on "Mexico: Power and Turmoil," pages 65-67]. Most importantly, he established an independent electoral commission to oversee elections, despite the objection of his party.

Governor Fox

By 1995, when Fox made another run at becoming Guanajuato's governor, the political climate had changed enough that fair elections would be ensured. In a staggering victory, Fox beat his opponent by a two-to-one margin. This was the most dramatic win by an opposition candidate in a gubernatorial election in Mexico's history.

Fox made it his mission while governor of Guanajuato to improve the economic well-being of the state. He relied on his varied experience as a businessman—both as an executive in the large corporate enterprise of Coca Cola and as a director of a family business. With this experience, Fox saw commerce as the way to improve the lives of the people.

Fox traveled constantly, both within the state of Guanajuato and also to the United States and other Latin American countries. Throughout his travels, he sought further business development and opportunity for the state. Under his direction and leadership, Guanajuato became the fifth wealthiest state in Mexico.

One of Fox's concerns was the migration of Mexican labor to the United States. Laborers could earn $60 a day in the United States, instead of an

Mexico: Power and Turmoil

For centuries, Mexico has seen one power struggle after another. In pre-Columbian times (before Columbus came to the New World), Mexico was inhabited by highly advanced cultures. The Olmecs, Mayans, and Aztecs were civilizations that had complex governmental systems, large-scale war, slavery, and taxes. In contrast to the natives of what is now the United States, the indigenous Mexicans had huge cities and large population centers.

The Spanish conquistadors (conquerors and explorers) led by Hernando Cortes landed in Mexico in 1519. The Spanish colonized and enslaved the native peoples, and power shifted from the war-like Aztecs to the militarily superior Europeans. In addition, conquistadors crushed the native religions, which often involved ritual human sacrifice, and people were forced to convert to Catholicism.

Three hundred years of oppression by the Spanish throne came to a close in 1810, when Mexico declared its independence. Eleven years of bloody fighting followed before Spain recognized Mexico's sovereignty. A number of governments followed in the next ninety years, some of them resembling Old World monarchy, some of them mimicking the United States, at least in the name of the office of president. During this time, California, Texas, New Mexico, and Arizona, which had been part of Mexico, became part of the United States, resulting in war and the loss of resources.

The Mexican Revolution, which was a violent and bloody uprising, began in 1910. Pancho Villa and Emiliano Zapata became folk heroes because of the armed bands they led, and some of their Robin Hood-like escapades. The Mexican Revolution sought three goals: to reduce the power of the Catholic church; to remove land from the hands of a few and distribute it to the people; and to take control of precious natural resources (gold, silver, and oil) from foreign interests.

In 1917 a new constitution was created. It signaled the beginning of a federal democratic system that loosely resembled that of the United States. The new government established 31 states (the actual official name of Mexico is *Los Estados Unidos de Mexico,* or the United States of Mexico) and a federal district. A representative congress was formed, and regular elections were established. The executive office of president was created to allow for one term only, with no opportunity for re-election.

The group of revolutionaries who drafted the new constitution became the Institutional Revolutionary Party, which is *Partido Revolucionaria Institucional* in Spanish, known as PRI. This party represented a seat of power that dominated the Mexican government for the next 71 years.

Technically and legally speaking, Mexico was a democracy with its citizens free to create competing political parties. But in reality, it was very difficult to ensure fair election practices. The PRI has been compared with earlier oppressive regimes in the country and has been charged with corruption, deception, censorship of the press, fraud, and theft. And in more recent

average $5 a day in Mexico. This difference has prompted many Mexicans, especially young men, to leave their country to work in the U.S. and send money home. Fox instituted a program to persuade Mexican workers abroad to send 25% of their earnings to be put into what he called "productive investment," like shops or factories, instead of just consumption (living expenses). And the state would match whatever funds were accumulated. This program resulted in 35 new enterprises, creating jobs that made it possible for workers to stay home and work instead of leaving the country.

years, the PRI has been implicated in the killings and disappearance of individuals who opposed their control of the country.

The PRI has held an iron grip on many social institutions, including government, business, and labor. Still, other major parties have slowly emerged. The two most important are the National Action Party, which is *Partido Acción Nacional* in Spanish, known as PAN, and the Party of the Democratic Revolution, which is *Partido Revolucionaria Democratica*, known as PRD. Opposing the PRI, however, was dangerous at times and often unfruitful, as the PRI controlled the whole election process, including the counting of ballots and voter registration.

In the 1980s and 1990s, however, democracy began to make some gains. In the 1994 presidential elections a record 78% of registered voters cast ballots. Ernesto Zedillo of the PRI won with 49% of the votes. The PAN candidate won 26% and the PRD candidate won 17% of the votes. Also, many congressmen and governors were elected from the opposition parties. The PRI was beginning to lose power.

During Zedillo's presidency, massive election reforms took place, including the establishment of an electoral college and equal public funding of political campaigns. These reforms resulted in an electoral process not unlike that of the United States. In fact, in the presidential election of 2000, one of the people entrusted with observing a fair election was former U.S. President Jimmy Carter. That process resulted in the election of PAN candidate Vicente Fox to the presidency.

With the election of President Fox, many Mexicans and foreign observers see the realization of democracy and the opportunity for Mexican citizens to have greater control of their government.

The Road to *"Los Pinos"*

Though intently focused on improving the state of Guanajuato, Fox's sights were set on the Mexican presidency. He made his intentions for the 2000 race public while he was still governor. He announced his candidacy in mid-1997, giving him a full two-and-a-half years to campaign and defeat the PRI.

Fox campaigned aggressively, traveling across Mexico and meeting with people at all levels of society. His working man's appearance and straight

President Vicente Fox, accompanied by his daughter, Paulina, and his son, Rodrigo, wave to the crowd en route to the National Palace following his inauguration ceremony, December 2000.

talk got the attention of poor people, while his business experience and his ideas for economic development attracted middle- and upper-class people. Fox's popularity grew as people became more aware of what kind of person he was.

Fox's political style was aptly described by journalist Dick Reavis, writing for *Texas Monthly*: "The Mexican masses noted Fox's pigstickers [cowboy boots] and rodeo-style belt buckles when they saw him on TV, and they chuckled when they heard him give voice to words from their own blue vernacular. The few of them who read newspapers or tuned into pundits found nothing in the rest of him but confirmation of what those symbols plainly said: that Vicente Fox was a president who would speak from the heart of the common man. Against this message, the PRI was nearly powerless."

Electoral reforms instituted by then-President Zedillo made funds available for television advertising for the first time to a non-PRI candidate. This helped Fox immensely, and he hired people to "sell" him in the same way that advertisers would sell any product. Fox campaigned on promises to end corruption in the government, improve economic growth, and focus on building the educational system in Mexico. And for the first time in Mexican history, the elections would be administered by an independent group of observers—not controlled by the PRI.

On Election Day 2000, the confidence of the people was high, resulting in 64% of Mexico's registered voters casting ballots. The PRI opposition was strong, but its influence was not strong enough to impede what many regard as the first fair election in Mexican history. On July 2, 2000, Fox defeated PRI candidate Francisco Labastida and PRD candidate Cuahtemoc Cardenas, who was Mexico City's mayor. Fox won with more than 43% of the vote. He was the first non-PRI president to occupy the presidential residence, *Los Pinos*, since the Mexican Revolution more than 70 years earlier.

The Challenge of Keeping Promises

On President Fox's inauguration day, he spent the morning having breakfast with street children in Mexico City's toughest neighborhood, Tepito. It was his way of saying he would not forget Mexico's poor or the tradition of crime and conflict that have been such a large part of Mexico's history.

"My commitment will be to move Mexico from a path of corruption and impunity, from a path where no one pays attention to education and human capital, and move on to a path of high-speed growth, with a state of law and with an educational revolution," Fox stated early in his presidency. Even after being elected, Fox offered promises of more jobs, better education, and more opportunity for growth.

—— **"** ——

"The Mexican masses noted Fox's pigstickers [cowboy boots] and rodeo-style belt buckles when they saw him on TV, and they chuckled when they heard him give voice to words from their own blue vernacular. The few of them who read newspapers or tuned into pundits found nothing in the rest of him but confirmation of what those symbols plainly said: that Vicente Fox was a president who would speak from the heart of the common man. Against this message, the PRI was nearly powerless." —Dick Reavis, **Texas Monthly**

—— **"** ——

But being the country's first president who wasn't supported by the PRI, Fox did not have the power base to effect change easily. Much of the legislature and the federal government was made up of PRI supporters. His desire to reform and to eliminate corruption met with opposition in many cases.

Other circumstances that have nothing to do with Mexico's political make-up have prevented noticeable progress. A week before the terrorist attacks on the United States on September 11, 2001, Fox was in Washington, D.C., proposing increased cooperation between the United States and Mexico. He has made no secret of his belief that the U.S. and Mexican economy are closely linked. In his visit with President Bush on September 8, 2001, Fox proposed more lenient immigration standards for Mexicans. Fox hoped that through more open immigration policy, money from émigrés to the United States would fuel economic growth back home. The theory is that products, labor, and money would flow more freely across the border, benefitting both countries.

> *"My commitment will be to move Mexico from a path of corruption and impunity, from a path where no one pays attention to education and human capital, and move on to a path of high-speed growth, with a state of law and with an educational revolution,"* Fox stated early in his presidency.

But with the attacks on September 11, the Bush administration quickly became focused on combating terrorism and addressing the faltering economy in the United States. Mexico and other countries have also shared the economic slump that has affected the United States. While Fox had promised to create 1.5 million jobs during his administration, he had to admit that more than 200,000 jobs had been lost during his first year in office.

Battling Corruption and Criticism

Fox has also been the object of criticism in his pledge to fight corruption in Mexico, particularly in the area of human rights. Early in his administration, key drug lords were arrested who had formerly been protected by corrupt law enforcement. These arrests earned him high praise. He made an open agenda of battling *la impunidad* (Spanish for "the impunity," or lack of consequences for wrongdoing among government officials and police). He initiated new access to government files on incidents that had

President Vicente Fox and his wife Martha Sahagun attend a state dinner at the
White House with President George W. Bush and First Lady Laura Bush,
September 2001.

been questionable in the past. Most notable was the opening of a long-secret file on the 1968 massacre of hundreds of protesting students.

Despite these early actions, many have voiced concern that Fox was not doing enough to reform the corrupt system that had been in place for years. This criticism increased with the assassination in October 2001 of Digna Ochoa, a key human rights leader. Ochoa was a human rights attorney who gained popularity by representing people who accused the police and military of kidnaping, torture, and murder. A note found at the scene of her murder made it clear that she was killed for her human rights work.

Opponents of Fox have claimed that he has not done enough to solve Ochoa's murder. Fox did, however, initiate a commission to investigate the disappearances and deaths of more than 500 anti-government activists since the late 1970s. For the first time in Mexican history, an official report admitted government involvement in some of the cases.

Despite such criticism, Fox remains committed to change for Mexico. In an address in June 2002 that marked the one-year anniversary of his inauguration, Fox said, "Friends, I am a man of my word and I know how to keep my word—this is what I learned from my parents, and I will try to keep my word to all of you. All the promises made during my campaign are being met. One year has not been much time to achieve the great objectives I proposed during the campaign. However, it has been more than enough time to show clearly that we are ready to guarantee the enormous changes that we wanted for our country, for our people, for our families, for our daughters and sons.... The future is ours."

> "Friends, I am a man of my word and I know how to keep my word—this is what I learned from my parents, and I will try to keep my word to all of you. All the promises made during my campaign are being met. One year has not been much time to achieve the great objectives I proposed during the campaign. However, it has been more than enough time to show clearly that we are ready to guarantee the enormous changes that we wanted for our country, for our people, for our families, for our daughters and sons.... The future is ours."

Fox has set an ambitious series of goals for his presidency, and whether he will be able to achieve all these goals in his six-year term remains to be seen. He will, however, be regarded in Mexican history as the leader who successfully broke the rule of the PRI and challenged the corrupt systems that have plagued Mexico for centuries.

MARRIAGE AND FAMILY

In 1971, Fox married Lillian de la Concha, who worked as a secretary at Coca Cola at the time they met. They adopted four children, two daughters (Ana Cristina and Pauline) and two sons (Vicente and Rodrigo). The couple divorced in 1991, and Fox has retained custody of the four children.

During Fox's campaign for the presidency, he became close with his spokesperson, Martha Sahagun. After he was elected, he named her press secretary. One morning, about a year after he was elected, Sahagun was in his office, taking notes on scheduled tasks. "July 2, 8 a..m.," Fox said. "Okay," Sahagun replied, as she noted the date. "What do you want me to do then?" "Marry me," was Fox's reply. July 2 would be a special day: it was the one-year anniversary of Fox's election, and also his birthday.

Fox's remarriage caused some criticism, especially from devoted Catholics. Church custom dictates that if a person hopes to marry a second time, their first marriage should be officially annulled (the church saying in effect that the marriage never existed). Both Fox and Sahagun were divorced, and neither had sought annulments. This caused scandal among some, and signaled to others liberalization from repressive religion. The two were married at *Los Pinos* in a civil ceremony on July 2, 2001.

Vicente Fox and Martha Sahagun smile as they pose during a private wedding ceremony at the presidential residence, Los Pinos, July 2001.

HONORS AND AWARDS

Civic Man of the Year (Alianza Civica
— Civic Alliance): 1991
Man of the Year (*Latin Finance*): 2001

FURTHER READING

Books

Contemporary Hispanic Biography, Vol. 1, 2002
Encyclopedia of World Biography Supplement, Vol. 21, 2001
Fox, Vicente. *Vicente Fox a Los Pinos*, 1999 (in Spanish)
Paprocki, Sherry Beck, *Vicente Fox (Major World Leaders)*, 2003
Who's Who in America, 2002

Periodicals

Atlanta Journal-Constitution, Nov. 11, 2001, p.A5
Current Biography Yearbook, 2001
Hispanic Magazine, May 2001
Newsweek, Nov. 26, 2001, p.66

Texas Monthly, Dec. 2000, p.126
Time, Oct. 15, 2001, p.80
Washington Post, Sep. 4, 2001, p.C1

Online Resources

Biography Resource Center Online, 2003, articles from *Contemporary Hispanic Biography,* 2002, and *Encyclopedia of World Biography Supplement,* 2001

ADDRESS

Presidente Vicente Fox
Los Pinos, México, D.F.
Mexico

WORLD WIDE WEB SITE

http://www.vicentefox.org.mx

Millard Fuller 1935-

American Attorney, Business Leader, and
Philanthropist
Founder of Habitat for Humanity International

BIRTH

Millard Dean Fuller was born on January 3, 1935, in Lanett,
Alabama. He is the son of Render Alexander Fuller, a grocery
store owner, and Estin Cook Fuller. Fuller's mother died when
he was only three. His father later remarried, and his new stepmother was Eunice Stephens Fuller. Fuller has two younger
half-brothers, James Doyle and Render Nicholas, who are the
sons of Fuller's stepmother.

YOUTH

From a very early age Millard Fuller had the makings of a successful businessman—he was an entrepreneur at heart, and he drew his strength to be independent from his family. Although his mother died when he was only three, he grew up in a loving, supportive, and religious family. His father remarried when Fuller was six, and he soon had two half-brothers. Their home community in Sumter County, Alabama, was very poor, and the Fullers struggled as much as anyone there. Fuller's grandfather had been a sharecropper (someone who farms a piece of land owned by someone else), and the family never had a permanent home. "We were always shifting around," Fuller remembered. "That's why I think interest in housing is so deep in my psyche."

Fuller's father worked hard to support his family, and his work ethic rubbed off on his son. "My father ran a grocery store and a soft ice cream shop on the edge of Lanett," Fuller recalled of his childhood years. "I worked there and flipped thousands of hamburgers and made thousands of milkshakes. He later was a cattle farmer, and I helped him sell cattle. I worked planting the fields, harvesting the grain, and baling the hay."

But the young boy did more than help his father; he also ran many of his own business ventures. "Since I was a boy," he said, "I was involved in several business enterprises. When I was six years old, my father bought me a pig and set me up a bookkeeping system where I could keep track of the expenses and income and profit when I sold the pig. My father was my mentor and inspiration for business. I sold chickens, rabbits, firecrackers, and a few used automobiles. At 19 I was the nation's youngest program director of Junior Achievement in Opelika, Alabama." Fuller also started his own worm farm, selling his product as bait for fishermen.

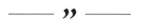

> "Since I was a boy, I was involved in several business enterprises. When I was six years old, my father bought me a pig and set me up a bookkeeping system where I could keep track of the expenses and income and profit when I sold the pig. My father was my mentor and inspiration for business. I sold chickens, rabbits, firecrackers, and a few used automobiles. At 19 I was the nation's youngest program director of Junior Achievement in Opelika, Alabama."

By the time he was 10 years old, Fuller had also gained his first experience in construction. His father had bought 400 acres of land, and there was a small, tumbledown house on it that he helped his father remodel. Little did he know at the time that this early job in construction would serve him so well in running Habitat for Humanity.

EDUCATION

Fuller continued to rely on his business acumen to earn money during his high school and college years. While in high school, he studied, worked on the family farm, was president of the Southeast Conference of Congregational Christian Churches (which later became the United Church of Christ), and raised and sold cattle for money that he saved for college. In 1953 he was accepted for admission at Auburn University, in Auburn, Alabama, where he studied economics and graduated with a B.S. degree in 1957. After receiving his bachelor's degree, Fuller decided he wanted to become a lawyer. He therefore enrolled at the University of Alabama's School of Law. In addition to his studies there, he wrote for the student newspaper and campaigned, unsuccessfully, for student body president. It was there, too, that he met his similarly ambitious friend and business partner, Morris S. Dees, Jr.

Together, Fuller and Dees launched a direct marketing business while they were still in law school, selling anything that seemed to have a customer demand, including holiday wreaths, doormats, bookends, lamps, and even a student directory. They delivered birthday cakes under the company name Bama Cake Service, and they also invested in real estate. Buying a number of rundown houses near the university, Fuller gained more construction experience renovating these homes, which he and Dees would then rent out. "We had a burning desire to be fabulously rich," he said, adding that "we were making $50,000 a year by the time we graduated from law school."

In 1960, Fuller received his law degree; also that year, he served briefly in the U.S. Army as a lieutenant. As he related, he and Dees then went down to Montgomery, Alabama, and opened up a law office. Again, the point of practicing law was to "make money: get the cases that would produce the most money. No interest in how we could right some wrong."

FIRST JOBS

The first few years of Fuller's career after college were marked by the relentless pursuit of wealth. With his law office partner, he also founded the

Fuller working on a house for Habitat for Humanity.

Fuller and Dees Marketing Group in 1960. Both Fuller and Dees were marketing wizards. Just like when they were in school, they sold whatever they could find a demand for, including tractors, tractor cushions, and cookbooks. In fact, their cookbooks did so well that they launched a smaller company called Favorite Recipes Press, publishing such popular works as *Favorite Recipes of American Home Economics Teachers*. "We sold them by the millions," stated Fuller. "But all of that was for one purpose: making a lot of money."

By the age of 29, everything seemed to be going great for Fuller. He was married with children, and he was already a millionaire. "It was a very quick success track," he remarked. "We made a lot of money and got everything that money gets for you: a Lincoln Continental, a cabin on the lake, two speedboats, 2,000 acres of land, 25 horses, hundreds of head of cattle, maids. We were living a fast and very successful life in terms of worldly standards. But the price you pay for that is that something has to give."

—— *"* ——

"It was a very quick success track. We made a lot of money and got everything that money gets for you: a Lincoln Continental, a cabin on the lake, two speedboats, 2,000 acres of land, 25 horses, hundreds of head of cattle, maids. We were living a fast and very successful life in terms of worldly standards. But the price you pay for that is that something has to give."

—— *"* ——

CHOOSING A CAREER

What started to give in Fuller's life was his family life, and it was this difficult time that caused him to change his career goals. His wife, Linda, was miserable, because her husband worked so hard that she and the kids never saw him. Even when Fuller came home to dinner, he was often with Dees, and the two would just talk business and ignore everyone else. "Me and the kids were on the fringe," Linda Fuller said. "That wasn't my idea of family." In 1965 she told her husband that she was considering divorcing him, and she took an airplane to New York City to gain some space, talk to a pastor, and think about the future.

At the same time that his wife left, Fuller was suffering from breathing and other health problems that his doctor told him were stress related. When his wife left him, it was a wake-up call that his workaholic lifestyle was ruining everything he really cared about. "I lost my mother when I was three," he commented, "and now through my own stupidity I was about to lose my wife. It was a very sobering and shocking revelation for me." Determined not to let his family fall apart, he flew to New York to put his marriage back together. Meeting his wife, the two of them decided that they could remain married, but things would have to change—drastically. Then, while riding in a taxicab, Fuller suddenly had a revelation. "I think Linda felt it too," he said of that moment. "It was nothing spooky or mysterious. I didn't hear any bells or choirs singing or anything like that. I just had a sensation of light. And I turned to Linda and I said, 'I think what we should do is leave business and give all our money away and make ourselves poor again and throw ourselves on God's mercy to find out what He wants to do with our lives. We've messed them up.'"

Fuller had been a religious man all his life, but until that moment his Christian faith had always taken a back seat to his quest for money. But at that moment, his life was filled with religious purpose. His wife agreed wholeheartedly with his plan. Although their friends and family all thought he was crazy, Fuller sold his share of his business to Dees and proceeded to give all his money and possessions to charity. Immediately, he and Linda felt relieved. But the question then became: what to do next?

> While riding in a taxicab, Fuller suddenly had a revelation. "I think Linda felt it too," he said of that moment. "It was nothing spooky or mysterious. I didn't hear any bells or choirs singing or anything like that. I just had a sensation of light. And I turned to Linda and I said, 'I think what we should do is leave business and give all our money away and make ourselves poor again and throw ourselves on God's mercy to find out what He wants to do with our lives. We've messed them up.'"

MAJOR INFLUENCES

The answer to their search for a new goal in life came unexpectedly from a man they had never heard of before: Clarence Jordan. Several weeks after deciding to abandon most of their worldly possessions, Fuller decided to visit a friend who lived at a Christian commune called Koinonia Farm near

Americus, Georgia. Koinonia comes from the Greek word meaning "fellowship." The community was run by Clarence Jordan, a doctor of theology who founded Koinonia in order to create a community where Christians could live a simple country life in racial harmony. Fuller was immediately impressed with this man. Instead of just staying a few hours to meet his friend, he decided to stay at Koinonia for a month.

"Clarence Jordan thought more like Jesus than anybody I ever met," Fuller once said of the theologian. "I had never been exposed to the thinking that I was hearing from Clarence," he also said. "He said every character he read about in the Bible he met in Sumter County. I never thought like that. He related the Bible to now. So many Christians keep the Bible in some far distant past. He saw black people as totally equal and for a white boy that was totally revolutionary. He said everyone was made in God's image and his whole thinking was about unlimited love. Most people put limits on their love: 'I love MY wife, MY children, MY clan, MY race, MY nation.' Clarence said you have to take all the boundaries away."

But Jordan's ideas of racial tolerance outraged the local residents. Black residents were suspicious of the motives of this white man, and white residents despised Jordan's desire to have the two races living in the same community. There had been many incidents when the locals had burned down buildings and even fired guns at the commune. Koinonia was founded in 1942 with several dozen residents, but by the time the Fullers arrived there were only a few families left. Despite its lack of growth, Koinonia and its founder greatly impressed Fuller, who felt that Jordan's ideals, wisdom, and tolerance for others were the embodiment of Christianity. "I really believe that God brought me and Clarence together because Clarence was a big dreamer and I'm a practical man attracted to idealism," Fuller said. "Because of him, I've been able to weave those things together."

After having many conversations with Jordan, Fuller decided to find a worthwhile organization to work for, one whose goal wasn't just to make money. So in 1966 he took a position as development director at Tougaloo College in Mississippi, a nearly all-black college that was church supported. Working out of New York City, he helped raise funds for Tougaloo for two years, sometimes traveling around the world to do so. One trip in particular took him to Zaire (now the Democratic Republic of the Congo), where Fuller was appalled by the conditions of the shanty towns in which the people lived. He remembered that one of Jordan's dreams was to build decent housing for the poor, and this led his thoughts back to Koinonia.

CAREER HIGHLIGHTS

By the late 1960s, all of Fuller's skills and experiences — including his religious upbringing, his familiarity with construction, his business sense, and his desire to do something worthwhile with his life — finally came together in what would become his mission to help the less fortunate.

From Koinonia to Zaire

In 1968 Fuller and his family returned to Koinonia Farm. There, Jordan had an idea to create the Fund for Humanity, which would seek donations and use that money to help create self-sufficient farms where poor people could live. Both Jordan and Fuller recognized that these people would need more than just farmland — they would need good homes. Together they established Koinonia Partners, which would build houses for low-income residents and give them no-interest loans. Fuller was named director of the new organization, and construction was started. Unfortunately, before the first building was completed, Jordan died of a heart attack on October 29, 1969. With the founder gone, Koinonia was managed by a board of directors. Fuller remained there for the next four years, helping to raise funds and working on public relations.

But Fuller was not content now that Jordan was gone, and so in 1973 he resigned his position at Koinonia and took his family to Mbandaka, Zaire, and the shantytowns he remembered there. "I was not at all happy with how things were being run [in Koinonia]," he recalled. "I discovered something about myself, and that was that I was not happy to be a part of something that I didn't have a very significant role in being the leader of. That inspired the move to Africa. I think it was a divine discontent." Beginning with a few thousand dollars donated by the Disciples of Christ Church, Fuller was challenged by the oppressive Zairian government, supply shortages, and difficult working conditions. Despite these problems, he managed to construct over 100 cement-block homes for the people there. He also set up funds to provide amputees with artificial legs and an eyeglass donation program where people in the United States would mail their used glasses to those who needed them in Zaire. He wrote about these experiences in his first book, *Bokotola*.

The Beginning of Habitat for Humanity International

After spending three years in Zaire, Fuller felt the urge to return to Georgia. Once back at Koinonia, he learned that the board of directors had decided to build homes only in the Americus area. This upset Fuller, who felt that their mission should not be limited to the local community, so he broke away from Koinonia to establish Habitat for Humanity International in 1976. Setting up an office in Americus in 1977, Fuller also started a law practice to earn some income for his family while working on Habitat.

Fuller calls Habitat for Humanity the "economics of Jesus, or Bible economics. The Bible teaches if you lend money to the poor, not to charge interest. And so, we charge no interest. We add no profit, charge no interest, and that makes a house affordable to very low income families. Part of the economics of Jesus is also seen in the Bible where the laborers in the vineyard who work different amounts of time all got paid the same, not according to the amount they produced, but according to their need."

The ambitious vision for Habitat is to provide descent housing for everyone who needs it—not just in the United States, but all over the world. But Fuller didn't want to establish a housing charity and just give people homes: he felt that most people, including the poor, don't really value

Fuller working on a house for Habitat for Humanity.

something that is provided for free. Instead, he wanted to give the poor affordable housing that was well built. So he created a non-profit organization where members would actually build homes. The construction work for Habitat is done almost entirely by volunteers, and much of the land and materials are donated. So Fuller was able to keep costs down. Low-income people who needed a home could then apply for a house, which could be purchased at a reduced rate and with a no-interest loan. Furthermore, the family that received the loan would have to assist with the construction of the house and promise to volunteer some of their time toward the building of homes for other people, something that Fuller calls "sweat equity." That helps the families feel like they've contributed to earning their homes.

Fuller calls his system the "economics of Jesus, or Bible economics. The Bible teaches if you lend money to the poor, not to charge interest. And so, we charge no interest. We add no profit, charge no interest, and that makes a house affordable to very low income families. Part of the economics of Jesus is also seen in the Bible where the laborers in the vineyard who work different amounts of time all got paid the same, not according to the amount they produced, but according to their need." Fuller also

> **"Habitat for Humanity is not charity. All we give away is an opportunity. The families have to help build their own houses."**

added that "Habitat for Humanity is not charity. All we give away is an opportunity. The families have to help build their own houses." He also believes that providing better houses for the poor has other benefits, such as children doing better in school: "Their grades go up when you get them into a better living situation. Their health improves. Many poor families in this country are living in houses with lead-based paint, and that has the effect of dulling the brain, and children don't do well in school." Therefore, he has come to the conclusion that "building homes is not just good religion... . It's good politics, it's good sociology, it's good economics. It's just plain good common sense."

Controversy Turns to Support

Following the ideals of Clarence Jordan, Fuller set an ambitious goal for Habitat: to house every man, woman, and child on the planet who needed shelter. And he put no limits on race or religion, which offended many of the residents of Americus. In the early years of Habitat, Fuller had to overcome a great deal of prejudice and suspicion against his organization. Because Habitat built homes without the intention of making a profit, the Fullers were accused of being Communists, as well as being some sort of religious cult. His family was also harassed. When the Fullers first moved to Americus, broken glass was thrown on their driveway every day, and his children were shunned at school by the other kids. But Fuller fought back with kindness. Going through the local newspaper, he wrote congratulatory letters to residents about whom he had read positive stories in the paper, and he gradually won friends. Also, as Habitat grew, the organization began employing the townspeople. Slowly, people in Americus began to see Habitat as a good thing for their community.

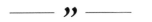

"[Children's] grades go up when you get them into a better living situation. Their health improves. Many poor families in this country are living in houses with lead-based paint, and that has the effect of dulling the brain, and children don't do well in school." Therefore, Fuller has come to the conclusion that "building homes is not just good religion. . . . It's good politics, it's good sociology, it's good economics. It's just plain good common sense."

Jimmy Carter Lends a Hand

But Habitat got a real boost in public relations when, in 1984, former U.S. President Jimmy Carter announced that he and his wife, Rosalyn, would like to volunteer their support to Fuller's cause. Carter's home is in Plains, not far from Americus, and he had known about Koinonia and Habitat for years. In 1982 he publicly addressed Habitat's annual meeting, saying, "I am proud to be a neighbor of Koinonia. . . . To have seen, from perhaps too great a distance, the profound impact of Clarence Jordan. . . . I think I will be a better Christian because of Clarence Jordan, Koinonia, and Habitat. And I hope to grow the rest of my life with you." Lending his full support as a director, financial partner, and volunteer (Carter is a capable carpenter), Carter helped Fuller begin the Jimmy Carter Work Project, a once-a-year event in which Habitat holds a week-long building marathon on a particular project. The first of these was a renovation project in New York City, where the volun-

Former president Jimmy Carter and his wife, Rosalynn Carter, stand between Millard Fuller, left, and Leroy Troyer, right, leader of Habitat's Los Angeles Projects, as they review building plans for 20 houses in Los Angeles, June 1995.

teers, including Jimmy and Rosalyn Carter, made an old 19-unit building suitable for new residents.

Carter also helped Fuller in another, unexpected way. In 1990, Fuller found himself in a serious controversy when several women who had worked for Habitat accused him of sexual harassment. Fuller has always been an out-wardly affectionate man, and he said that the contact he had made with these women had only been in the form of hugs. However, the women felt these gestures were inappropriate, and the board of directors wanted to strip Fuller of his powers as executive director of Habitat and place him in a more ceremonial role. Fuller, however, would have none of this, and he decided to resign.

After Fuller left, Habitat lost a $2 million line of credit. The organization began to suffer financial problems and ended up laying off 43 of its em-ployees. Carter was angry over the board's decision, and he told them frankly that he would quit Habitat unless they reinstated Fuller. Under this kind of pressure, the members of the board relented and asked

Fuller to return. However, he would no longer run the day-to-day operations of Habitat, a responsibility that now fell to executive vice president Jeff Snider, whom Fuller had hired for the role. Fuller is now president of Habitat and in charge of promoting the organization and being its spiritual center. From the harassment accusations he learned that, especially as a public figure, he had "to be more careful about who you touch and how you hug somebody, because the rules are different."

"I have had the experience,"
Fuller said proudly,
"of walking into the home of
a family who had been living
in a very bad situation and
have the members of that
family grab and hug me with
tears pouring down their
faces saying, 'You have made
it possible to have a decent
life.' What's that worth?
It's priceless."

Amazing Growth

With the crisis of leadership behind it, Habitat for Humanity enjoyed a period of exponential growth during the 1990s. By 1995, the organization had constructed 12,000 homes, including 4,000 in the United States and 8,000 abroad. Fuller challenged Habitat and its many affiliates to push the limit and build more homes every year. The result was that by 2002, just seven years later, Habitat had multiplied its 1995 total ten times, completing 120,000 homes (including 20,000 in Africa) while expanding to 2,000 affiliate branches worldwide. Today, Habitat for Humanity continues to work toward its goal of housing the world's people. And Fuller's dream has already become a reality in Habitat's base in Sumter County, where every single shack has been replaced by a good quality home. In 1999, the organization launched its 21st Century Challenge, in which it asked all of its affiliates to do the same for their counties as the Americus headquarters did for Sumter County.

Although he gave up his fortune and material wealth, Fuller considers himself richer than ever before. He has won numerous awards, including several honorary doctoral degrees, but it is not for these honors that he works so hard. Rather, it is for the joy he and his wife have been able to bring to others. "I have had the experience," he said proudly, "of walking into the home of a family who had been living in a very bad situation and have the members of that family grab and hug me with tears pouring down their faces saying, 'You have made it possible to have a decent life.' What's that worth? It's priceless."

MARRIAGE AND FAMILY

Fuller married Linda Caldwell on August 30, 1959. The two originally met while he was a junior in law school and she was a junior in high school. She has a degree in elementary education and, as part of a special Habitat mission, she currently focuses on providing homes for those who are struggling with mental diseases. They have four children: Christopher, who is a pastor; Kimberly, who is a flight attendant; Faith, who is a television newscaster; and Georgia, who is a teacher. For years, the family lived in one of the Habitat-built homes in a low-income area of Americus, but recently they moved into a larger home in a better area.

WRITINGS

Bokotola, 1978

Love in the Mortar Joints: The Story of Habitat for Humanity, 1980 (With Diane Scott)

No More Shacks: The Daring Vision of Habitat for Humanity, 1986

The Excitement Is Building: How Habitat for Humanity Is Putting Roofs over Heads and Hope in Hearts, 1990

The Theology of the Hammer, 1994

A Simple, Decent Place to Live, 1995

More than Houses, 1999

Cotton Patch for the Kingdom: Clarence Jordan's Demonstration Plot at Koinonia Farm, 2002 (With Ann Louise Coble)

Building Materials for Life: Radical Common Sense, the Power of Right Thinking, Persistence, Plowing New Ground, Relevant Religion, and 35 Other Essays on How to Enhance Your Life, 2002

AWARDS AND HONORS

Clarence Jordan Exemplary Christian Service Award (Southern Baptist Theological Seminary): 1986

Dr. Martin Luther King Jr. Humanitarian Award (Martin Luther King Jr. Center): 1987

Distinguished Christian Service in Social Welfare Award (North American Association of Christians in Social Work): 1988

International Humanity Service Award (American Overseas Association): 1989

Public Service Achievement Award (Common Cause): 1989
M. Justin Herman Memorial Award (National Association of Housing and
    Development Officials): 1989
Temple Award for Creative Altruism: 1990
Professional Achievement Award (Partnership for Affordable Housing):
    1993
Harry S. Truman Public Service Award (City of Independence, Missouri):
    1994
Builder of the Year (*Professional Builders Magazine*): 1995
Faithful Servant Award (National Association of Evangelicals): 1996
Spirit of Georgia Award: 1996
National Housing Hall of Fame: 1996
Presidential Medal of Freedom (United States Government): 1996
Jefferson Award: 1999, for outstanding contributions to his community
Mark O. Hatfield Leadership Award (Council for Christian Colleges and
    Universities): 2001, for demonstrating uncommon leadership that re-
    flects values of Christian higher education

FURTHER READING

Books

Contemporary Heroes and Heroines, Vol. 3, 1998
Encyclopedia of World Biography Supplement, Vol. 18, 1998
Who's Who in America, 2002

Periodicals

Boston Globe, Dec. 28, 1997, National/Foreign section, p.A1
Chicago Tribune, May 14, 1995, WomanNews section, p.3
Christian Science Monitor, Apr. 9, 1986, p.7; Aug. 7, 1987, p.21; Dec. 28,
    1990, p.13
Christianity Today, June 14, 1999, p.44; June 10, 2002, p.28
Current Biography Yearbook, 1995
Los Angeles Times, Aug. 6, 1988, part 2, p.7; Nov. 4, 2001, p.E2
National Review, Dec. 30, 1988, p.40
New York Times, May 25, 1982, p.A16; Sep. 3, 1984, section 1, p.1
Time, Jan. 16, 1989, p.12

Online Database

Biography Resource Center Online, 2003, articles *Contemporary Heroes and
    Heroines*, 1998, and *Encyclopedia of World Biography Supplement*, 1998

ADDRESS

Millard Fuller
Habitat for Humanity International
121 Habitat Street
Americus, GA 31709-3498

WORLD WIDE WEB SITE

http://www.habitat.org

Josh Hartnett 1978-

American Actor
Star of the Hit Films *Pearl Harbor, O,* and
Black Hawk Down

BIRTH

Joshua Daniel Hartnett was born on July 21, 1978, in St. Paul, Minnesota. His father, Daniel Hartnett, is a former professional guitar player who later became a building manager. His mother is a teaching assistant. Josh's parents divorced when he was quite young, and his mother moved to San Francisco, California. Josh was raised primarily by his father and stepmother, Molly, who is an artist. He has three younger siblings: Jessica, Jake, and Joe.

YOUTH

The Hartnett family has lived in St. Paul since 1865. Josh's great-great-grandfather went to Minnesota to work on the railroads, and his mother's family arrived in St. Paul around 1900. He grew up, therefore, with a deep attachment to the Minneapolis-St. Paul area.

Josh first learned what it was like to perform in front of an audience by serving as an altar boy. He and his friends often volunteered to serve as altar boys at funerals because they would be paid five dollars and get a day off school. When he was a little older, he worked in a video store, and this is where he fell in love with movies. He even remembered saying to himself, "People in Hollywood are doing work like that? I want to go out there!" Josh's father recognized his interest in the entertainment business and suggested classic movies that he should check out. To this day, Hartnett idolizes Jimmy Stewart, the actor who starred in many of the films he watched as a youngster.

When he was 16, Hartnett and some of his friends made a short film about a robbery at a Dairy Queen—until a passerby thought a real robbery was taking place and called the police. "It's a good thing we were taking a break and eating Dilly Bars [when the police arrived]," recalled Hartnett. "If we'd had our fake yellow pistols in our hands, we probably would have all been goners."

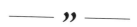

When he was 16, Hartnett acted in a short film that he and some of his friends made about a robbery at a Dairy Queen. His performance as one of the robbers was so convincing that a passerby thought a real robbery was taking place and called the police. "It's a good thing we were taking a break and eating Dilly Bars [when the police arrived]," he recalled. "If we'd had our fake yellow pistols in our hands, we probably would have all been goners."

EDUCATION

Hartnett attended Nativity of Our Lord School in St. Paul before starting high school at Cretin-Derham Hall. At the end of his sophomore year, he transferred to South High School in Minneapolis, which was known for putting on three or four huge theatrical productions every year. His high school theater coach, Louise Bormann, remembers casting him as gambler Sky Masterston in the musical *Guys and Dolls*. Even at this young age, Hartnett showed impressive poise and professionalism. "It was like, 'Whoa! Here's a kid I don't need to coach,'" Bormann said.

Although Hartnett was an intelligent boy, he was a mediocre student. "I hated school," he admitted. "I loved learning, but I hated doing all the busywork." He was more interested in playing football, but he had to quit the team when he tore a ligament in his knee at 16. At this point his aunt, who was very interested in theater, talked him into auditioning at the Youth Performance Company. This community theater group for young actors in Minneapolis was putting on *Tom Sawyer*. Hartnett agreed to audition and ended up winning the role of Huckleberry Finn. "It started with me just being competitive and wanting to see if I could beat out the other kids," he acknowledged. "[But] I kind of just took to it. I loved the immediate gratification of being onstage."

———— **"** ————

Hartnett claims that his acting career "started with me just being competitive and wanting to see if I could beat out the other kids [for parts]. I kind of just took to it. I loved the immediate gratification of being onstage."

———— **"** ————

By the time he graduated from South High School in June 1996, Hartnett had appeared in several television commercials and hired a manager who specialized in handling talented young Minnesota actors. He soon began attending the theater program at the State University of New York at Purchase, but he left before completing his freshman year because of a disagreement with the university's administrators. "They didn't really kick me out; they just said I could leave if I wanted to," Hartnett explained. Never an enthusiastic student, he decided to take his manager's advice and move to Los Angeles.

CAREER HIGHLIGHTS

The "Hottie of Horror"

Hartnett arrived in Los Angeles in February 1997. He immediately signed with a Hollywood- based agent and started going out for three or four auditions a day. "I was kind of a romantic and deluded kid," he admitted. "I

Josh Hartnett sits behind the wheel in a scene from The Faculty.

thought that I was going to walk in and say, 'I'm here.' And they'd be like, "You're our guy.'" In fact, Hartnett landed his first role—in the television detective drama "Cracker"—within a couple of months of his arrival in Los Angeles. He played the troubled 17-year-old son of a police psychologist. "My first scene on national television, I was sitting on a toilet," he recalled. "My dad said I could only go up from there." The show was canceled after nine episodes, but it gave Hartnett the introduction to Hollywood that he needed.

The cancellation of "Cracker" freed Hartnett to accept his first big screen role, as Jamie Lee Curtis's son in *Halloween: H20,* a teen slasher movie in the "Halloween" series. Curtis plays Laurie Strode, sister of the Halloween murderer Michael Myers. He is believed to be dead—but of course is very much alive. To escape from her homicidal brother, Laurie fakes her own death in a car accident, moves to California under an assumed name, and starts a new life as headmistress of an elite California boarding school. Most of the school's faculty and students go off on a camping trip to Yosemite. But Laurie's son John, played by Hartnett, manages to stay behind, putting himself in serious jeopardy. Although the movie itself received poor reviews, a critic from *Interview* magazine praised Hartnett for his "thoughtful, brooding presence tempered by good humor." He was also nominated for an MTV Movie Award for Best Breakthrough Performance.

Not long after the 1998 release of *Halloween: H20,* Hartnett appeared in another horror movie, *The Faculty.* This time the villain is an alien that shows up at a high school in Ohio and begins to take over first the faculty and then the students. Hartnett played Zeke Tyler, a drug-dealing underachiever who is repeating his senior year. Zeke unexpectedly rises to the challenge and decides to do something about the "invasion of the body-snatchers" taking place at his school. This film received even worse reviews than *Halloween: H20,* but Hartnett's performance led *Seventeen* magazine to call him the "unofficial hottie of horror."

Branching Out

Hartnett recognized the danger in being typecast as a teenage horror movie star, so he made a deliberate effort to find roles that would broaden his acting experience. In 2000 he worked on five different films. The first, *Here on Earth,* provided him with an opportunity to play a romantic leading role. Hartnett played Jasper, a farm boy who is dating his childhood sweetheart, Samantha (played by Leelee Sobieski), a waitress at a local diner. His main rival for Samantha's affection is Kelley (played by Chris Klein), an arrogant preppy and class valedictorian. Kelley challenges Jasper to a drag race that ends up destroying the diner, which is owned by Samantha's mother. Their punishment is to rebuild the place, and Kelley moves in with Jasper and his family until the work is done. The developing relationships among the three teens provide the crux of the story. Like most of the films in which Hartnett had appeared to this point, *Here on Earth* was panned by the critics.

Soon after *Here on Earth* was released, Hartnett appeared in *Blow Dry.* He played an ambitious young hairdresser from Yorkshire, England, who enters a national hairstyling competition. The competition triggers an intense rivalry between two beauty salons in the same small town. Hartnett had to master a British accent for the role. It also gave him a chance to play opposite Rachel Leigh Cook, who graduated from the same Minneapolis high school as Hartnett, only two years later. Although the role was a departure for him, Hartnett was able to tap into his own competitiveness to play it convincingly. Still, the movie itself failed to attract much notice.

Hartnett's third movie of 2000, *The Virgin Suicides,* was the first film in which he appeared that earned wide critical acclaim. Adapted from a novel by Jeffrey Eugenides and directed by Sophia Coppola, daughter of the legendary director Francis Ford Coppola, the film tells the story of the five

Hartnett and co-star Julia Stiles at the premiere of the movie O.

mysterious Lisbon sisters. The youngest daughter kills herself, and the film explores the effect of her death on the remaining four sisters and their overly strict parents. The boys in their suburban Michigan neighborhood are fascinated by the Lisbon sisters — particularly Lux, the eldest (played by Kirsten Dunst) — and spend most of their time fantasizing about what might happen if the girls ever escaped their parents' control. Hartnett plays Tripp Fontaine, a 1970s teenage heartthrob who develops an obsession for Lux. Sophia Coppola cast him in the role without even meeting him in person. "You just knew he had it," she recalls. Although Dunst attracted most of the critical attention for her portrayal of Lux, Hartnett also received praise for his skillful portrayal of the seductive and irresponsible Tripp. (For more information on Dunst, see *Biography Today Performing Artists*, Vol. 1.)

The fourth movie that Hartnett worked on in 2000 was *Town & Country*, a divorce comedy that was not released until the following year. Hartnett plays a relatively minor role as the son of the film's two stars, Warren Beatty and Diane Keaton. The film follows two middle-aged couples and explores their marital problems. But despite a talented cast that also included Goldie

Hawn, Andie MacDowell, Garry Shandling, and Nastassja Kinski, *Town & Country* was a colossal failure among critics and at the box office.

Hartnett's fifth movie of 2000 was *O*, a modern-day retelling of Shakespeare's *Othello* set in an elite boarding school. "O" is the nickname of Odin James (Mekhi Phifer), the school's only black student and its star basketball player. O is in love with the dean's daughter, Desi (Desdemona in Shakespeare's original), played by Julia Stiles. The dean is torn between wanting to end his daughter's interracial romance and wanting the school's basketball team to win the state finals. Martin Sheen plays the school's basketball coach, and Hartnett plays the role of Hugo Goulding, the coach's son. Just like the character Iago in *Othello*, Hugo is jealous of O's stardom and the close relationship that develops between his father and the star athlete. As a result, Hugo tries to destroy O by convincing him that Desi is in love with another boy on the team, who happens to be O's best friend.

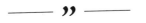

> "I knew [Pearl Harbor] was going to be huge," Hartnett remembered. "I was afraid I wouldn't be able to walk around and live my life the way I always had."

Although *O* was filmed in 2000, its release was delayed until the summer of 2001. Many movie studio executives worried that the film's grim and violent ending was too similar to the real-life 1999 student shooting incident at Columbine High School in Colorado. The delay proved fortunate for Hartnett, because in the meantime he appeared in the blockbuster *Pearl Harbor* and became a star. But even though Hartnett's name brought his fans to the theaters, *O* was not well received by critics. *Variety* magazine attacked the film for its "thoroughly misguided effort to make a classic tale somehow topical and relevant."

Pearl Harbor

When Hartnett was first approached about appearing in *Pearl Harbor* — a big-budget action movie about the Japanese attack on the U.S. Navy base in Hawaii on December 7, 1941 — he was hesitant about accepting the role. "I knew this movie was going to be huge," Hartnett explained. "I was afraid I wouldn't be able to walk around and live my life the way I always had." He went home to Minnesota and talked to his father about his fears. His father pointed out that fame was only temporary, but that the regret he might feel if he turned the role down could last a lifetime.

Producer Jerry Bruckheimer, cast members Josh Hartnett, Kate Beckinsale, and Ben Affleck, and director Michael Bay pose together prior to the world premiere of the motion picture Pearl Harbor.

Director Michael Bay had no hesitation at all about casting Hartnett in one of the lead roles. "He was this grunge kid from Minnesota," Bay recalls. "As soon as I screen-tested him, I knew. I got so excited. I called [producer Jerry Bruckheimer] on the phone. I said, 'Jerry, this guy is awesome.'" Still, Bay was determined not to hire the first young actor he saw. He kept Hartnett waiting for three months while he auditioned others. But the director ultimately gave Hartnett the role of Danny Walker, a young American fighter pilot who is stationed in Hawaii at the time of the Japanese attack. "He had comic timing, sincerity, and a genuine shyness that really worked," Bay says.

In the movie, Danny and Rafe (played by Ben Affleck) are ace fighter pilots and best friends. They also fall in love with the same woman, a young nurse named Evelyn (played by Kate Beckinsale). The resulting love triangle is played out against the backdrop of World War II and the attack on Pearl Harbor. To prepare for their roles as military men, Hartnett, Affleck, and several of the film's other actors were sent to an Army boot camp on the Hawaiian island of Oahu, where Pearl Harbor is located. "We were there for about four or five days and it felt like seven, eight, nine years,"

Hartnett said. "They were supposed to break us down and then build us up again like they do in the Army. They didn't have time to build us back up. They broke us down and said, 'Go, make a movie. Have fun.'" But Hartnett emerged from the experience with great respect for members of the military, whom he says "work harder than most people I've ever met."

Hartnett also learned a great deal from talking to World War II veterans about their experiences. "I talked for hours with a guy who was a number-one ace pilot in the Pacific, shooting down Japanese planes," he said. "We met right off the bat, but the conversation stuck with me throughout the whole film shoot."

Although *Pearl Harbor* received a huge amount of publicity and attracted many moviegoers, it received mixed reviews and never made the anticipated box-office history. It did, however, turn Josh Hartnett into a recognizable Hollywood name. When asked how he felt about the fact that the movie received some harsh reviews, Hartnett responded with characteristic nonchalance: "I don't want people to think that I'm ungrateful for what I've been given," he said. "But at the same time my life is not completely run by the movie business. I have friends and family that I really care about and lots of things that I love to do aside from this. So it's nice when things go well, and it's too bad when things don't."

40 Days and 40 Nights

After wrapping up *Pearl Harbor,* Hartnett switched gears and appeared in a lighthearted romantic comedy, *40 Days and 40 Nights.* His character, Matt Sullivan, has just gone through a bad breakup with his longtime girlfriend. He decides to give up sex for Lent, a 40-day period in which many Christians fast and ask forgiveness for their sins in preparation for Easter. Unfortunately, the day after he makes his decision he meets Erica (Shannyn Sossamon), the girl of his dreams. She and everyone around him — including his ex-girlfriend and his buddies at the office — seem determined to make him break his vow.

Hartnett tried to get into his role by abstaining from all sexual activity, even hugging and kissing, during the filming. But the main result of this decision was that he endured constant teasing from the cast and crew. "It was pretty much embarrassing for me from beginning to end," he recalled. However, he did appreciate the fact that the film gave him his first chance to play a comic leading role.

40 Days and 40 Nights aroused a certain amount of controversy upon its release, which took place during the middle of Lent. Some religious organizations objected to the film's subject matter and claimed that it was disrespectful of the traditions of Lent. It received only lukewarm reviews, but Hartnett was given most of the credit for its modest success. A writer for *WWD* noted that his "knack for projecting authenticity" made a film that might otherwise have come across as absurd seem both humorous and believable. And the *Virginia Pilot* claimed that "the comedy works" because "Hartnett plays his role with earnestness. If Adam Sandler had been cast instead, this would have been a fiasco. Hartnett is hilarious."

Black Hawk Down

Hartnett's personal favorite among all of his films is *Black Hawk Down,* which was released in 2002. Directed by Ridley Scott and produced by Jerry Bruckheimer, who also produced *Pearl Harbor,* it is based on a bestselling true-life story by journalist Mark Bowden. *Black Hawk Down* follows a group of American soldiers who take part in a disastrous mission to capture members of a rebel clan in Mogadishu, Somalia. The doomed mission, which took place in 1993, resulted in the deaths of 18 American soldiers and more than 500 Somalis.

Hartnett played Matt Eversmann, a U.S. Army Ranger who takes part in what is supposed to be a swift and efficient military action. The mission is intended to stop the activities of a Somali warlord who is stealing the food and supplies that are intended for his starving countrymen. The warlord has also killed 24 members of

Working on **Black Hawk Down** *gave Hartnett greater respect for members of the military."[The U.S. soldiers] put themselves in situations where it's life or death, and they've got to make these huge moral decisions that I would never want to have to make," Hartnett said. "Hopefully, when a movie like this comes out, people will think twice about sending our troops on the ground into a land that we don't know anything about, to be slaughtered."*

the United Nations peacekeeping force in the area. When the Rangers arrive on the scene, they quickly find themselves trapped in a deadly fight for their lives on the city's rubble-strewn streets. Attempts to rescue them fail when two Black Hawk helicopters are shot down. The chaotic 15-hour battle ends with three dead American soldiers being dragged through the streets of Mogadishu. The movie included a re-creation of this event, which aired repeatedly around the world on television news networks.

Promotional posters for Black Hawk Down *emphasized Hartnett's starring role.*

Black Hawk Down focused on telling the story exactly as it occurred, without taking sides or trying to be patriotic. While shooting the film in Morocco, Hartnett met several of the soldiers who actually participated in the ill-fated military operation. The experience gave Hartnett even greater respect for members of the military, but it also increased his doubts about how the United States sometimes chooses to use its military strength. "[The soldiers] put themselves in situations where it's life or death, and they've got to make these huge moral decisions that I would never want to have to make," he commented. "Hopefully, when a movie like this comes out, people will think twice about sending our troops on the ground into a land that we don't know anything about, to be slaughtered."

Hartnett received star billing for *Black Hawk Down,* which won Academy Awards for both film editing and sound. The movie also received a great deal of critical praise. Writing in *Time,* Richard Schickel claimed that it deserves a place "on the very short list of the unforgettable movies about war and its ineradicable and immeasurable costs." The *Atlanta Journal-Constitution,* meanwhile, described the film as a "stunning depiction of war."

Black Hawk Down featured a large cast, and it was more concerned with showing the terrible battle that unfolded in Mogadishu than with character development. Nonetheless, a number of reviewers singled Hartnett out for delivering a strong performance. The *San Francisco Chronicle,* for example, declared that "Hartnett's beautifully delivered final scene" helped turn *Black Hawk Down* into an "exceptional accomplishment."

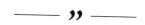

"You get the sense that Josh isn't acting," says Jerry Bruckheimer, who produced **Pearl Harbor** *and* **Black Hawk Down.** *"With some actors, you see the wheels turning, but not with him. Josh has an inner peace and a strength on screen that bring Gary Cooper to mind."*

After wrapping up the filming of *Black Hawk Down,* Hartnett decided to take some time off. He was upset by the poverty he saw around him while shooting the movie in Morocco. These feelings intensified after the terrorist attacks on the United States of September 11, 2001. The United States responded to the attacks on the World Trade Center and the Pentagon by invading Afghanistan, a Central Asian country where terrorists responsible for the September 11 attacks were believed to be hiding. Hartnett opposed the invasion of Afghanistan, arguing that it mainly hurt innocent people. "Suddenly we hate all these people over there who, most of them, have nothing to do with terrorism and are the innocent victims of our brashness," Hartnett stated. "Suddenly it was us against the world."

Hartnett, co-star Harrison Ford (left), and director Ron Shelton (center) on the set of Hollywood Homicide.

During Hartnett's one-year break from moviemaking, he stated that he wanted to "discover who I am as a person" and to recover from "some important mistakes in my choices," both as an actor and in his personal life. With these goals in mind, he returned to Minnesota to spend time with family and friends.

One year later, Hartnett resumed his acting career by appearing in *Hollywood Homicide,* a comedy about a pair of mismatched police detectives. Hartnett plays K.C. Calden, an easygoing rookie cop who moonlights as a yoga instructor for classes full of beautiful women and aspires to become an actor. Harrison Ford plays his grumpy veteran partner, Joe Gavilan, who sells real estate on the side in order to pay alimony to his many ex-wives. The partners have a number of comic disagreements as they investigate a murder at a rap club. *Hollywood Homicide* received poor reviews upon its release in 2003. *Newsweek* reviewer David Ansen, for example, called it a "numbingly formulaic action comedy" that is "oddly listless from the get-go."

Fame a Mixed Blessing

Now that he is a star and can pick and choose among the scripts that he is offered, Hartnett has vowed to concentrate on "stretching" himself as an actor and finding roles that are unlike those he has already played. He has established his own production company and has agreed to star in an upcoming romantic comedy called *Bob,* about an engaged man who falls in love with an older woman who has children. He has also signed on to star in *Wicker Park,* a psychological drama about a man who is obsessed with the search for a former lover. Reluctant to star in another blockbuster, Hartnett turned down an offer to play Superman in a three-film series. "It didn't feel like the right thing for me," he explained. "Am I going to feel fulfilled doing [the series]? Probably not. It was three films over many months, and I decided that putting on the tights just didn't make sense."

Everyone who has worked with Hartnett comments on his modesty and genuineness. "You get the sense that Josh isn't acting," says Jerry Bruckheimer, who produced *Pearl Harbor* and *Black Hawk Down.* "With some actors, you see the wheels turning, but not with him. Josh has an inner peace and a strength on screen that bring Gary Cooper to mind." Hartnett does not try to attract attention to himself, although he is usually very polite to the fans and autograph-seekers who now dog his every step. "I'm pretty good at returning to life after my work is done," Hartnett said. But he admitted that fame can be a mixed blessing. "It's made it a lot easier to get good projects coming around. I was getting good scripts before but we couldn't get them made into movies because it wasn't commercially viable and so that's changing," he says. "But I've got people sitting in their cars and looking in my windows in front of my house, and that's a little weird."

> **""**
>
> *"I'm pretty good at returning to life after my work is done," Hartnett said. But he admits that fame can be a mixed blessing. "I've got people sitting in their cars and looking in my windows in front of my house, and that's a little weird."*
>
> **""**

HOME AND FAMILY

Hartnett recently bought a house in Minneapolis, where he can be near his family and escape the trappings of Hollywood. "It's one of those ideal places to raise a family," he explained. "It's safe, it's beautiful, there are lakes and cabins." He often stops in to see shows at the Youth Performance

Company, where he got his start in theater. His girlfriend, Ellen Fenster—whom he describes as "a normal person" he would rather keep out of the limelight—is a Minneapolis theater director. He likes to get together and jam with his father, a former guitarist, and his younger siblings, all of whom play musical instruments.

Hartnett describes his family as a group of "very intelligent people who see things for what they are at all times. . . . My family doesn't have to try too hard to maintain balance. It's just natural for them to be able to pick out the BS and choose not to deal with it." Although he occasionally thinks about moving to New York City, Hartnett appreciates the fact that "people in Minneapolis have been very good, extremely polite and reserved. As long as it stays that way, it is my home."

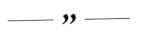

> *Hartnett describes his family as a group of "very intelligent people who see things for what they are at all times. . . . My family doesn't have to try too hard to maintain balance. It's just natural for them to be able to pick out the BS and choose not to deal with it."*

FAVORITE BOOKS AND MOVIES

Hartnett is a big fan of the Beat writers (a group of novelists and poets whose work was popular in the 1950s). In fact, he claims that Jack Kerouac's classic novel *On the Road* changed his life. "It gave me this wanderlust," he recalled. "It made me want to move." One of the highlights of his life was when Lawrence Ferlinghetti, another Beat author, visited the set of *40 Days and 40 Nights* in San Francisco. "I can't even tell you how cool that was," he said.

Trainspotting remains one of his favorite movies. He first saw it when he was a high school student working in a video store. "You see that kind of work and you want to be part of it," he said. Two of the film's stars, Ewan McGregor and Ewen Bremner, later appeared with Hartnett in *Black Hawk Down*. Other recent film favorites include *12 Monkeys*, *The Usual Suspects*, and *Basquiat*, which he described as "beautifully made, beautifully acted. It's so honest, so spot-on and has such a beautiful message on fame."

HOBBIES AND OTHER INTERESTS

Hartnett has always loved to paint. "It relaxes me because it's just me and the canvas and there's no right way or wrong way," he explained. He also enjoys playing sports — especially baseball, basketball, football, and hockey. But his favorite way to spend time when he is not working is to be with his family in St. Paul.

SELECTED CREDITS

Films

Halloween: H20, 1998
The Faculty, 1998
Here on Earth, 2000
Blow Dry, 2001
The Virgin Suicides, 2000
Town & Country, 2001
Pearl Harbor, 2001
O, 2001
Black Hawk Down, 2001
40 Days and 40 Nights, 2002
Hollywood Homicide, 2003

Television Series

"Cracker," 1997-98

FURTHER READING

Books

Contemporary Theatre, Film, and Television, Vol. 29, 2000
Lanum, Lorelei. *Josh Hartnett: American Idol,* 2002

Periodicals

Atlanta Journal-Constitution, Jan. 18, 2002, p.P1
Details, June/July 2003, p.146
Interview, Jan. 1999, p.68; Feb. 2000, p.146
Minneapolis Star-Tribune, June 1, 2003, p.A1; June 13, 2003, p.E11
New York Times, Mar. 17, 2002, p.17
Newsweek, June 23, 2003, p.63
Observer (London), Apr. 21, 2002, p.14
People Weekly, June 11, 2001, p.69
San Francisco Chronicle, Jan. 18, 2002, p.D1
Seventeen, Mar. 2000, p. 189
Teen People, Feb. 1, 2002, p.58

Vancouver (BC) Province, June 8, 2003, p.D3
Vanity Fair, July 2001, p.83
Virginia Pilot, May 2, 2002, p.E4
YM, Feb. 2002, p.69

Online Databases

Biography Resource Center Online, 2003, article from *Contemporary Theatre, Film, and Television,* Vol. 29, 2000

ADDRESS

Josh Hartnett
Iris Burton Agency
8916 Ashcroft Ave.
Los Angeles, CA 90048

Dolores Huerta 1930-
American Labor Leader
Cofounder of the United Farm Workers

BIRTH

Dolores Huerta was born Dolores Fernandez on April 10, 1930, in Dawson, New Mexico. She was the second of three children born to Juan Fernandez, a coal miner and migrant farm worker, and Alicia (Chavez) Fernandez, a waitress and factory worker. Huerta's parents divorced when she was five years old, and her mother eventually became a restaurant owner and hotel manager. Huerta has two brothers, Juan and Marshall, as well as two much younger half-sisters from her mother's later marriages.

YOUTH

Huerta was born at the beginning of the Great Depression, a time of great economic hardship for many Americans. The tough economic conditions made it tremendously difficult for Alicia Fernandez to support her three children after the divorce. She moved them first to Las Vegas, New Mexico, and then to Stockton, California, a city located in a vast farming region known as the San Joaquin Valley. Hernandez maintained an exhausting schedule to support her children, working as a waitress during the day and toiling in a cannery at night. Huerta and her brothers, meanwhile, took care of laundry and other housecleaning chores under the supervision of their widowed grandfather. His nickname for Huerta was "seven tongues" because she was so talkative. "[My grandfather's] influence was really the male influence in my family," she recalled.

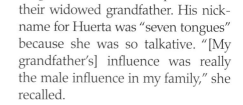

Huerta and her brothers took care of household chores under the supervision of their widowed grandfather. "[My grandfather's] influence was really the male influence in my family," she recalled.

As Huerta grew older, her mother remarried and had another daughter. Alicia Fernandez and her new husband bought a restaurant and a small hotel, where farm workers and their families often stayed. Huerta and her brothers worked there during their summer vacations. During this time, they met many Mexican *braceros*— day laborers who had been hired to work on the valley's fruit and vegetable farms because so many American men were off fighting in World War II. The *braceros* were paid less than regular workers, and Alicia Fernandez often let them stay at her hotel for free. During these summers, young Dolores also came to known and appreciate members of Stockton's other ethnic groups, including Chinese, Japanese, Filipino and Jewish people.

By the early 1950s, Alicia Fernandez had skillfully built the hotel into a successful business enterprise. She divorced her second husband around this time and married Juan Silva, with whom she had another daughter. During this time, she encouraged her eldest daughter to participate in a wide range of activities. Huerta recalled that she pleased her "motivated and ambitious" mother by taking piano, violin, and dancing lessons, singing in the church choir, and serving as a Girl Scout for many years.

Even as a young woman, Huerta was heavily involved in campaigns to improve the lives of migrant farmworkers.

Huerta did not see her father very often when she was growing up, but she never lost contact with him entirely. Her father divided his time between laboring in local coal mines and traveling throughout the American West to harvest crops on big farms. During his travels, he and many other

Mexican-Americans—the primary ethnic group involved in migrant farm work—often endured terrible working conditions. They were paid very low wages for hours of difficult, physically draining labor in the hot sun. Work breaks were often nonexistent, and laborers often had to handle crops that had been treated with pesticides. This constant exposure to pesticides placed their health at significant risk. Working conditions were poor in many other ways as well. For example, many farms did not provide outdoor toilets for workers to use, so workers were forced to suffer the humiliation of squatting down in the fields or hiding behind bushes. The nature of migrant farm labor also forced migrant families to spend much of their

Defining Ethnic Heritage in the Latin American Community

Many different terms are used to define ethnic heritage in the Latin American community. The terms *Chicano* (masculine—pronounced chi-KAHN-oh or shi-KAHN-oh) and *Chicana* (feminine) refer to a person who comes from Mexico or is of Mexican descent. The term comes from the Mexican Spanish word *mexicano,* meaning 'Mexican.' A person of Mexican descent who is a resident or citizen of the United States is often referred to as a *Mexican-American.*

The terms *Latino* (masculine—pronounced la-TEEN-oh) and *Latina* (feminine) refer to a person of Latin-American descent who is living in the United States. Latin America includes all of Mexico as well as other Central and South American countries where Spanish or Portuguese is the national language.

The term *Hispanic,* from the Latin word for "Spain," refers to a person living in the U.S. from any of the countries in either the Northern or Southern hemisphere where Spanish is the primary language. A native of Spain, for example, is a Hispanic but not a Latino.

Although the U.S. government uses the broadest term, *Hispanic,* when referring to members of the Spanish-speaking community, some people find the term offensive. It doesn't sound as Spanish or as culturally authentic as *Latino,* and it doesn't have a feminine form like *Latina.*

To make matters even more confusing, certain terms are preferred in certain parts of the country. For example, *Latino* is used widely in California, while *Hispanic* is more common in Florida and Texas. But even in these states, it is not unusual to find the two terms used interchangeably.

time traveling from farm to farm as various crops became ready for harvest. As a result, migrant workers and their children spent many nights sleeping in their cars or in shacks without heat, plumbing, or running water. Worst of all, young children often ended up working all day alongside their parents because it was the only way the family could earn enough money to survive.

These awful living conditions led Juan Fernandez to become an active participant in labor union activity. Labor unions are organizations formed by workers to protect their rights and interests against unfair or dangerous business practices. In the 1930s he formally joined the local chapter of a union known as the Congress of Industrial Organizations. His union activities eventually brought him into the world of politics. In 1938 he was elected to the New Mexico state legislature, where he worked hard to pass laws that would help migrant workers. He was voted out of office after only one term.

After losing his seat in the legislature, Fernandez worked for a time as a traveling salesman. At age 11, Huerta even spent most of one summer accompanying him on his travels. He eventually moved to Stockton and became a union activist. During this period, he visited his children much more regularly. Looking back, Huerta has expressed pride in her father's efforts on behalf of migrant farmers and other workers. But she also notes that her father held very chauvinistic attitudes toward women. She believes that her father's conviction that men are superior to women was typical of most Chicano (see box) men of his generation.

EDUCATION

Huerta attended Lafayette Grammar School, Jackson Junior High, and Stockton High School. She was a popular student who participated in a variety of extracurricular activities. During her high school years, however, she also experienced several disillusioning instances in which she was the victim of racial prejudice. On one occasion, for example, she organized a teen center that attracted young people from many different ethnic backgrounds. But local police did not like the idea of white teenagers socializing with Chicanos and other minorities, so they closed the center down. Dolores also recalled that she sold more war bonds than anyone else in a school-sponsored contest, but she never received the trophy that had been promised to the winner. She contended that school officials wanted to ignore the contest results because they were embarrassed that a Mexican-American student had out-performed everyone else. "If you were black or brown," she concluded, "you got treated differently."

Huerta walks with Senator Robert F. Kennedy (left) during a 1968 UFW rally.

During the 1940s and 1950s, few Hispanic women were able to go to college. When Huerta graduated from high school in 1948, however, her mother's success as a hotel owner made it possible for her to continue her education. Dolores enrolled at Stockton College, but dropped out before earning her degree to marry her high school boyfriend. They had two children, but the marriage only lasted three years before it ended in divorce. Dolores then returned to Stockton College — now affiliated with University of the Pacific and known as Delta Community College — in the early 1950s. She earned an associate's degree with a certificate in teaching in 1953.

FIRST JOBS

Dolores held a number of jobs in Stockton before she graduated from college. She worked in her mother's hotel during the summers and managed a small grocery store owned by her mother. When the store went out of business, she worked as a secretary at the local U.S. Navy supply base and at the sheriff's office.

After receiving her teaching certificate, Dolores became an elementary school teacher in Stockton. Many of her students came from poor families that supported themselves through migrant farm labor. The sight of barefoot, malnourished children crowding into her classroom every day finally became too much for her to take. She decided to quit her teaching job and get more directly involved in helping farm workers fight poverty. "It just hit me that I could do more by organizing farm workers than by trying to teach their hungry children," she explained.

CAREER HIGHLIGHTS

Becoming a Labor Activist

During the 1950s, many minorities in the United States began to challenge the discriminatory practices that existed in nearly every aspect of American society. This dissatisfaction brought about the civil rights movement, which eliminated many laws that discriminated against black Americans and other minorities. During this same period, labor unions delivered higher wages and safer workplace rules for their members. But many migrant farm workers were left behind by these trends. For example, the Fair Labor Standards Act of 1938 established a minimum wage for workers and placed limitations on the amount of overtime a company could demand of its workers. But the law did not cover agricultural workers, most of whom were minorities. Similarly, the National Labor Relations Act of 1935 gave most American workers the right to join or form labor unions and to bargain collectively (as a group) with their employers for decent wages and working conditions. But this law excluded farm workers as well.

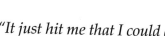

"It just hit me that I could do more by organizing farm workers than by trying to teach their hungry children," Huerta said.

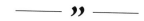

Determined to improve the lives of poor migrant families, Huerta decided to work as a volunteer for the Community Service Organization (CSO). This Mexican-American self-help group provided civic and educational programs for Hispanic-Americans, including citizenship classes and voter registration drives. It also pressured local communities with high Hispanic populations to hire more Hispanic police officers and to provide Spanish-speaking people in hospitals, community centers, and government offices so that Mexican-Americans could be guaranteed the same services that white people received. The CSO also encouraged Hispanic-Americans to bring about changes in their schools and their communities by organizing group actions that would draw attention to their needs.

In 1955 Huerta helped establish a CSO chapter in Stockton. She hoped the organization could help the Chicanos and other minority farm workers who came to the San Joaquin Valley every year to harvest crops. As the months passed by, she also launched voter registration drives and publicized incidents in which migrant workers were mistreated by employers, police, and city officials. Over time, Huerta became so skillful at lobbying local government officials on behalf of migrant workers that the CSO hired her as a full-time lobbyist for the organization. As a result, she spent much of her time in the state capital of Sacramento, urging lawmakers to pass laws that would benefit Mexican-Americans.

———— " ————

"[The grape boycott] was like a war," recalled Huerta. "We never slept. We'd get up at 3 or 4 a.m. and then we'd go till 11 p.m. because we'd always have a meeting."

———— " ————

In 1960 Huerta founded an organization known as the Agricultural Workers Association (AWA). Over the next two years, Huerta and the AWA helped persuade California lawmakers to pass more than a dozen laws giving non-citizen workers retirement benefits, medical and disability insurance, and financial support for their families when they were unemployed. Legislators even passed laws that allowed migrant workers to vote and to take their driver's license exams in Spanish.

A Union for Farm Workers

During Huerta's employment at CSO, she also established a strong working relationship with a man named Cesar Chavez. (For more information on Chavez, see *Biography Today,* September 1993.) A former migrant farm worker himself, Chavez had joined the CSO in 1953. By the late 1950s he had gained a reputation as a tireless worker who was determined to improve the lives of the migrant families toiling on the farms of the American West.

In the late 1950s Chavez and Huerta repeatedly tried to persuade the CSO to devote more attention to rural field workers. But the CSO leadership continued to focus most of its efforts on improving the lives of Mexican-Americans located in cities. As a result, Chavez and Huerta left the organization. They moved to Delano, California, where they founded a farm workers' union called the National Farm Workers Association (NFWA) in 1962.

Huerta carries campaign literature during the UFW's grape pickers' strike.

In the beginning, convincing migrant farm workers to join the NFWA was a difficult task. In many instances, their *patrones* (employers) had threatened to fire them and send them back to Mexico if they attended union meetings. Some farm workers had been beaten for trying to join unions, and many were afraid they would be killed. But by visiting the workers in the fields and talking to them face-to-face about what the NFWA could do

245

for them, Chavez and Huerta eventually won their trust. The NFWA gradually became one of the country's most popular organizations for Mexican-Americans.

As time passed, it became clear that Huerta and Chavez were a good team. Chavez possessed a vibrant personality and strong leadership qualities that inspired many workers to join the union. Huerta, meanwhile, excelled as an organizer and negotiator. Time after time, she sat down with fruit and vegetable growers and convinced them to sign contracts in which they promised to provide decent wages and housing for their workers. "I think we really built on each other's strengths," Huerta recalled.

As the NFWA increased in size, it launched several successful lobbying campaigns to improve the lives of its membership. For example, the union urged lawmakers to raise the minimum wage for farm workers. It also worked to establish a credit union and an insurance program for migrant workers, and to allow them to bargain collectively with their employers. The NFWA's lobbying activities also helped convince lawmakers to eliminate a federal law that allowed growers to hire Mexican migrant workers for less money than they paid their American workers.

The Table Grape Boycott

In 1965 Filipino grape pickers who were members of a labor union called the Agricultural Workers Organizing Committee (AWOC) in Delano walked off the job. They declared that they would not return until the growers who employed them raised their wages and contributed to the union's health and welfare fund. This action — called a strike — attracted the support of the NFWA. Led by Chavez and Huerta, the NFWA members joined the strike, boosting the total number of protesting workers to more than 5,000.

Initially, the grape growers who employed the pickers reacted angrily. They used violence and threats in an effort to frighten the workers into ending their strike. But the unions did not back down. Instead, they launched a nationwide table grape boycott — an effort to convince grocery stores and consumers to stop buying grapes that had been grown in California and harvested by underpaid migrant workers. Huerta was the boycott's main organizer. She traveled around the country, raising money to help the strikers and participating in protests designed to draw attention to strikers' demands. In New York, for example, Huerta and various supporters of the boycott — including students, political activists, community and religious groups, and consumers from many different races — picketed in front of grocery stores that sold table grapes until they agreed to take the grapes off the shelves. "It was like a war," Huerta recalled. "We never slept. We'd get up at 3 or 4 a.m. and then we'd go till 11 p.m. because we'd always have a meeting."

In 1966 the AWOC and the NFWA merged to form the United Farm Workers (UFW). That same year Huerta negotiated a new labor contract with Schenley Industries, one of California's grape growing businesses. This contract was a major triumph, for it marked the first time that an agricultural employer had negotiated a collective bargaining agreement with its workers. "Women are particularly good negotiators because we have a lot of patience and no big ego trips to overcome," Huerta later commented. "It unnerves the growers to negotiate with us."

Unfortunately, the other growers did not immediately follow Schenley's lead. The UFW engaged in five more years of strikes and boycotts before the other Delano growers agreed to bargain with union representatives. The resulting contracts gave grape pickers fairer wages, established vacation and holiday pay, and included measures for companies to contribute to the union's health and welfare fund.

"[Cesar Chavez and I] always worked as a team, but we used to argue a lot," Huerta admitted. *"We had different thoughts on strategies. . . . Sometimes he would win, and sometimes I would win."*

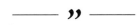

The UFW launched other boycotts in the 1970s and 1980s in an effort to improve the lives of its membership. In 1975, for example, a UFW boycott of grapes, lettuce, and Gallo wines was so successful that it led to the passage of the Agricultural Labor Relations Act (ALRA) in California. This law — the first of its kind — forced growers to acknowledge farm workers' right to meet with union organizers. It also forced growers to recognize whatever union the workers chose to represent them.

Huerta and Chavez worked closely together to coordinate these boycotts, but their relationship was a fiery one. "We always worked as a team," she explained, "but we used to argue a lot. We had different thoughts on strategies. . . . Sometimes he would win, and sometimes I would win." On several occasions, Chavez became so angry with Huerta that he fired her. But she always returned to her job within a day or two, and they would start working together again as if nothing had happened.

Huerta and Cesar Chavez (right) were a formidable team for the UFW. They are pictured here with posters of Robert F. Kennedy and Mahatma Gandhi.

Victories for the UFW

By the late 1970s Huerta was in charge of all the UFW's political activities. She spent much of the next several years lobbying Congress to pass a federal law giving amnesty (freedom from punishment) to more than a million illegal immigrants who lived, worked, and paid taxes in the United States but had never become citizens. After years of hard work, the Immigration Act of 1985 was finally passed into law. Years later, Huerta described the act as one of the UFW's most important achievements.

Huerta continued to travel back and forth across the country throughout the 1980s. During this time, she helped establish a United Farm Workers radio station, KUFW-Radio Campesina. In addition, she worked tirelessly to promote Chavez's "Wrath of Grapes" campaign, which focused attention on how pesticides were harming farm workers and their children. "No march is too long, no task too hard for Dolores Huerta if it means taking a step forward for the rights of farm workers," Chavez said. "[She is] totally fearless, both physically and mentally."

"No march is too long, no task too hard for Dolores Huerta if it means taking a step forward for the rights of farm workers," said Chavez. "[She is] totally fearless, both physically and mentally."

The UFW campaign eventually succeeded in forcing growers to stop using pesticides such as DDT and parathion, which had been linked to cancer and birth defects. But the victory was not a total one. Some growers continued to use other chemicals on crops without regard for the potential impact on the health of workers.

In 1988 Huerta traveled to San Francisco, where Vice President George Bush was campaigning for president (he eventually became the 41st president of the United States). She joined a protest that had been organized outside a Bush campaign event. The aim of the protest was to publicize the UFW's boycott activities, highlight its campaign to reduce worker exposure to dangerous agricultural chemicals, and criticize Bush's views on worker issues. But as the protest continued, tensions rose between participants and police officers responsible for controlling the crowd. At one point, Huerta was clubbed by an officer. The injuries forced her to a local hospital, where she had emergency surgery to remove a ruptured spleen and repair several broken ribs.

Huerta speaks at a rally in the 1970s.

Huerta later sued the city for the officer's actions. She eventually received an $825,000 settlement from the city, which also agreed to make changes in the methods its police department used to control large crowds. After recovering from her injuries, Huerta returned to the UFW, where she continued to attend farm workers' rallies, participate in strikes, and negotiate contracts with growers.

Decline of the UFW

Membership in the UFW had peaked at about 100,000 in the 1970s. In the 1980s, however, it underwent a steady decline, dropping to fewer than 40,000 members. Some observers claimed that the UFW was hurt by the conservative, pro-business administration of President Ronald Reagan, who served from January 1981 to January 1989. Others pointed to diminished media coverage of UFW boycotts, which limited their effectiveness. Some critics also claimed that members left because the union failed to bring about major improvements in the lives of farm workers and their families. For example, most farmer workers still earned less than the minimum wage in the early 1990s. It seemed to many people that farm workers had no more money or job security than they'd had before the union came along.

In 1993 the struggling union suffered another serious blow when Cesar Chavez died. "That was one of the saddest days I have ever known," Huerta said. "I think his death was a loss for all mankind. He was a real leader, like Mahatma Ghandi or Martin Luther King, and like them he believed in nonviolence." Chavez's son-in-law, Arturo Rodriguez, became the union's new president, and together he and Huerta worked harder than ever to keep the UFW alive. For example, they devoted a great deal of energy in the mid-1990s to establishing a union presence in the strawberry industry. But in 1996 their efforts were rejected by the strawberry workers. Many of these workers viewed the UFW as "a family business driven by money and power" rather than as an organization that could help them.

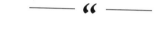

"If we are ever going to have justice in the world, we have to start by balancing the relationship between men and women in our society," *Huerta declared.*

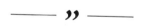

Huerta remained strong in the face of these disappointing events. In fact, she expanded the scope of her activities. In addition to her UFW work, she became heavily involved in specific efforts to improve the lives of Latino women. For example, she helped launch campaigns to eliminate sexual harassment of female farm workers and support the election of women to public office. She also helped found the Coalition of Labor Union Women (CLUW), a group aimed at increasing women's participation in union activities. "If we are ever going to have justice in the world, we have to start by balancing the relationship between men and women in our society," she explained.

Many women were inspired by Huerta's leadership in these areas. "Mexican women used to do what the men said, but Dolores Huerta was our example of something different," said one female union member. "She was always out in front, and she would talk back. She wasn't scared of anything."

*Huerta speaks out against cuts in state education funding at a
2003 rally in California.*

In the late 1990s, meanwhile, the UFW tried to revitalize itself through a
shift in strategy. It placed less emphasis on strikes, which were not always
effective and sometimes resulted in violence. Instead, the union's leadership relied more heavily on tactics like Huerta's "Five Cents for Fairness"
campaign. Under this strategy, the UFW urged consumers to pay five cents
more for a basket of strawberries so that the strawberry pickers could earn
higher wages. In addition, the union began to place more emphasis on organizing entire industries instead of individual farm operations.

A Lifelong Crusader

In 1999 Huerta left her position as vice president of the UFW to work for Al
Gore's presidential campaign. She was about to leave on a campaign trip
through the state of California when she was admitted to the hospital. At
first, doctors thought that she was suffering from a bleeding ulcer. They
eventually realized, however, that she had a bleeding artery in her intestine.
Her condition remained critical for several days as doctors treated her. She
then spent the next several months recovering. But even during her recovery, she spent much of her time drawing up plans to establish a leadership
foundation that would train young people as community organizers.

In 2002, at the age of 72, Huerta participated in a 165-mile walk through searing temperatures in California's Central Valley to the state capitol at Sacramento. Once she and other demonstrators arrived at the capitol, they urged California Governor Gray Davis to sign a bill that would end a stalemate in negotiations between growers and farm workers. Davis eventually signed the bill, and the new law went into effect in September 2002.

Huerta no longer holds an active position in the union, but she continues to promote its causes in her usual energetic fashion. In recent years she assisted in the establishment of a retirement village for farm workers. She also helped pass a ban on the use of short-handled hoes for harvesting, because the use of these tools often caused serious back problems for pickers. In addition, she helped agricultural workers gain greater access to medical insurance, pensions, educational funds, vacation and overtime pay, and other benefits. "My vision is for the farm workers to have the same rights, protection, and wages that other workers in this country have," she explained. "As long as my health holds out I want to pass my experiences along to help other people."

Huerta thinks that the UFW's nonviolent approach to confrontations with growers has been its most enduring contribution. "I think we brought to the world, the United States anyway, the whole idea of boycotting as a nonviolent tactic. I think we showed the world that nonviolence can work to make social change. . . . I think we have laid a pattern of how farm workers are eventually going to get out of their bondage."

> **"**
>
> *"I think we brought to the world, the United States anyway, the whole idea of boycotting as a nonviolent tactic," Huerta said. "I think we showed the world that nonviolence can work to make social change. . . . I think we laid a pattern of how farm workers are eventually going to get out of their bondage."*
>
> **"**

MARRIAGE AND FAMILY

Huerta married Ralph Head when she was a college student. They had two daughters—Celeste and Lori—before their marriage ended after three years. She later married her second husband, Ventura Huerta, and had five children—Fidel, Emilio, Vincent, Alicia, and Angela. Their marriage fell apart when it became clear, in Dolores's words, "that I cared more about helping other people than cleaning our house and doing my hair." In the early 1970s Huerta became romantically involved with Richard Chavez, Cesar Chavez's brother. Although they never married, they had four children together—Juanita, Maria Elena, Ricardo, and Camilla—and their relationship continues today.

Huerta, who lives in Bakersfield, California, admits that her 11 children have had to make sacrifices because of her UFW work. For many years they depended on donations for their food and clothing, and their mother's hectic travel schedule forced them to spend long periods living with friends or moving from school to school. Her daughter Lori says, "I remember, as a child, one time talking to her about my sadness that she wasn't going to be with me on my birthday. And she said that the sacrifices we as her children make would help hundreds of other children in the future. How can you argue with something like that?"

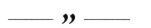

> *"I don't feel proud of the suffering that my kids went through. I feel very bad and guilty about it, but by the same token I know that they learned a lot in the process."*

For her part, Huerta admits that her kids endured difficult childhoods. "I don't feel proud of the suffering that my kids went through," she said. "I feel very bad and guilty about it, but by the same token I know that they learned a lot in the process." She believes that her children, several of whom have inherited their mother's devotion to activism, are better off as adults because of the values their mother instilled in them. "I expect them to follow their dreams, to change the world, to make the world a better place," she says.

HONORS AND AWARDS

Outstanding Labor Leader Award (California State Senate): 1984
National Women's Hall of Fame: 1993
Outstanding American Award (Eugene V. Debs Foundation): 1993
Roger Baldwin Award (American Civil Liberties Union): 1993
Ellis Island Medal of Freedom Award (National Ethnic Coalition of
    Organizations): 1993
Earl Warren Civil Liberties Award (American Civil Liberties Union): 1996
Eleanor Roosevelt Human Rights Award (U.S. Government): 1999

Hispanic Heritage Award: 2000
Puffin/Nation Prize for Creative Citizenship (Puffin Foundation and
Nation Institute): 2002

FURTHER READING

Books

Latinas! Women of Achievement, 1996

Periodicals

Hispanic, Aug. 1996, p.41
Latino Leaders, Feb.-Mar. 2000, p.49
Los Angeles Times, Apr. 29, 1999, Metro section p.1; Aug. 15, 1999, p.NA
Minneapolis Star Tribune, May 16, 1995, p. D1
Ms., Nov. 1976, p.11; Jan.-Feb. 1998, p.46
The Nation, Feb. 23, 1974, p.232; Dec. 23, 2002, p.7

Online Articles

http://www.latinoleaders.com
    (*Latino Leaders,* "Dolores Huerta: Secretary-Treasurer/United Farm
    Workers of America," Feb.- Mar. 2000)
http://www.hispaniconline.com
    (*Hispaniconline.com,* "For the Sake of Good: Civil Rights Activist Dolores
    Huerta Proves that Ordinary People Can Stand Up for Justice — and
    Win," May 2003)

ADDRESS

Dolores Huerta
United Farm Workers of America
P. O. Box 62
Keene, CA 93531

WORLD WIDE WEB SITES

http://www.ufw.org/
http://www.nwhp.org/

Sarah Hughes 1985-

American Figure Skater
Winner of the Gold Medal in Figure Skating at the
2002 Winter Olympics

BIRTH

Sarah Elizabeth Hughes was born in Great Neck, New York, on May 2, 1985. She comes from a family of athletes. Her grandfather on her father's side came from Ireland, where he played professional soccer in the 1930s. His son John (Sarah's father) was the captain of his college national championship hockey team in 1970 and even tried out for the Toronto Maple Leafs professional team. He decided, though, that he would only make a mediocre pro player and instead became a lawyer. Sarah's mother, Amy, worked in accounting, but she became a full-time home-maker when they started a family.

John's parents had cared for foster children when he was growing up, and he and Amy wanted a large family. When he was young, John says, "there always was a baby around. Eighteen kids passed through, so we always had diapers in the house. And then I got married and we had six kids, and for 16 years there always were diapers in our house." John and Amy Hughes have six children: Rebecca, David, Matt, Sarah, Emily, and Taylor. They live in Great Neck, Long Island, about 25 miles from Manhattan. It is an upper-middle-class community known for its good schools and well-to-do residents who commute to work in New York City. Their large, eight bedroom ranch home gave plenty of room for their growing family.

YOUTH

Sarah Hughes grew up in the midst of this large, happy family. She is often noted as being different from other figure skaters. Typically, top figure skaters live away from home so they can work with a top coach. But Sarah still lives with her family and is not the center of attention because of her skating career. All of her siblings are busy, successful young people. Her parents focus on helping all their children pursue their talents while stay-ing normal, well-rounded people. Rebecca says, "We're not the average American family. We're all very busy. We run around. But when all of us are home, Sarah is just one of us, and that's a rare thing for an elite ath-lete. We're her friends." The family even has a motto—work hard and stick together.

When the children were young, John Hughes made a hockey rink in the backyard during the winter. He began teaching his boys to play hockey, as he had in college, and Sarah was invited to play, too. But she didn't like hockey—she was afraid of the puck. Still, she loved skating by herself. When she was three, her mother took her to the skating rink along with Rebecca, David, and Matt. Amy Hughes sat her four children down and began lacing up their skates, starting with the youngest first. She moved on to Matt, and then noticed that Sarah was gone. She looked out on to the crowded rink and there was little Sarah, making her way among all the whizzing skaters. "I was pregnant with Emily then, and I ran out to the rink, shouting: 'Stop that kid! She's going to get killed!' After that, I would line them up in age order and tie Sarah's skates last."

But Sarah was determined to skate—she learned to tie her own skates by the time she was four. "It wasn't so important for me to tie my skates first.

It was because I was the only one who could do it right, how I liked it." When someone asked the young skater what she liked best about skating, she replied dreamily, "The ice." Skating has been important for many of the Hughes—two of her brothers have been hockey players, and two of her sisters have been figure skaters. Hughes said, "I was always very competitive, regardless of what it was. I tried to skate faster than [my brothers and sisters]. I always wanted to be the first to do everything."

EDUCATION

Since Hughes was a young girl, skating and school have been the two major features of her life. She likes school and is a good student, which is important in order to keep up with the demands of competitive skating. Through junior high school, she was able to keep a fairly normal school schedule. She attended regular school most of the time and even played the violin in the orchestra, except when she was traveling for competitions and some tours. She would practice in the morning and arrive at school late, then train again for several hours after school.

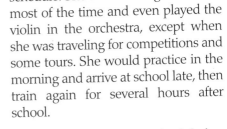

"I was always very competitive, regardless of what it was. I tried to skate faster than [my brothers and sisters]. I always wanted to be the first to do everything."

But as her competitive schedule became more demanding, with appearances in major competitions around the world, Hughes was able to attend school less and less. The competitive skating season is during late fall and winter, so Hughes is often traveling then. And when the competitive season ends and she is not on the road, she spends much of her time training at the skating rink. With this rigorous schedule, coach Robin Wagner wanted her to stop attending school completely in favor of individual tutoring. But her parents wanted her to stay in school, for whatever amount of time possible. So whenever she's not traveling, she gets up early each morning and goes to school for biology, Advanced Placement history, or another class.

Hughes's self-discipline and sharp mind make her both a good skater and a good student. History teacher Susan Babkes says, "What I feel in Sarah is the same discipline she has for skating, she has for her studies. It's the person she is. She's gifted, she has discipline, and she has focus." Hughes's favorite subjects are math and science. She attends classes when she can, and stays in touch with her teachers by email, phone, and fax when she is out of town. Some subjects she studies independently, with the help of tutors. Sometimes they will meet at Starbucks, or at her home. They have to be very flexible to work with Hughes. "I've faxed lots of stuff to various hotel rooms around the country," said Babkes. "She'll be away for a month, but I'm able to give her a task, several essay questions, and she'll call or e-mail to talk about her impressions." One teacher, Maggie Goldberger, said, "She doesn't come to class . . . then when she comes she does better than anybody." Hughes's organizational skills help her stay on track with her studies. When she's traveling to competitions, she often takes school work with her, although she usually doesn't do any on the day of a big competition. She even had her SAT study book with her at the Nationals.

Hughes also catches up on her homework while in the car. When she's not traveling to competitions, she trains at a skating rink in New Jersey. She has a one-and-a-half hour commute each way to the rink. So after her early morning classes at school, she meets her coach Robin Wagner in the parking lot of the local mall to begin their commute to the rink. Skating talk is off-limits during this time, so they often discuss current events. Other times, Hughes does homework or reads assigned books like *Ethan Frome* (which she didn't like) or David McCullough's biography of John Adams. Wagner often makes phone calls with her headset cellular phone — to sets up appointments for fittings or photographs, to arrange trip details, or do other skating business.

CAREER HIGHLIGHTS

Early Training and Coaches

Hughes first experiences with skating took place when she was about three, with her brothers and sisters at the local rink and in their back yard. Her father said, "There were probably more snowball fights on that rink than serious skating." She remembers that "it wasn't a great rink. The ice was bumpy. We took our family Christmas picture on it once, so there are a lot of fond memories." Then Hughes began to take lessons. By age five, she was already showing great talent. She could do Axel jumps, double Salchows, and double toe loops, and even won local competitions. Her father said, "She would get on the ice and she wouldn't want to come off. And she would be the first one out there, and the Zamboni would be honking the horn to get her off."

Hughes had several coaches when she was young, before her parents asked Robin Wagner to be her full-time coach. Wagner had been doing choreography for Hughes since she was about nine, and had about 30

other students at the time. She had been a serious competitive skater herself in her teens, and she had experience in fashion and business. Hughes's parents were impressed with her abilities and her desire to make "a lady out of Sarah, and not just a figure skater." Her job would be more than just the technical training. Wagner would take Sarah to the rink each day and coach her on a daily basis, but she would also plan special coaching sessions with people who could help her work on new skills, such as a triple Axel jump. She would continue to choreograph routines, but would also plan costumes and hire costume designers. She would arrange publicity shoots when needed, coordinate Hughes's other workout and therapy sessions, and travel with her around the world to competitions. She was in charge of "the total package." It was up to her to design the strategy that would make Hughes an Olympic champion, from the spins and jumps to the sequins and the hairstyle. It was a huge responsibility and opportunity for Wagner.

The family's decision to choose Wagner as coach was an important and somewhat risky one. She was not a well-known coach with a proven track record. Most other ambitious skaters' families were willing to move across the country or divide up their families to be near the best, most famous coaches. But the Hughes family was committed to keeping Sarah at home and living the most normal life possible. Wagner lived nearby and could make that happen, while Sarah could still train competitively. It was an important connection that would be pivotal to the rest of Hughes's skating career.

Competitive History

High-level competitive ice skating is a complicated business. The performances that the public sees require an incredible amount of work. The U.S. Figure Skating Association has eight levels of proficiency: pre-preliminary, preliminary, pre-juvenile, juvenile, intermediate, novice, junior, and senior. The senior level is the most visible. The best seniors compete at the World Championships and the Olympics. Competitions include two events: the short (or technical) program and the long (or freeskate) program. The short program requires a number of specific elements. The long program doesn't have required elements; instead, skaters are expected to show their technical and artistic skills. The judges base their scores for each portion on technical and artistic merit. For the overall score, the short program counts for less than the long program.

Hughes has been determined to master the skating proficiency levels since she was very young. Her family has a video of an eight-year old Sarah confidently telling the camera, "I want to be in the Olympics and get a gold medal. I can't wait for that to happen." Hughes started her climb to the gold medal podium with Novice competitions when she was about ten. She came in third in the North Atlantic Region, which allowed her to compete in the Eastern Sectional, where she came in tenth. The following year, in 1997, she won a gold medal at the regional and placed 6th at the sectional, but didn't advance to the Novice Nationals like she hoped. But instead of waiting to place higher at the Novice level, she decided, with her coach and family, to go ahead and move up to the Junior division. She was confident that she had the skills to do it.

Moving Up to the Junior Division

Hughes was training harder than ever to compete in the Junior division, the second-highest level in ladies' figure skating. Then the Hughes family received terrible news — Amy Hughes had breast cancer. They had to work together to help the family manage and to support Amy during her treatment. Older sister Rebecca began flying home from Harvard on the weekends to take care of Emily and Taylor. John worked long hours at his business and managing the children's lives and came to the hospital in the evenings. And Sarah became more determined than ever to do well at skating. She "took ownership of her own skating" at that point, her father said. She had read about Scott Hamilton, an Olympic gold medalist who beat cancer. She knew when she did well in skating it helped her mother feel better, and she was determined to win.

Entering her first Junior competition, Hughes stunned the crowd and her family by winning first place at the North Atlantic Regionals. Then she moved up to the Eastern Sectionals and won first place there, too. She was headed to her first Junior Nationals competition. But her mother could not be there to watch — she was in the hospital to have some of her own stem cells taken for transplant as part of her cancer treatment. John took his cell phone to the arena in Philadelphia and held it up so Amy could listen to the music as Sarah skated. A little while later, he called back. Sarah was in first place after the short program. Amy was thrilled, and the next day, the doctors were amazed to find that they had more stem cells from her blood than usual, so she could go home. She was able to make the trip to Philadelphia the next day in a friend's limousine to see Sarah skate the long program. Amy was in the audience as her daughter performed a beautiful program with a perfect triple Lutz/double toe jump combination, which won her the gold medal in the 1999 Junior National Championship. Amy remembers, "I'm sitting there saying this is the best medicine I ever had." And Sarah Hughes had a new nickname: Dr. Sarah.

Hughes performs her short program during the Winter Olympics, February 2002.

Hughes went on to win the silver medal at the World Junior Championships. She was invited to compete all over the world at events on the Junior Grand Prix circuit—the Hungarian trophy, the Mexico cup, and others. She was only in the eighth grade, and she and Wagner were traveling the world. They took time to see the sights—attending the opera in Vienna, eating sushi in Japan, shopping in Paris, and going to museums in Russia. Hughes was improving dramatically, and she was doing the five triple jumps that the senior women skaters performed. She and Wagner decided that it was time to move up again, this time to the final stage of skating: the senior division.

Moving Up to the Senior Division

In 1999, at 13 years old, Hughes arrived at the Senior Nationals competition in Salt Lake City, Utah. She was in awe of being in the same competition as Michelle Kwan and Irina Slutskaya from Russia, the top female skaters in the world. Michelle Kwan had been the dominant U.S. figure skater for years and had given the most perfect performances in U.S. Nationals history in 1998. She had competed in two Olympics already, once in 1994 as the youngest competitor ever, and again in 1998, when she was favored to win. But the gold medal slipped from her grasp after Tara Lipinski skated a brilliant performance. Hughes was excited just to be at the Senior Nationals competition. "It was so cool. I think every girl who goes to Seniors for the first time probably walks in the dressing room and thinks, 'Oh my god! There's Michelle Kwan!' My problem was that I almost said, 'Oh my god! There's Michelle Kwan!'"

Hughes's short program was excellent, and she was shocked to find herself in second place, right after Kwan, her idol. But her long program didn't go as well. She fell twice, but then landed a triple-toe/triple toe combination that had only been done once before in national competition, by Tara Lipinski. After it was over, Hughes ended up with fourth place—a pewter medal. But the silver medalist was too young to go to Worlds, so Hughes took her place and found herself ranked seventh in the world.

Hughes's skating career continued to take an amazingly perfect upward spiral. She had virtually no set-backs. At the next U.S. championship, she took third. In three years at Worlds, she moved from seventh to fifth to third. At Skate America, she took fourth and then second twice. A big breakthrough came at Skate Canada in 2001. She took the gold medal, beating both Michelle Kwan and Irina Slutskaya. She was now a serious medal contender for the 2002 Olympics. The U.S. Nationals were held in January 2002, and all skaters had their eyes on the three spots open for women on the U.S. Olympic team. But then the skater Sasha Cohen made a spectacular come-back after being missing for months because of injury. Cohen took the silver and Kwan the gold, leaving Hughes with her second bronze medal at the U.S. Nationals. It may not have been what she wanted, but it was enough to get her to the Olympics.

The 2002 Olympics

The 2002 Winter Olympics were held in Salt Lake City, Utah. For Hughes, the month between the Nationals and the Olympics was frantic with preparation. Robin Wagner decided that this was Sarah's big chance. It was no time to be conservative, coming in as a young third-place finisher at Nationals. Hughes and Wagner continued to rework her faulty triple Lutz jump. Figure skate blades aren't flat — they have two edges like an upside-down u, and the Lutz must start from the back outside edge. Takeoff had been a continual problem for Hughes, and she and Wagner worked hard to correct it. They added another triple/triple jump combination, a risky move that would put Hughes ahead of the other skaters in terms of the difficulty of her program. They created a new ending for the long program, one with a more thrilling musical climax and choreography. "It made all the difference," Hughes later said about enhancing the difficulty and drama of the performance. "It was the most instrumental thing we did, and one of the greatest moves I've ever made. And one of the most risky moves. I knew it would be really great or really terrible."

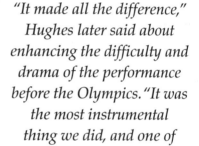

"It made all the difference," Hughes later said about enhancing the difficulty and drama of the performance. "It was the most instrumental thing we did, and one of the greatest moves I've ever made. And one of the most risky moves. I knew it would be really great or really terrible."

In addition, Hughes and Wagner worked on her look. They ordered two additional costumes from a new designer, Jef Billings, as well as new practice costumes (the judges attend practices and take notes). Hughes had her hair cut by a new stylist in Manhattan, one known for celebrity clients. Soon the media began to pay close attention to Hughes and the other figure skaters. She was featured on the cover of *Time* magazine, while Kwan was on *Newsweek* and Slutskaya on *Sports Illustrated*.

Hughes performs her long program during the Winter Olympics, February 2002.

Hughes arrived in Salt Lake City to attend the opening ceremonies, where she posed with President George W. Bush for pictures. She spent two nights in the Olympic Village to get to know some of the other athletes and have some fun, then flew to Colorado Springs to spend a week training in the high altitude before her event began. During that week, controversy erupted as the judging scandal broke during the pairs event. The Canadian pairs team Jamie Sale and David Pelletier skated a clearly superior performance, yet they were awarded a silver medal. Many felt that they deserved the gold. Then the French judge admitted to being part of an agreement to "trade" votes for key performances. The world's eyes were turned on the women skaters as they began one of the final, and most watched, events of the Olympics.

Skating the Short Program

A week of strong practices brought Hughes to the short program with a confident attitude. She went fifth, early in the evening, which is not a good position because the judges leave room in the scores for later skaters to do better. She began well, skating to *Ave Maria* with her new costume, when her first error caught her. The triple Lutz she had worked so hard on came off with the same old problem—she took off on the wrong edge of the skate. Then she came too close to the boards on the edge of the rink and had to pull her leg in to avoid colliding, which would give a major deduction. But the rest of her jumps went well, and there were no more mistakes. All in all, it was a good performance. But Sasha Cohen shone her way to third, Irina Slutskaya jumped to second, and Michelle Kwan sailed to first place with her lovely artistry. Hughes was in fourth. It meant she could still earn a medal, but that she could also come away with nothing.

> *According to coach Robin Wagner, "Sarah's better as a chaser, not as the one being chased. It fires up something inside of her."*

Fortunately, Hughes loves competition and a challenge. Robin Wagner said, "Sarah's better as a chaser, not as the one being chased. It fires up something inside of her." As Wagner's husband, Jerry, looked at the scores and calculated the complex scoring system, he announced that Sarah could actually still win the gold—as long as in the long program she performed absolutely brilliantly, Sasha Cohen didn't do well, and Irina Slutskaya topped Kwan's score. Sarah said, "Okay. I'll do it!"

Skating the Long Program

The day of the long program finally came, after Hughes spent the night answering hundreds of good-luck emails and sleeping in her lucky Peggy Fleming T-shirt. She practiced, took a nap, and arrived early at the arena. Of the four top skaters, she was first again. This time, she had nothing to lose.

The music started and Hughes nailed her first two jumps — the double Axel and the triple Salchow/triple loop, her most difficult jumps. The crowd responded with roaring cheers. She was the first American to skate at the most popular event at an Olympics on home soil. In that highly patriotic year, shortly after the terrorist attacks of 9/11, the crowd was on her side. Hughes felt her confidence grow. She came to the troublesome triple Lutz and nailed it perfectly. Then she flew through another triple, and the crowd began to go wild. There was magic in the air as a superb performance began to unfold. The next triple/triple combination came, and Hughes nailed that one perfectly, too. She was the first woman to land two triple/triple combinations in competition. The audience was on its feet as she sailed through the last section of the program, to the new triumphant ending she and Wagner had worked on. She finished in a spectacular spin and then clapped and laughed in amazement as the fans cheered. She looked to her coach in astonishment — it was the most perfect performance she had ever given, at the most perfect time. Afterwards, skating enthusiasts called it a beautiful blend of athleticism and artistry, skated with a sense of freedom and joy. The performance, they said, showcased her love of skating.

Her scores were good, but with enough room to allow one of the other skaters to deliver a perfect program, too. Hughes and Wagner went to an empty locker room to celebrate and wait for the other 22 skaters to perform. A camera crew followed them in. They weren't watching the ice or even thinking about the medals at that point — they were just enjoying the moment. As the other skaters came and went, though, their attention began to turn to the ice. Sasha Cohen fell in her program — she couldn't top Hughes's score. Then the skater everyone was waiting for — Michelle Kwan. Everyone knew that Kwan was determined to win the gold medal she had missed in 1998, when she lost to Lipinski. But as she skated her program, Kwan began to make small errors. She doubled a triple jump and landed on two feet. She touched the ice as she fell out of a triple flip. The confidence drained out of her, despite the warm crowd, and she came off the ice terribly disappointed. Then Irina Slutskaya took over. She also doubled a jump and almost fell. Her performance was good, but it wasn't great. The judges tallied: Slutskaya beat Kwan, but Hughes had been brilliant. It was the one-in-a-million scenario that Jerry Wagner had described. It was the biggest upset in figure skating history. Sarah Hughes had come from fourth place to win the gold medal.

The cameraman in the locker room listened to his headset and was the first to give the news to Hughes and Wagner — Hughes had won the gold.

The three medal winners in figure skating at the 2002 Winter Olympics: Hughes, gold (center); Slutskaya, silver (left); and Kwan, bronze (right).

They fell on the floor laughing and crying in shock and amazement. Out in the hallway, John, Amy, and Matt Hughes were gasping in astonishment, just like everyone watching the event. Even Scott Hamilton, the sports commentator, was shouting on TV, "What an upset!" The rest of the evening, and night, went by in a rush. Hughes was interviewed, awarded her medal, and rushed to a victory party. She ended up at dinner with her jubilant family, who all wanted to see her medal immediately, at 1:30 in the morning. "I never let them stay up this late!" her mother said. Sarah said, "You know, I didn't even think it was possible. I knew mathematically it was possible, but I didn't think that could happen. I never dreamed that I'd skate so well. Although I've been training very hard for this, and I had a really good feeling about tonight. My coach and I just decided that I'd go out and have fun. I wasn't skating for a gold medal. I wasn't really skating for anything in particular. I was just skating because — just to have fun and enjoy the experience. And it was great."

After the Olympics

The days and weeks after the Olympics were a whirlwind. Within hours, offers were pouring in. There were so many invitations that Hughes couldn't begin to accept them all, so her father and Wagner helped her choose. She was on several of the morning news shows and Jay Leno's "Tonight Show." She hosted "Saturday Night Live," met *N Sync privately, appeared at the Grammy Awards, opened the New York Stock Exchange, and went to the White House to meet the president. She appeared on the Wheaties box, had a sandwich at her favorite deli named after her, and went home to a parade with 60,000 people cheering for her. Her first day back to school weeks later came with 60 reporters in attendance. She was so tired out that she was unable to train for the World Championships and had to miss the event. She began touring with Stars on Ice, but found that their constant circuit of cities was leaving her exhausted.

The future for Sarah Hughes looks great. Experts said that she could expect to bring in one to four million dollars in the next year and up to $10 million in the future. Another Olympic appearance in 2006 is still a possibility. And of course, with her family's emphasis on education, Hughes plans to attend college.

> "You know, I didn't even think it was possible [to win the gold medal]. I knew mathematically it was possible, but I didn't think that could happen. I never dreamed that I'd skate so well. Although I've been training very hard for this, and I had a really good feeling about tonight. My coach and I just decided that I'd go out and have fun. I wasn't skating for a gold medal. I wasn't really skating for anything in particular. I was just skating because—just to have fun and enjoy the experience. And it was great."

HOME AND FAMILY

Hughes's self-confidence and determination undoubtedly grew out of her family's strong love, support, and work ethic. She has been very fortunate to be able to live with her family and still train as an elite skater. Other top skaters like Michelle Kwan and Tara Lipinski had to move across the country and be separated from some of their family members for years in order to work with the best coaches. Her father was opposed to Sarah moving away from home to train. "I wouldn't want her going away and just hanging around a rink when she wasn't skating. She'll do fine with her skating. It's after her skating that I'm worried about."

Hughes poses for photographers with her parents, after winning the gold medal.

Hughes has received a tremendous amount of support from her whole family, but especially from her father. John Hughes uses his skills as an attorney to negotiate Sarah's contracts for tours and endorsements (Robin Wagner helps him; Sarah does not have an agent). But his first priority is being her father. He makes sure that her skating is balanced with her education and the family. His wife Amy, referring to his care for the family during her encounter with cancer, said, "He is the anchor of this ship."

Her mother's battle with cancer has had a big impact on Hughes. After the Olympics, she felt that she was in a position to speak up and to make a difference. "One of the biggest things that's happened over this year is that now I have a platform to be an advocate for causes that I'm passionate about, especially breast cancer awareness," Hughes said. "My mom, Amy, was diagnosed with breast cancer when I was 12. She was courageous and strong, and she kept going—through the first surgery, through the bone marrow transplant, through chemotherapy and radiation. She's always had a positive outlook. (Today she's been cancer-free for four years.) Seeing how well her doctors took care of her made me want to be a doctor."

HONORS AND AWARDS

U.S. Championship, Junior: 1998, Gold Medal
Mexico Cup: 1998, Silver Medal
Hungarian Trophy: 1998, Silver Medal
World Junior Championships: 1999, Silver Medal
U.S. Championships: 1999, fourth place; 2000, Bronze Medal; 2001, Silver
    Medal; 2002, Bronze Medal
International Skating Union Junior Grand Prix: 1999, Silver Medal
Vienna Cup: 1999, Gold Medal
Skate America: 1999, fourth place; 2000, Silver Medal; 2001, Silver Medal
Trophee Lalique: 1999, Bronze Medal; 2001, Silver Medal
Nation's Cup: 2000, Silver Medal
Cup of Russia: 2000, Bronze Medal
Grand Prix Final: 2001, Bronze Medal; 2002, Bronze Medal
World Championships: 2001, Bronze Medal
Skate Canada: 2001, Gold Medal
Olympic Winter Games: 2002, Gold Medal

FURTHER READING

Books

Ashby, R.S. *Going for the Gold*, 2002 (juvenile)
Krulik, Nancy. *Sarah Hughes: Golden Girl*, 2002 (juvenile)
Sivorinovsky, Alina. *Sarah Hughes: Skating to the Stars*, 2001 (juvenile)

Periodicals

Chicago Tribune, Jan. 4, 2002; January 6, 2002, p.C1; May 3, 2002, p.N1
Newsday Feb. 11, 2002, p B7
Newsweek, Dec. 31, 2001, p.87
People, Mar. 26, 2001, p.105; Mar. 11, 2002, p.58; Sep. 2, 2002, p.24
Sports Illustrated, Feb. 21, 2002, p.12; Mar. 4, 2002, p.48
Sports Illustrated for Kids, Sep. 2001, p.90
Sports Illustrated Women, Mar. 2001, p.96
Teen People, Nov. 2002, p.126
Time, Feb. 11, 2002, p.44

Online Articles

http://www.newsday.com/sports/olympics/ny-questforgold.htmlstory
    (*Newsday,* "The Making of a Champion," multiple articles, local paper
    tribute to its local star)

ADDRESS

Sarah Hughes
USFSA
20 First Street
Colorado Springs, CO 80906

WORLD WIDE WEB SITES

http://www.usfsa.org
http://www.usolympicteam.com

Enrique Iglesias 1975-

Spanish-Born American Singer
Creator of the Hit Albums *Enrique* and *Escape*

BIRTH

Enrique Iglesias Preysler was born on May 8, 1975, in Madrid, Spain. His father, Julio Iglesias, is a well-known international singer who has sold 250 million records during his career. His mother, Isabel Preysler, is a journalist and actress who was born in the Philippines. Spanish family names are often made up of both the father's and the mother's family names, but may be shortened to just one name, usually the first of the two. That's why Enrique uses just Iglesias for his last name. He has an older sister, Chabeli, who is a talk show host on Spanish television, and an older brother, Julio Jose, who is a model, actor, and singer. He also has several younger half-siblings from his parents' later relationships.

YOUTH

Growing up as the son of a famous singer and ladies' man was not always easy for Enrique. His father was often away from home at recording sessions or on concert tours. In fact, Julio Iglesias has readily admitted that he put his career ahead of his family. "My profession is the most important thing in my life," he stated. "If I said that my family and my children were more important, then I would be lying." Enrique's parents divorced in 1979, when he was four years old. His father moved from Spain to the United States at this time, and his mother remarried a short time later. For the next few years, Enrique and his siblings divided their time between their mother's home in Madrid and their father's home in Miami, Florida.

In 1981 Enrique's grandfather was kidnapped by political terrorists. They demanded that Julio Iglesias pay a huge ransom for his father's safe release. Fortunately, Spanish authorities were able to find the kidnappers and rescue the hostage before the ransom was paid. But the incident sent shock waves through Enrique's family. They felt vulnerable and started paying greater attention to security. By 1984 Enrique's parents felt that they could no longer ensure the safety of the children in Madrid. Enrique and his siblings were sent to Miami to live with their father. "It broke my heart to send them away," his mother stated. "But we had to for security reasons."

"I remember coming to the U.S. in a huge plane, and when it landed in Miami, there were FBI agents everywhere, and we were getting picked up by helicopter, and I was like, 'Whoa, cool.'"

At first, nine-year-old Enrique found the whole experience very exciting: "I remember coming to the U.S. in a huge plane, and when it landed in Miami, there were FBI agents everywhere, and we were getting picked up by helicopter, and I was like, 'Whoa, cool.'" He soon settled into his father's Miami mansion, which featured a pool and tennis courts. But he rarely saw his father, and he was raised mostly by a nanny, Elvira Olivares. "In a way, she was the closest to being a mother," Enrique noted. Before long, the young boy grew lonely. "I missed all my friends from Spain, and

Enrique Iglesias with his parents, Julio Iglesias and Isabel Preysler, on the eve of his first communion.

my mother, and it was pretty hard. I used to cry every single day," he recalled. "I didn't know anyone in America. It was like starting over."

In order to overcome his feelings of loneliness, Iglesias spent a lot of time at the beach and learned to love water sports, especially windsurfing. He also poured out his emotions on paper in the form of song lyrics. "I realized writing songs was the way for me to truly express myself, to let my emotions come out," he noted. "Those songs were like a diary to me. People keep their most personal thoughts in a diary, and mine were coming out as songs." Unbeknownst to his family, Iglesias had secretly dreamed of becoming a singer for many years. "I used to pray I'd grow up to be a singer," he recalled. "I'd sing along to the radio and TV, but it was stupid stuff like that that helped me to learn how to feel music. But I kept my dreams a secret and never told anybody. I strived to be independent. I matured in that way, I guess, because my dad was always working and never around, and the rest of my family was in Spain."

Iglesias loved listening to music as a teenager, though he never listened to his father's records—which contained mostly slow, romantic songs sung in Spanish. Instead, he preferred popular music by performers like Dire Straits, Billy Joel, the Police, U2, Bruce Springsteen, Marvin Gaye, and Otis Redding. "I'm one of those that can listen to so many different styles of music," he explained. "Even if I don't like it as much, there's always something I can learn." When he was 16, Iglesias began singing with a make-shift band that practiced in a friend's garage. "The songs were real cheesy. I used to cry about how bad they sounded. That was the hardest part, getting used to my voice, getting used to feeling good about what I was singing and writing. It took a long time," he recalled. "It's not like I was looking for a record deal then. I did it because I loved it. I never told anyone. For me it was a getaway to sing, one of those things I didn't want anyone to screw up."

EDUCATION

Iglesias attended an English school in Spain, so he was able to speak English when he arrived in the United States. He acted up a bit in elementary school as he struggled to make the transition to living with his father in Miami. In fact, he was once suspended for putting a lizard on his teacher's back. But his behavior improved by the time he reached junior high.

Iglesias went to a private high school in Miami called Gulliver Preparatory School. He recalled that he was short and skinny and did not hang out with the popular crowd. Amazingly, the young man who would later be named "sexiest man in the world" by the Spanish-language edition of *People* magazine often got turned down for dates and went to the senior prom alone. "It was very hard for me to get a date when I was in high school," he noted. "I was very shy with girls and scared of being rejected. I'm still shy, I think—though it's a lot easier to get a date now."

After graduating from high school in 1993, Iglesias enrolled at the University of Miami as a business major. But he had trouble concentrating on his studies because he had his heart set on becoming a singer. "I used to be in math class and it was all I used to think about," he remembered. "When I was at the university, that's all I heard in my mind." Iglesias dropped out of college during his sophomore year in order to pursue a career in music.

> *It's hard to believe that the young man who has been called the "sexiest man in the world" often got turned down for dates and went to the senior prom alone.*
> *"It was very hard for me to get a date when I was in high school. I was very shy with girls and scared of being rejected. I'm still shy, I think—though it's a lot easier to get a date now."*

CAREER HIGHLIGHTS

Getting Started as a Singer

Throughout Iglesias's teen years, no one but his musician friends and his nanny knew that he longed to be a singer. He continued practicing in secret until he finally decided he was ready to sing in public. In 1994, shortly after he dropped out of college, Iglesias made a mysterious phone call to Fernan Martinez, his father's agent and a family friend. Without saying what he wanted, he asked Martinez to meet him. "My first reaction was: He's in trouble!" Martinez remembered. "I thought it was something with a girl, he was so mysterious and secretive. I had no clue." Iglesias took the confused agent to his friend's garage and sang several songs for him — some in English and some in Spanish. He then asked Martinez to give him an honest assessment of his skills as a singer.

———— " ————

"It's pathetic. Even after I won the Grammy, I heard this girl say, 'Oh, you won a Grammy because your dad is Julio Iglesias.' And you know the funny thing is that last year my dad was nominated for a Grammy and he didn't win. I don't like to get into it but I'm tired of hearing, 'Do you think you sell more records because of your dad?' Well, right now in the U.S. I sell more records than my father. So it would seem a little contradictory that people are buying the records only for who my dad is."

———— " ————

Martinez recognized that Iglesias had talent and recommended that he make a demo tape of his singing. In order to avoid telling his family about his secret passion, Iglesias borrowed money from his nanny to make the recording. He gave the tape to Martinez, who planned to play it for record company executives. But Iglesias imposed an important condition: Martinez was not allowed to tell anyone that they were listening to the son of the famous Julio Iglesias. Instead, the agent was supposed to say that the artist on the tape was an unknown singer from Columbia named Enrique Martinez. "I wanted them to buy my music, not my name," Iglesias explained. "I figured if I take the easy way, I might get there faster, but I won't last as long. People won't care if you're the son of the king of the world. If you're not good, people are not going to be listening."

After being rejected by several major record labels, Iglesias finally signed a $1 million contract with Fonovisa Records to produce three Spanish-language albums. It was only when he signed the contract that Fonovisa executives discovered his true identity. Iglesias continued to keep the secret from his family. In fact, Julio Iglesias learned about his son's record deal from a friend at a party. "He was a little shocked," Enrique remembered. "But all he told me was to do it right or not even try it at all. Besides that, so far I haven't asked him for advice, not a single time."

Iglesias released his first album, *Enrique Iglesias,* in 1995. Fonovisa support-ed the album with the largest promotional push ever given to a Latin singer. In fact, Iglesias did 400 interviews in a matter of months to support the launch of his debut album. *Enrique Iglesias* became a hit, selling a mil-lion copies within three months and going on to sell nearly six million copies worldwide. The album featured the hit single "Si Tu Te Vas" ("If You Go"), which reached number one on *Billboard* magazine's Latin music charts. Four songs from the album — some of which Iglesias had written in high school — eventually hit number one.

Iglesias was beginning to establish himself as a successful performer in his own right. He even won a Grammy Award in 1996 for Best Latin Pop Per-formance, for *Enrique Iglesias.* Yet he was often compared to his famous fa-ther, and some people even suggested that his name was the reason for his success. "It's pathetic," Enrique stated. "Even after I won the Grammy, I heard this girl say, 'Oh, you won a Grammy because your dad is Julio Iglesias.' And you know the funny thing is that last year my dad was nominated for a Grammy and he didn't win. I don't like to get into it but I'm tired of hearing, 'Do you think you sell more records because of your dad?' Well, right now in the U.S. I sell more records than my father. So it would seem a little contradictory that people are buying the records only for who my dad is."

Reinventing Spanish Music

With the release of his first album, Iglesias became part of a new generation of recording artists. When he came on the scene, most recording artists who were singing in Spanish were older and performed mostly traditional songs. He and other singers that emerged around the same time, like Ricky Martin, adopted a modern pop sound that was faster and more sophisticated, to appeal to a younger audience.

In 1997 Iglesias followed up the success of his first album with the release of *Vivir* ("Living"), which sold five million copies worldwide. The young singer supported the album with a world concert tour that stopped in 13 countries. In 1998 Iglesias released his third album, *Cosas del Amor* ("Things of Love"). He wrote six of the songs on this album.

In 1999 Iglesias signed a $44 million recording contract with Interscope Records/Universal Music Group, making him one of the highest-paid Latino artists of all time. Under the terms of the contract, Iglesias would produce six albums—three in English and three in Spanish. He released his first English-language single, "Bailamos" ("We Dance"), a short time later. This song was featured on the soundtrack of the movie *Wild Wild West*, which starred Will Smith. The upbeat "Bailamos" became a monster hit, reaching number one on the pop charts in 16 countries. The single brought Iglesias even greater fame among American listeners and marked his emergence as a mainstream pop star.

Reaching New Fans by Singing in English

Iglesias made a smooth transition to singing in English. "After all, I've grown up in the U.S.," he explained. "I used to write [songs] in English. My first demo was in English." He also felt that singing in English would help distinguish him from his father, who sang primarily in Spanish. Iglesias released his first English-language album, *Enrique*, in 1999. It sold seven million copies around the world and produced two number one singles. Although *Enrique* was a mainstream pop album, Iglesias claimed that

it was not too different from his earlier albums. "That's what I used to do in Spanish," he noted. "They called it Latino music, because I sang in Spanish and I'm Latino, but the albums themselves were mainstream."

Enrique features a cover of "Sad Eyes," a little-known Bruce Springsteen ballad. "I thought, 'What are critics going to think about me, a Latino, doing a Bruce Springsteen cover? You can't get any more American than that!'" Iglesias said. "But at the same time, I love Bruce Springsteen, and I fell in love with the song. It's such a simple song—simple and direct, but beautiful." The album also includes "Could I Have This Kiss Forever?" which Iglesias sang as a duet with Whitney Houston. Iglesias received mostly positive reviews for his English-language debut. For example, Arion Berger of *Entertainment Weekly* praised Iglesias for "an alluring voice, rich and controlled, with appealing scratched-up edges and a masterful sense of musical balance."

Iglesias experienced the ups and downs of pop stardom in the United States. On the plus side, he was invited to perform live during the Super Bowl halftime show in 2000. But he ran into controversy later that year, when outspoken radio personality Howard Stern accused him of lip-synching in his live shows. Stern even played a tape on the air that he claimed was Iglesias singing off-key. Iglesias responded by flying to New York and singing live on Stern's radio show in order to prove himself. Though he never pretended to have the best voice in the world, he wanted to make sure his fans felt that they got their money's worth. "I've always said, 'There are millions of people who can sing.' My backup singers sing better than me," he stated. "But how come they don't have solo deals? Can they really do an album and not bore you? That's really what it comes down to. It's about telling a story and having people believe it."

> "*Touring is my favorite thing to do. I love the adrenaline I feel when I'm on stage and the energy I get from my fans. I love my audience. I feel so protected when I'm around them. You can't really explain what you feel. That's what pushes you. That's when you say, 'All the work, all the traveling, all the interviews, all the sleepless nights, all the hotels, all that — it's all worth it as long as you feel that.*"

In 2001 Iglesias released *Escape,* his second English-language album. It sold eight million copies worldwide and produced three hit singles. One of the best-known songs from the album is "Hero," a ballad that provided comfort to many Americans in the wake of the September 11 terrorist attacks. In 2002 Iglesias released *Quizas* ("Maybe"), his first Spanish-language album in five years. "The power of music in Spanish is so strong that I couldn't stay away from it any longer," he explained. "It has been great to record an entire record in Spanish again. My fans have been by my side throughout my journey, and I hope they will enjoy taking this step with me." Iglesias wrote all but one song on the album.

Connecting with Fans

In just a few years as a recording artist, Enrique Iglesias has sold 25 million albums worldwide. He has become tremendously popular, especially among young women. In fact, his face has graced the covers of over 250 maga-

Iglesias performing live in Times Square in New York City, September 2002.

zines. He claims that he enjoys all the attention he receives from fans. "Touring is my favorite thing to do. I love the adrenaline I feel when I'm on stage and the energy I get from my fans," he stated. "I love my audience. I feel so protected when I'm around them. You can't really explain what you feel. That's what pushes you. That's when you say, 'All the work, all the

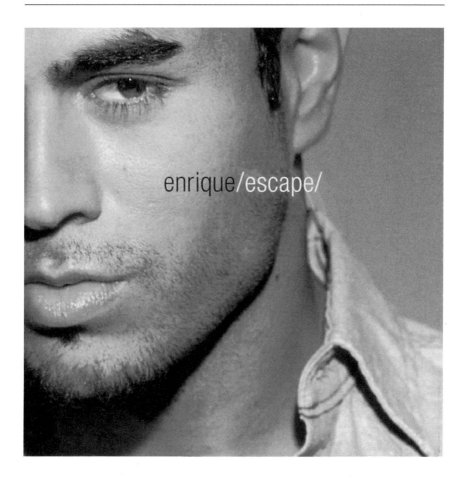

traveling, all the interviews, all the sleepless nights, all the hotels, all that — it's all worth it as long as you feel that."

Iglesias has recorded songs in Spanish, Italian, Portuguese, and English. He continues to write many of the songs he records. "Writing songs is very difficult for me," he admitted. "I am not a professional songwriter. I cannot write about a given subject, nor at any time I wish. It has to be something that has happened to me or which comes to me perhaps in a strange manner, and then I spend many hours revising what I have written, changing it until I arrive at the final result. There are many songs that die in the attempt."

Though Iglesias has earned his own spot in the music world, people continue to ask him about his famous father. He still struggles to understand why people try to make comparisons between the two singers. "If my name were Pepe Grillo, you'd never think of Julio Iglesias after hearing my voice," he noted. "Of course, there are things here and there, because I think my father is the greatest. But my thing is completely different." For his part, Julio Iglesias says that he is proud of his son's accomplishments. "I think it is amazing," he stated. "He is an amazing kid. He has a lot of class, a lot of charm, a lot of talent. Sometimes I look at him and I don't believe this guy is so young and so successful."

Enrique says he is particularly grateful to Julio for teaching him about the music business and preparing him to handle fame. "I am not impressed by money or fame. I've been lucky. I grew up around that," he stated. "I knew that if I failed I would always have something to eat. And in terms of fame and adulation I have grown up around my father. I've seen it up close, and I've learned a lot. Some people think because of that I would be even more egotistical, and it's exactly the opposite. That's my advantage. I assure you that if what had happened to me . . . had happened to a 21-year-old kid who's had nothing, it would have destroyed him psychologically."

Iglesias is thrilled to be living his boyhood dream and connecting with people as a singer. "Maybe 20 percent of the people in the world, or less, have a job they love," he noted. "I have one of the best jobs in the world. I wake up every single day and feel blessed. So I might as well keep on working as hard as possible. I gotta go all the way."

> ———— **"** ————
>
> *"Writing songs is very difficult for me. I am not a professional songwriter. I cannot write about a given subject, nor at any time I wish. It has to be something that has happened to me or which comes to me perhaps in a strange manner, and then I spend many hours revising what I have written, changing it until I arrive at the final result. There are many songs that die in the attempt."*
>
> ———— **"** ————

HOME AND FAMILY

Iglesias, who is single, lives in Miami with his two dogs. For the time being he's happy to date, but he says that he would like to get married and have a family someday. "I've been in love one and a half times, and I've had my heart broken many, many times. But I don't like to talk about that stuff," he said. "When I do settle down, though, I want to be with a girl who has a great smile, a great sense of humor, and a strong, independent streak."

HOBBIES AND OTHER INTERESTS

In his spare time, Iglesias enjoys participating in water sports, such as windsurfing, waterskiing, and scuba diving. He donates a portion of the proceeds from his concert tours to charity, including Ronald McDonald House.

RECORDINGS

Enrique Iglesias, 1995
Vivir ("Living"), 1997
Cosas del Amor ("Things of Love"), 1998
Enrique, 1999
The Best Hits, 2000
Escape, 2001
Quizas ("Maybe"), 2002

HONORS AND AWARDS

Grammy Award (National Academy of Recording Arts and Sciences): 1996, Best Latin Pop Performance, for *Enrique Iglesias*
Latin Music Award (*Billboard* magazine): 1997, 1998, Hot Latin Tracks Artist of the Year
Sexiest Man in the World (*People en Espanol*): 1998

FURTHER READING

Books

Contemporary Musicians, Vol. 27, 2000
Furman, Elina, and Leah Furman. *Enrique Iglesias: An Unauthorized Biography,* 2000
Granados, Christine. *Enrique Iglesias,* 2001 (juvenile)
Marquez, Heron. *Latin Sensations,* 2001 (juvenile)

Periodicals

Billboard, Aug. 31, 2002, p.5
Boston Herald, Mar. 24, 2002, p.57
Cosmopolitan, Jan. 2000, p.140

Current Biography Yearbook, 1999
Los Angeles Times, Nov. 29, 1995, p.F1; Nov. 23, 1997, Calendar sec., p.5; Dec. 2, 1999, p.F6
Miami Herald, Nov. 10, 1996, p.I1; Feb. 12, 1999, p.G29
Newsday, Mar. 15, 1999, p.B6
People, Apr. 22, 1996, p.144
Rolling Stone, Apr. 13, 2000, p.104
Seventeen, Jan. 2000, p.74
USA Today, July 14, 2000, p.E5
Washington Post, Jan. 28, 1999, p.C1

Online Databases

Biography Resource Center, 2002, article from *Contemporary Musicians,* 2000

ADDRESS

Enrique Iglesias
Interscope Records
10900 Wilshire Boulevard
Los Angeles, CA 90024

WORLD WIDE WEB SITES

http://www.enriqueiglesias.com
http://www.mtv.com/bands/az/iglesias_enrique/artist.jhtml

Jeanette Lee 1971-

American Professional Pool Player Known as
"The Black Widow"
The Most Visible and Popular Women's Pool Player
in the World

BIRTH

Jeanette Lee was born on July 9, 1971, in Brooklyn, New York.
She was the younger of two girls born to Bo Chun Lee, who
owned a tobacco shop, and Sonya Lee, who worked as a nurse.
Her parents had been born in Korea and immigrated to the
United States. When Jeanette was five years old, her father left

the family and returned to Korea. She had no further contact with him until she visited Korea as an adult. Her mother eventually remarried, and from that time on Jeanette and her older sister were raised by their stepfather.

YOUTH

The Lee family had very little money and lived in one of Brooklyn's tough neighborhoods. In fact, Jeanette often got beaten up for being one of the few Koreans in the neighborhood.

Lee's family tried to combine the cultural traditions of Korea with those of their new homeland. For example, they emphasized the Korean value of hard work as well as the American vision of opportunity. The Lees dreamed of a future in which Jeanette completed school and then married a Korean doctor.

Her parents were bilingual, meaning that they spoke two languages, English and Korean, but Jeanette spoke only English. Growing up she felt closest to her grandmother, even though her grandmother spoke only Korean. Her stepfather worked long days and Jeanette did not get to spend much time with him. But she respected him because he made her mother happy.

Lee was a shy child, but she had a strong competitive streak. She rebelled against her parents' strict rules as she got older. For example, she began wearing her trademark all-black outfits in her youth because it upset her mother. When she was 11, Jeanette moved out of her family's house and lived with a variety of friends and one of her teachers before eventually returning home.

At the age of 13, Jeanette was diagnosed with scoliosis, a medical condition that causes the spine to curve. It's a spinal deformity that most often appears during adolescence. Her mother first noticed the S-shaped curve in her back when the family was at the beach. That started a very tough time for Jeanette. She went through eight surgeries and had metal rods inserted into her spine to keep it straight. Afterward, she had to wear a back brace and was unable to play sports with her friends and schoolmates. She also had to wear thick glasses to correct her terrible eyesight, which was so poor that she was classified as legally blind.

Lee later said that these things made her feel like a "monster" during her teen years. Her competitive nature made it even more difficult for her to handle these physical limitations. She ended up spending a lot of time playing cards when she was young because it provided an outlet for her competitiveness.

EDUCATION

Lee was an excellent student and was accepted to the prestigious Bronx Science School in New York. For many years, she dreamed of becoming an elementary school teacher. The details of her education are unclear, but it appears that she dropped out of the Bronx Science School before graduating and earned her high school diploma elsewhere. She later attended Queens College, but she dropped out before earning a degree in order to focus on pool.

CHOOSING A CAREER

Lee first played pool at camp at the age of ten. She also accompanied a few boyfriends to pool halls over the years. But it was only after she saw "The Color of Money"—a 1989 movie about a pair of professional pool players (portrayed by Paul Newman and Tom Cruise)—that she became truly intrigued by the game. Lee went to a local pool hall called Chelsea Billiards to check it out first hand. While there she was mesmerized by the play of Johnny Ervolino, an older regular at the club who was poetry in motion on the pool table.

Lee's deep fascination with the game of pool began when she was 18 years old. At this point in her life, she had dropped out of college and was working at a series of odd jobs. For example, she worked as an editorial assistant in a Korean computer company and as a hostess at a rhythm and blues club in Manhattan. "I was an aimless party girl who woke up every morning wishing I could be anybody but who I was," she recalled. "Then I discovered pool. And once I did, I was not to be stopped. Before pool, I had no reason to wake up in the morning, and after pool there is not enough time in the world." Pool was a sport Lee could play despite her bad back, and as she improved her pool-playing skills she developed the self-confidence she had lacked as a child.

Within two months Lee was playing pool for money. She started out hustling tables at pool halls, meaning that she accepted challenges to play against other people with bets riding on the outcome. According to one tale from these early days, Lee once won $90,000 in a 23-hour period by taking wagers from challengers.

For many years, she played pool nearly every night of the week. For the record, Lee claims that she never "sand-bagged," or pretended to be a poor player in order to set up men to be beaten. However, she admits that most men's egos were so big that they did not believe any woman—no matter how good—could beat them. And she gladly took advantage of this foolish notion since she needed the money to survive.

Learning to play pool was hard work for Lee. She practiced every day, sometimes more than 15 hours a day. She once played non-stop for 37 hours, although she was in such pain afterward that her friends had to carry her home. She even slept with her hand taped in the cue bridge position (the way the hand sits on the pool table to prop the cue stick steadily). While Lee gained both the skills and the mental toughness necessary to be a champion, she also began to learn some important lessons about life. "I honestly don't think it matters if your passion is pool or business or building a family or all three," she explained. "What matters is that you find the strength and the courage and the means to achieve your goal."

> "I honestly don't think it matters if your passion is pool or business or building a family or all three. What matters is that you find the strength and the courage and the means to achieve your goal."

Within five years, Lee was the top-ranked female pool player in the world. As she wrote in her book *The Black Widow's Guide to Killer Pool*, "I could have quit a thousand times, after bitter losses, close calls, and hospital visits, but I never did, because in my heart I knew I could make it, even though everyone else thought it was unrealistic." At first, Lee's parents did not support her decision to become a professional pool player. They worried about her staying out late into the night and hanging out at pool halls where most of the patrons were men. But when she started winning tournaments, her mother conceded, "You know, as much as we think you're fooling around the pool room, you can't win all these tournaments unless you've really been working."

CAREER HIGHLIGHTS

"The Black Widow" Emerges

Lee turned professional in 1993. Women's pool (or billiards) tournaments are organized by the Women's Professional Billiard Association (WPBA). This organization sponsors a number of tournaments around the world each year. Participants earn points based on their finish at each professional tournament, and they are ranked each month based on their total points

Lee in action during a tournament in Minneapolis, February 1996.

over the preceding 12-month period. Many professional pool players also take part in other tournaments sponsored by pool halls, casinos, and resorts. Although these tournaments do not count toward the WPBA rankings, they do offer prize money.

Shortly after turning pro, Lee earned the nickname "The Black Widow." The nickname was partly based on her jet black hair, all-black attire at tournaments, and sleek look. But the name was also appropriate from a competitive standpoint, because she often devoured her opponents the way a black widow spider eats its mate. The nickname originally came from Gabe Vigorito, the owner of the Howard Beach Billiard Club. He once said that "Jeanette walked in as a beautiful, young thing but when she started shooting, she killed her opponent. She went from a butterfly to a black widow." The nickname remained a private joke until Lee let it slip to a reporter who then used it in the *New York Times*. Lee's mother tried to change her nickname to "The Lily of the Valley," but "The Black Widow" fit Lee's mystique, and the name stuck.

Unfortunately for Lee, her nickname only added to the negative perceptions of her held by other players. They initially viewed Lee as aggressive and cocky, and they did not particularly like her. She earned some of the criticism by stomping around after missing shots, and glaring at both the table and her opponents. She also once stated early in her career that she wanted to be the best and intended to crush anyone who got in her way. But some fellow players resented her simply because she was young, attractive, fashionable, ambitious, and highly competitive.

Rising to the Top

Lee made a splash almost immediately upon joining the WPBA tour, when she took second place at the 1993 World Championships in Konigswinter, Germany. She also learned a great deal in this important tournament. Lee was on fire early in the competition, sinking difficult shot after difficult shot. Her confidence irritated players who were more experienced than her. Although Lee had worked hard and practiced thousands of hours, she was still considered a rookie who had not yet paid her dues.

As Lee advanced through the tournament, other players started booing her. In the first set of the finals—in which the winner had to take two out of three sets—Lee got flustered and was blown out by her opponent, Loree Jon Jones. Lee then realized that she was playing right into the hands of her tormentors, and she regrouped to dominate the second set. As the crowd geared up to watch the deciding third set, however, she panicked. As she

> "You have to figure out what happened," she reflected about a tough tournament loss. "Don't ignore the wound and hope it closes by itself. If you do, you'll be left with a terrible scar. Use pain as your motivation— not just to get angry, but to do something about it. I won the next tournament, and the one after that, and by the end of the next year I was the number-one-ranked professional in the world. And it wouldn't have happened without that loss in Germany."

thought about how significant it was that she was playing for the world championship as a 23-year-old rookie, a flood of nervousness washed over her. Lee was unable to shake these feelings, and Jones easily won the decisive third set to claim the championship.

But Lee was wise enough to learn from that event and apply what she learned to her future play. "You have to figure out what happened," she explained. "Don't ignore the wound and hope it closes by itself. If you do, you'll be left with a terrible scar. Use pain as your motivation—not just to get angry, but to do something about it. I won the next tournament, and the one after that, and by the end of the next year I was the number-one-ranked professional in the world. And it wouldn't have happened without that loss in Germany."

In 1993 Lee moved to Reno, Nevada, where there were more competitive pool opportunities. In 1994 she won five of the 12 WPBA tournaments and rose into the top 10 in the WPBA rankings. She also won the U.S. Open Championships and took second place for the second consecutive year in the WPBA World Championships. These accomplishments earned her the WPBA's Player of the Year award.

> "I have learned how to compete, how to lose gracefully and win frequently. I have come to understand the psychology of success, the importance of mental toughness. I have learned the difference between competing against men and against women. I know how to stay focused under pressure, and how to achieve goals in the face of seemingly impossible odds."

In 1995, less than two years after turning pro, Lee became the top-ranked female pool player in the world. In 1998, following multiple tournament wins, she was named the WPBA Sportsperson of the Year. In 1999 Lee played as the in-house professional at the Amsterdam Billiard Club for the National Straight Pool Championship. (In straight pool, players shoot for all 15 balls, each of which is worth a point.) She was one of only two women competing in the tournament against 80 men. In one round of the tournament she played Johnny Ervolino—the old man who inspired her ten years earlier with his fluid play—and she beat him.

Taking a Break

Although Lee had a successful year in 1999, she struggled against severe back pain throughout the season. She decided to take the first half of 2000 off in order to undergo more back surgery. Over the course of her career, Lee has had surgery on her neck, shoulder, and back, for herniated discs, tendinitis, and a tumor. She also had the metal rod that had been inserted in her back when she was a teenager replaced. Because of these rods she

Lee lines up a shot during a guest appearance at an exhibition in Boston, February 2001.

cannot lean forward at more than an 80 degree angle, which is barely far enough to break on a billiard table. This limitation makes her status as one of the world's top pool players even more remarkable.

During her time off from pool, Lee co-authored a book called *The Black Widow's Guide to Killer Pool.* She had the following advice for women who want to become professional pool players: "You have to understand the level of commitment that goes towards being a top pro. You have to know that it's going to be tough out there, and unless you love it more than anything, you're not going to make it. You have to have a tough mind, and you have to be willing to take hard losses, so when you overcome them, the win is so great. Stay focused and no matter what gets you down, just believe in your heart whatever your dreams are. Set real goals and be willing to back it up with hard work."

Back to the Game

The layoff from the tournament circuit caused Lee to drop to number five in the world rankings. She returned in the second half of 2000 determined to reclaim her number one spot, but she failed to win any tournaments that year. In 2001, however, Lee came back to win a gold medal at the World Games in Akita, Japan. This marked the first time that pool was included in the World Games, which is the first step for the sport to gain official recognition for the Olympic Games. Lee also placed in the top 10 in five of the six tournaments she entered that year.

> "I've grown up a lot. I know more about how to deal with the other players and the press, and how to handle myself at tournaments. But some things haven't changed — the World Nine-Ball Championship isn't a Miss Congeniality contest sponsored by Martha Stewart. And I'm not out there looking to make friends. I'm still looking to kick butt and take names."

Lee was honored when ESPN voted her the third-sexiest female athlete in the world behind track star Marion Jones and tennis player Anna Kournikova. "I think women should be very proud to be women and celebrate their femininity, and that's something that I do," she stated. "I'm very proud to be a woman. I want to be feminine and still be able to be great and hold myself with class and dignity, and that's what I try to do."

Because of her good looks and aggressive style of play, Lee has become a prominent personality in the pool world and beyond. She has appeared on a number of television programs, including "Good Morning America," "Extra," "Hard Copy," and "MTV Sports," as well as in such publications as *People, Glamour,* and *Sports Illustrated.* "I think I've opened up a lot of eyes," she noted. "I've brought a lot of media attention to the sport [of pool], in a very positive way. It was thought of as Men's Pool. I represent Women's Billiards and it is awesome and cool and fun. I do take some credit for that."

Lee is the highest-earning pool player in the world today. Thanks to her exotic beauty, fierce attitude in competition, and diligent effort, she has earned several endorsement deals that bring in 90 percent of her income.

Lee has appeared in advertisements for whiskey and for pool gloves and equipment (through a major long-term deal with Imperial International). She also developed her own line of pool cues and an Interplay video game. In addition, Lee is a model, actress, and motivational speaker. She has appeared in the HBO TV series "Arliss," the movie *The Other Sister*, and a commercial for ESPN's "SportsCenter."

Lee has worked hard to change the arrogant reputation she acquired early in her professional career. She has grown and learned from her experiences over the years. "I have learned how to compete, how to lose gracefully and win frequently," she said. "I have come to understand the psychology of success, the importance of mental toughness. I have learned the difference between competing against men and against women. I know how to stay focused under pressure, and how to achieve goals in the face of seemingly impossible odds."

Billards player Jeanette Lee attends the Women's Sport Foundation Annual Gala in New York City, October 15, 2001.

At the same time, Lee remains a fierce competitor with supreme confidence in her abilities. "I've grown up a lot," she noted. "I know more about how to deal with the other players and the press, and how to handle myself at tournaments. But some things haven't changed — the World Nine-Ball Championship isn't a Miss Congeniality contest sponsored by Martha Stewart. And I'm not out there looking to make friends. I'm still looking to kick butt and take names." Lee's outgoing and flamboyant personality make her a crowd favorite. She lets her emotions show whether she is playing well or not, sharing her passion and her pain with fans.

Lee credits attitude as the determining factor that separates a true champion from a good pool shooter. "It's all about meeting the challenge," she stated. "Because life does not just line up for you to conquer it. If it were that easy, we wouldn't need 80 years to get it right. The essence of competition is pushing your limits, testing yourself against the best. That is

———— " ————

*"People don't know
what scoliosis does to those
who have it. It just
destroys your self-esteem,
going to school in a
cast or a brace looking
like a monster and
having no one to talk
to who can understand
and support you. A huge
part of my [own] healing
process was learning
to feel good about myself
and turn that part of my
life into a positive. . . ."*

———— " ————

the best way to improve, and the only way to become a champion. If you don't have that attitude, you might as well pack your bags. Even if you win the tournament against watered-down competition, you are never going to get anywhere in life ducking challenge after challenge."

As of January 2003, Lee ranked fourth in the WPBA based on the number of points earned in major tournaments over the previous year. And she shows no signs of slowing down. "I love playing pool and I don't see myself stopping anytime soon—at least not until I get back to being number one in the world again," she said. "If I have to, I'll use my cue as a cane to get around the table. Just as long as I can keep playing." Lee wants to leave her mark on history as the best pool player who ever lived. She also hopes to earn enough money to help her parents retire and put her cousins through college.

MARRIAGE AND FAMILY

In 1996 Lee married fellow professional pool player George Breedlove (nicknamed "The Flamethrower" because of his strong breaks), whom she met at a tournament in Los Angeles. Breedlove proposed marriage after just three dates with Lee. They currently live in a large ranch house in Indianapolis, Indiana, with George's two teenage daughters, Morgan and Olivia. They are hoping to have more children in the future, although doctors are concerned that Lee's back is not strong enough for her to carry a child to term. She can have corrective surgery in the future to improve her chances of a successful pregnancy, but she would have to give up her professional career to do so.

Breedlove no longer plays pool professionally and has started a business making custom furniture. The couple has promised each other never to be apart for more than seven days, and Lee calls her husband every day that she's away. She admits that Breedlove's best game is better than hers, but says that she can beat him when he is not focused on playing up to his full potential.

HOBBIES AND OTHER INTERESTS

Lee works out every day with a personal trainer. In addition to trying to maintain flexibility in her back, she also works on breathing and upper arm strength. She also practices pool six to eight hours a day and travels up to 300 days a year.

When she's not practicing pool, Lee likes to play with the kids in her neighborhood or with her dog, Sandy, and cat, Lucky. Her favorite non-pool sports to play are golf and bowling. She also enjoys going to the spa and shopping for make-up and clothes (she especially likes shoes and purses). She has also taken up painting, another activity she can pursue despite her bad back.

Lee is involved in charitable activities that mirror her own personal experiences. She is a national spokesperson and vice president of the board of directors for the Scoliosis Association. She also established the Jeanette Lee Foundation in 1998 to raise money for scoliosis research.

"People don't know what scoliosis does to those who have it," said Lee. "It just destroys your self-esteem, going to school in a cast or a brace looking like a monster and having no one to talk to who can understand and support you. A huge part of my [own] healing process was learning to feel good about myself and turn that part of my life into a positive. When you're young, you don't know why things happen to you. But if anything good comes out of this, it's when you learn that you can overcome it and perhaps be an inspiration to someone out there who is going

"When you're young, you don't know why things happen to you. But if anything good comes out of this, it's when you learn that you can overcome it and perhaps be an inspiration to someone out there who is going through something similar. They're going to know that there is at least one person they can talk to and realize that you're not offering them pity, you're offering them inspiration."

through something similar. They're going to know that there is at least one person they can talk to and realize that you're not offering them pity, you're offering them inspiration."

Lee is also on the board of the Billiard Education Foundation, which encourages young people to get a good education and allows them to earn money for college through playing pool. She also promotes causes on behalf of women athletes on the Diverse Races Committee of the Women's Sports Foundation. She recently met with President George W. Bush at the White House to fight for equal funding for men's and women's college sports. Finally, Lee is an active member of the WPBA board, which is responsible for the rules and regulations of professional billiards.

WRITINGS

The Black Widow's Guide to Killer Pool, 2000 (with Adam Scott Gershenson)

HONORS AND AWARDS

WPBA Player of the Year (*Billiards Digest*): 1994
WPBA Player of the Year (*Billiards Magazine*): 1994
World Billiards Championships: 1994, silver medal; 1995, silver medal
WPBA Sportsperson of the Year Award: 1998
Akita World Games: 1999, gold medal
Billiard Congress of America Open Nine-Ball Champion: 2001

FURTHER READING

Books

Lee, Jeanette. *The Black Widow's Guide to Killer Pool,* 2000 (with Adam Scott Gershenson)

Periodicals

Chicago Daily Herald, Jan. 12, 2002, Sports sec., p.1
Current Biography Yearbook, 2002
Daily Telegraph (London), Mar. 19, 1997, p.69
Indianapolis Star, Feb. 21, 1999, p.J1; June 3, 2000, p.E2
Oregonian, Jan. 17, 2002, p.D1
People, Mar. 13, 1995, p.86
Sports Illustrated, July 8, 1996, p.7
St. Petersburg Times, Feb. 18, 2002, p.D1
USA Today, Mar. 12, 1997, p.C2

ADDRESSES

Jeanette Lee
Jeanette Lee Foundation
1427 West 86th Street
Suite 183
Indianapolis, IN 46260

Jeanette Lee
Scoliosis Association
P.O. Box 811705
Boca Raton, FL 33481
Phone: 800-800-0669

WORLD WIDE WEB SITES

http://www.jeanettelee.tv
http://www.scoliosis-assoc.org
http://www.womenssportsfoundation.org
http://womensportsonline.com

John Lewis 1940-

American Political Leader
U. S. Representative to Congress
Leader of the U.S. Civil Rights Movement

BIRTH

John Lewis was born on February 21, 1940, in Pike County,
Alabama, in his family's rural home. He was the third of ten
children born to Eddie and Willie Mae Lewis, who worked as
farmers to support their family.

YOUTH

Growing Up Under the Shadow of Segregation

Lewis grew up during a period of U.S. history in which black Americans did not have the same rights and opportunities that white Americans enjoyed. The inferior social position of African-Americans was especially apparent in the country's southern states. This region of the country had practiced slavery until 1865, when the North defeated the South to end the American Civil War. Still, racist attitudes towards black people remained strong in many white communities. In fact, all of the southern states built political and social systems that were blatantly unfair to African-American citizens. For example, states like Alabama embraced the system of segregation, which kept white and black people separated from one another in most aspects of everyday life. The state enforced segregation in restaurants, theaters, buses, and other public places. Alabama and other states even established separate public drinking fountains for white and black people. In nearly every instance, the facilities that were designated for white people were much nicer and cleaner than those that were assigned to members

"Even a six-year-old could tell that this sharecropper's life was nothing but a bottomless pit. I watched my father sink deeper and deeper into debt, and it broke my heart. More than that, it made me angry. There was no way to get ahead with this kind of farming. The best you could do was do it well enough to keep doing it."

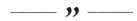

of the black community. Alabama also supported separate schools for white and black children. This was perhaps the most destructive element of segregation, since these schools provided an inferior education that further limited opportunities for African-Americans.

Many African-American people resented the unequal system in which they lived. But the black communities of the American South felt powerless to change things. White men occupied nearly every important political and law enforcement office across the South, and most of them did not want African-Americans to gain greater political, economic, or social power. As a result, white officials used a variety of means to keep black families "in their place." For example, some officials forced African-Americans to pass extremely difficult written tests before they would allow them to register to vote. The poll tax — a tax that a person must pay before being permitted to vote — was another popular tool to repress the black vote, because most black people were so poor that they could not afford the expense. Finally, whites used violence and intimidation to make sure that African-Americans remained in their inferior position in society.

A Happy Childhood

During his first years of childhood, Lewis was not aware of the segregated world that awaited him. Instead, he spent nearly all of his time playing and working on the farm that his family tended. His parents worked as share-croppers, farming land that belonged to a wealthy white landowner. In return for the use of the landowner's property, Lewis's parents had to give the landowner a sizable portion of the profits from the sale of their crops. In addition, they had to pay the landowner for seed, fertilizer, equipment, and other materials used in farming the land. As a result, the Lewis family — like most sharecropping families — always owed the landowner money and never had much money leftover for clothing, food, or other basic needs. "Even a six-year-old could tell that this sharecropper's life was nothing but a bottomless pit," Lewis recalled. "I watched my father sink deeper and deeper into debt, and it broke my heart. More than that, it made me angry. There was no way to get ahead with this kind of farming. The best you could do was do it well enough to *keep* doing it."

> "You had to bend down to pick cotton. Eight to ten hours of stooping like that and your back would be on fire. It would ache all night, and still be aching when you got up the next morning to go out and do it all over again."

Still, Lewis recalls his early years on the family farm with fondness. "It was a small world, a safe world, filled with family and friends," he remembered. In fact, the world of his early childhood was so small that he only saw two white people — the mailman and a traveling salesman — until he was six years old.

As he grew older, Lewis joined his older siblings out in the fields, where they spent long hours picking cotton and other crops. "You had to bend down to pick cotton," he explained. "Eight to ten hours of stooping like that and your back would be on fire. It would ache all night, and still be aching when you got up the next morning to go out and do it all over again."

Lewis also was responsible for caring for the chickens on the family farm. But unlike cotton picking, he greatly enjoyed this chore. "I named them, talked to them, assigned them to coops and guided them in every night and when one of them died, I preached his funeral and buried him," he recalled. "I also protested when one of them was killed for food. I refused to eat. I guess that was my first protest demonstration. . . . The kinship I felt with these other living creatures, the closeness, the compassion, is a feeling I carried with me out into the world from that point on."

A picture of Lewis in the early 1960s.

Growing Awareness of Social Injustice

At age 11, Lewis joined one of his uncles on an extended visit to Buffalo, New York. This adventure made an enormous impression on the young boy. He was stunned to see black and white people shopping, traveling, and eating together, and was amazed to see African-American families living in clean neighborhoods lined with warm and spacious homes. "Home would never feel the same as it did before that trip," he admitted. "The signs of segregation [in the American South] that had perplexed me up till then now outright angered me."

During his teen years, Lewis sensed that black unhappiness with segregation and institutional racism was on the increase in Alabama and other southern states. In 1955, for example, civil rights activist Rosa Parks refused to give up her seat to a white person on a city bus. That action prompted civil rights leader Martin Luther King Jr. and other black citizens to organize a boycott of the bus system in Montgomery, Alabama, to protest the poor treatment they received. Elsewhere, brave black students began challenging southern colleges and universities that had long refused to open their doors to African-Americans. These courageous actions inspired Lewis to think about what he might do to advance the cause of civil rights.

In the meantime, Lewis devoted much of his time to his deep religious faith. "More than anything else — besides work, of course, which became the center of my life as soon as I was big enough to join my parents in the fields — the most important thing in my family's life, and in almost every family's life around us, was church," he recalled. By age 16, he was regularly giving sermons in black churches in surrounding communities, and he was formally ordained as a minister while he was still a teenager.

EDUCATION

When Lewis was growing up in Pike County, Alabama, there were two separate school systems for white and black children. As was the case throughout the South, the school buildings and supplies set aside for the black children were not nearly as good as those that were available to white children. Lewis's elementary school, for instance, was a two-room wooden shack, and the schoolbooks he received were old ones that had been discarded by nearby white schools.

"I loved school, loved everything about it, no matter how good or bad I was at it. My penmanship was poor—it's gotten a little better over the years, but just a little—yet the thrill of learning to write was intense."

Nonetheless, Lewis thrived in school. "I loved school, loved everything about it, no matter how good or bad I was at it," he said. "My penmanship was poor—it's gotten a little better over the years, but just a little—yet the thrill of learning to write was intense." His parents recognized his genuine thirst for knowledge, and they encouraged him to develop his reading, writing, and math skills. But the demands of farming sometimes interfered with his schoolwork. On some days, he and his brothers and sisters had to stay home from school to help harvest crops. This upset Lewis so much that he sometimes tried to sneak away to catch the school bus when no one was looking.

Lewis attended Dunn's Chapel Elementary School through sixth grade. He then completed grades seven through nine at a local junior high school. After completing ninth grade, he had few options for continuing his education since there was not a single high school in the county that was open to African-Americans. He ended up enrolling at Pike County Training School, a school that taught black youth about farming and housekeeping—careers that were seen as unthreatening to the dominant white power structure.

In 1954 the U.S. Supreme Court ruled that segregated schools were unconstitutional. "We rejoiced [at the ruling]," recalled Lewis. "It was like a day of jubilee." But this happiness did not last for long. Alabama and other Southern states defied the law and kept their schools segregated, and the federal government took little action to enforce the Supreme Court ruling and to force the Southern states integrate the schools.

In 1957 Lewis left Alabama to attend the American Baptist Theological Seminary in Nashville, Tennessee. Normally, he would not have been able to afford a college education. But the school charged no tuition. Instead, students paid for their classes by working for the school. Lewis enjoyed his classes, but he spent much of his time studying the growing civil rights movement. In 1958 he approached Martin Luther King Jr. and another civil rights leader named Ralph Abernathy with a plan to integrate Troy State in Alabama. Lewis volunteered to try to enter the school, which refused to admit black students. King and Abernathy vowed to support the young man's brave plan. But his parents recognized that the plan might put their son's life in danger, and they refused to give their consent. Their opposition killed the plan, since Lewis was still a minor.

During the late 1950s, Lewis set aside his college education in order to work in the civil rights movement. In 1961, however, he received a gift from the Southern Christian Leadership Conference (SCLC), a civil rights organization founded by Martin Luther King Jr. and others to apply the principles of nonviolent resistance throughout the South. SCLC gave college scholarships to Lewis and several other young activists. This gift enabled Lewis to attend Fisk University in Nashville, where he later earned a bachelor's degree in philosophy in 1967.

CAREER HIGHLIGHTS

Demonstrations and Sit-Ins

John Lewis began to emerge as one of the most influential leaders of the civil right movement while he was living in Nashville and attending American Baptist Theological Seminary. It was during that time that his interest in civil rights prompted him to attend workshops on nonviolent forms of protests. He learned how to demonstrate for equal rights in a peaceful manner. The workshops taught the activists how to respond — and how *not* to respond — when confronted by hostile opponents. The workshops also taught them how to resist in a nonviolent way, even when faced with violence. "The workshops became almost like [another college course] to students like me," he recalled. "It was the most important thing we were doing. I'd finally found the setting and the subject that spoke to everything that had been stirring in my soul for so long."

Soon Lewis joined the Student Nonviolent Coordinating Committee (SNCC), which was dedicated to ending segregation in the South. SNCC (pronounced "snick") was founded in 1960 to coordinate and organize nonviolent protests, primarily by students. With SNCC, Lewis and other young civil rights activists began participating in lunch counter "sit-ins." In these demonstrations, they would take seats at whites-only lunch counters. White reaction to these peaceful protests was swift and cruel. Lewis and other participants were taunted, insulted, and physically abused by crowds of angry white people. On many occasions, they were arrested by white police officers who charged them with disturbing the peace or trespassing. Time after time, Lewis and other brave young activists were led away to jail in handcuffs as mobs of white onlookers cheered. In fact, Lewis was arrested more than 40 times from 1960 to 1965 for participating in peaceful civil rights demonstrations. These encounters with the law horrified his family. They viewed their son's repeated arrests as a source of deep shame and embarrassment. But their disapproval failed to shake his dedication to the civil rights cause. Lewis felt that he was involved in a "holy crusade," and he saw his arrests as "a badge of honor."

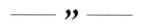

"I will never, ever forget that moment," Lewis said about being physically assaulted as a Freedom Rider. "I was 21. I was a sharecropper's son from a farm near Troy, Alabama. Yet somehow I learned that where there is injustice, you cannot ignore the call of conscience."

Becoming a Freedom Rider

In 1961 Lewis decided to work with the Congress of Racial Equality (CORE), a civil rights group that had been founded in 1942 to fight for equal rights for blacks. Lewis got involved with the group after a 1960 government decision to ban segregation in interstate travel facilities. CORE decided to test the federal government's willingness to enforce the ruling — in other words, would the U.S. government actually ensure that interstate bus and train lines were integrated. So Lewis volunteered to work with CORE and become a "freedom rider." Freedom riders were volunteers in mixed groups of blacks and whites who would board commercial buses and travel around the south to challenge segregation in buses and bus stations.

Lewis and several other freedom riders rode a bus that traveled out of Alabama into South Carolina. When the bus arrived at the small town of Rock Hill, Lewis and the others stepped down from the bus and entered

Two blood-spattered Freedom Riders, Lewis (left) and James Zwerg (right), stand together after being attacked and beaten by pro-segregationists in Montgomery, Alabama, May 20, 1961.

With a taped X marking the spot where he was struck on the head, Lewis enters a police van. He and 26 other Freedom Riders were arrested in Jackson, Mississippi, May 24, 1961.

309

the bus station. Despite the Supreme Court ruling, the station was still segregated — there were separate waiting rooms for black and white passengers. When Lewis tried to sit in the white waiting room, he was physically assaulted. "I will never, ever forget that moment," Lewis said. "I was 21. I was a sharecropper's son from a farm near Troy, Alabama. Yet somehow I learned that where there is injustice, you cannot ignore the call of conscience."

> "Courage is a reflection of the heart — it is a reflection of something deep within the man or woman or even a child who must resist and must defy an authority that is morally wrong. Courage makes us march on despite fear and doubt on the road toward justice. Courage is not heroic but as necessary as birds need wings to fly. Courage is not rooted in reason but rather courage comes from a divine purpose to make things right."

Over the ensuing months, Lewis and other civil rights activists embarked on numerous freedom rides, even though they knew that they were risking their lives. Indeed, many buses carrying freedom riders were attacked by whites wielding baseball bats, firebombs, and other weapons. The rides became so dangerous that some volunteers wrote out their wills or said tearful goodbyes to loved ones before boarding buses. Even the police were no help — Lewis and other freedom riders were attacked and beaten by uniformed police officers and state troopers throughout the segregationist South. As columnist Mary McGrory noted, "Lewis [received] an unremitting diet of violence and hatred from uniformed fellow Americans. He was slammed around without mercy by sheriffs, herded into paddy wagons with electric prods, flung onto jailhouse floors, shoved, kicked, and beaten."

Yet Lewis stayed true to his philosophy of nonviolent resistance, and he never let the punishment and hatred that he experienced turn him away from his goal of establishing equal rights for African-Americans across the country. "Courage is a reflection of the heart — it is a reflection of something deep within the man or woman or even a child who must resist and must defy an authority that is morally wrong," Lewis explained. "Courage makes us march on despite fear and doubt on the road toward justice. Courage is not heroic but as necessary as birds need wings to fly. Courage is not rooted in reason but rather courage comes from a divine purpose to make things right."

Lewis speaking to marchers at the Lincoln Memorial at the March on Washington, August 28, 1963.

In 1962 Lewis was named to the executive committee of SNCC, and one year later he was elected chairman of the civil rights organization. His election surprised some people outside the group. After all, he was only 23 years old, and he did not possess an eloquent public speaking style or outgoing personality. But fellow members of SNCC admired his courage and his faith in the principles of nonviolent resistance, and they recognized that he possessed a fierce dedication to civil rights.

After his election, Lewis moved to Atlanta, Georgia, where he spent much of his time engaged in fundraising activity. But he also continued to organize and participate in civil rights protests and other events. In August 1963, he joined Martin Luther King Jr. and other civil rights leaders in a meeting with President John F. Kennedy. A few weeks later, he participated in the famous March on Washington. Hundreds of thousands of Americans from all racial and social backgrounds converged in front of the Lincoln Memorial to show their support for civil rights and the vision of an America undivided by racial lines. It was at this momentous event that Martin Luther King Jr. delivered his famous "I Have a Dream" speech. But other organizers, including Lewis, delivered impassioned speeches as well. "By the force of our demands, our determination, and our numbers, we shall splinter the desegregated South into a thousand pieces and put them back together in the image of God and democracy," Lewis told the crowd

———— " ————

"That was a long summer, that summer of '64. Intense. Confusing. Painful. So hopeful in the beginning, and so heartbreaking in the end. . . . For all the positive seeds that were planted that summer . . . the end result for most of the people who experienced it was pain, sorrow, frustration, and fear. No one who went into Mississippi that summer came out the same. . . . "

———— " ————

to thunderous applause. "We must say 'Wake up, America. Wake up! For we cannot stop and we will not be patient!"

Freedom Summer

By 1964 the battle to gain equal rights for African-Americans had captured the attention of the entire nation. All across the South, civil rights organizations—like CORE, SNCC, the National Association for the Advancement of Colored People (NAACP), and the Southern Christian Leadership Conference (SCLC)—were leading demonstrations and protests calling for the end of segregation and the beginning of a new age of racial brotherhood. These activities sparked violent, hateful resistance from white political leaders and many white citizens. As clashes between the two sides became more frequent, tensions rose throughout the country. But activists knew that if their dream of securing equal rights was to come true, they had to keep pushing for change.

In the summer of 1964 Lewis and other leaders of the civil rights movement launched a new initiative called the Mississippi Summer Project. This program was a massive effort to register African-American voters in Mississippi, which had a long history of denying black people the right to vote. Such tactics as poll taxes, literacy tests, and outright intimidation were commonly used to prevent African-Americans from exercising their right to vote. The Mississippi Summer Project eventually succeeded in adding 17,000 black voters to the state's voting register. As the program got underway, the civil rights movement celebrated the passage of the Civil Rights Act of 1964. This law, signed by President Lyndon B. Johnson on July 2, 1964, prohibited segregation of public places like hotels, libraries, playgrounds, and restaurants anywhere in the United States. It also made it illegal for companies to discriminate against blacks in their hiring practices.

These developments led some people to refer to the summer of 1964 as "Freedom Summer." But as Lewis later admitted, those months also featured explosions of violence and hatred that took a heavy toll on members of the civil rights movement: "That was a long summer, that summer of '64. Intense. Confusing. Painful. So hopeful in the beginning, and so heartbreaking in the end." Indeed, over the course of the summer SNCC documented 450 violent incidents against civil rights activists and black citizens in Mississippi alone, including 30 bombings, 35 church burnings, and 80 beatings. "For all the positive seeds that were planted that summer . . . the end result for most of the people who experienced it was pain, sorrow, frustration, and fear," said Lewis. "No one who went into Mississippi that summer came out the same. So many young men and women, children really, teenagers, 18 and 19 years old, went down there so idealistic, so full of hope, and came out hardened in a way, hardened by the hurt and the hatred they saw or suffered, or both. So many people I knew personally, so many people I recruited, came out of that summer wounded, both literally and emotionally."

In 1965 civil rights leaders turned their attention to Lewis's home state of Alabama, another place where African-Americans had long been denied the right to vote. As activists spread out across the state, they organized peaceful demonstrations that aroused the fury of white communities. Sometimes these confrontations ended in episodes of ugly violence that were reported across the country. But as Lewis noted, "what tends to be forgotten among the dramatic photographs and news accounts of the moments of violence . . . were the days and days of uneventful protest that took place outside courtrooms and jails. People silently walked a picket line for hours on end, or sang freedom songs from dawn to dusk, or simply stood in line at a door they knew would not be opened, hour after hour, day after day."

"So many young men and women, children really, teenagers, 18 and 19 years old, went down there so idealistic, so full of hope, and came out hardened in a way, hardened by the hurt and the hatred they saw or suffered, or both. So many people I knew personally, so many people I recruited, came out of that summer wounded, both literally and emotionally."

Bloody Sunday

On March 7, 1965, Lewis and fellow civil rights leader Hosea Williams led a group of 600 silent and peaceful marchers in Alabama. These marchers intended to walk from Selma to Montgomery to protest Alabama's re-

At the Edmund Pettus Bridge in Selma, Alabama, on Bloody Sunday, March 7, 1965, moments before the Alabama state troopers attacked Lewis and the group. Lewis is on the right, in the light coat.

fusal to allow blacks to register to vote. They stopped, however, when they reached a large bridge that led out of Selma — the Edmund Pettus Bridge. "There, facing us at the bottom of the other side [of the bridge], stood a sea of white-helmeted, blue-uniformed Alabama state troopers, line after line of them, dozens of battle-ready lawmen," recalled Lewis. As the marchers watched, the troopers pulled on gas masks and issued a warning to the demonstrators to turn around within two minutes or face the consequences. Lewis and the marchers responded to the threat by kneeling in prayer. One minute later, the state troopers launched a furious assault on the peaceful, praying demonstrators. The troopers ran through the kneeling marchers, swinging their batons at the heads of men and women with all their might, as reporters looked on in horror. Lewis himself suffered a fractured skull in the attack, and many other demonstrators were injured as well.

The attack in Selma quickly came to be known as "Bloody Sunday." The event was filmed by television news cameras, and it horrified the nation. The police response was so terrible and vicious that within the next few days, demonstrations in support of the marchers were held in 80 cities. Thousands of religious and lay leaders, including Martin Luther King, Jr., flew to Selma. Outraged citizens flooded the White House and Congress with letters and phone calls. Bloody Sunday convinced President Lyndon B. Johnson to send new voting-rights legislation to Congress. "At times history and fate meet at a single time in a single place to shape a turning

*Civil rights leader Hosea Williams, left, leaves the scene as state troopers
break up the demonstration on Bloody Sunday. Behind him, at right,
Lewis is forced on the ground by a trooper.*

*Lewis, in the light coat in the center, attempts to ward off the blow as a state trooper
swings his club at Lewis's head. Lewis suffered a fractured skull in the attack.*

point in man's unending search for freedom," Johnson declared. "So it was at Lexington and Concord. So it was a century ago at Appomattox. So it was last week in Selma, Alabama. . . . Their cause must be our cause, too. Because it is not just Negroes, but really it is all of us who must overcome the crippling legacy of bigotry and injustice. And we shall overcome."

—————— **"** ——————

"At times history and fate meet at a single time in a single place to shape a turning point in man's unending search for freedom," President Lyndon Johnson declared. "So it was at Lexington and Concord. So it was a century ago at Appomattox. So it was last week in Selma, Alabama. . . . Their cause must be our cause, too. Because it is not just Negroes, but really it is all of us who must overcome the crippling legacy of bigotry and injustice. And we shall overcome."

—————— **"** ——————

On August 6, 1965, Johnson signed the Voting Rights Act into law. It ended literacy tests and poll taxes and ordered the appointment of federal voting registrars who would ensure the rights of black voters. Lewis attended the signing ceremony, and the president even gave him one of the pens he used in the ceremonial signing event. Years later, Lewis called the Selma campaign and the passage of the Voting Rights Act "probably the nation's finest hour in terms of civil rights."

Leaving SNCC

Life for African-Americans began to improve with the passage of the 1964 Civil Rights Act and the 1965 Voting Rights Act. But racism and social inequality still reigned in many areas of the United States. During this time, many black activists expressed anger with the slow pace of change. They believed that the country's major political parties and its leading lawmakers were not truly dedicated to improving the lives of African-Americans. As a result, SNCC and other black organizations turned to leaders who emphasized "black power" and independence from white society. Lewis and other civil rights activists who remained devoted to the ideals of integration and nonviolence were pushed aside.

Lewis's ouster from the leadership of SNCC took place in May 1966, when members voted to make the radical activist Stokely Carmichael the new chairman. Lewis was hurt and disappointed by the decision, but it did not shake his faith in his own beliefs. After spending several months in New

Part of a sit-in protest in Jackson, Mississippi, June 15, 1965. Lewis, here seated (center), was among an estimated 175 people arrested.

York, he moved to Atlanta to work as a community organizer for the Southern Regional Council. It was during this time that he met a librarian named Lillian Miles, who eventually became his wife.

In 1968 Lewis took a leave of absence from his job with the Southern Regional Council to work on Robert F. Kennedy's presidential campaign. A few weeks later, on April 4, 1968, Martin Luther King Jr. was assassinated in Memphis, Tennessee. "When he was killed I really felt I'd lost a part of myself," Lewis later wrote. Two months later, on June 4, 1968, Kennedy was shot and killed by another assassin. Lewis had greatly admired these two men, and losing both of them in the space of two months took a heavy emotional toll on him. "It hurt so incredibly much when they were taken away," he recalled. "It was like trusting yourself to fall in love again after you've given your heart once and had it broken. . . . What could we believe in now?"

In 1970 Lewis assumed leadership of the Southern Regional Council's Voter Education Project. Under his guidance, the program held voter registration drives and rallies, provided rides to courthouses and polling places for people without reliable transportation, and provided assistance to African-American politicians. In 1976, Lewis became interested in running

Congressman Lewis speaks at home in Atlanta, January 1985.

for Congress. Andrew Young had left his spot in the Georgia delegation of the U.S. House of Representatives to take a position in President Jimmy Carter's administration. Four years earlier, Young had become one the first African-Americans elected to Congress to represent the South in the 20th century, along with Barbara Jordan of Texas. Lewis decided to try to win Young's Congressional seat, but his first campaign for public office ended in defeat. In July 1977 Carter asked Lewis to run VISTA, a national volunteer program managed by the federal government. Lewis headed this effort for two years, then worked as a business manager in the private sector for a short time before winning election to the Atlanta City Council in November 1981.

During Lewis's first four-year term on the city council, he gained a reputation as a tireless champion of the people of his district. His high ethical standards and blunt talk sometimes produced clashes with other council members. But the citizens of Atlanta liked and respected him, and in 1985 he was elected to a second term by a large percentage of the vote.

Dedicated Legislator

In 1986 Lewis decided to take another run at a seat in the U.S. House of Representatives. Since the district he targeted favored candidates from the Democratic Party, Lewis knew that the winner of the party's nomination would win the seat. But he faced tough competition for the seat from state senator Julian Bond, who also had been a major figure in the civil rights movement of the 1960s. Bond had the support of the Democratic Party's leadership, and his good looks and articulate manner made a good impression on television and in the newspapers. But Lewis campaigned with his usual dogged determination. "Throughout my years in the movement and throughout this new political career of mine, people had always underestimated me," he said. "With my background—the poor farm boy from the woods—and my personality—so unassuming and steady—people tended to assume I was soft, pliable, that I could be bent to meet their needs. They were always amazed, those who didn't know me, to see me dig in and stand my ground. Independence and perseverance — people had shortchanged me on those qualities all my life, often, in the end, to their dismay."

When the votes from the August 1986 primary were tallied, Bond fell just short of the 50 percent majority he needed to clinch the nomination. A runoff election was scheduled for September 2 between Bond and Lewis, who had finished second in the primary voting. Most political observers thought that Bond would claim an easy victory. But Lewis performed strongly in three televised debates and he pulled off what the *New York Times* described as "a stunning upset." Two months later, Lewis defeated Republican candidate Portia Scott to claim his place in the U.S. Congress.

In January 1987 Lewis was sworn in as a member of the 100th Congress in the U.S. House of Representatives. He has remained a member of Congress ever since, winning re-election eight consecutive times. "I have continued to tend to the hands-on needs of my constituents [during that time]," Lewis wrote. "But beyond that, my overarching duty, as I declared during that 1986 campaign and during every campaign since then, has been to uphold and apply to our entire society the principles which formed the foundation of the movement to which I have devoted my entire life, a movement I firmly believe is still continuing today. I came to Congress with a legacy to uphold, with a commitment to carry on the spirit, the goals, and the principles of nonviolence, social action, and a truly interracial democracy. ... [Government's] first concern should be the basic needs of its citizens — not just black Americans but *all* Americans — for food, shelter, health care, education, jobs, livable incomes, and the opportunity to realize their full potential as individual people."

"[As a representative to Congress], my overarching duty, as I declared during that 1986 campaign and during every campaign since then, has been to uphold and apply to our entire society the principles which formed the foundation of the movement to which I have devoted my entire life, a movement I firmly believe is still continuing today. I came to Congress with a legacy to uphold, with a commitment to carry on the spirit, the goals, and the principles of nonviolence, social action, and a truly interracial democracy."

Throughout his years in Washington, Lewis has been a quiet but steady advocate for Americans who are poor and politically powerless. He admits that other politicians are better at grabbing the spotlight and making speeches. But he feels that his own low-key style has been effective as well. "People who are like fireworks, popping off right and left with lots of sound and sizzle, can capture a crowd, capture a lot of attention for a time," he acknowledged. "But I always have to ask, where will they be at the end? Some battles are long and hard, and you have to have staying power. Firecrackers go off in a flash, then leave nothing but ashes. I prefer a pilot light — the flame is nothing flashy, but once it is lit, it doesn't go out."

> *"People who are like fireworks, popping off right and left with lots of sound and sizzle, can capture a crowd, capture a lot of attention for a time.*
>
> *But I always have to ask, where will they be at the end? Some battles are long and hard, and you have to have staying power.*
> *Firecrackers go off in a flash, then leave nothing but ashes. I prefer a pilot light — the flame is nothing flashy, but once it is lit, it doesn't go out."*

At times, Lewis's refusal to compromise on his life-long pursuit of peace and racial unity has led him to take unpopular positions on certain issues. For example, he was one of the few in Congress who voted against the 1991 Persian Gulf War. He also refused to participate in the October 1995 Million Man March on Washington. In this event, which was organized by Nation of Islam leader Louis Farrakhan, hundreds of thousands of African-American men from around the country gathered in Washington to renew their dedication to their families and communities. But to Lewis and many others, Farrakhan's history of racist statements cast a shadow over the event. "I supported the ideas and goals of that march," said Lewis. "I did not march because I could not abide or overlook the presence and central role of Louis Farrakhan, and so I refused to participate. I believe in freedom of speech, but I also believe that we have an obligation to condemn speech that is racist, bigoted, anti-Semitic or hateful. Regardless of the race of the speaker, I won't be a party to it. . . . I am committed to bringing the people of this nation together, not pushing them apart."

Lewis and President Bill Clinton at an event commemorating the 1963 March on Washington, August 26, 1998.

Walking with the Wind

In 1998 Lewis published an autobiography called *Walking with the Wind: A Memoir of the Movement.* The book was warmly received by readers and critics across the country. The *Washington Post* described it as a "definitive account of the civil rights movement" and claimed that "it is impossible to read this inspirational and hideous story of courage and cruelty without being moved." Writing in the *Los Angeles Times,* Jack Nelson offered similar praise for the book and its author: "A shy, humble man of deep convictions, Lewis lacked the charisma of such civil rights figures as [Martin Luther King Jr.], Jesse Jackson, Julian Bond, and Stokely Carmichael. Yet his compelling autobiography, *Walking with the Wind,* helps us understand how this son of poor Alabama sharecroppers not only survived the turbulent 1960s but rose to become a heroic figure and an influential member of Congress." Nelson went on to say that *Walking with the Wind* is "destined to become [a classic] in civil rights literature." In 1999 *Walking with the Wind* won the Robert F. Kennedy Book Award. In announcing the award, the chair of the selection committee described Lewis's book as "an honest and trenchant memoir that powerfully conveys the anguish and hope of tragic days. It is both a superb contribution to the history of our times and a moving evocation of a gallant spirit."

———— " ————

"There is an old African proverb: 'When you pray, move your feet.' As a nation, if we care for the Beloved Community, we must move our feet, our hands, our hearts, our resources to build and not to tear down, to reconcile and not to divide, to love and not to hate, to heal and not to kill. In the final analysis, we are one people, one family, one house — the American house, the American family."

———— " ————

Honors for Lewis's long and distinguished record of civil rights activism and public service continued in 2002. In that year, he received both the Martin Luther King Memorial Award from the National Education Association and the prestigious Spingarn Medal from the NAACP. The Chairman of the NAACP, Julian Bond — Lewis's old civil rights ally and political opponent — declared that Lewis was a worthy recipient for the honor. Bond described him as "a true American hero" whose "bravery and solid commitment to justice and dignity are legendary."

Lewis appreciates the recognition he has received in recent years. He is also proud of the progress that the United States has made in improving race relations and addressing social problems. "No one, but no one, who was born in America 40 or 50 or 60 years ago and who grew up and came through what I came through, who witnessed the changes I witnessed, can possibly say that America is not a far better place than it was," he said. But Lewis recognizes that there is still a lot more work to be done. "There is an old African proverb: 'When you pray, move your feet,'" he said. "As a nation, if we care for the Beloved Community, we must move our feet, our hands, our hearts, our resources to build and not to tear down, to reconcile and not to divide, to love and not to hate, to heal and not to kill. In the final analysis, we are one people, one family, one house — the American house, the American family."

MARRIAGE AND FAMILY

John Lewis married Lillian Miles on December 21, 1968, in a ceremony officiated by the Reverend Martin Luther King Sr. She currently serves as an administrator for the Office of Research and Sponsored Programs at Clark-Atlanta University. They have one son, John Miles Lewis, whom they adopted in 1976.

HOBBIES AND OTHER INTERESTS

Lewis enjoys collecting antiques and rare books about African-Americans.

WRITINGS

Walking with the Wind: A Memoir of the Movement, 1998 (with Michael D'Orso)

HONORS AND AWARDS

Best Nonfiction Book of the Year (*Booklist*): 1998, for *Walking with the Wind*
Robert F. Kennedy Book Award: 1999, for *Walking with the Wind*
Four Freedoms Award (Franklin and Eleanor Roosevelt Institute): 1999
John F. Kennedy Profile in Courage Award for Lifetime Achievement (John F. Kennedy Library): 2001
Martin Luther King Memorial Award (National Educational Association): 2002
Spingarn Medal (National Association for the Advancement of Colored People — NAACP): 2002

FURTHER READING

Books

Contemporary Black Biography, Vol. 2, 1992
Egerton, John. *A Mind to Stay Here: Profiles from the South,* 1970
Encyclopedia of World Biography, 1998
Halberstam, David. *The Children,* 1998
Hampton, Henry, and Steve Fayer. *Voices of Freedom: An Oral History of the Civil Rights Movement from the 1950s through the 1980s,* 1991
Hill, Christine M. *John Lewis: From Freedom Rider to Congressman,* 2002 (juvenile)
Kennedy, Caroline, ed. *Profiles in Courage for Our Time,* 2002
Lewis, John, and Michael D'Orso. *Walking with the Wind: A Memoir of the Movement,* 1998
McGuire, William, and Leslie Wheeler. *American Social Leaders,* 1993
Who's Who in America, 2002

Periodicals

Atlanta Journal-Constitution, Dec. 4, 1994, p.E1; Mar. 8, 1999, p.A3; Apr. 24, 1999, p.E2; June 29, 2000, p.J3; Apr. 8, 2002, p.C1
Christian Century, July 15, 1998, p.689

Current Biography Yearbook, 1980
Dissent, Winter 1997, p.9
Ebony, July 1967, p.146; Oct. 1971, p.104; Nov. 1976, p.133; Oct. 1999, p.182
Jet, Dec. 28, 1998, p.14; June 11, 2001, p.4; July 15, 2002, p.4
Los Angeles Times, June 14, 1998, p.5
National Geographic, Feb. 2000, p.98
New Leader, June 29, 1998, p.20
New Republic, July 1, 1996, p.19; Oct. 5, 1998, p.12
New York Times, Sep. 4, 1986, p.A1; July 6, 1991, p.A8; Mar. 8, 1999, p.A12
New York Times Magazine, June 25, 1967, p.5
Newsweek, June 1, 1998, p.69
Parade, Feb. 4, 1996, p.8
People, Aug. 24, 1998, p.125
Time, Aug. 4, 1986, p.26
Washington Monthly, May 1998, p.38
Washington Post, Sep. 7, 1986, p.C7; June 9, 1998, p.D1; Mar. 6, 2000, p.C1

Online Articles

http://www.cs.umb.edu/jfklibrary/newsletter_summer2001_07.html
   (*John F. Kennedy Library and Foundation Newsletter*, "Remarks by John
   Lewis," Summer 2001)
http://www.time.com/time/community/transcripts/1999/022399lewis.html
   (*Time.com*, Transcript of interview with John Lewis, Feb. 23, 1999)

Online Databases

Biography Resource Center Online, 2002, articles from *Contemporary Black
   Biography*, 1992, and *Encyclopedia of World Biography*, 1998

ADDRESS

John Lewis
343 Cannon
Washington, DC 20515

WORLD WIDE WEB SITES

http://www.house.gov/johnlewis
http://memory.loc.gov/ammem/today/mar07.html
http://www.pbs.org/newshour/forum/july98/lewis.html

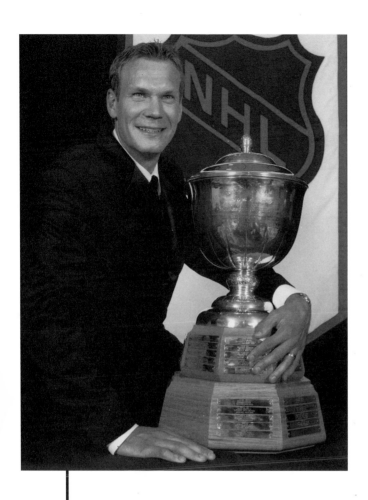

Nicklas Lidstrom 1970-

Swedish Professional Hockey Player for the Detroit
Red Wings
Three-Time Winner of the Norris Trophy as the NHL's
Best Defenseman

BIRTH

Nicklas Lidstrom was born on April 28, 1970, in Vasteras, Sweden, a city located about 60 miles from the national capital of
Stockholm. His father, Jan-Eric Lidstrom, worked as an engineer for the Swedish highway system. His mother's name is
Gerd.

YOUTH AND EDUCATION

Lidstrom was raised in Avesta, a town near Vasteras. His father claims that Lidstrom was a spirited and outgoing boy. "He was a little warrior, always joking and doing little things to get into trouble," Jan-Eric Lidstrom recalled. But Lidstrom has described himself as a more laid-back youngster. "I've always been quiet," he said. "Ever since I was a little kid, I've always been quiet."

As was the case in most other Swedish communities, many children in Avesta played ice hockey at an early age. By the time Lidstrom started playing hockey at age 7, he recalled that "all the kids where I lived were already playing hockey. . . . It was natural for me to get involved." Within a few months of lacing up his skates, he was one of the top players in his age group in all of Avesta.

Lidstrom enjoyed other sports, too, of course. For example, he displayed top soccer skills at an early age. But hockey gradually emerged as his favorite. He spent hours competing in youth leagues and in pick-up games at local rinks. "When I first started out, I just wanted to play on the big team in my hometown," he recalled. "When I was 13 or 14, I wanted to play in the Elite league [the top pro hockey league in Sweden]. It wasn't until I was about 16 that I started to think about the NHL." Indeed, Lidstrom spent many evenings watching broadcasts of National Hockey League (NHL) games. He especially enjoyed watching the Toronto Maple Leafs, which featured Borje Salming, one of the first Swedish players ever to play in the NHL. "He was a hero, for sure," remembered Lidstrom. "My idol."

Lidstrom attended school in Avesta as well. In the Swedish school system, all students start learning the English language at age 10. As a result, he became proficient in English by his mid-teens. Years later, when he became a player in the NHL, his mastery of the English language made it much easier for him to make the transition to living in the United States.

CAREER HIGHLIGHTS

From Sweden to Detroit

By his late teens, Lidstrom was one of Sweden's most promising young hockey players. Even in Sweden's elite competitive leagues, his all-around abilities attracted notice. Before long, the talented young defenseman was playing in front of crowds that included NHL scouts from the United States and Canada.

In 1989 the NHL's Detroit Red Wings selected Lidstrom in the third round of the league draft with the 53rd selection overall. Jimmy Devellano, who was the club's general manager in 1989, later admitted that he drafted the young Swedish player without ever seeing him play. "You have to believe in your scouts, and that's what we were doing," he explained. "You have to understand, we're drafting kids 17, 18 years old. All you're doing is projecting how they will develop. You do the best you can do, evaluating them. But you never know."

Lidstrom was delighted that the Red Wings drafted him. "The NHL seemed so far away," he said. "You read and heard about the players, but you never imagined you'd be part of it. I wanted to see what it was like." But instead of leaving immediately for the NHL, Lidstrom stayed in Sweden to play hockey for the next two years. This decision met with the approval of the Red Wings organization. Detroit's staff knew that the young Swede would have the opportunity to play a lot of hockey in his homeland, but that he would get only limited playing time in the ultra-competitive NHL.

Lidstrom spent the 1990 and 1991 seasons playing for Vasteras in the Swedish Elite League. He also helped Team Sweden win a gold medal at the 1991 World Championship. These experiences allowed him to hone his defensive skills against star players from Sweden and other countries. "I was glad that I waited a couple of years after I was drafted to come to the NHL," he later admitted. "I was more confident. Playing at the World Championships in 1991 against NHL players also helped my confidence."

——— *"* ———

"When I first started out, I just wanted to play on the big team in my hometown," Lidstrom recalled. *"It wasn't until I was about 16 that I started to think about the NHL."*

——— *"* ———

Lidstrom finally joined the Red Wings for the 1991-92 season. "When I first came over, I thought I might stay two or three years," he said. "I just wanted to see if I could play at this level." As it turned out, the young defenseman made an immediate impact. Impressed by his smart and steady play, Red Wings coaches gave him lots of "ice time" — playing time — from the very first game. By the end of the season, Lidstrom had earned a spot on the NHL All-Rookie Team. He also finished second to rookie sensation Pavel Bure in the balloting for the Calder Trophy, given each season to the league's top first-year player. In addition, Lidstrom helped Detroit post a 43-25-12 (43 wins, 25 losses, 12 ties) record and a first-place finish in their

Lidstrom carries the puck down the ice in a 1997 game.

division. "Just the way he stepped in and played right away, the ability he showed, you knew he had a chance to be a special player," recalled Devellano. "He helped us a lot that season."

After the season was over, Lidstrom admitted that the year had taken a lot out of him. "When I first came over here, I didn't know anything," he explained. "How to order a phone, find an apartment, things like that." In addition, he said that the NHL's 82-game regular season was "definitely an adjustment. We'd play 40 games in the regular season [back in Sweden], and there were many breaks. We'd get almost three weeks off for Christmas, and breaks before the national tournament. Just a lot of time off. The NHL isn't like that."

Developing into a Quiet Star

Over the next several seasons, Lidstrom developed into one of the most important players on the Wings. His playmaking abilities and sound defensive skills contributed to Detroit's emergence as one of the NHL's most dangerous teams. Indeed, from 1992-93 to 1995-96, the Red Wings earned three division titles and two President's Trophies, given each year to the NHL team with the best regular season record. But in each of these seasons, the club fell short in its bid to win the Stanley Cup as NHL champions.

Lidstrom's teammates recognized that he was an important factor in the team's success. Outside of Detroit, however, the defensive ace received little recognition. "He always seems to be the forgotten guy," said fellow Red Wing Darren McCarty. "We were perfectly happy to keep him a sleeper."

Many of Lidstrom's teammates attributed his low public profile to his refusal to seek out publicity. "It's refreshing to see an athlete who's just down-to-earth," said teammate Mike Ramsay. "Somebody that doesn't think the world owes him something. Some people like to be in the limelight, they want to be on TV every day. Other people are happy sitting in the shadows, being their own man. I'm sure he'd love to get the recognition that he deserves. But you're not going to see him go out and pound the drums for it." For his part, Lidstrom simply observed that "I'm pretty calm and quiet. I don't really avoid attention, but I don't look for it either, in the locker room or on the ice."

"It's refreshing to see an athlete who's just down-to-earth," said one of Lidstrom's teammates. "Somebody that doesn't think the world owes him something. Some people like to be in the limelight, they want to be on TV every day. Other people are happy sitting in the shadows, being their own man. I'm sure he'd love to get the recognition that he deserves. But you're not going to see him go out and pound the drums for it."

Winning the Stanley Cup

As the 1996-97 season unfolded, Lidstrom took his game to a new level. In addition to playing his usual flawless defense, he used his skating, shooting, and puckhandling skills to give Detroit another major scoring threat.

During the 1990s Lidstrom emerged as one of the league's best defensemen.

Many of his goals and assists came on the Wings' power play. (In hockey, players who commit penalties must leave the ice for a set period of time. That gives the opposing team a "power play" in which they can attack with an extra skater on the ice.) "All through my career I've been used on the power play," Lidstrom said. "I have to play a solid game overall and play well defensively, but I think people expect me to play well offensively, especially on the power play."

By the end of the regular season, Lidstrom's 57 points (15 goals, 42 assists) ranked third among all NHL defensemen. These totals — along with his smothering defense — helped boost Detroit to a 38-26-18 record and another playoff berth. The quiet Swede excelled in the playoffs as well, as the Wings marched to a spot in the 1997 Stanley Cup finals against the Philadelphia Flyers. The Red Wings overwhelmed the Flyers in four straight games to clinch the club's first NHL championship in 42 years.

Many Red Wings played important roles in the team's championship drive, but hockey experts claimed that Lidstrom was particularly valuable. For example, Head Coach Scotty Bowman often used Lidstrom against Philadelphia superstar Eric Lindros during the finals. Other teams had failed to contain Lindros, one of the league's biggest and strongest players. But Lidstrom used his smarts and skating ability to thoroughly neutralize the bigger man's game. "We like to have him out there against the other team's top offensive line," Bowman acknowledged. "His main job is to prevent goals, not to score them. He's very underrated defensively."

Stardom Finally Arrives

Lidstrom maintained his excellent standard of play during the 1997-98 season. He finished second on the team in points (with 59 points, including 17 goals and 42 assists) and led the entire league in scoring by a defenseman. He also made his second straight appearance in the NHL All-Star Game, and finished second in the voting for the Norris Trophy, given each year to the league's best defenseman. Most important, he helped the Red Wings clinch a second straight Stanley Cup. The team posted a 44-23-14 record in the regular season, then marched through the playoffs to claim another championship. During Detroit's playoff run, Lidstrom set team records for most assists (13) and points (19) by a defenseman in a single playoff year.

"Nick plays more quality minutes than maybe anyone in the NHL," said Steve Yzerman. "He kills penalties, plays on our power play, and he's always out there on defense against the opposing team's best players. I'd hate to have to find out just how ordinary we'd be without him."

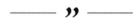

The 1998-99 season came to a disappointing close for Lidstrom. The team posted a 43-27-7 record and clinched another division title, but it failed in its quest to win a third straight Stanley Cup. Still, Lidstrom could take comfort in the fact that he emerged as a true NHL star during the course of the season. He was voted to start in the NHL All-Star Game for the first time, and praise for his mistake-free style poured in from all corners of the league. "Lidstrom's game is fueled by his incredible hockey sense," wrote analyst Karl Samuelson for NHL.com. "An excellent skater with tremendous vision on the ice, the talented defenseman has an effortless way of accomplishing his dominance on the blue line. Lidstrom does not crush his opponents through the glass . . . nor does he try to skate through the other team. Instead, he establishes his superiority in an understated manner."

At season's end, Lidstrom once again finished second in the voting for the Norris Trophy. He also finished second in the voting to Wayne Gretzky for the Lady Byng Trophy, which is awarded to the player who exhibits the best sportsmanship. Many of Lidstrom's teammates expressed deep satisfaction with the belated recognition. "Nick plays more quality minutes than maybe anyone in the NHL," said teammate Steve Yzerman. "He kills penalties, plays on our power play, and he's always out there on defense against the opposing team's best players. I'd hate to have to find out just how ordinary we'd be without him."

———— **"** ————

"The issue all along has been to do what's best for our kids," Lidstrom said about deciding when to return to Sweden. "What finally made the difference was that we talked to several friends that lived in the States for a time and then returned to Sweden. Like us, they felt it was important to raise their families in Sweden. But they all agreed that there was no problem with their kids living there longer than what we already have."

———— **"** ————

Considering a Return to Sweden

In the summer of 1999, Lidstrom shocked Detroit hockey fans with an announcement that he was thinking about leaving the NHL and taking his family back to Sweden. "My family comes first, I've always said that," he said. He noted that he liked living in the Detroit area, but that his closest friends and family still lived in Sweden. He also wanted to make certain that his children appreciated their Swedish heritage.

Over the next several weeks, Lidstrom struggled with the decision. He knew that he could make much more money playing hockey in the United States, but he missed his friends and family. Another important factor to consider was Sweden's shorter hockey season, which would leave him with more time to spend with his family. Ultimately, however, Lidstrom decided to remain with the Red Wings. In September 1999 he agreed to a new contract that paid him $22 million over three years. "The issue all along has been to do what's best for our kids," he said. "What finally made the difference was that we talked to several friends that lived in the States for a time and then returned to Sweden. Like us, they felt it was important to raise their families in Sweden. But they all agreed that there was no problem with their kids living there longer than what we already have."

In the 1999-2000 campaign, Lidstrom maintained his steady standard of excellence. He finished second in the voting for both the Norris Trophy and

Lidstrom uses skating ability and positioning to collar opposing players.

the Lady Byng Trophy. He also set career bests in several categories, including goals (20), power play goals (9), and power play points (31). In addition, he led all NHL defensemen in points (73) and was named captain of the World Team in the 2000 NHL All-Star Game. The Red Wings, meanwhile, remained one of the league's top teams. They finished the season with a

48-24-10 record and entered the playoffs as a Stanley Cup favorite, only to see the New Jersey Devils claim the title.

In 2000-01, Lidstrom finished second on the Wings in points (71) and set a new career mark for assists (56). His 71 points placed him second among all NHL defensemen in scoring and helped Detroit march to a division-best 49-20-9 mark. As season's end, Lidstrom finally claimed the Norris Trophy as the league's best defenseman, after three straight years of being runner-up. According to Red Wings General Manager Ken Holland, no other player in the NHL was more deserving of the honor. "Nick is a solid all-around player in every aspect of the game," declared Holland. "He can score and is a great passer. Nick knows when to jump into the play and is excellent defensively. He is not overly physical, but doesn't get beat one-on-one because he is so smart. He knows how to position himself and has such quick feet and skating ability that he knows how to adjust to situations. . . . Nick is so smooth in everything he does on the ice. He is almost like silk."

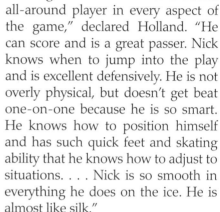

> "I was really surprised to win [the Conn Smythe Trophy]," Lidstrom admitted. "It's an honor I'll never forget. . . . I'm not a flashy player, but I do my job out there playing a lot of minutes. It's a tremendous honor to receive this award."

Winning the Conn Smythe Trophy

Lidstrom enjoyed another banner season in 2001-02. He represented Sweden in the 2002 Winter Olympics in Salt Lake City, Utah, and in December 2001 he signed a new contract with Detroit that pays him $10 million a season through 2003-04. By season's end he had tied for the league lead in points by a defenseman (59) and earned his second straight Norris Trophy.

Best of all, the Red Wings claimed the Stanley Cup for the third time in six seasons. Armed with a roster of future Hall of Famers, including Steve Yzerman, Brett Hull, and Dominick Hasek, the Red Wings finished the regular season with an amazing 51-17-10 mark. Detroit then dropped the first two games of the playoffs to the underdog Vancouver Canucks. But Lidstrom scored the winning goal in Game Three, and the Wings dominated the series from that point forward. Detroit then marched to the Western Conference finals, where they knocked off their archrivals, the Colorado Avalanche, in a tense seven-game series. In the Stanley Cup finals, Detroit lost the first

Lidstrom celebrates winning both the Stanley Cup and the Conn Smythe Trophy as most valuable player of the 2002 NHL Playoffs.

game to the Carolina Hurricanes. But in Game Two, Lidstrom delivered another game-winning goal. After punching the puck into the net, he pumped both fist and roared at his ecstatic teammates. "I guess my teammates were surprised I showed emotion," he later said. "It's the old Swedish stereotype [that] I don't get excited, don't show it as much as others."

After tying the series at one game apiece, the Wings went on to win the next three games and claim the Cup. As the Wings celebrated, Lidstrom (5 goals, 11 assists in the playoffs) learned that he had been awarded the Conn Smythe Trophy as the Most Valuable Player of the playoffs. He thus became the first European player, the second non-Canadian, and the seventh defenseman ever to receive the Conn Smythe Trophy. "I was really surprised to win it," he admitted. "I wasn't even thinking about it, really. You want to win the Stanley Cup. But it's an honor I'll never forget. . . . I'm not a flashy player, but I do my job out there playing a lot of minutes. It's a tremendous honor to receive this award."

Lidstrom's teammates were happy for him, too. "He's been our best player for a long time now," claimed Yzerman. "He's a quiet guy, but he's the best guy I've ever played with. You have to watch him closely to appreciate how good he is." Teammate Boyd Devereaux offered similar praise. "He totally deserved it," said Devereaux. "I'm the biggest fan of Nick. He's the greatest guy in the world."

As Lidstrom prepared for the 2002-03 season, he learned that *Hockey News* had ranked him as the best player in the NHL. Lidstrom appreciated the kind words, but he did not let them distract him from his on-ice responsibilities. He performed at his usual high level, and at midseason he was rewarded by fans, who cast more All Star votes for him than any other player in the league. By season's end, Lidstrom had earned his third consecutive Norris Trophy as the league's best defenseman. He also finished second in the voting for the Lady Byng Trophy for the fourth time in five years. "He's like a Swiss watch, always in control," marveled first-year head coach Dave Lewis, who replaced the retiring Scotty Bowman. "He's just such a complete player, so very efficient. You look at the amount of ice time he plays, and the type of level he plays at, it's quite remarkable."

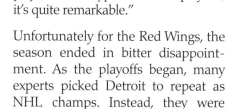

> "He's like a Swiss watch, always in control," said Coach Dave Lewis. "He's just such a complete player, so very efficient. You look at the amount of ice time he plays, and the type of level he plays at, it's quite remarkable."

Unfortunately for the Red Wings, the season ended in bitter disappointment. As the playoffs began, many experts picked Detroit to repeat as NHL champs. Instead, they were swept from the playoffs in the opening round by the Anaheim Mighty Ducks. This loss shocked everyone in the Detroit clubhouse. But despite this setback, analysts, coaches, and players around the league believe that Lidstrom and his teammates will be Stanley Cup contenders for the next several seasons.

MARRIAGE AND FAMILY

Lidstrom and his wife Annika have three sons, Kevin, Adam, and Samuel. During hockey season, the Lidstrom family lives in Novi, Michigan, a suburb of Detroit. They also own a home in Vasteras, Sweden, where they spend the offseason. Lidstrom has repeatedly stated that he intends to move his family to Vasteras permanently after his NHL playing career is over.

After the Red Wings won the 2002 Stanley Cup, Lidstrom's sons Adam (center) and Kevin (right) joined their father on the ice for the post-game celebration.

HOBBIES AND OTHER INTERESTS

Lidstrom is a big sports fan. He especially enjoys American football. "I enjoy the games and the action," he said. "I've been to a few [Detroit] Lions games. I like sitting in the crowd and watching the games. It's fun."

HONORS AND AWARDS

World Hockey Championship: 1991, gold medal
NHL All-Star: 1996, 1998-2003
NHL First Team All-Star: 1998-2003
World Cup: 1996, as member of Team Sweden
Olympic Hockey: 1998, 2002, as member of Team Sweden
Norris Trophy: 2001-2003, for NHL's best defenseman
Conn Smythe Trophy: 2002, for most valuable player of the playoffs

FURTHER READING

Books

Cotsonika, Nicholas J. *Hockey Gods: The Inside Story of the Red Wings' Hall-of-Fame Team,* 2002
Duff, Bob. *History of Hockeytown: Detroit Red Wings, 75 Years,* 2002
Fischler, Stan. *Detroit Red Wings: Greatest Moments and Players,* 2002
Romanuk, Paul. *Hockey Superstars, 1998-1999,* 1998 (juvenile)

Periodicals

Chicago Tribune, May 7, 1999, p.N1
Denver Post, Apr. 6, 2001, p.D13
Detroit Free Press, Oct. 30, 1991, p.C2; Jan. 19, 1996, p.C5; Apr. 15, 1997, p.D1; June 7, 1997, p.B1; Feb. 24, 1998, p.D1; June 11, 1998, p.D2; Jan. 23, 1999, p.B1; June 14, 2001, p.C7; June 15, 2001, p.D1; Dec. 8, 2001, p.B1
Detroit News, June 15, 2001, p.A1; Jan. 28, 2003, p.1 (Special); June 13, 2003, p.H3
Grand Rapids (Michigan) Press, June 14, 2002, p.B2
New York Times, June 8, 2002, p.D3
Sporting News, Sep. 6, 1999, p.90
Sports Illustrated, June 2, 1997, p.54; June 16, 1997, p.28; Jan. 12, 1998, p.66; Apr. 3, 2000, p.70; June 17, 2002, p.58; June 27, 2002, p.74
Sports Illustrated for Kids, Jan. 1, 2003, p.48
Windsor (Ontario) Star, Feb. 7, 1992, p.B1

Online Articles

http://www.asapsports.com
  (*ASAP Sports Web Site*, "An Interview with Nicklas Lidstrom,"
  June 13, 2002)
http://www.nhl.com
  (*NHL.com*, "Dependable Lidstrom Stands Alone," Jan. 23, 2003;
  "Lidstrom: No Need to Plan Ahead," Jan. 23, 2003; "Lidstrom Plays
  'Swede' Music in Detroit," Jan. 23, 2003)
http://www.washingtonpost.com
  (*Washington Post Online*, "For Wings' Lidstrom, No Place Like Home,"
  June 15, 1998)

Online Databases

Biography Resource Center Online, 2002, reproduced in *Biography Resource
  Center*, 2003

ADDRESS

Nicklas Lidstrom
Detroit Red Wings
Joe Louis Arena
600 Civic Center Drive
Detroit, MI 48226

WORLD WIDE WEB SITES

www.nhl.com
www.nhlpa.com
www.detroitredwings.com

Clint Mathis 1976-

American Professional Soccer Player
Forward for the New York/New Jersey MetroStars and
for the U.S. National Team

BIRTH

Clint Mathis was born on November 25, 1976, in Conyers,
Georgia. He is the son of Pat Mathis, who works as a bank
manager, and Phil Mathis, a former preacher who is currently
an insurance salesman. Pat and Phil Mathis divorced in 1988,
when Clint was about 12. The youngest of four children, Clint
has two older brothers and an older sister.

YOUTH

According to his parents, Mathis was born to be an athlete. "As soon as he was born I said, 'Oh, my gosh, he looks like a ballplayer,'" said his mother. He was walking from the time he was just nine months old, and he was already playing with a soccer ball when he was three. His mother quickly realized that her son had great potential in the sport. "I used to take him to the field in his stroller to watch his brothers," she remembered. "He just started walking. Then he was kicking paper cups, balls of paper, whatever. It's like he always played." She added, "When Clint was a little bitty thing, I told him, 'I feel like God has given you a gift.' He had such knowledge so young. He was four and yelling at other kids about being offsides."

Mathis played with his soccer ball indoors and out. A favorite family story relates how he used to kick the ball against a curio cabinet. He would break the glass so often that, after a while, the repairman stopped charging the family for the glass. His brothers also played soccer, so when Clint got a little older, they were his first coaches. In the backyard, they made their younger brother maneuver the soccer ball using only his left foot. Like most people, Mathis is right-handed and right-footed, so the purpose of the exercise was to make him equally adept using either foot. Because the rules of soccer prohibit using your hands to touch the ball, the ability to use both feet is crucial. The young boy also imaginatively invented a game he called "soccer croquet" in which he had to kick the ball between multiple obstacles. This helped him develop dexterity.

> "
>
> *"I used to take him to the field in his stroller to watch his brothers," his mother remembered. "He just started walking. Then he was kicking paper cups, balls of paper, whatever. It's like he always played. . . . When Clint was a little bitty thing, I told him, 'I feel like God has given you a gift.' He had such knowledge so young. He was four and yelling at other kids about being offsides."*
>
> "

Mathis's current coach for the MetroStars, Octavio Zambrano, believes that this type of unstructured practice helped him become the player he is today: "[In the U.S.] we have a system where we have youth soccer leagues, where young players are constantly being coached and supervised by adults who often have very little experience in soccer. Clint grew up playing the game in a different environment than most Americans, in one that resembled much more my own youth in Ecuador. That form of play allows for the growth of creativity, for imagination to flourish, and you see that in what Clint does. In a sense, he grew up in a pure soccer culture that does not yet exist in this country."

By the time he was five, Mathis was playing magnet ball, a kind of simplified soccer for little kids. When he was nine, his mother received an invitation in the mail for her son to become part of an Olympic development team. Pat Mathis was a single mother raising four children by working multiple jobs—at the time, she worked in a dentist's office, cleaned houses, and sold jewelry and antiques. So she didn't have very much money to spend on traveling around the country so her son could play soccer. However, she was determined not to let money stop her, and cut back on every expense she could. Other parents, she said, "didn't know I was eating crackers and Coke in the room for dinner." But the sacrifices she made would prove to be well worth it.

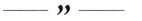

> "Clint loved every sport, but after that . . . he'd say he was going to play basketball, then [he'd say], 'Well, that might mess up my soccer, I'd better not.' He played basketball for fun. Soccer was way too serious."

CHOOSING A CAREER

Besides soccer, Mathis played other sports, including football, when he was a little kid. But when he was just nine years old he saw something that inspired him to focus on soccer. When he was watching television one day, he saw the World Cup quarterfinal game between the national teams for England and Argentina. One of the stars of the Argentine team, Diego Maradona, made two brilliant goals that led to a victory for his country. One goal has since become known to soccer fans as the legendary "Hand of God" goal. Mathis later recalled, "I saw Diego Maradona dribbling through seven or eight guys [when he scored]. Not the 'Hand of God' goal, but the other goal. It was amazing. I said, 'Man, I want to do that.'" Although soccer still wasn't a big sport in America, he said "that is when I first realized how big the World Cup was around the world."

Mathis became a devoted Maradona fan, and he loved the Maradona jersey that his mother bought for him. "He wore it night and day," she said, adding that "Clint loved every sport, but after that . . . he'd say he was going to play basketball, then [he'd say], 'Well, that might mess up my soccer, I'd better not.' He played basketball for fun. Soccer was way too serious."

EDUCATION

Mathis was a bright student who started high school one year earlier than most teens, but what he enjoyed most about school was, of course, playing soccer. As a teenager, he attended Heritage High School in Conyers, Georgia, where he was on the varsity team and impressed his coach, Karl Bostick. "I've seen him play twice and he took four shots. He scored four goals," Bostick said in 1994. "I have no doubt he's the best scorer in the state. He rockets everything." Mathis was the lead scorer on his team, leading it to two state championships in 1992 and 1993, and he was named "Georgia Player of the Year." But he didn't stop there. In addition to his high school team, he also played for the South Metro Lightning, which won a state championship, the State Select Team, and the U.S. National Junior Team, all while still getting good grades and graduating in 1994.

Not surprisingly, Mathis was recruited by many colleges and universities. He accepted a scholarship from the University of South Carolina to begin the next chapter of his up-and-coming career. At USC he studied exercise science and, of course, played soccer for the USC Gamecocks. He also played soccer for a U.S. Youth Soccer Association team called the Lightning Soccer Club, which went to its first national championship with Mathis as a star player, and he was on the U.S. Under-20 National Team in 1995. In the meantime, at USC he scored 53 goals from 1994 to 1997, had 15 assists, was named All-American twice, and was nominated three times for the Hermann Trophy for best college player—like a soccer version of the Heisman Trophy in football. He helped the Gamecocks go to the NCAA Tournament in 1995, and the USC team was ranked among the top five university soccer teams while he was there. In 1997, he also played for Team USA, which won a bronze medal at the World University Games in Italy. Mathis might have accomplished even more during his college years, had he not injured his knee in 1996. Despite missing some games, his record at USC demonstrated that he was professional material.

CAREER HIGHLIGHTS

When Mathis entered the world of professional soccer in 1998, the sport was just barely beginning to attract the attention of Americans, who have never been as enthusiastic about soccer as the rest of the world. Mathis would soon help to change all that.

A Brief History of Soccer

The game of soccer, which is more commonly called "football" outside the United States, was invented in England in the third century A.D. The game was first organized under the London Football Association in 1863 and became popular in continental Europe. In 1904, with soccer spreading throughout Europe, the Federation Internationale de Football Association (FIFA) was created to standardize rules and regulate international competition. Today, soccer is the most popular sport around the world. There are hotly competitive leagues in Europe and in South America, in particular. Children there grow up cheering their favorite soccer teams, rather than football, baseball, or basketball teams.

Meanwhile, in the United States, American "football," which actually more closely resembles the English game of rugby, was becoming a popular sport. In the U.S., American football quickly gained many more fans than soccer, which was regarded as a less exciting, foreign sport. Nevertheless soccer grew in popularity among children and teens in the 1980s and 1990s, and a movement began to grow to create professional leagues. The North American Soccer League was formed, and in 1996, Major League Soccer was established with 12 professional teams. Americans were beginning to get interested in the World Cup, which is the international soccer competition played once every four years. Countries around the world form national teams from their best players. Teams play in a series of qualifying games to get into the World Cup, and only 32 teams qualify. Those teams compete in a month-long competition of elimination. The World Cup is the most popular sporting event in the world. The American men's team has been very weak, and it rarely even qualified to play for the Cup. In 1998 the men's national team finished dead last in the competition. Happier news came from the U.S. women's team, however, which won world championships in 1991 in China and in 1999 in Brazil. But America was yearning to show that it could have a world-class men's team, too.

Playing for the Los Angeles Galaxy, Mathis takes the ball down field in this game against the Dallas Burn, March 1999.

The Los Angeles Galaxy

After finishing college, Mathis was immediately drafted in 1998 by the Los Angeles Galaxy, a Major League Soccer team. Excelling at passing the ball, free kicks, and wild, risk-taking goals, the young player was a top-scoring rookie who helped his team go to the MLS Cup final in 1999. Although easygoing off the field, he gained a reputation for being a loose cannon on the field who had a highly unconventional playing style. "When I play," Mathis once said, "I like to try to catch people off guard. People don't expect the unexpected, and that's what I try to do. You can call it arrogance or confidence. I call it competitiveness. I wouldn't want to be on the field if I could accept losing." He also continued to develop a reputation—begun in college—for being a bit of a showboat. Sometimes he will take his shirt off after scoring a goal (something for which he has been penalized) or do a victory "worm dance" where he flops on the ground on his stomach and bounces up and down. Mathis at times also lets his temper get the best of him, and he has been ejected from games for yelling at officials. "I'm a nice guy off the field," he said, "but on it, I guess you could say I'm [a jerk] out there."

> "When I play, I like to try to catch people off guard. People don't expect the unexpected, and that's what I try to do. You can call it arrogance or confidence. I call it competitiveness. I wouldn't want to be on the field if I could accept losing."

Mathis was unique among professional soccer players in America at the start of his career because, at the time, many teams were still recruiting players from other countries who were more skilled at the game. Because of his Southern background, accent, and goofy sense of humor his teammates jokingly nicknamed him "Cletus," implying that he was a backwoods bumpkin. Yet "Cletus" chalked up an outstanding record with the Galaxy, scoring 43 goals in the regular season from 1998 to 2000.

In 1998, the same year Mathis joined the Galaxy, the U.S. national team's star player Claudio Reyna was injured. That created an open spot on the National team roster, and Mathis was selected to fill it. Although he didn't get much playing time during his first two years with the national team, Mathis was voted MVP in a game against Australia in 1998 and scored his first goal in 2000 in a World Cup qualifying game against Barbados. But despite his record, the Galaxy team left him unprotected in 2000 so that they could obtain Mexican player Luis Hernandez. This meant that any team in the MLS could snatch up Mathis, which is just what the New York/New Jersey MetroStars did.

Playing for the New York/New Jersey MetroStars, Mathis dribbles the ball during a game against the Los Angeles Galaxy, August 2002.

The New York/New Jersey MetroStars

MetroStars coach Octavio Zambrano was happy to acquire Mathis for his roster in 2000. "It was clear to me that he was one of the best on the field, if not the best," said Zambrano. "I thought he would go earlier [in the draft]. I was extremely surprised — and ecstatic." Mathis was happy as well, because he didn't get as much playing time as he wanted with the Galaxy and was moved around a lot to different positions. "I have a lot more freedom [with the MetroStars]," he said. "This is the first time I've had a solid position [as a forward]. That gives me confidence, and more freedom to produce chances for the team." And even though he came from a small-town background, Mathis enjoyed New York City and soon purchased a newly built townhouse in nearby New Jersey. To show his appreciation for his fans with his new team, when he scored his first goal against his former Galaxy teammates as a MetroStar he took off his jersey to reveal a T-shirt that said "I Love New York." It was a gesture that his new fans really appreciated.

In 2000, Mathis scored 16 goals and had 14 assists, won the Honda MVP/Budweiser Scoring Championship, and set an MLS single-game record by scoring five goals in one match. The 2001 season, therefore, seemed to hold a lot of promise for the young star. He was excited to keep playing for the MetroStars, but at the same time something even bigger was looming over the horizon: the 2002 World Cup.

World Cup Hopes

During the first half of 2001, everything was going great for Mathis. Every game he played for the MetroStars ended in either a victory or a tie. In one game, he scored a hat trick in a 4-1 victory over the Kansas City Wizards, using his head, his right foot, and his left foot to score goals. In another game, he rocketed 60 yards, weaving past Dallas Burn defenders to score what *Sports Illustrated* called "one of the most electrifying strikes in United States soccer. The goal, the replays of which were aired worldwide, . . . evoked heady comparisons to Maradona." Mathis said that "I try to play on instinct. I just go. The moment I start thinking on the field is the moment I start messing up."

Mathis was also a valued player on the National Team, assisting his team to a victory over Mexico in February and beating the Honduras team in March. With his success in the United States, he began to eye prospects in Europe, where the competition was more intense and the pay much better. He had aspirations to join one of the Premier League teams in England because he liked the way the English played soccer — fast, just like him. If he could get a playing spot there, he could triple his American salary of about $200,000 a year, even if he spent all his time on the bench. However, Mathis had a contract with MLS and the MetroStars that didn't expire until 2003, and the star player was unlikely to be released from his obligation.

Bad news came in June 2001 when Mathis tore his right anterior cruciate ligament (ACL), a critical tendon behind the knee. The injury put him out of action for the rest of the year. Despite being sidelined with this injury, though, he was still making news in the media. In May 2002 Mathis was featured on the covers of *Sports Illustrated* and *ESPN: The Magazine,* the first American men's soccer player to have done so.

On the eve of the 2002 World Cup, many viewed Mathis as a potential savior for American soccer. According to Jeff Z. Klein in the *New York Times,* "What makes Mathis such a prized commodity is his ability to create goals at any time and from any place on the field, the rarest and most precious skill in a sport where a final score of 2-1 reflects a fiesta of rollicking, high-octane offense. No American has ever scored at such a prolific rate as Mathis over the past season and a half or so. . . . The goals he scored and set up in 2000 and 2001 propelled the United States to four victories in the early part of the World Cup qualification process. . . . This year, he returned from the injury and performed brilliantly in several World Cup tuneup games, showcasing not only his magic with the ball but also his fiery temperament and, as important to soccer stardom as anything, his charismatic ability to entertain the crowd." That view was echoed by Giorgio Chinaglia, a leading scorer in the 1970s and 1980s on an Italian premier team and also a member of the New York Cosmos. "Clint Mathis is hungry, he's greedy, and he has a certain selfishness—all the strikers, we have this knack," Chinaglia says. "He's for real, the type of player the U.S. has never had before. He wants the ball, he demands that his teammates provide for him the ball, and when he gets it, he does things no one can imagine him doing. This is a rare skill. He'll go far, because all the teams in Europe, they're looking for someone who can score."

The 2002 World Cup

By the time Mathis returned to play, the National Team was gearing up for the 2002 World Cup. In the first qualifying round, the U.S. played against Portugal, South Korea, and Poland. Mathis wanted to play, but National Team coach Bruce Arena didn't feel he was in good enough condition to do so at first. In fact, Arena benched him during the first qualifying game against Portugal, which the American team ended up winning with a score of 3-2. The coach criticized Mathis's trash talk to opponents and his confrontational approach to referees, with resulting yellow cards. He also accused him of partying too much and not working hard enough to get into playing shape. "I'm not too worried about the trash talk, because no one playing for Portugal or South Korea or Poland is going to understand him

> "
>
> "Clint Mathis is hungry, he's greedy, and he has a certain selfishness — all the strikers, we have this knack," said Giorgio Chinaglia, a leading scorer in the 1970s and 1980s on an Italian premier team and a former member of the New York Cosmos. "He's for real, the type of player the U.S. has never had before. He wants the ball, he demands that his teammates provide for him the ball, and when he gets it, he does things no one can imagine him doing. This is a rare skill. He'll go far, because all the teams in Europe, they're looking for someone who can score."
>
> "

The United States National World Cup Soccer Team, 2002.

anyhow," Arena said. "I'm not too worried about the [yellow] cards, because that just shows his competitiveness. I am worried about his work ethic. It took him nearly seven months to heal from ACL surgery. Other players have done it in nine weeks. The greatest players work the hardest. He's going to have to learn that if he wants to play for a big club." Mathis responded by saying, "I definitely don't think that's the case. I work hard, just like everybody else, in order to enjoy my life and do the things I enjoy. If I continue to do my job on the field . . . I don't think it's anybody's business what I do off the field, as long as I get the job done."

Fans were surprised by Mathis's reduced playing time in the early World Cup games, but when he did play his contributions were significant. In a shootout against Canada, it was his successful penalty kick that put the U.S. team into the finals; he scored twice in the 4-0 victory over Honduras, and had an assist in the 1-0 victory over Ecuador. The German team, however, proved too much for the U.S. Even though Mathis scored twice, his team lost 4-2. They also lost to Ireland and the Netherlands, but won against Uruguay, Jamaica, and Portugal. A score by Mathis late in the game brought a 1-1 tie against the South Koreans in June, followed by a loss against Poland and a win over Mexico. Meeting the Germans again on June 21 in the quarterfinals, the Americans were defeated 1-0 when Michael Ballack butted the ball into the net with his head. The Americans went home without the cup, but they still had done better than any other U.S. men's team. A good deal of the credit went to Mathis.

Disappointment . . . and Hopes for the Future

Controversy and a disappointing scoring season plagued Mathis in 2002. His coaches complained about his outrageous Mohawk haircut. He hurt his right knee in July, had knee surgery, and spent some time in recovery. He missed several games before returning in mid-August and scored only four goals with the MetroStars during the year. About his weak 2002 season with the MetroStars, he commented, "I can't pinpoint it. I got mentally drained, got away from what I needed to do. I was disappointed. I was so tired. I took it out on the referees. That's just not me." Coach Octavio Zambrano felt that his temper on the field was getting out of control. There was an incident in which Mathis stepped on an opposing player — something he said was an accident — and received a major penalty. Afterwards, Zambrano even told the media that he thought Mathis could use some psychological therapy. Mathis disagreed, telling newspapers that "Octavio believes there is a problem there and the only reason he is bringing it up publicly is to get my attention. That's fine. We'll do whatever we have to do to fix it."

— " —

"As much as I love soccer and I wouldn't want to be doing anything else," Mathis said, "I have to look at it as a business, too. I have to look at what will benefit me and my future family down the road if I get hurt. So maybe I have to look at leaving down the road. I mean, I'd love to stay here and help soccer grow. Being an American, I would love to see my kids and grandkids playing in a soccer league based here which is run very well like they are in Europe. I'll try to do whatever is in my power to help the league grow, but at the same time, I'm realistic."

— " —

With his contract for the MetroStars running out in 2003, Mathis is seriously considering going to an overseas team. He has already traveled to Germany to talk with the Bayern team there. "As much as I love soccer and I wouldn't want to be doing anything else," he said, "I have to look at it as a business, too. I have to look at what will benefit me and my future family down the road if I get hurt. So maybe I have to look at leaving down the

*Mathis celebrates after he scored the 1-0 goal during the
U.S. World Cup match against South Korea, June 2002.*

road. I mean, I'd love to stay here and help soccer grow. Being an American, I would love to see my kids and grandkids playing in a soccer league based here which is run very well like they are in Europe. I'll try to do whatever is in my power to help the league grow, but at the same time, I'm realistic."

HOME AND FAMILY

Mathis is currently single and lives in a new townhouse in New Jersey. When Mathis isn't training or playing soccer, his favorite thing to do is to hang out with his friends in his basement. He remodeled his basement in 2001 when he was recovering from knee surgery. It includes a large-screen television, a pool table, and a 12-foot-long couch. "This is my pride and joy," said Mathis, who added, "My idea of an ideal Saturday night is hanging out here with friends, watching movies, playing pool." He is also involved in some charitable work, serving in 2001 as the national spokesman for the MLS New York Life Dribble, Pass, and Shoot, a national youth skills competition for kids ages six to 14.

HONORS AND AWARDS

High School Player of the Year (*Atlanta Journal-Constitution*): 1993
Gatorade Player of the Year in Georgia: 1993
First Team All-American: 1995
Third Team All-American: 1997
Goal of the Year Award (Major League Soccer): 2000
Budweiser Scoring Championship (MetroStars): 2000, 2001

FURTHER READING

Periodicals

Los Angeles Times, May 12, 2002, Part 4, p.3
New York Times, May 28, 2001, section D, p.4; Dec. 18, 2001, p.S6; May 12, 2002, p.L1
New York Times Magazine, May 26, 2002, p.40
Soccer Digest, October 2000, p.26; Feb.-Mar. 2002, p.16; June-July 2002, p.14
Sports Illustrated, May 14, 2001, p.R4; May 27, 2002, p.60; Feb. 17, 2003, p.R2
Times (London), June 5, 2002, p.2

ADDRESS

Clint Mathis
MetroStars
One Harmon Plaza, 3rd Floor
Secaucus, NJ 07094

WORLD WIDE WEB SITES

http://www.metrostars.com
http://www.mlsnet.com
http://www.ussoccer.com
http://www.ussoccerplayers.com

Donovan McNabb 1976-

American Professional Football Player with the
Philadelphia Eagles
Considered One of the Top Quarterbacks in the NFL

BIRTH

Donovan Jamal McNabb was born on November 25, 1976, in
Chicago, Illinois. His father, Samuel, is an electrical engineer
who works for the power company. His mother, Wilma, is a
registered nurse. Donovan has one brother, Sean, who is four
years older.

YOUTH

Until Donovan was eight years old, the McNabb family lived on Chicago's South Side — an area that has experienced problems with drugs and crime. Then they moved half an hour away to the quiet, middle-class suburb of Dolton, Illinois. The McNabbs were the first African-American family to move into their new neighborhood. Although many people were friendly and welcoming toward them, a few people were prejudiced against them because of their race. Before they moved into their new house, some vandals spray-painted nasty messages on it and smashed the windows. But the situation improved quickly once the McNabbs settled into their new home. Donovan, in particular, had an easy time adapting to the all-white neighborhood. He was a bright, funny child who soon attracted a wide circle of friends.

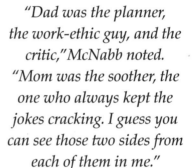

"Dad was the planner, the work-ethic guy, and the critic," McNabb noted. "Mom was the soother, the one who always kept the jokes cracking. I guess you can see those two sides from each of them in me."

Donovan grew up as part of a close-knit family that taught him the value of discipline and hard work. "You cannot be successful unless you have discipline in your life," his father stated. "What I tried to convey to both sons is that you have to be willing to work hard in life. Nothing comes easy." Although Donovan took his father's message to heart, he also developed a mischievous sense of humor as a boy. In fact, his mother always thought that he would become a comedian when he grew up. "Dad was the planner, the work-ethic guy, and the critic," Donovan noted. "Mom was the soother, the one who always kept the jokes cracking. I guess you can see those two sides from each of them in me."

Donovan loved sports as a child and covered the walls of his bedroom with pictures of professional athletes. But the person he admired most was his older brother, who was an outstanding young football player. When Donovan reached the seventh grade, he decided that he wanted to follow in Sean's footsteps and join the middle-school football team. But his mother told him he was too skinny and refused to let him play. Luckily, the coach recognized Donovan's talent and convinced his mother that he would not get hurt. Donovan played quarterback and quickly learned to avoid being hit by bigger, older boys. "At that age, you try to use a lot of juke moves because you don't want to be hit as a young child, playing football for the first time," he explained. "You watched so many big hits on TV, you don't want to be one of them. You make a lot of moves and see if you can avoid some people. Try to limit it to as few hits as you can."

EDUCATION

McNabb attended Mt. Carmel High School in Chicago—a private, all-boys' Catholic school with a reputation for both academic and athletic excellence. During his first two years of high school, it took him an hour to get to school on public transit. Once he learned to drive, however, his commute to school was cut to a half-hour. McNabb was a very good student whose favorite subject was math. But his sense of humor also came through, and he was known among his fellow students as a class clown.

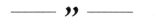

In high school, McNabb enjoyed playing both basketball and football. "They're both fun," he said at the time. "When you're playing one, it takes your mind off the other. I don't know which sport I'm going to play in college. Right now I want to see what I can do at both sports."

McNabb was an outstanding athlete at Mt. Carmel. He played point guard on the varsity basketball team and was a strong defender. After leading the team to a 25-4 record during his senior season, he was named to the all-area team by the Chicago press. McNabb was also a star on the football field. As a sophomore, he played quarterback on the scout team offense that helped the starting defense prepare for that week's opponent. The defense usually preferred to play against real teams, however, because McNabb was so hard to catch. He became Mt. Carmel's starting quarterback as a junior and helped the team average over 35 points per game during the 1992 season.

McNabb enjoyed playing both basketball and football. "They're both fun," he said at the time. "When you're playing one, it takes your mind off the other. I don't know which sport I'm going to play in college. Right now I want to see what I can do at both sports." Throughout his high school career, Wilma McNabb would pay her son $10 for every touchdown he scored. Though she paid out a lot of money during football season, she always made it back during basketball season by charging him $1 for every free throw he missed.

By his senior year, McNabb had attracted the attention of college scouts across the country. Several large schools recruited him to play football. He eventually chose to attend Syracuse University in New York. Syracuse had a solid football program under Head Coach Paul Pasqualoni. In addition, Pasqualoni agreed to let the young quarterback try out for the university's powerful basketball team. Another factor in McNabb's decision was that Syracuse had a strong communications program that had produced many well-known broadcast journalists, including Bob Costas. If he was unable to make a career for himself as a professional athlete, McNabb planned to become a sportscaster. He graduated from Mt. Carmel in the spring of 1994 and entered Syracuse that fall. He earned his bachelor's degree in speech communications from the university in December 1998.

CAREER HIGHLIGHTS

College — The Syracuse University Orangemen

But of course the whole time he was at Syracuse he was also playing football. McNabb was "redshirted" during the 1994 football season, meaning that he practiced with the team but did not appear in any games. According to college athletic rules, athletes are eligible to play a sport for up to four years. Major college football programs often redshirt promising athletes during their freshmen year to give them time to adjust to the college game while retaining their full four years of eligibility. This decision paid off with McNabb, who was ready to become the starting quarterback for the Syracuse University Orangemen in the 1995 season. He led the team to a 9-2 record and was named Big East Conference Rookie of the Year. Although Syracuse lost the conference championship game to the Miami Hurricanes, they still appeared in the Gator Bowl, where they defeated the Clemson Tigers by a score of 41-0.

McNabb's parents traveled ten hours by train from Chicago to attend every Syracuse home game. They also kept in close touch with their son by telephone to make sure that he did not let his success as a big-time college quarterback change him. "I would call him periodically just to see where he was," his father recalled. "I wanted to make sure that I didn't have to come over there to Syracuse and start bursting egos. Fortunately, I didn't have to do that. He was very focused on what he wanted to do."

Immediately after the 1995 football season ended, McNabb joined the Syracuse men's basketball team. Although he spent most of his time on the bench, he still accompanied the team to the NCAA Finals, where they lost to Kentucky. McNabb's success on the football field continued during

Quarterback McNabb of the Syracuse Orangemen drops back to pass during a game against the Pittsburgh Panthers, November 1995.

the 1996 season. The sophomore quarterback led his team to a 9-3 record and a share of the Big East Championship, then helped the Orangemen defeat Houston in the Liberty Bowl. At the end of the season, McNabb was named Big East Player of the Year. He continued to be a dual-sport athlete by playing basketball again in 1996-97, but after spending another season on the bench he decided to concentrate on football.

During the 1997 football season, McNabb set a new school record with 2,892 yards in total offense. Syracuse beat Miami to win the Big East Conference, but then lost to Kansas State in the Fiesta Bowl. McNabb received Big East Player of the Year honors a second time for his performance as a junior. Syracuse had an up-and-down year in 1998, losing three straight games before turning it around. One of the highlights of McNabb's senior season came before the final home game against Miami, when he received a long, loud standing ovation from the crowd. "To be received the way I was, that was something special for myself and my parents," he stated. "That was a memorable event. It's second to none. It's something that I never expected to happen."

Syracuse went on to beat Miami 66-13 — thus handing its bitter rival its worst loss in 50 years — to win the Big East title. McNabb rushed for three touchdowns and passed for two more during the game. The Orangemen's victory over the Hurricanes earned them a trip to the Orange Bowl, where they lost to Florida in McNabb's final college game. The quarterback was named Big East Player of the Year for an unprecedented third time at the conclusion of the season.

One of the highlights of McNabb's senior season came before the final home game, when he received a long, loud standing ovation from the crowd. "To be received the way I was, that was something special for myself and my parents," he stated. "That was a memorable event. It's second to none. It's something that I never expected to happen."

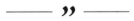

McNabb left Syracuse as one of the most decorated athletes in school history. McNabb led the Orangemen to a 33-12 record in his four years as a starting quarterback. He set school records with 8,389 yards passing and 9,950 yards total offense in his career. He also established a Big East record for career touchdown passes with 77.

McNabb also earned the respect of his coaches and his fellow players with his dedication, hard work, and positive attitude. "I think he fits into the history of our program as one of the all-time great players at Syracuse," said Coach Paul Pasqualoni. "I think he fits into that from a character standpoint in the mold of unbelievable kids. He is as well-loved in the community as he is as a player. He's been perfect. He's been a role model for every kid in New York and a tremendous representative of Syracuse and a tremendous representative of Division I college football in the 1990s. The guy came in humble. He does not have a selfish bone in his body."

"I think he fits into the history of our program as one of the all-time great players at Syracuse," said Coach Paul Pasqualoni. *"I think he fits into that from a character standpoint in the mold of unbelievable kids. He is as well-loved in the community as he is as a player. He's been perfect. He's been a role model for every kid in New York and a tremendous representative of Syracuse and a tremendous representative of Division I college football in the 1990s. The guy came in humble. He does not have a selfish bone in his body."*

NFL — The Philadelphia Eagles

McNabb's fine college football career attracted the attention of coaches and scouts from the National Football League (NFL). It soon became clear that he would be among the players selected in the first round of the 1999 NFL draft. But his draft position was unclear, since a number of promising young quarterbacks were turning pro that year. Most football analysts appreciated McNabb's strong arm and athletic ability, but a few questioned whether he would be able to direct a complicated, pro-style offense.

In the weeks leading up to the draft, McNabb underwent interviews and workouts with several of the teams that held high draft picks. The Philadelphia Eagles — one of the worst teams in the NFL with a 3-13 record in 1998 — held the second overall pick in the draft. McNabb visited Philadelphia and impressed the Eagles coaching staff with his work ethic, leadership skills, and knowledge of the game. During one part of the interview process, quarterbacks coach Brad Childress tried to confuse McNabb by firing questions at him and forcing him to make quick decisions. "Brad was just spitting things at him, and Donovan was answering at a rapid-fire pace," Eagles Head Coach Andy Reid recalled. "Finally Brad was like, 'Slow down, would you? I can't keep up.' But that's how Donovan's mind works. He's incredibly sharp."

By the time McNabb left Philadelphia, the Eagles were certain that they had found the player they wanted to draft. Unfortunately, some Philadelphia fans had other ideas. They hoped that the Eagles would draft Ricky Williams, a powerful running back who had just won the Heisman Trophy as the best player in college football. In fact, Philadelphia Mayor Ed Rendell sponsored a city council resolution urging the team to draft Williams.

On draft day, the Cleveland Browns selected Kentucky quarterback Tim Couch with the first overall pick. The Eagles followed and selected McNabb, making him the highest-drafted African-American quarterback in NFL history. The Philadelphia fans in the audience, many of whom wore Ricky Williams jerseys, were disappointed and booed loudly when McNabb's name was announced. But McNabb took the fans' reaction in stride. He walked up to the podium and smiled, then set out to prove all the doubters wrong. "Fans are always going to state their opinion, and I respect them for that," he said. "I've learned it doesn't matter what fans say in the beginning, just as long as they are cheering in the end."

The negative reaction McNabb received on draft day bothered his friends and family members more than it bothered him. His father compared it to the situation the family faced when they moved to an all-white suburb. "What we learned from our move to Dolton is that not everyone will be happy for you when you make a success of your life," Samuel McNabb stated. "I'm constantly reminding Donovan that although he's enjoyed great popularity, not everyone's happy for him. They'll boo him again if given the chance, and they'll say ugly things about him. What's important to understand is that it's going to happen and not to let it rattle you or stop you from being the person you are."

Other McNabb supporters claimed that it was only a matter of time before Eagles fans recognized what a great choice the team had made. "They don't know it yet, but they're going to love him in Philadelphia," said Syracuse Coach Paul Pasqualoni. "It's a great marriage. In that city, with that offense, if they just give him a chance, they'll find out what a special player they've got."

Even before the football season began, McNabb began winning over the people of Philadelphia with his charm and sense of humor. For example, he appeared at a public reception and received a gift from Mayor Ed Rendell. McNabb responded by giving the major a special Eagles jersey that had McNabb's number 5 on one side, and Ricky Williams' number 34 on the other. After lengthy contract negotiations, McNabb signed a seven-year contract worth $54 million. The contract made him the highest-paid player in Eagles history and one of the highest-paid in the NFL. "I'm excit-

Philadelphia Eagles quarterback McNabb (#5) runs with the ball against the New York Giants, September 2000.

ed," McNabb noted. "I'm pretty anxious to get started. This is another step toward fulfilling my goals."

Learning the Pro Game

When McNabb joined the Eagles, the team was coming off a disastrous season in which they had ranked last in the NFL in many offensive categories. But they had recently hired a new head coach, Andy Reid, who put many new strategies in place. Reid decided to bring his rookie quarterback along slowly to help ease his adjustment to the pro game. McNabb thus began the 1999 season as the Eagles' backup quarterback. "It was frustrating at times," he admitted. "Early on, I felt I should have been in there, but I never went up to Andy and said, 'Am I going to play this week?' or 'How much am I going to play?' And you know, I didn't know what I know now. I definitely didn't grasp the magnitude of the game early on."

McNabb made his first NFL appearance during the second half of a September 19 game against the Tampa Bay Buccaneers. He was sacked six times by the tough Bucs defense. McNabb's first starting assignment did not come until November 14 against the Washington Redskins. At this point the Eagles had a 2-7 record and looked like they were headed for another disappointing season. But McNabb gave the Philadelphia fans some hope for the future by running for 49 yards, passing for another 60 yards, and leading the Eagles to a 35-28 victory.

"It was frustrating at times," McNabb said about playing backup during his first season with the Eagles. "Early on, I felt I should have been in there, but I never went up to Andy and said, 'Am I going to play this week?' or 'How much am I going to play?' And you know, I didn't know what I know now. I definitely didn't grasp the magnitude of the game early on."

The rookie quarterback kept his starting job for the rest of the season. McNabb threw his first NFL touchdown pass the following week against the Indianapolis Colts, but he also committed six turnovers in a 44-17 loss. "Things are a little faster than college," McNabb admitted. "But the biggest thing is that you have to eliminate the mistakes. You have to take care of the little things." He ended the year with 948 yards passing for 8 touchdowns, and 313 yards rushing. Although the Eagles were still bad, they had managed to win five games — three of them with McNabb as the starting quarterback. The fans had reason to be optimistic about the team's prospects for the following year, especially when the Eagles picked up several good players in the college draft and the free-agent market.

McNabb worked hard to improve his skills and conditioning during the off-season. In fact, he spent much of the summer at an elite training facility for college and professional athletes in Phoenix, Arizona. His trainers put him through such unusual drills as throwing footballs from a balance beam to improve his coordination, playing with blinders on to improve his peripheral vision, and chasing balls designed to bounce unpredictably to improve his quickness. "I was a guy coming into my second year who sat out as a rookie for most of the season and I knew I was going to start and I had to improve myself," he explained. "It was really important to get better. They paid a lot of attention to detail, to my drops, to my fundamentals, to my conditioning. . . . I left there a lot better in everything than when I started."

Making the Playoffs

McNabb entered the 2000 season as the Eagles' starting quarterback and soon became one of the NFL's rising stars. Thanks to his unique style — which combined traditional drop-back passing, passing on the run, and running with the ball — McNabb was sometimes referred to as the "quarterback of the future." He started all 16 games in his second year as a pro. He finished the season with an impressive 3,365 passing yards for 21 touchdowns and 13 interceptions. He added an amazing 629 rushing yards — an average of nearly 40 yards per game — which was the fourth-highest total for a quarterback in NFL history. With 4,000 total offensive yards, McNabb accounted for nearly 75 percent of Philadelphia's yards from scrimmage over the course of the season.

For McNabb, the most important statistic was the Eagles' 11-5 record. The team won more games than in the previous two years combined and earned a spot in the NFL playoffs. They won in the first round but were defeated in the second round by the New York Giants. Nevertheless, Philadelphia fans were thrilled with the team's quick turnaround and excited about their hot young quarterback. McNabb's performance helped him finish second in the voting for the NFL's Most Valuable Player to running back Marshall Faulk of the St. Louis Rams.

McNabb had another great year in 2000. He again started all 16 games, during which he completed 285 of 493 passes for 3,233 yards and 25 touchdowns, with 12 interceptions. He also added 482 yards rushing for 2 more touchdowns. The Eagles started the season slowly but won eight straight games at the end to earn their first division championship since 1988. They defeated Tampa Bay in the first round of the playoffs, 31-9, but then lost in the second round to the eventual Super Bowl champion Rams, 29-24. "We had a long run. We had a great run," McNabb said afterward. "We're looking forward to what we can do next year."

Before the 2002 season began, McNabb signed a 12-year, $115 million contract with the Eagles. The contract made him the highest-paid player in

NFL history and virtually guaranteed that he would play out the rest of his career in Philadelphia. "It means a lot," he noted. "You see players who were great players and Hall of Fame players who just didn't stay with their given team. To know that I'll be locked into the Philly area is a wonderful feeling for me and for my family."

Injury Threatens Playoff Run

The Eagles started out well in the 2002 season, posting a 6-3 record. But then an injury to their star quarterback threatened to keep the team out of the playoffs. McNabb suffered a broken fibula—the outside bone in the ankle—on November 17 during the third play of the Eagles' game against the Arizona Cardinals. He left the game for a few plays but then returned to action, not realizing that his ankle was broken. "I've always said that you have to put everything on the line," he explained. "That's the only way you get trust from your teammates. That's what I did. I didn't know the ankle was broken because I'd never broken anything in my life. I thought it was a high ankle sprain. I wasn't going to take myself out of the game because of a nagging injury. I had worked too hard in the off-season and set my goals too high to take myself out of a game for something I thought was little."

> "I've always said that you have to put everything on the line," McNabb explained. "That's the only way you get trust from your teammates. That's what I did. I didn't know the ankle was broken because I'd never broken anything in my life. I thought it was a high ankle sprain. I wasn't going to take myself out of the game because of a nagging injury. I had worked too hard in the off-season and set my goals too high to take myself out of a game for something I thought was little."

Although McNabb was limping noticeably, he still managed to complete 20 of 25 passes for 255 yards and four touchdowns. His outstanding performance lifted the Eagles to a 38-17 victory. However, the game marked the first time in his career that he did not have a rushing attempt. Once the game ended, McNabb submitted to an X-ray and learned the truth about his injury. The broken ankle forced him to the bench after 10 games. By this point in the season, McNabb had already completed 211 of 361 passes for 2,289 yards and 17 touchdowns, with only 6 interceptions. He had also added 460 yards rushing for 6 touchdowns.

Philadelphia Eagles quarterback McNabb looks for an open man during this divisional playoff game against the Atlanta Falcons, January 2003.

McNabb ended up spending the next six weeks watching from the sidelines. "I saw the game from a different perspective. I learned things," he recalled. "I got my pen and paper out and wrote down some things I thought would help me out." To the surprise of many fans, the Eagles won five of their next six games under the guidance of veteran backup quarterbacks Koy Detmer and A.J. Feeley. Philadelphia claimed the top playoff seed in the National Football Conference, which earned them a bye in the first round. This gave McNabb an extra week to recover from his injury and get ready to return to the starting lineup. "It takes an entire team to win, and that's what we've done," he stated. "I couldn't be more proud of the way the guys played with me on the sidelines. I'm excited for what the team accomplished and I'm excited about returning for the playoffs."

McNabb started at quarterback on January 11 during the Eagles' playoff game against the Atlanta Falcons. Though he looked a little rusty at times, he completed 20 of 30 passes for 247 yards and also ran four times for 24 yards to lead his team to a 20-6 victory. The following week the Eagles played against the Tampa Bay Buccaneers for the right to represent the NFC in the Super Bowl. Unfortunately, Tampa's attacking defense proved too much for McNabb, who looked tentative throughout the game. Although he completed 26 of 49 passes for 243 yards, and added 17 yards rushing, most of these yards came when the result of the game was no longer in doubt. McNabb also fumbled the ball twice and threw an interception that led to a key Buccaneer touchdown. The Eagles lost 27-10 in their last home game at historic Veterans Stadium.

McNabb accepted full responsibility for the team's failure to reach the Super Bowl. "I played poorly. No reason. I just played poorly. It all starts with the quarterback. I had the opportunity to make plays. And, being the leader of the team, I had to make them. It happens. You want [the game] back, but there's nothing you can do. All you can do is put it behind you and live your life. I'm going to use this as motivation in the off-season."

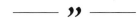

McNabb accepted full responsibility for the team's failure to reach the Super Bowl. "I played poorly. No reason. I just played poorly. It all starts with the quarterback. I had the opportunity to make plays. And, being the leader of the team, I had to make them," he acknowledged. "It happens.

You want [the game] back, but there's nothing you can do. All you can do is put it behind you and live your life. I'm going to use this as motivation in the off-season."

Quarterback of the Future

With his strong arm and great running ability, McNabb is often considered to be at the forefront of a new generation of athletic quarterbacks. He has enhanced his natural talents and earned the respect of his teammates and coaches with hard work and dedication to the game of football. He arrives at the Eagles practice facility at 6:30 every morning, spends the whole day working out, practicing with the team, meeting with the coaches, and studying game films, and finally returns home at 6:30 at night. McNabb recognizes that his position as quarterback makes him a leader on his team, so he tries to set a good example for his fellow players. "When you go in the huddle and you go up to the line of scrimmage, you have to look guys in the eye," he stated. "And, once you look them in the eye, and they can see how serious you are about the game, how much you love the game, then it'll rub off on some other players."

> "My dad told me something when I was younger that I'll never forget. He said there will always be somebody out there who's better than I am, and the only way I'll beat this guy is to outwork him. I believe that. I can't let up because right now someone is out there studying film, lifting weights, and running and throwing passes. He wants to be better so that he can help his team win. I can see this guy. I always keep him in mind...."

Even though he works hard and takes the game seriously, McNabb has maintained his sense of humor over the years. In fact, he is regarded as one of the funniest and best-liked players in the Eagles' locker room. McNabb is particularly known for his impersonations of the Philadelphia coaches and his fellow players. When he pretends to be Head Coach Andy Reid, he pulls his shorts up until the waistband reaches his chest and then stomps around the locker room. "I walked in on a team meeting, and Donovan was up at the front, talking and acting like me," Reid recalled. "The whole team was cracking up. He had imitated every coach—a whole stand-up comedy routine."

McNabb is not satisfied with his current level of success. He plans to continue striving to be the best player he can be and ultimately lead his team to the Super Bowl. "It's not time to relax yet," he stated. "My dad told me something when I was younger that I'll never forget. He said there will always be somebody out there who's better than I am, and the only way I'll beat this guy is to outwork him. I believe that. I can't let up because right now someone is out there studying film, lifting weights, and running and throwing passes. He wants to be better so that he can help his team win. I can see this guy. I always keep him in mind. . . . I play this game to be the best. And the only sure way I know to be the best is to outwork everybody else. Some people take one step toward their dream, accomplish a little something, and then feel like that's it. Not me. I'm never satisfied."

> "*. . . I play this game to be the best. And the only sure way I know to be the best is to outwork everybody else. Some people take one step toward their dream, accomplish a little something, and then feel like that's it. Not me. I'm never satisfied.*"

HOME AND FAMILY

McNabb lives in Cherry Hill, New Jersey — a suburb of Philadelphia — in a house he shares with his older brother and his two dogs, a boxer named Sinbad and a Rottweiler named Diego. In May 2002 he became engaged to his longtime girlfriend, Raquel Nurse (known as Roxi). The couple met during their freshman year of college. Nurse was a star guard on the Syracuse women's basketball team. In fact, she still holds the school record for career assists with 530, and she was named Big East Conference scholar-athlete of the year for 1997-98. McNabb proposed marriage while they were together on a vacation cruise. "My girlfriend's been there for me when things were pretty tough, and there when they were going well," he explained. "She's been there when I wasn't the Donovan McNabb everyone in Philly knows about, when I was a rinky-dink kid in college trying to win a starting job on the football team."

McNabb remains close to his parents, who still travel from Chicago to attend many of his home games. The fact that McNabb is wealthy and famous makes no difference in the way his parents treat him. In fact, his mother still calls to scold him if she sees a picture of him on TV or in a magazine wearing pants that need to be pulled up. "My mother and father have always been there for me, in anything I do . . . to make me a better person," McNabb stated. "That's where it all starts. They gave me guidance and advice, whether I asked for it or not. They've been my number one fans, and my number one critics."

HOBBIES AND OTHER INTERESTS

McNabb tries to lead a normal life outside of football. He enjoys relaxing with friends, playing video games, watching movies, and attending Philadelphia 76ers basketball games. "I do the same things everybody else does. It's just you might see me on Sunday playing football," he said. "People say, 'He's in the NFL, his head's going to blow up. He's a young guy. He doesn't know what he has.' Man, I know what I have. It's just that I don't show people. I just take things in stride, know what I'm saying? You won't see me in flashy cars or flashy clothes. That's just me."

> "My mother and father have always been there for me, in anything I do . . . to make me a better person," McNabb stated. "That's where it all starts. They gave me guidance and advice, whether I asked for it or not. They've been my number one fans, and my number one critics."

McNabb enjoys using his wealth and fame to help others. For example, he donated $100,000 to help renovate the football locker room at Syracuse University. "I am delighted to pay back, in some small way, all that I have gained from having graduated from Syracuse University and for having been a part of the great Syracuse football tradition," he said of the gift. "It's just a little appreciation for everything that they've done throughout my college career." In 2002 the university invited McNabb to become the youngest member on its board of trustees. McNabb has also donated money for scholarships to help deserving students attend Mt. Carmel High School.

The cause that is closest to McNabb's heart is the fight against diabetes. Diabetes is a disease in which the body does not produce or properly use insulin, a chemical that aids in the digestion of sugar. It is a serious, chronic condition that has no cure. The disease often causes complications such as blindness, heart disease, and kidney failure. Diabetes affects over 15 million people in the United States and is the nation's seventh-leading cause of death. McNabb's grandmother died from diabetes, and his father has been diagnosed with the disease. "My father Samuel was diagnosed with Type 2 diabetes five years ago," he noted. "What both of us learned along the way motivated us to help people avoid or minimize the consequences of this terrible disease."

McNabb serves as a national spokesperson for the American Diabetes Association. He also sponsors an all-star weekend each year to raise money for diabetes research. The event includes a football clinic with several big-name NFL players, a gala awards dinner, a prayer brunch, and a celebrity all-star basketball game. Finally, McNabb is active in charitable events in the Philadelphia area. For example, every year at Christmastime he dresses up as Santa Claus and distributes gifts to needy children at a local community center. In addition to his charity work, McNabb also does a lot of paid endorsements. One of his favorites is a humorous commercial for Campbell's Chunky Soup that also features his mother.

HONORS AND AWARDS

Big East Conference Rookie of the Year: 1995
First Team All-Big East Conference Quarterback: 1995, 1996, 1997, 1998
Big East Conference Offensive Player of the Year: 1996, 1997, 1998
Gator Bowl Most Valuable Player: 1996
Big East Conference Player of the Year (*Football News*): 1998
Big East Conference Player of the Decade: 1990s
NFL Player of the Year (CBS Radio): 2000
Offensive Most Valuable Player (Philadelphia Eagles): 2000
Terry Bradshaw Award (Fox Sports): 2000
NFL Pro Bowl: 2000, 2001, 2002
Wanamaker Award (City of Philadelphia): 2002

FURTHER READING

Books

Contemporary Black Biography, Vol. 29, 2001
Who's Who among African Americans, 2002

Periodicals

Chicago Sun-Times, July 21, 1992, p.74
Fort Lauderdale Sun-Sentinel, Dec. 29, 1998, p.C8
New York Times, Aug. 25, 1996, Sec. 8, p.7
Philadelphia Daily News, Sep. 6, 2001, p.E3; Jan. 18, 2002, p.E8; May 18, 2002, Sec. Local, p.3; Jan. 13, 2003, Sec. Sports, p.120; Jan. 20, 2003, Sports sec., p.134

Philadelphia Inquirer, July 22, 1999, p.D1; July 31, 1999, p.C1; Dec. 5, 1999, p.A1; Jan. 18, 2002, p.E4; Sep. 28, 2002, p.D1; Nov. 18, 2002, p.A1; Jan. 13, 2003, p.D6; Jan. 18, 2003, p.D1; Jan. 20, 2003, p.E14; Jan. 22, 2003, p.D7
Sporting News, Apr. 20, 1998, p.59; Dec. 18, 2000, p.18; June 18, 2001, p.52
Sports Illustrated, Aug. 1, 1996, p.50; May 17, 1999, p.38; July 30, 2001, p.58; Jan. 28, 2002, p.38; Jan. 20, 2003, p.44; Jan. 27, 2003, p.48
Sports Illustrated for Kids, Sep. 1, 2001, p.41
St. Louis Post-Dispatch, Sep. 9, 2001, p.E1
USA Today, Jan. 20, 2003, p.C6

Online Articles

http://www.phillyhealthandfitness.com/Interviews/McNabb.htm
(*Philly Health and Fitness,* "The Sorcery behind the Spiral: McNabbracadabra!" Dec. 2, 2002)
http://www.superbowl.com/insider/story/6111179
(*NFL Insider,* "McNabb: If I Have to Run, I'll Run," Jan. 7, 2003)

Online Database

Biography Resource Center Online, 2003, article from *Contemporary Black Biography,* 2001

ADDRESS

Donovan McNabb
Philadelphia Eagles
One Navacare Way
Philadelphia, PA 19145

WORLD WIDE WEB SITES

http://www.donovanmcnabb.com
http://www.nfl.com/players/playerpage/133361
http://www.philadelphiaeagles.com/store/the_team/players.asp?id=2
http://www.jockbio.com/Bios/McNabb/McNabb_bio.html

Nelly 1974-

American Rap Artist
Creator of the Chart-Topping CDs *Country Grammar*
and *Nellyville*

BIRTH

Nelly was born Cornell Haynes, Jr., on November 2, 1974, in
Austin, Texas. Nelly's record company, however, has repeatedly claimed that he was born in the late 1970s to make it appear
that he is closer in age to rap music's teenage fan base. His
nickname is actually a shortened version of "Nelly Nel," which
he was called in his youth. Nelly's father is Cornell Haynes,

Sr., who served as a non-commissioned officer in the U.S. Air Force. His mother, Rhonda Mack, worked in fast food restaurants. Nelly's parents divorced when he was seven years old. He is the only offspring of his parents' marriage, but he is believed to have a half-sister and a step-brother.

YOUTH

When Nelly was a small child, he and his mother followed his father on military assignments around the world. They eventually settled in St. Louis, where they lived in a poor neighborhood filled with condemned buildings and empty lots. After his parents divorced, Nelly remained with his mother. But Rhonda Mack became concerned about the influence of older neighborhood boys on her son. In addition, she decided that she could not support her son on the modest wages she earned at fast food restaurants. As a result, she sent him to live with various relatives and friends over the next several years. "I never spent more than three years in one household," Nelly said. "I had to basically raise myself because I was constantly on the move. I learned to depend on myself, which is good, but as a kid you look at it like, 'Why don't nobody want me?'"

> "I never spent more than three years in one household," Nelly said. "I had to basically raise myself because I was constantly on the move. I learned to depend on myself, which is good, but as a kid you look at it like, 'Why don't nobody want me?'"

This unsettled existence continued until Nelly's teen years, when his mother managed to find a home for them in University City, a middle-class, integrated suburb of St. Louis near Washington University. Nelly's mother hoped that as her son became accustomed to his new home, he would be less vulnerable to street gangs and other negative influences.

At first, the move to University City seemed to be a positive one for Nelly. He started playing baseball — a game at which he proved to be very talented — and became a big fan of hip-hop and rap artists such as LL Cool J, Run-DMC, Goodie Mob, OutKast, and Jay-Z. He soon discovered that he possessed a gift for rhyming and storytelling, and before long he was spinning out rap songs of his own.

For a while it appeared that Nelly might be headed for a career as a professional baseball player. A star shortstop in the St. Louis Amateur Baseball

Nelly's favorite rap subjects include partying, women, and cars.

Association, his performance caught the attention of a number of major league scouts. He was even invited to training camps held by the Atlanta Braves and the Pittsburgh Pirates. But Nelly lacked the discipline and dedication that the sport required. Instead of focusing on baseball, he became heavily involved in dealing drugs and other illegal activities. "I wanted the cars, I wanted the jewelry. I wanted all that [crap] I didn't really need at the time," Nelly confessed. "So I kind of got out of the baseball thing and went back to the 'hood."

EDUCATION

Nelly attended eight different schools in 12 years. Throughout, his school record was marked by poor grades, fights, and expulsions for disruptive behavior. In fact, he was expelled from four different schools during his youth. "He was a handful," agreed his mother, "but what child isn't?" By the time he reached high school, his studies had taken a back seat to making money. At first, he earned his money honestly by working as a cashier at McDonald's and loading trucks for the United Parcel Service (UPS). But as time passed, he turned to drug dealing and street crimes to put money in his wallet.

As a senior at University City High School in 1993, however, Nelly became involved in a musical venture that changed his life forever. He joined together with Robert "Kyjuan" Cleveland, Tohri "Murphy Lee" Harper, "Big Lee" Ali Jones, Corey "Slo Down" Edwards, and Lavell "City Spud" Webb. Together they formed a rap group called the St. Lunatics, an African-American nickname for "St. Louis." As the weeks passed by, music became a positive outlet for the group's members. In fact, Nelly and the other group members made a vow to each other that they would stay away from illegal activities and focus instead on getting jobs and earning enough money to record their songs.

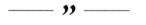

> **"We said, yo, let's not talk about killing and robbing," explained one St. Lunatics member. "Let's just talk about partying and having fun, get the whole world — black people, white people — into our music."**

At first, the St. Lunatics performed "gangsta' rap," in which inner-city violence and crime are major themes. But when "Big Lee" left the group to attend college, it made the other members think about life beyond the streets of St. Louis. When Big Lee came home to visit, he advised his fellow band members to listen to other rap groups and develop a sound that would set their own music apart. Day after day, Nelly and his friends went to the studio to work on developing their own unique style. They finally decided that instead of performing rap tunes about street life and crime, they would write songs with a more positive message. "We said, yo, let's not talk about killing and robbing," explained Ali Jones. "Let's just talk about partying and having fun, get the whole world — black people, white people — into our music."

CAREER HIGHLIGHTS

Climbing to the Top

In 1996 the St. Lunatics recorded a song called "Gimme What Ya Got" that a local newspaper described as a "a heavy-on-the-bass ditty that challenges rappers to come up with decent lyrics." Nelly and his friends quickly distributed the song to record stores and radio stations around the city. To everyone's surprise, it became the number one tune on the most popular hip-hop station in St. Louis, and it eventually sold 10,000 copies.

Nelly poses with members of the St. Lunatics.

Energized by the success of "Gimme What Ya Got," the St. Lunatics put together another single called "Who's the Boss," which was also a local hit. But despite these successes, the group failed to attract the attention of the big rap record labels. Executives with the major rap record companies seemed to be interested only in rap artists based in New York, Los Angeles, and other major cities on the East and West Coasts. The group decided that its best bet for success was for Nelly, who had the rhyming skills and stage presence to sell himself as a solo artist, to seek a recording contract on his own. If he succeeded, he would be able to help the rest of the group reach stardom as well.

In 1999 Nelly secured a solo recording contract with Fo'Reel Entertainment/Universal Records. "When I met Nelly, his whole charisma and style [were] just different," recalled Fo'Reel executive Cudda Love. "Like when you heard [the rap artist Notorious] B.I.G. for the first time, he didn't sound like anybody. 2Pac didn't sound like anybody. Snoop Dogg didn't sound like anybody. It was the same way with Nelly."

Country Grammar

After signing with Universal, Nelly called on the St. Lunatics to join him in the recording studio. Backed by his old friends, Nelly released his first solo effort on the Universal label in 2000. Called *Country Grammar*—a reference to the local dialect spoken by black communities in St. Louis—the

Nelly's Country Grammar *made the rap artist a nationally recognized star.*

album caused an immediate sensation in the music world. It quickly rose to number one on the *Billboard* album charts and stayed there for several weeks. The single most popular track on the CD was the title song, "Country Grammar," which showcased Nelly's ability to combine singing with rapping. It also highlighted the singer's ability to build a song out of simple elements. For example, the tune's refrain — "down, down baby" — was taken from a children's game that Nelly and his friends had played while growing up. The single ultimately reached the top of the *Billboard* rap singles chart and stayed there longer than any other rap song released that year.

The runaway success of *Country Grammar* put St. Louis on the hip-hop map. Reviewers noted that the songs on *Country Grammar* had a different style than those performed by popular East and West coast rappers. Nelly's songs did explore many of the same themes as rap songs from the coasts, such as sex, crime, violence, and expensive cars. But the influence of St. Louis, where the blues and jazz are very popular, could be clearly heard throughout Nelly's work. Many music critics loved Nelly's approach. *Time,* for example, praised the album for "what many other current hip-hop releases lack: strong, sure hooks. The rhythms are vigorous, the production is crisp, and Nelly's rapping manages to be both laid back and engaging." Several songs on the album, including "Batter Up" and "Steal the Show," featured the St. Lunatics, and it was clear that Nelly had no intention of leaving the group behind. "The biggest surprise on *Country Grammar,*" said the *Washington Post,* "is Nelly's crew. The St. Lunatics appear on most of the album and . . . each member seems to be a credible talent in his own right."

Country Grammar sold 10 million copies in the two years following its release, surpassing the sales of such established stars as Eminem, Britney Spears, and 'N Sync. Nelly also raked in an array of honors for the recording, including a 2000 World Music Award (as Best-Selling New Artist) and two Grammy nominations. He was even invited to perform at the 2001 Super Bowl. But as Nelly's fame and fortune grew, he also drew criticism from some people for his lyrics and subject matter. Many listeners were offended by his swearing and his album's focus on sex and partying. St. Louis Mayor Clarence Harmon even refused to issue a proclamation honoring the local rap artist in 2000 because one of his song titles contained a four-letter word.

"When I met Nelly, his whole charisma and style [were] just different," said one record executive. "Like when you heard [the rap artist Notorious] B.I.G. for the first time, he didn't sound like anybody. 2Pac didn't sound like anybody. Snoop Dogg didn't sound like anybody. It was the same way with Nelly."

Less than six months after the release of *Country Grammar,* Nelly starred in *Snipes,* an independent movie set in the world of hip-hop. He plays the role of a rap star named Prolifik who is kidnapped by gang members the night before his highly anticipated first album is scheduled for release. After the film's release, director Richard Murray gave high marks to Nelly for his professionalism. "I know how musicians and recording artists approach acting," he said. "They take it as a joke. No such case with Nelly. He really approached it from a standpoint of someone taking the challenge as an actor." Unfortunately, the film did not attract large numbers of moviegoers, and it received mostly harsh reviews. A critic writing for the *Indianapolis Recorder*, for example, claimed that the film "reduces the African-American inner-city experience to a glorified ghetto . . . where guns, knives, expletives, and racial epithets lead and reason lags far behind."

Back to the Recording Studio

Nelly used his success with *Country Grammar* to help the St. Lunatics land a record deal of their own with Universal. He also performed with them on the resulting CD, which was released in 2001. Unfortunately, one of the group's members was not around to share in the achievement: Lavell Webb — known as "City Spud" to the St. Lunatics — had been sent to prison in November 1999 for his involvement in an armed robbery. The group named their album *Free City* in his honor, and Nelly started wearing a Band-Aid on his left cheek as a "symbol of solidarity" with City Spud.

> *"I don't sound like anyone [else], I've got a style that's all my own,"* declared Nelly. *"I like to think of my music as a jazz form of hip-hop."*

Bristling with head-bobbing rhythms and lyrics celebrating a hard-partying lifestyle, the songs on *Free City* immediately caused a buzz in the music world. The album debuted at No. 3 on the Billboard 200 album charts, and it eventually sold more than one million copies. *Free City* also confirmed the St. Lunatics' pride in their St. Louis roots. The band members even chose the song "Midwest Swing," which describes their hometown in positive terms, as the album's lead single.

Indeed, while some other popular singers and bands have tried to downplay their local origins so that their music will appeal to the widest possible audience, Nelly has never tried to deny his Midwestern background. Nelly's brand of rap "has a relaxed feel that gives the rhythms and the rhymes their distinctive flavor," the London *Independent* observed. But Nelly himself prefers the word "swing" — the jazzy form of hip-hop characteristic of St. Louis — to describe his more "soulful" style of rap. "Swing is a Midwest thing," Nelly explained to one interviewer. "It's in our walk, the way we dance, our swagger."

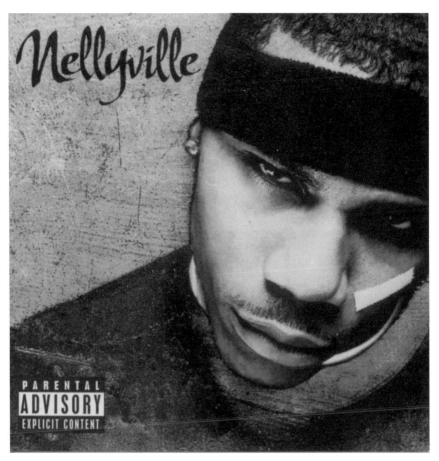

Nellyville *featured hit tracks such as "Hot in Herre" and "Dilemma."*

Nellyville

Shortly after the release of Free City, Nelly and the St. Lunatics joined the 2001 MTV Total Request Live Tour. Nelly then returned to the recording studio, where he put together his second solo album for Universal. The final product, called *Nellyville,* was released in 2002. As with his earlier recordings, Nelly paid tribute to his hometown in a song. The title track describes an idealized version of the crime-ridden neighborhood in which he grew up. "Imagine blocks and blocks of no cocaine with no gunplay/ ain't nobody shot, so ain't no news that day," Nelly sings, adding that in his dream world, everyone has "40 acres and a pool/6 bedrooms, 4 baths with a jacuzz/6-car garage, full paved and smooth/Full front and back deck/Enough room to land a jet."

Another *Nellyville* song, called "#1," describes what it's like to be a hip-hop star. The tune was selected for the soundtrack of the movie *Training Day,* starring Denzel Washington. But it also triggered angry words from hip-hop artist KRS-One. He felt that Nelly's song was full of empty boasts and claimed that one of the song's lines — "Boat sank and it ain't left the dock, mad /cause I'm hot, he just mad 'cause he's not" — was aimed directly at him. KRS-One also accused Nelly of "selling out" because he invited white pop artists like 'N Sync's Justin Timberlake to make guest appearances on the album.

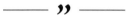

> "I think that nowadays people are turning to music for the positive side," said Nelly. "With all the stuff that been going on in the world, I think people are starting to realize that, yo, maybe we do need to chill out a little more."

Critical reaction to *Nellyville* was mixed as well. *Rolling Stone* claimed that Nelly had "one of the catchiest rhyme flows to ever hit the pop charts" and praised him for being "clear-eyed about his success, his art, who he is and where he's headed." But the magazine accused him of "going through the motions" on some of his songs. *Time,* meanwhile, called Nelly's rhymes "emptier than the St. Louis arch," but admitted that he "raps in a Southern-inflected sing-song so bouncy and joy-filled that he could read the Cardinals' box scores and the world would bob its collective head." For his part, Nelly strongly defends his emphasis on partying and fun times in his lyrics. "I think that nowadays people are turning to music for the positive side," he said. "With all the stuff that been going on in the world, I think people are starting to realize that, yo, maybe we do need to chill out a little more."

In any event, negative comments from critics did not seem to have any effect on the album's sales. *Nellyville* sold two million copies within a month of its release, and it eventually netted Nelly two Grammy Awards and six Billboard Music Awards. Two of the tracks on *Nellyville* proved particularly popular. "Hot in Herre" (pronounced "hurr" in imitation of the way people from St. Louis draw out their r's) describes a party in which everyone is so hot they start taking their clothes off. "Dilemma," which featured singer Kelly Rowland from Destiny's Child, tells the story of a young woman with a baby who isn't happy with the baby's father but can't seem to turn her back on him. "Dilemma" climbed to the top spot on the Billboard charts

Nelly performs with Kelly Rowland at the 2003 Grammy Awards.

and stayed there for 10 weeks, the longest period in which any rap song had claimed the No. 1 spot. When asked to explain the popularity of these and other songs, Nelly simply declared that "I don't sound like anyone [else]. I've got a style that's all my own. . . . I like to think of my music as a jazz form of hip-hop."

Reaching Out to Kids

During his recording career, Nelly has paid tribute to his St. Louis roots in several songs. But he has also devoted time and money to improving the lives of the children growing up in the city's poorest neighborhoods. After the release of his first album, he started visiting inner city high schools to try to convince kids not to drop out. And after *Nellyville* rocketed to the top of the charts, he promised to make appearances at St. Louis schools on days when state-required standardized tests were being given. He and the St. Lunatics subsequently popped up to play basketball and talk to stu-

Nelly and fellow rapper P. Diddy (left) perform during a 2003 appearance on the "Tonight Show."

dents at a number of schools in inner-city St. Louis. School administrators later claimed that Nelly's efforts gave a tremendous boost to school attendance.

In 2002 Missouri Governor Bob Holden issued a proclamation praising Nelly and the St. Lunatics for their involvement in the schools. Some people criticized the proclamation, given the rough language and heavy sexual content of their songs. But the governor's office defended the decision. "The governor is not saying he agrees with the lyrics' content," said a spokesperson. "But what he does agree with is . . . that these young men used their success to improve the quality of education in St. Louis."

HOME AND FAMILY

Nelly has one daughter, Chanel, and one son, Cornell III (who is called Tre). He and the children's mother were together for several years, but he does not like to comment publicly on the current status of their relationship. "Right now, we each do our thing, and take care of the kids the way it's supposed to be."

When he is not touring, Nelly lives in St. Louis, where he currently owns two houses. "I'm just more of a Midwest guy," he likes to say. He bought one of the houses for his mother, Rhonda Mack, who retired in 2000 after 30 years in the fast food business. Today, Mack, who describes herself as her son's biggest fan, helps manage Nelly's charitable activities.

MAJOR INFLUENCES

One of Nelly's first childhood heroes was Ozzie Smith, a defensive shortstop for the St. Louis Cardinals baseball team in the 1980s and 1990s. "I wanted to be him. He had fundamentals and flash," he says. "Ozzie was the best shortstop ever. I used to do back flips when I played shortstop because he did it. I wanted to be Number One because that's the number he wore."

Nelly also admires pop star Michael Jackson. "He was the king, regardless of what he's doing or how he looks today. He's like history—he captured the whole world. He paved the way for a lot of [us]."

HOBBIES AND OTHER INTERESTS

Nelly still loves to play baseball, although he does not play as often as he would like. "I don't get much free time," Nelly admits, "so when I have some I really just like to chill out. It depends on where I am. If I'm at home in St. Louis, I'll go to the community center and play with the same Little League guys I've been playing with since I was 12."

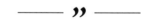

"I don't get much free time," Nelly admits, "so when I have some I really just like to chill out.... If I'm at home in St. Louis, I'll go to the community center and play with the same Little League guys I've been playing with since I was 12."

Nelly has used the proceeds from his albums to establish a foundation called 4Sho4Kids. This charitable organization seeks to improve the quality of life for children with developmental disabilities, especially those born with Down Syndrome or drug addictions. "A large portion of my audience is kids and if I can help them as well as they've supported me, it's beautiful for both sides," Nelly declared. In addition, the rap star has expressed interest in starting a nationwide donor drive on behalf of patients in need of bone marrow transplants. With this purpose in mind, Nelly's foundation has announced a "Jes Us 4 Jackie" campaign. The campaign is named for his sister Jackie Donahue, who suffers from leukemia and needs a bone marrow transplant to help her fight off the disease.

Nelly's commercial ventures include a line of urban streetwear for young men between the ages of 13 and 30 called Vokal (Very Organized Kids Always Learning). To promote Vokal, he recently became one of the first African-Americans to become part-owner of a NASCAR racing team. He hopes to hire a minority driver for the team some day. In addition, Nelly has started a production/management company to represent up-and-coming rap and hip-hop artists from the St. Louis area.

RECORDINGS

Country Grammar, 2000
Free City, 2001 (with the St. Lunatics)
Nellyville, 2002

HONORS AND AWARDS

Source Award: 2000 (two awards), Best New Artist of the Year and Best
    Album of the Year, for *Country Grammar*
BET Award (Black Entertainment Television): 2001, Best New Artist
MTV Video Music Award: 2001, Best Rap Video, for "Ride Wit Me"
Soul Train Music Award: 2001, Best R&B/Soul or Rap New Artist, for
    "Country Grammar"; 2003, for Entertainer of the Year
American Music Award: 2002, Favorite Rap/Hip-Hop Artist
Grammy Award: 2003 (two awards), Best Male Rap Solo Performance, for
    "Hot in Herre," and Best Rap/Sung Collaboration (with Kelly Rowland)
    for "Dilemma"
American Music Award: 2003, Fan Choice Artist

FURTHER READING

Books

Contemporary Black Biography, 2002

Periodicals

Current Biography Yearbook, 2002
Daily Telegraph (London), Nov. 2, 2000, p.25
Ebony, Sep. 2002, p.142
Entertainment Weekly, Aug. 2, 2002, p.38
Indianapolis Recorder, Sep. 6, 2002, p.3

Interview, Sep. 2002, p.88
Jet, July 30, 2001, p.32
Los Angeles Times, July 21, 2002, p.F4
New York Times, June 23, 2002, p.L1
Newsweek, Nov. 11, 2002, p.71
Rolling Stone, Nov. 9, 2000, p.55; Sep. 14, 2000, p.64
Seventeen, Mar. 2003, p.147
USA Today, Sep. 29, 2000, p.E5; Sep. 3, 2002, p.D1
YM, Apr. 2003, p.6

Online Databases

Biography Resource Center Online, 2003, article from *Contemporary Black Biography,* 2002

ADDRESS

Nelly
Uptown/Universal Records
1755 Broadway
New York, NY 10019

WORLD WIDE WEB SITES

http:// www.nelly.net

Andy Roddick 1982-

American Professional Tennis Player
Winner of Five Career Association of Tennis
Professionals (ATP) Tournaments

BIRTH

Andy Roddick — known to his friends as "A-Rod" — was born
on August 30, 1982, in Omaha, Nebraska. His father, Jerry, was
a private investor and businessman. His mother, Blanche, was
a schoolteacher and homemaker. He has two older brothers,
Lawrence and John.

YOUTH

Roddick's family moved to Austin, Texas, when he was five years old. But Andy still considers Omaha his hometown. "It's small-town USA, I guess," he stated. "I was brought up with good family values. You won't find people there with a lot of attitude, I'm pretty laid back mentally. I haven't been back to Nebraska for a few years now, what with all the traveling, but I suppose there's a lot of the state still in me."

Older Brothers Fire Competitive Instincts

Roddick grew up in a competitive family that enjoyed all kinds of sports. Both of his older brothers were good athletes, and Andy followed them around and tried to imitate them from an early age. His brother Lawrence was a competitive diver who eventually made the U.S. Senior National Team. Young Andy often accompanied him to the pool and jumped off of the 30-foot-high diving platform. "I would see him do it and try to copy him," he remembered. "Of course, it would usually end up with me doing a belly flop."

His brother John was an outstanding junior tennis player. Inspired by John's success, Andy began taking tennis lessons at the age of six, and he played in his first tournament a year later. He also spent hours in the garage playing imaginary matches against the great professional tennis players of the era. "Oh yeah, I destroyed all the big names — [Pete] Sampras, Andre Agassi, Boris Becker, you name it," he recalled. "Of course I did it when I was eight, practicing in my garage."

In 1993, the Roddick family moved from Austin to Boca Raton, Florida, so that John could attend a tennis academy and play year-round. Andy attended many of his brother's matches and dreamed of equaling his accomplishments. "I remember being in the newspaper once when they took a picture of him and I was in the background," he noted. "I was all stoked because my hat was in the picture. I was like, 'Yeah man, I'm famous!'" John Roddick went on to become a three-time all-American at the University of Georgia. Although John's hopes for a professional career were ended by a back injury, he became a successful college tennis coach.

A Rising Star in Junior Tennis

When the Roddick family moved to Florida, 11-year-old Andy began concentrating on tennis as well. For a while he trained under Rick Macci, a well-known tennis coach who contributed to the early development of top

———— **"** ————

"I would say it was the most embarrassing day I've ever had. I was 12, I guess, and I was playing this kid I didn't like. I thought he'd cheated once before. I just did not like this kid at all. I lost the first set and this kid was really annoying. So he runs up to the net, hits a little ball, and I hit it as hard as I can right at him. But he ducks and it goes out. And instead of calling it out, he gives me the finger. This drove me nuts. I lost it. 'I hate you! You're so mean!' I was shouting. I couldn't express my anger. So Mom came up and said: 'All right, you're off the court.'"

———— **"** ————

women's players Venus and Serena Williams. Although Roddick became a star in junior tennis, his parents made sure that he kept his feet on the ground. His mother, in particular, would not tolerate bad manners and once pulled Andy off the court in the middle of a match. "I would say it was the most embarrassing day I've ever had," he remembered. "I was 12, I guess, and I was playing this kid I didn't like. I thought he'd cheated once before. I just did not like this kid at all. I lost the first set and this kid was really annoying. So he runs up to the net, hits a little ball, and I hit it as hard as I can right at him. But he ducks and it goes out. And instead of calling it out, he gives me the finger. This drove me nuts. I lost it. 'I hate you! You're so mean!' I was shouting. I couldn't express my anger. So Mom came up and said: 'All right, you're off the court.'"

As Roddick made his way up through the ranks of junior tennis, his main goal was to earn a college scholarship, like his brother had done. But in 1998 two factors combined to make Roddick raise his goals. First, he started an impressive growth spurt that added almost a foot to his height, which improved his chances of becoming a professional tennis player. Second, he began working with a new coach, Tarik Benhabiles. "It was during a rain delay at the American Junior Nationals," Roddick recalled of the chance first encounter with Benhabiles. "Mom and I were sitting under the same canopy as him. We just starting talking and it turned out he lived three streets away from me." Benhabiles had reached the top 20 himself on the professional tennis tour and had also coached French pros Cedric Pioline and Nicolas Escude into the world rankings.

With the help of Benhabiles, Roddick made rapid improvements in both his mental and physical game. "It's so important to have the right people, to be around positive people," said his mother. "The kid has to look in his coach's eyes and has to see that he believes in him." Benhabiles felt that his new student had the potential to be a solid professional tennis player. "He has no holes in his game. He is a powerful player but also has finesse in his game. He moves unbelievably well for his size," the coach said. "Andy's work ethic and his intensity level are tremendous for a kid his age. I tell him not to worry about the future, because if his dedication stays the same, there's no limit."

EDUCATION

Roddick attended a private high school called Boca Prep. He maintained a 3.5 grade point average, even though he freely admits he was "not the most studious guy in the world." Roddick was a popular student who often entertained his classmates and annoyed his teachers. "I was the class clown at high school," he recalled. "Smart comments and stuff. There was this one teacher that would make me write 500-word essays as punishment whenever I spoke out of turn or did something bad. So one Sunday I decided I'd write five or six of 'em and when she said, 'Write, 500-word essay!' I just pulled one right out of my desk. She made me write 1,000 for that one."

Against the advice of his tennis coach, Roddick played on his school's varsity basketball team. In fact, he once snuck out of his parents' house to play in a big game. "I looked at the newspaper the next day and there was Andy's name," his mother remembered. "Zero points. Five rebounds. Hmm. And he told me he was just going out with his friends for a while." Roddick graduated from Boca Prep in May 2000. Although tennis commitments forced him to miss his graduation ceremony, he did attend the senior prom, where he was named Prom King. After graduation, Roddick put his college plans on hold to play professional tennis.

"I was the class clown at high school. Smart comments and stuff. There was this one teacher that would make me write 500-word essays as punishment whenever I spoke out of turn or did something bad. So one Sunday I decided I'd write five or six of 'em and when she said, 'Write, 500-word essay!' I just pulled one right out of my desk. She made me write 1,000 for that one."

Roddick returning a serve at the Monte Carlo Tennis Open, April 2002.

CAREER HIGHLIGHTS

Turning Pro

By the time Roddick turned professional during the 2000 season, he had already gained a reputation as one of the biggest servers in the game. His serves sometimes reached speeds of 140 miles per hour, and some observers claimed that he might someday beat Greg Rusedski's record serve of 149 miles per hour. In addition to his overpowering first serve, Roddick had a strong second serve, a good baseline game, and a high-energy, enthusiastic court presence.

In 2000, Roddick appeared in some professional tournaments while also continuing to play junior tennis. At one professional tournament in Washington, D.C., he defeated players ranked 24th, 61st, and 89th in the world before losing to Agassi in the quarterfinals. By the end of the year, Roddick's world ranking had rocketed from 800 to 160. Meanwhile, he won the junior division of the Australian Open and the U.S. Open. These two events, along with the French Open and Wimbledon, make up the Grand Slam of tennis, the most presigious events on the pro tour. He also finished the season as the world's top-ranked junior player, becoming the first American man to achieve this feat in eight years.

In 2001—his first full season on the professional tennis tour—Roddick earned a string of impressive victories that convinced some observers that he represented the future of American men's tennis. The first indication of his talent came in March, when he defeated Pete Sampras at the Ericsson Open in Miami, Florida. Sampras had won a record 13 Grand Slam titles over the course of his 13-year career, making him one of the best tennis players in history. Roddick admitted that it felt strange to face one of his childhood idols across the net. "I was trying to keep it just another match," he recalled. "Then, during the warm-up, I kind of sneaked a look over the net and thought, 'Oooohhh-kaaayyy, I'm playing Pete Sampras, in front of 15,000 people, and it's on national television.'"

Roddick quickly overcame his nerves and began blasting away with his powerful serve. Over the course of the match, he hit seven aces, winning serves that go untouched by the opposing player. Some of his serves were so fast that Sampras was unable to get out of the way. "He just throws it up and swings as hard as he can," Sampras noted. "A couple of them went into my body, just kind of caught me off guard. He really can crack it pretty good." To the amazement of the crowd, Roddick dominated the match and went on to become the first player outside the top 100 to beat Sampras in seven years. Afterward, Sampras had nothing but praise for the rookie: "The way he played today, the future of American tennis is looking very good. The way he competes and the way he plays, he really is the future." But Roddick tried to deflect some of the praise. "I'm not a hero. I'm a tennis player," he stated. "I'm not the president or anything special. Pete Sampras and Andre Agassi are still my heroes."

> *Roddick admitted that it felt strange to face one of his childhood idols across the net. "I was trying to keep it just another match. Then, during the warm-up, I kind of sneaked a look over the net and thought, 'Oooohhh-kaaayyy, I'm playing Pete Sampras, in front of 15,000 people, and it's on national television.'"*

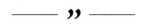

Claiming His First Professional Tournament Victory

In April 2001, Roddick won his first professional tournament at the Verizon Tennis Challenge in Atlanta, Georgia. He claimed the title in only his tenth event as a pro—faster than such American greats as Agassi, Sampras, Michael Chang, or Jim Courier. "Last year, I was going in to compete. I was basically going to the court to take my beating and then leave," Roddick said afterward. "This year, I thought if I played well and stuck around, I could get some opportunities, and I did."

———— **"** ————

Roddick learned about the power of crowd support at this tournament, when his semifinal match was interrupted by a several-hour rain delay. "Finally, at 11 p.m., we got back out to finish and there were still about 250 fans, all psyched to see the end of the match," he remembered. "I was feeling sluggish, not into playing, until I saw those fans. Then all of a sudden I really wanted to win. They got me pumped. I won . . . and as I signed autographs, the fans were thanking me. I thought it should be the other way around. "

———— **"** ————

Roddick proved that the victory had been no fluke a week later, when he captured his second career title at the U.S. Men's Clay Court Championships in Houston, Texas. Roddick learned about the power of crowd support at this tournament, when his semifinal match was interrupted by a several-hour rain delay. "Finally, at 11 p.m., we got back out to finish and there were still about 250 fans, all psyched to see the end of the match," he remembered. "I was feeling sluggish, not into playing, until I saw those fans. Then all of a sudden I really wanted to win. They got me pumped. I won . . . and as I signed autographs, the fans were thanking me. I thought it should be the other way around. Something clicked in my head. Maybe I could thank them—in a different way. So I got the umpire's mike and announced that anyone who didn't have a ticket for the final the next day should go and pick one up at the box office on the way out, that it was on me."

At the French Open, his first Grand Slam event of the year (he did not play in the earlier Australian Open), Roddick played an epic second-round match against fellow American Michael Chang. Chang had won the French Open title 12 years earlier by overcoming terrible cramps to defeat Ivan Lendl. "One of the matches that got me interested in tennis was the one here between Michael and Ivan Lendl —you know, where Michael started cramping so badly, he served underhand," Roddick recalled. "But he hung in and won and went on to become the youngest player to win the French Open. That was 1989. I was six."

Strangely, history seemed to repeat itself during the match. Roddick began experiencing severe cramps during the fifth set, but he showed great determination and won the four-hour contest by a score of 5-7, 6-3, 6-4, 6-7 (5-7), 7-5. (In men's tennis, a player wins a match by defeating his opponent in 3 of 5 sets — except in the early rounds of some tournaments, when he must win 2 of 3 sets. The first player to win 6 games usually wins the set, but if the margin of victory is less than 2 games, the set is decided by a tie-breaker. Shorthand notation is often used to show the score of a tennis match. For example, 6-2, 4-6, 7-6 means that the player in question won the first set by a score of 6 games to 2, lost the next set 4 games to 6, and came back to win the match in a third-set tie-breaker.) Roddick hit a tournament record 37 aces during the match against Chang. "Relief, joy, you can't even explain moments like that," he said afterward. "I almost wanted to cry, but I wanted to scream and yell at the same time. That's what I play tennis for." Unfortunately, Roddick pulled a hamstring muscle during his third-round match against Lleyton Hewitt and was forced to retire from the tournament.

At the 2001 Grand Slam event at Wimbledon, Roddick lost in the third round to eventual winner Goran Ivanisevic. In August Roddick claimed his third career title at a tournament in Washington, D.C. Later that month he made it to the quarterfinals of the U.S. Open before suffering a heartbreaking five-set loss to eventual winner Lleyton Hewitt, 6-7 (7-5), 6-3, 6-4, 3-6, 6-4. Roddick was trailing in the fifth set when he hit a backhand that TV replays showed landed in his opponent's court. The line judge called the ball correctly, but umpire Jorge Dias overruled the call from his chair on the other side of the court. Roddick was outraged at what he felt was an irresponsible decision by the umpire. He went crazy on the court, yelling at the umpire and calling him a "moron." "That's the worst I've ever lost it on a tennis court, but I had a good reason to. He can't overrule that ball in that situation," Roddick explained. "No umpire in his right mind would make that call. That's not a ball he can say — and this is the rule of umpires — 'I saw it clearly, 100 percent, no doubt in my mind out.' If he can say that, he's a liar." The bad call threw off Roddick's concentration, and he lost the match a short time later.

Although the 2001 season held its share of disappointments for Roddick, he still performed remarkably well for such a young player. He claimed the first three tournament titles of his career, and he saw his world ranking rise from 160 to 16. He thus became the first American teenager to be ranked in the top 20 since Michael Chang a decade earlier. He was also selected to represent the United States as part of the Davis Cup team, which played a series of tournaments against other countries. Roddick won the only

Roddick at Wimbledon, June 2002.

match he played and became friends with several other American players, including Jan-Michael Gambill and Andre Agassi.

Continuing to Learn and Improve

Roddick started off the 2002 season with a bang, claiming his fourth career singles title in February at the Kroger St. Jude tournament in Memphis, Tennessee. He also played well on the Davis Cup team, winning his first seven matches of the year and clinching a victory for the American team over Spain. Roddick helped boost the Americans into the semifinals, where they lost to a strong French team. In April 2002 Roddick captured his fifth tournament victory in Houston, Texas, defeating Pete Sampras in the final.

Despite his success in lesser tournaments, some critics claimed that Roddick would not be considered among the top names in tennis until he won a Grand Slam event. But Roddick's string of bad luck continued in the 2002 Grand Slam tournaments. He was forced to retire in the second round of the Australian Open with an ankle sprain, then he lost in the first round at the French Open and in the third round at Wimbledon. "In Grand Slam, I just haven't put it together," he admitted. "But there's still some tennis to be played this year. I'm going to get back to the drawing board and see what I can do with the rest of it."

By August 2002, Roddick had broken into the top 10 in the world rankings. He played well at the U.S. Open and reached the quarterfinals, where he faced Pete Sampras. Fans and the media eagerly anticipated this match, which was billed as a battle between the current and future generations of American men's tennis. By that time Sampras had gone two years without winning a Grand Slam title, and some people wondered whether the aging champion's skills were fading. "I'm excited about playing Pete," Roddick said. "We're from the same country, from kind of generations that are overlapping. I grew up idolizing him. I have a great deal of respect for Pete and what he's done. It will be a very special moment for me out there. But, you know, having said that, I want to go out there and play some ball."

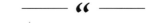

"I'm excited about playing Pete [Sampras]. We're from the same country, from kind of generations that are overlapping. I grew up idolizing him. I have a great deal of respect for Pete and what he's done. It will be a very special moment for me out there. But, you know, having said that, I want to go out there and play some ball."

Unfortunately for Roddick, the match was a bit of a letdown. Sampras proved his critics wrong and easily defeated the younger player in straight sets, 6-3, 6-2, 6-4. "It's a learning experience," Roddick said afterward. "I'll try my best to soak it up. I'll have my moment here someday. I'll have to keep working hard and take something away from these losses, as well as the wins." Sampras went on to win the U.S. Open championship—the 14th Grand Slam of his remarkable career.

High Hopes for the Future

As the 2002 season came to a close, Roddick had posted a career singles record of 98-40, with five titles and $1.8 million in prize money. He consid-

A smashing serve at the Mercedes-Benz Cup, July 2002.

ers himself fortunate to be able to make a living as a professional tennis player. "It is definitely something I dreamt about growing up," he stated. "I never thought it would come true, but now that it has I will never take a day of it for granted." Roddick has won over many tennis fans with his laid back style and his fun-loving, enthusiastic approach to the game. "I'm not good when I keep everything pent up inside," he explained. "I'm an emotional player. I'm sure I'll never be one of those players who never say anything. I like to leave it out there."

Despite his early success, Roddick remains committed to working hard and improving his game. "The fact that I am doing ok on tour now but feel that I have a lot of room for improvement keeps me optimistic about the future," he noted. "I don't know what the future holds. Your guess is as good as mine. But if I don't make it as big as Pete and Andre, which I probably won't, considering they're two of the greatest ever, I just said it's not going to be because of lack of hard work or effort on my part."

Many observers have commented that Roddick has the potential to fill the gap that will be left in men's tennis when the current generation of stars retire. "Andy will certainly help the men's game, because we all know the men's game can use a big kick in the butt," said Patrick McEnroe, captain of the U.S. Davis Cup team. "I think we're all wondering what's going to happen when Agassi and Sampras are gone—and Andy could be it. He has so much raw energy and enthusiasm. He enjoys the pressure and the challenge. He has the pizzazz." Although Roddick would love to achieve the success of his idols, he is determined to play his own game. "I said all along that I'm not going to replace Sampras and Agassi," he stated. "I'm going to try to do my own thing and hope that works out well."

"Andy will certainly help the men's game, because we all know the men's game can use a big kick in the butt," said Patrick McEnroe, captain of the U.S. Davis Cup team. "I think we're all wondering what's going to happen when Agassi and Sampras are gone—and Andy could be it. He has so much raw energy and enthusiasm. He enjoys the pressure and the challenge. He has the pizzazz."

HOME AND FAMILY

Roddick recently purchased a home in a gated community near Boca Raton. His top priority was peace and quiet, so he appreciates the fact that most of his neighbors are senior citizens. Roddick remains close to his parents and calls home often when he is traveling. "Whenever I need advice I first go to my parents," he stated. "For sure."

Roddick, who is single, claims that his lifestyle leaves little time for dating. "I'm starting to see how playing tennis around the globe doesn't exactly help the boyfriend-girlfriend thing," he admitted. "I'm not about to get married, but it would be great to have someone who I could just [hang out] with after matches."

HOBBIES AND OTHER INTERESTS

In his spare time, Roddick enjoys playing golf and basketball, riding mountain bikes and jet skis, listening to music, and shopping for furniture and decorations for his new house. He also likes watching sports on TV and is a big fan of the University of Nebraska Cornhuskers football team.

Roddick's good looks, outgoing personality, and success on the court have provided him with many opportunities outside of tennis. For example, he made a guest appearance on the TV series "Sabrina, the Teenage Witch," in which he taught star Melissa Joan Hart to play tennis. Roddick was included on *Us* magazine's list of the world's sexiest athletes, and he placed in the top 10 of a poll of the most marketable athletes in sports. His current sponsors include Reebok, Babalot rackets, Sports Authority, and Pristine trading cards.

FURTHER READING

Periodicals

Daily Telegraph (London), June 25, 2001, p.65
Fort Lauderdale Sun-Sentinel, Dec. 13, 1999, p.D12
Houston Chronicle, Apr. 21, 2002, p.1; Apr. 29, 2002, p.1
Los Angeles Times, Apr. 2, 2001, p.D5; June 2, 2001, p.D5; June 28, 2001, p.D7; July 15, 2001, p.D1; July 22, 2001, p.D3; Sep. 7, 2001, p.D1; Sep. 6, 2002, p.D1
Miami Herald, Dec. 14, 1999, p.D1
New York Times, Aug. 31, 2002, p.D5; Sep. 6, 2002, p.D1
Palm Beach Post, Sep. 11, 2000, p.C1; Mar. 26, 2001, p.C1; Mar. 3, 2002, p.B7; Aug. 26, 2002, p.C1
Rolling Stone, Sep. 27, 2001, p.48
Sports Illustrated, Feb. 21, 2000, p.R6
Sports Illustrated for Kids, July 1, 2002, p.41
Tennis, Dec. 2001/Jan. 2002, p.22; Feb. 2002, p.11; Apr. 2002, p.72; Sep. 2002, p.48
USA Today, Dec. 21, 1999, p.C16; Feb. 9, 2001, p.C8; Mar 28, 2001, p.C10; May 9, 2001, p.C1
Vogue, Sep. 2001, p.472

ADDRESS

Andy Roddick
ATP Tour
200 ATP Tour Boulevard
Ponte Vedra Beach, FL 32082

WORLD WIDE WEB SITES

http://www.andyroddick.com
http://www.atptennis.com
http://www.usopen.org

Gwen Stefani 1969-

American Singer and Songwriter
Lead Singer for the Rock Band No Doubt

BIRTH

Gwen Renee Stefani was born on October 3, 1969, in Fullerton, California. Her father, Dennis, is a marketing consultant. Her mother, Patricia, is a full-time homemaker. Both of her parents are devout Catholics of Italian descent. Stefani is one of four children. Her older brother Eric founded the band No Doubt in 1987 and later worked as an animator on the TV show "The Simpsons." She also has a younger sister, Jill, and a younger brother.

YOUTH

Stefani grew up in Anaheim, California, 30 miles south of downtown Los Angeles. The family's home was so close to Disneyland that ashes from the Disney fireworks displays sometimes floated into their front yard. Looking back on her childhood, Stefani claimed that she was an ordinary, suburban girl from a "goody-two-shoes" but warm and loving family. She also indicated that she was "chubby" throughout her youth, a condition that eventually prompted her to compete on her high school's swim team. "I joined the swim team because I wanted to get skinny," she said. "I grew up ten pounds overweight and never had a date."

Stefani was exposed to music at an early age. Her parents played folk music themselves, and they enjoyed listening to many different styles of music in their home. As a child, Stefani particularly liked soundtracks from such musicals as *Evita, Annie,* and *The Muppet Movie.* She especially loved the 1960s movie musical *The Sound of Music.* "The whole soundtrack is really special to my heart," she said.

Stefani's older brother Eric also loved music. "Growing up, my brother was the one with all the talent and all the focus," she recalled. "I had him, so I didn't have to do anything, you know?" She even credits Eric with introducing her to ska music, a form of dance music similar to reggae. "[Eric was] a really quirky, creative guy who discovered ska music, and we all became attracted to the hyperactivity and energy," she explained. "My brother was sort of the leader of the family so the rest of us became obsessed with it."

——— " ———

"I was rebellious in the sense that I wasn't into popular music," Stefani stated. "It was like, 'I'm into ska, nobody knows what it is. I'm cool, you're not.' I wasn't a cheerleader, never had a lot of girlfriends — just one best girlfriend."

——— " ———

By Stefani's teen years, ska music had achieved cult favorite status in Southern California. But she credits one particular ska band, called Madness, for her enduring affection for the musical genre. In 1983, when Stefani was about 14, she was thrilled to hear that Madness was opening for English rock star David Bowie at a nearby concert hall. "My brother got to go, but my dad said I was too young. I cried myself to sleep on the couch because Madness is my favorite band of all time," Stefani remembered. "The next thing I know, my mom put the phone on my ear, and it was my dad saying, 'Are you too tired to go to the concert? I got tickets.' I was mesmerized by Madness."

As a teen, Stefani even saw her love for ska music as a way of establishing a unique identity. "I was rebellious in the sense that I wasn't into popular music," she said. "It was like, 'I'm into ska, nobody knows what it is. I'm cool; you're not.' I wasn't a cheerleader, never had a lot of girlfriends—just one best girlfriend."

The other major area in which Stefani proclaimed her individuality was in the clothes she wore. "Ever since puberty, it has been all about doing something that was a little bit different from everyone else, while at the same time showing off my favorite features and hiding the ones I'm not a fan of," Stefani explained. During high school she combed through thrift stores or sewed her own clothes to get the look she wanted. Sometimes, her mother's skills as a seamstress came in handy as well. For example, her mother helped her make a high school prom dress that was a replica of the one Grace Kelly wore in the Alfred Hitchcock film, *Rear Window.* "I've always been obsessed with the days of the Hollywood starlet," Stefani declared.

> "When I look back at some of the horrible things people did to others in high school, it breaks my heart," Stefani said. "When you judge people and say things that may hurt someone else, it may go deeper than you think. So try to be as open-minded as you can. At this age, you're still trying to find yourself."

EDUCATION

Stefani grew up with a form of dyslexia, a type of learning disability that causes readers to confuse the order of letters in words. As a result, she struggled in many of her classes. "I had a really hard time learning in school," she admitted. For many years, she did not even know that she was suffering from a dyslexic condition. "I didn't know that and it was really challenging for me," she said. "I had horrible fights with my mom because I was frustrated that I couldn't learn."

Stefani also has mixed memories of high school's social scene. Her love for music blossomed during this period of her life, but she witnessed numerous instances when students were cruel to one another. "When I look back at some of the horrible things people did to others in high school, it breaks my heart," she said. "Think about the fact that you don't know everything about another person. You don't know where they are coming from. You don't know the circumstances in their family. For instance, one of my best friends and bandmates shot himself at age 18. We didn't even know the pain he was going through. . . . When you judge people and say things that may hurt someone else, it may go deeper than you think. So try to be as open-minded as you can. At this age, you're still trying to find yourself."

Despite her reading difficulties, Stefani graduated from Loara High School in Anaheim. She also attended Fullerton Junior College and California State University at Fullerton. "I wanted to be educated. I wanted to be a strong member of society and know what I was talking about," she said. "When I went to college, I said that I'm just going to try my hardest. Going to college saved me."

CAREER HIGHLIGHTS

Joining the Band

Stefani's brother Eric and a classmate named John Spence founded No Doubt as a ska band in December 1986. Named after Spence's habit of saying "no doubt" all the time, the band soon came to include Stefani. She initially shared lead and backing vocals with Spence, a high-energy performer known for his punk-style screaming and back-flips on stage. In December 1987, however, Spence shocked and saddened his bandmates by committing suicide. "He was a very important part of the band," Stefani said. "It still haunts us in a way. When your friend dies like that, and it's so unexpected, it's very traumatic. I think it taught us all a big lesson in how much one person can influence so many different people."

Less than two weeks after Spence died, the band kept an engagement in West Hollywood. During the show, a friend announced from the stage that it would be the band's last appearance. A short time later, though, the band members decided Spence would have wanted them to continue. His death turned out to be only the first of many hurdles that No Doubt would overcome over the years.

After Spence's suicide, Stefani was reluctant to take on the role of lead singer. For a year or so she shared the spotlight with bandmate Alan Meade. But when Meade left the band, Stefani nervously took center stage. "It took a lot of convincing to get her to the lead-singer position," recalled one former band member.

At first, Stefani worried that she was not aggressive enough to satisfy the band's high-energy fans. But she compensated by displaying a flair for sexy showmanship. Stefani soon perfected a highly energetic and theatrical style on stage, with a purring and growling sound that became a band signature. She also developed a striking appearance, sporting bleached plat-

No Doubt released its self-titled debut album in 1992.
Band members included (from right) Gwen Stefani, Tony Kanal,
Tom Dumont, Adrian Young, and Eric Stefani.

inum blond hair, dramatic make-up, and outrageous outfits that combined masculine and feminine qualities. For example, she often roamed the stage in baggy combat trousers and a push-up bra, wearing candy-apple-red lipstick and clunky Doc Martens shoes. She loved to bare her midriff, and her bare bellybutton became a trademark.

Stefani also credited No Doubt's surging popularity among California music fans to the band's mix of musical styles. Indeed, various band members brought different musical styles to No Doubt's mix, from funk and heavy metal to punk and classic rock. Stefani and her brother Eric, meanwhile, made sure that the band never strayed too far from its ska and reggae roots. "I always thought we could never be cool enough or tough enough or hard enough, because of me being a girl," she recalled. "But we could always mix it up a lot more—I love to sing all sorts of stuff, ballads and punk songs. Our show is so physical. The music is raw, broken down to the bare bones."

Yet despite their growing popularity, Stefani claimed that she and the other band members—brother Eric, bass player Tony Kanal, guitarist Tom Dumont, and drummer Adrian Young—never dared dream of major or long-term success. "We were doing it because we were passionate and couldn't help ourselves," she said. "We all went to school and went to college and we all had back-up plans. No one was ever intending for this to be our careers."

Reaching for Stardom

In 1992, No Doubt's popularity in southern California convinced the Interscope label to sign them to a record contract. Later that year, the band released their first album, *No Doubt*. Eric Stefani, who remained the artistic heart of the group, wrote most of the music and guided the production of the debut album. The release blended serious relationship songs with lighthearted pieces about "pigging out" and Eric's wisdom-tooth extraction, all set to a bouncy, fun beat. Unfortunately for the band, the recording was mostly ignored because it was so different from "grunge rock," the dominant musical style of the early 1990s. The group toured to support the record—an experience Eric Stefani clearly did not enjoy—but it remained a commercial disappointment.

> "I always thought we could never be cool enough or tough enough or hard enough, because of me being a girl," Stefani admitted. "But we could always mix it up a lot more—I love to sing all sorts of stuff, ballads and punk songs."

The album's poor performance concerned Interscope. When the band presented new material for a second album, Interscope repeatedly asking Stefani and her bandmates to go back and start over. The label's attitude angered the band, and in 1995 No Doubt took matters into their own hands. They distributed their second record, *The Beacon Street Collection*, as an independent release. The band liked the songs on *Beacon Street*, but it did not attract much attention from the public. Music critics gave it a mixed reception, too. At this point, Stefani and the other members of the band began to feel the stress of an uncertain future.

Around this time, however, the band caught the attention of a small record label called Trauma. The label's chief loved No Doubt's music and wanted to bring out their next record. That suited Interscope, which continued to serve as the band's distributor. The deal came as a great relief to the group, but it failed to soothe Eric Stefani, who was fed up with the hassles and uncertainties of the music business. By this time, he had even stopped coming to band practice sessions—even though they took place in his own house. It came as no surprise, then, when he announced his decision to leave the group to focus on a career as an animator.

Eric's departure forced the other band members to fill the creative and musical void he left behind. To her surprise, Stefani discovered she had more room to develop as a songwriter. "In the early days, my brother wrote most of the music and I was the one sitting on the couch watching *The Brady Bunch*," Stefani said. After he left the band, however, she wrote many of the lyrics and music for No Doubt's third album, *Tragic Kingdom.*

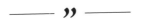

"*I'm a more old-fashioned kind of girl, a real girly-girl,*" *Stefani said. "At the same time, being in a band for eight years with all these guys, you really see the difference between being a girl and a guy."*

As it turned out, Stefani had plenty of real-life song-writing material for the record. In the midst of preparing the album, Stefani's eight-year romance with No Doubt bass guitarist Tony Kanal came to an end. She resisted the break-up—"the amputation," she called it—but when it happened, she tapped into her emotions to write several songs. In "Don't Speak," for example, she used lyrics that reflected the feelings of the heartbroken everywhere: "Don't speak/ I know just what you're saying/ So please stop explaining/ Don't tell me 'cause it hurts." In "Happy Now?" on the other hand, Stefani gently taunts a man who has ended a romance but then wants to get back together. And in songs such as "End It on This," Stefani declares her independence from boyfriends. Stefani later described the album as "happy music with bummed-out lyrics."

Tragic Kingdom Breaks Through

When *Tragic Kingdom* was released in late 1995, "we were hanging on a thread," Stefani admitted. "We carried this album for three years and it went through some hard times. By the end, we were back in school, had

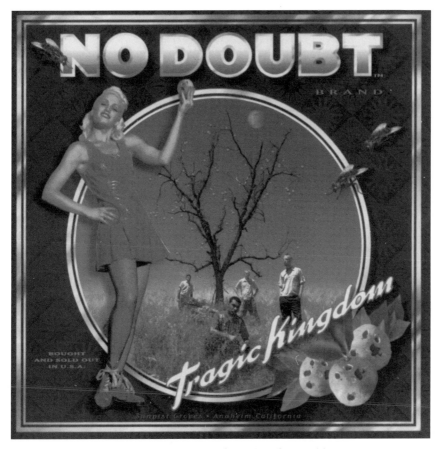

Tragic Kingdom *transformed Stefani and her*
bandmates into major rock stars.

jobs, had all our back-up plans in place [in case the album failed]." But instead, *Tragic Kingdom* took the music world by storm. Snapped up by
music fans eager for an upbeat alternative to grunge rock, the album
soared up the charts. *Tragic Kingdom* became one of the top-selling albums
of 1996, and it eventually sold 15 million copies worldwide.

To Stefani's surprise, the album's biggest hit was "Just a Girl," a song she
wrote about society's patronizing attitudes toward women. "I'm really not
the type of person that's a big feminist. I'm a more old-fashioned kind of
girl, a real girly-girl," Stefani said. "At the same time, being in a band for
eight years with all these guys, you really see the difference between being
a girl and a guy. The song kind of reflects those differences with a sarcastic
edge."

Stefani performs at a No Doubt concert in New York City.

After eight years together, the members of No Doubt regarded their "overnight" international success as if it were a happy dream. "That we got on the radio is the weirdest thing in the world," Stefani said. "I'm driving in my car, and the DJ's saying our name, and it's like, 'Hey, everybody, that's us!'" Stefani and her bandmates wore their success lightly, even as they savored every moment. "I really try to enjoy every second and be really aware," Stefani said. "I don't take it for granted when somebody says, 'Can I have your autograph?' I give it with joy."

During No Doubt's 1995 concert tour in support of *Tragic Kingdom,* Stefani emerged as the band's most visible member. Reviewing one concert appearance, *Hollywood Reporter* declared that she "practically radiated soon-to-be-huge stage presence, managing to come off sexy, coy, and ferocious simultaneously," But Stefani's growing stardom created tension with the band's three male members, all of whom felt that they were being ignored. The situation worsened when *Spin* splashed a photo of Stefani—without the other No Doubt members—on its cover. Stefani did what she could to discourage the favoritism, but it did not make her bandmates feel much better.

Meanwhile, Stefani and Kanal faced the difficulty of working together after their break-up. "You break up with your boyfriend that you've been with for almost eight years, and you're writing about him, and he's in your group and he's going to play the song that's about him," she said. "And then you travel with him on a bus 24 hours a day. It's a really weird situation—but we've made it work." She noted that neither of them has tried to hide the fact that many of *Tragic Kingdom* songs were inspired by their relationship. "Later, we started thinking we should be more quiet about it. But how could we know the band was going to get big?"

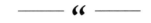

"You break up with your boyfriend that you've been with for almost eight years, and you're writing about him, and he's in your group and he's going to play the song that about him," said Stefani. "And then you travel with him on a bus 24 hours a day. It's a really weird situation—but we've made it work."

As the tour continued, Stefani met Gavin Rossdale, lead singer of the British rock band Bush. The two singers started a romance, but their busy touring schedules and home bases—hers in California and his in London, England—made it difficult for them to see one another.

Return of Saturn

No Doubt toured for more than two years after the release of *Tragic Kingdom*. The traveling took its toll, however. In the fall of 1996, for example, doctors ordered Stefani to stop singing temporarily after she devel-

Stefani and rap star Eve (right) teamed up to record the hit song
"Let Me Blow Ya Mind."

oped nodules on her throat. At the conclusion of the tour, she returned to her parents' home for a rest. But instead, she settled into what she described as "a weird kind of depression. Maybe not a depression so much as just a cloudy, confusing state for a couple of years."

Stefani gradually realized that she was not entirely happy with her life, despite her professional success. She was approaching 30 years of age, but she felt lonely and far away from her long-time dream of having children. "I think everyone gets to a point in their life where they grow up and go, 'Wow, this is me now. I'm not just a kid. This is what I'm doing,'" she said.

Stefani's bandmates were in a reflective mood, too. "I think we all knew it," said No Doubt guitarist Tom Dumont. "We got together and decided that rather than repeat *Tragic Kingdom*, we should have a goal—to improve as songwriters. To stretch." Stefani took this goal to heart. At Rossdale's suggestion, she began to keep a journal. She also studied the work of writers she admired, including folksinger Joni Mitchell and Sylvia Plath, a gifted American poet who killed herself in the early 1960s.

In 2000 No Doubt released its fourth album, titled *Return of Saturn*. The title refers to the 29 and a half years it takes the planet Saturn to revolve around the sun. Stefani reckons that this is about the same amount of time that most people need to figure out what they want to do with their lives.

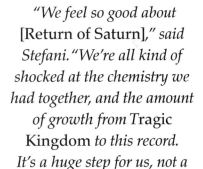

"We feel so good about [Return of Saturn]," said Stefani. "We're all kind of shocked at the chemistry we had together, and the amount of growth from Tragic Kingdom *to this record. It's a huge step for us, not a little baby one."*

Several of the songs on the album displayed the band's interest in exploring issues of personal growth and happiness. On "A Simple Kind of Life," for example, Stefani muses on the crossroads she faces at 30: "I always thought I'd be a mom/Sometimes I wish for a mistake/The longer I wait the more selfish I get." Stefani said that many people believe this song simply expresses her longing to get married and have babies. But she claimed that it is "more about how I used to think that's all I ever wanted and the confusion of realizing that I am more faithful to my freedom than I ever thought I could be. And that's scary." The song "Bathwater" rollicks like an old show song, but expresses more unfulfilled longing: "I still love to wash in your old bathwater/ Love to think that you couldn't love another." Stefani acknowledged that her boyfriend Rossdale inspired these songs, along with the not-so-subtle "Marry Me. "

All of the members of No Doubt expressed deep satisfaction with *Return of Saturn*. "We feel so good about it," confirmed Stefani. "We're all kind of shocked at the chemistry we had together, and the amount of growth from *Tragic Kingdom* to this record. It's a huge step for us, not a little baby one." But critics did not completely agree. *Time* praised the record and declared that Stefani performed her "bittersweet" songs very well. But *Entertainment Weekly* accused Stefani of having "regressed emotionally," claiming that Stefani's lyrics "incessantly circle around the same theme: terminal insecurity." *Rolling Stone,* meanwhile, praised it as a "subtle and heartfelt" album, but charged that some portions of it were "a little overcooked." Music fans also gave *Return of Saturn* a mixed reception. After debuting at No. 2 on the

Billboard chart of top-selling records, it slid down the chart fairly quickly. It eventually sold 1.4 million copies in the United States, a healthy total but far less than the sales reaped by *Tragic Kingdom.*

In 2001 Stefani stayed in the music spotlight with guest appearances on two songs recorded by other major musical stars. The first of these was "South Side," composed by electronica musician Moby. For the second, she teamed up with Philadelphia rapper Eve to record "Let Me Blow Ya Mind." Initially, Stefani was unsure about recording a song with Eve. "It was like, 'Should I be doing another side thing? Ya know, Are people gonna think that I'm just like the side sausage?" she recalled. But she desperately wanted to work with Eve's producer, hip-hop legend Dr. Dre. Stefani later admitted that the recording sessions for "Let Me Blow Ya Mind" wore her down. "I probably sang the chorus for like two-and-a half hours straight," she said. "[Dr. Dre] beat me up as a singer. He really challenged me. He had one thing in his head, and I wasn't hearing the same thing in my head." Ultimately, however, they recorded a song that everyone liked.

> "[We] were having dance parties every night, inviting people back and listening to a lot of Jamaican dancehall — just having the most fun," said band member Tony Kanal. "So, when we started making [Rock Steady], we decided to put everything else aside and just have a great time. The thinking was, 'While we're writing music, let's keep the fun going.'"

A few months later, Stefani and Eve received a 2002 Grammy Award for Best Rap Song Collaboration for "Let Me Blow Ya Mind." In addition, her work with Moby and Eve brought her to the attention of legions of electronica and hip-hop fans. "Even the big, beefy security guards now recognize me: 'Hey, Gwen, wazzzz up? You're dope, man.' I love that!" she said. "And all I did was sing on that song!"

Rock Steady

In 2001 No Doubt returned to the upbeat sound of their early days for *Rock Steady,* their fifth album. Bathed in good spirits and high times, it blended Jamaican dancehall (a form of slowed-down reggae), new wave, and hip-hop music into a crowd-pleasing series of songs. The recording also featured a wide array of guest stars from the worlds of ska, reggae, and funk.

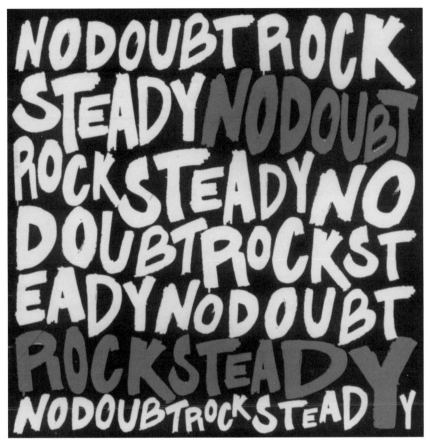

Rock Steady *was praised by critics as one of No Doubt's strongest releases.*

Kanal later said that the spirit of *Rock Steady* could be traced back to the band's *Return of Saturn* tour. "[We] were having dance parties every night, inviting people back and listening to a lot of Jamaican dancehall—just having the most fun," he said. "So, when we started making this record, we decided to put everything else aside and just have a great time. The thinking was, "While we're writing music, let's keep the fun going." With this perspective in mind, the band refused to spend months agonizing over every song. "We're not taking ourselves so seriously," Stefani said. "It's like, get over it. We're in a . . . band and we're really lucky to be doing what we do."

Reviewers loved the results. "As comebacks go, [*Rock Steady* is] up there with Elvis," pronounced the English music magazine *NME*. *Entertainment Weekly*—which had slammed *Saturn Returns*—heaped praise on the band as well. "[This] beat-heavy quickie turns out to be the best album they've ever hatched. . . . *Rock Steady* mostly ditches ska, not to mention the overthink of *Return of Saturn,* and replaces it with doses of the leaner, meaner pop No Doubt was born to make." *Newsweek,* meanwhile, called the album No Doubt's "most risky, varied and creative music to date." According to the review, Stefani's voice displayed a " new confidence: she's able to smooth out and flow on balmy, Caribbean-style ballads like 'Underneath It All,' then kick in hard on quirky, slamming dance tunes such as 'Hey, Baby' and 'Making Out'."

In the meantime, Stefani continued to be a fashion trendsetter. Long known for her appearance—an unlikely blending of Hollywood starlet and "riot grrrl" styles—she started to wear clothing by such top designers as Vivienne Westwood and John Galliano. She also has been credited with contributing to the popularity of everything from push-up bras and teeth braces to pink hair and Indian bindis (the stick-on jewel in the center of a woman's forehead). Stefani admitted that her influence on fashion continues to astonish her. "I was the type who thought I could never influence anyone, this loser from Anaheim," she said. "I think I've been able to fool a lot of people. Because I know I'm a dork, I'm a geek."

> ———— **"** ————
>
> *Stefani has admitted that her influence on fashion continues to astonish her. "I was the type who thought I could never influence anyone," said Stefani. "I think I've been able to fool a lot of people. Because I know I'm a dork, I'm a geek."*
>
> ———— **"** ————

The success of *Rock Steady* enabled No Doubt to claim a number of desirable touring slots. They shared the stage with the famous Irish rock band U2 on a number of dates, and even opened for the Rolling Stones. The album also earned the band its first ever Grammy Award, when "Hey, Baby" won the 2003 Grammy for Best Pop Performance by a Group.

Since the tour supporting *Rock Steady,* No Doubt has been on a break. Stefani has kept busy, however. In early 2003 she announced that she was preparing a line of leather goods, from CD cases to handbags, for a major manufacturer. She also has announced plans to launch her own ready-to-wear fashion line, called Lamb. Finally, Stefani is expected to make her acting debut in a film biography of the famous American millionaire Howard Hughes. The movie will be directed by Martin Scorcese, one of America's most respected filmmakers, and stars Leonardo DiCaprio in the role of

Hughes, along with an all-star cast. Stefani is slated to portray glamorous actress Jean Harlow.

MARRIAGE AND FAMILY

Stefani married her longtime boyfriend, Gavin Rossdale of the British grunge-rock band Bush, in September 2002. "It was fairly obvious that this was going to happen," stated Rossdale's father. "They are a good couple." Stefani has stated that she wants to start a family. "I feel very romantic about the idea because I think Gavin's going to be the most incredible dad," she said. "I'm excited about seeing him as a husband first. But if I got pregnant tomorrow, I'd be like, 'Yeeahhh'!"

Stefania and Bush lead singer Gavin Rossdale were married in September 2002.

HOBBIES AND INTERESTS

In addition to fashion and music, Stefani is interested in painting. "I always had this big fantasy that when I get pregnant I'm going to have this little mask on and sit and paint every day and get really fat and have a show at the end with all the paintings," she said. "'The Mind of a Pregnant Woman' would be the name of it."

SELECTED RECORDINGS

No Doubt, 1992
The Beacon Street Collection, 1995
Tragic Kingdom, 1995
Return of Saturn, 2000
Rock Steady, 2001

HONORS AND AWARDS

MTV Music Award: 1997, Best Group Video for "Don't Speak" (with No Doubt)

VH1/Vogue Fashion Awards: 1999, for Most Stylish Video for "New";
2000, for Most Stylish Video for "Ex-Girlfriend"; 2001, for Most
Fabionable Female Artist

Grammy Awards: 2002, for Best-Rap Song Collaboration for "Let Me Blow
Ya Mind" (with Eve); 2003, for Best Pop Performance by a Duo or Group,
for "Hey, Baby" (with No Doubt)

FURTHER READING

Books

Contemporary Musicians, Vol. 20, 1997

Periodicals

Billboard, Nov. 24, 2001, p.1
Entertainment Weekly, May 12, 2000, p.32
Los Angeles Times, April 13, 2000, p. F6; Mar. 16, 1996, p. F1; Apr. 2, 1992,
    p. F1
Newsweek, Dec. 17, 2001, p 67
People Weekly, May, 19, 1997, p.105
Rolling Stone, Nov. 8, 2001, p.27; Jul. 6, 2000, p.68; May 1, 1997, p.36
Scholastic Scope, Mar. 11, 2002, p.16
Teen People, Aug. 1, 2002, p.138
Vogue, Oct., 2002, p.354
Washington Post, June 15, 1997, p.G1

Online Databases

Contemporary Musicians, 1997, reproduced in *Biography Resource Center,* 2003

ADDRESS

Gwen Stefani
Interscope Records
2220 Colorado Ave.
Santa Monica, CA 90404

WORLD WIDE WEB SITE

http://www.nodoubt.com

Emma Watson 1990-

British Actress

Stars as Hermione in the Hit Films *Harry Potter and the Sorcerer's Stone* and *Harry Potter and the Chamber of Secrets*

BIRTH

Emma Charlotte Duerre Watson was born on April 15, 1990, and lives in Oxford, England. Her parents, Jacqueline Watson and Chris Watson, are both lawyers and are divorced. She has one brother, Alex, who is three years younger.

YOUTH

Emma Watson grew up with a very normal childhood in Oxford, England. Oxford is a city not far from London, and it is known for its famous university. She spends time with her brother and with each of her parents. She has two cats named Bubbles and Domino. She enjoys school (except for geography and math) and likes to play sports, such as hockey, rowing, tennis, and a game called rounders, which is similar to baseball. She attends The Dragon School, a private prep school, where she has many friends. Watson has participated in several of the school's dramatic productions, playing Morgan La Fay in *Arthur: The Young Years*, the swallow in *The Swallow and the Prince*, the angry cook in *Alice in Wonderland*, and a lead role in *The Happy Prince*. She also attended classes at Stagecoach Theatre Arts, a network of performing arts schools across England.

> *"I just stood there staring for it seemed like five minutes. It was just too much to take in," Watson said about being offered the role of Hermione. "It was the scariest thing that ever happened to me. It was the biggest thing that ever happened to me. It was the best thing that ever happened to me. I love the idea of people liking me and seeing me as a role model. I think that is very flattering."*

CAREER HIGHLIGHTS

Auditioning for the Role of Hermione

Watson says that she wanted to be an actress since she was three years old. She enjoyed being in school productions as she was growing up, but her big break came when moviemakers were searching all over England for the right child actors for the first Harry Potter movie. "My dad read me the first and second books, and I was in the middle of the third book when I started auditioning. I was a really big fan." Some of the auditions were held in the gym at Watson's school. The casting directors asked the school staff for the names of students who might fit the parts, and one of the teachers recommended Emma Watson. "It sounded like fun so I did it. I did the first one and got through to the second audition and that was a bit more serious because they had me on camera."

After the second audition, Watson was called to Leavesden Studios outside of London. She and Rupert Grint were called into producer David Hey-

A scene from Harry Potter and the Sorcerer's Stone, *2001.*

man's office and asked if they would like to play the parts of Hermione and Ron. "That was an amazing moment. My Dad was waiting outside. He thought it was just going to be about another audition." At first, she wasn't sure it was real. "I just stood there staring for it seemed like five minutes. It was just too much to take in." It was a turning point in Watson's life. "It was the scariest thing that ever happened to me. It was the biggest thing that ever happened to me. It was the best thing that ever happened to me. I love the idea of people liking me and seeing me as a role model. I think that is very flattering."

Harry Potter and the Sorcerer's Stone

Watson was offered the role of Hermione, one of the main characters in the Harry Potter books. Harry Potter is a young wizard, age 11 when the series begins, who doesn't know that he has magical powers. His parents died when he was a baby, and he has been living with his cruel aunt and uncle ever since. Harry's aunt and uncle have never told him that another magical world exists among the regular, non-magical "Muggle" world. After some amazing events, he comes to attend boarding school at the Hogwarts School of Witchcraft and Wizardry. He meets two other new students, Ron and Hermione, who become his closest friends. Hermione is the daughter of Muggle parents — she just happens to have magical powers. She is a very serious student who loves to learn, and she is quite determined to follow the rules and do things properly. Unfortunately, her friendship with the famous Harry Potter keeps getting her into all different kinds of trouble.

———— " ————

"I'm not obsessed with books," Watson said about how she's different from Hermione. "I'm not obsessed with school and homework, and I'm not obsessed with not getting into trouble. I'm not obsessed with woolly grandma-knitted jumpers, and I hope I've got a better sense of fashion. So no, I'm not like [Hermione]...."

———— " ————

Watson started shooting *Harry Potter and the Sorcerer's Stone* soon after the offer from producer David Heyman, and her dreams of being a movie star turned into the reality of hard work. "It's definitely not what you would call glamorous. You have to wake up really early in the morning. I think the earliest they ever called me in was a six o'clock pick-up, which means you have to be in the car and leaving by six. I prefer getting up late in the morning and coming back late at night. I did enjoy it though." Acting for the movies also means doing scenes over and over and over again. "When you do a scene 20 times it can get boring. But it's mostly great because every day you are doing a different scene with different people." There is also the hard work of doing some of the stunts herself, such as in the troll scene in *Harry Potter and the Sorcerer's Stone*. "In the girls toilets, they have these six cubicles and I have to climb under them. They put a safety mat under them but that made it very hard to do. We actually measured the space and there was only 30 cms clearance. I bumped my head every time I had to duck under one. I had to crawl along the sinks dodging the troll. That was fun!"

Watson has enjoyed working with director Chris Columbus, who has helped her make an easy transition from school plays to major film productions. "[He's] really good with working with children, and he really got us into the moment, and he made us feel really, really, comfortable. He's a great director." Some of Columbus's requirements were difficult, though—like keeping the stories' secrets until the premiere. "It was hard. I was frightened that in the press conferences I was going to tell everybody that it was all fake. A lot of it had to be secret even from my family, there were things I couldn't tell my grandmother."

Although she spent months on the set of *Harry Potter and the Sorcerer's Stone*, Watson had to wait along with everyone to see the finished product at the premiere. After watching it, she found that it met her expectations perfectly. "I feel like they've kind of just like taken a piece of my mind out from the book and just used it on the film, because it is exactly as I imagined it I—I mean, I suppose every actress, when they like see themselves on screen they're like, 'Oh, they cut out my best lines,' or 'Oh, I look so bad in that scene,' or 'Oh, my hair looks disastrous.' But I think everyone says that. So I'm very self-critical, but altogether I just loved the film. It's amazing."

Harry Potter and the Chamber of Secrets

Coming back to work on the second film, *Harry Potter and the Chamber of Secrets*, was much easier for Watson. "I enjoyed making the second one much more than I did the first one. . . . [We] knew the cast, we knew the crew, we knew the director, and let's face it, we knew what we were doing the second time around, which was good. Yeah, I think it was—I also enjoyed watching the second one a lot more. I think it's much, much better than the first one." Watson, along with Rupert Grint and Daniel Radcliffe as Ron and Harry, are all scheduled to appear in the third film as well. After that, no one is certain what will happen, especially as the young actors grow and mature faster than their screen characters.

Watson likes her character Hermione, who is fun, annoying, and demanding to play. "I reckon that Hermione is pretty bossy, pretty swotty, pretty teacher's pet." Her lines give Watson a challenging time occasionally. "I think Hermione gets all of the big words to say. Some of them are a real mouthful. She gets the long sentences and long complicated words, which even I can't understand. . . . It's like tongue twisters in every paragraph. But she does get good lines. It's hard, especially when you have to do it quickly. There are always so many things going on in your mind. You try and remember your lines but it's not just that. You have to get on your mark, make sure you are in the light, that the camera can see you, making sure you are not blocking the person behind you, and then you have to remember your lines with all of that." Watson thinks that Ron gets the brunt of Hermione's "snooty" lines. Her personal favorite, though, was, "We're going to get killed, or worse, expelled!"

"Instead of spending my time doing academic things like she does, I do lots more sports. I play hockey, tennis, and rounders at my school. I spend a lot of time with my friends and I like being at home a lot. It must be quite hard for Hermione to be away from home at Hogwarts."

A scene from Harry Potter and the Chamber of Secrets, *2002, of Watson brewing a potion in the girls' bathroom.*

Watson seems to like some of Hermione's character traits but not others. "She's self-assured, irritating, emotional, and loyal." As she has worked on the two films, she has gotten to know Hermione's character better and has grown to like her more. "I like the way she's developing. She's more interesting to play (in the second Potter film) because she is maturing, growing up. Emotionally, she's becoming more independent. And in the second film, she's the one who gets knocked down, but I thinks she winds up on top."

Working with an all-star cast has also been exciting for an aspiring young actress. One of her favorite scenes was in the second film. "That was really good to film. That was really good. I was also kind of nervous about meeting Gilderoy Lockhart—well, actually, Kenneth Branagh, who plays Gilderoy Lockhart, obviously, because he's like such an amazing Shakespearean actor and everything. . . . He is absolutely hilarious. He is so funny. But he's also really down to earth. He's just like a really nice guy."

Combining Acting and School

During filming, Watson and the other young actors are allowed to work between three and five hours a day. When they are not doing a scene, they work with a tutor to keep up on schoolwork. "It's one to one, so even though we do, like, half the amount we would do in a normal school day, you get just as much work done because it's one to one. And when you're in a class, you know, it takes a little longer." School on a film set also has other advantages. "We don't get any homework, which is cool, and no detentions, which is even cooler." Watson enjoys her regular school and misses her friends when she isn't there. But she doesn't overdo it, like Hermione. "I'm not obsessed with books. I'm not obsessed with school and homework, and I'm not obsessed with not getting into trouble. I'm not obsessed with woolly grandma-knitted jumpers, and I hope I've got a better sense of fashion. So no, I'm not like [Hermione]. Instead of spending my time doing academic things like she does, I do lots more sports. I play hockey, tennis, and rounders at my school. I spend a lot of time with my friends and I like being at home a lot. It must be quite hard for Hermione to be away from home at Hogwarts."

"I've been at my school for seven years so I know all my friends very, very well and I think they are just curious and interested, and otherwise they are exactly the same. I still see them. I still go to the cinema with them. It's quite hard to keep in touch with all of my friends when I'm filming but I do my best."

Watson's friendships seem to have withstood her new fame quite well. "I've been at my school for seven years so I know all my friends very, very well and I think they are just curious and interested, and otherwise they are exactly the same. I still see them. I still go to the cinema with them. It's quite hard to keep in touch with all of my friends when I'm filming but I do my best." When she is back at school full-time, though, some of the other students who she doesn't know as well aren't as calm about it. "I go to a very big school and some people give me a bit of stick. They walk past and go 'Wingardium Leviosa' for the billionth time that day, and I go aaagggghhhhh!"

———— **"** ————

"People stop me in the street. Everywhere. And mostly, they say, 'Hi, Hermione,' and I say, 'Hi,' back. But it's scary. It's quite scary to be 10 feet tall on the screen and that everyone knows everything about you, at least physically. You are kind of being watched all the time. Most people are really nice but some stare, like you're some kind of zoo exhibit and not a real person with real feelings."

———— **"** ————

Dealing with Fame

Watson went from being a normal pre-teen to one of the most famous faces on earth after *Harry Potter and the Sorcerer's Stone* opened to huge audiences in 2001. The success of *Harry Potter and the Chamber of Secrets* in 2002 made her even more recognizable. Life in public isn't the same anymore. "People stop me in the street. Everywhere. And mostly, they say, 'Hi, Hermione,' and I say, 'Hi,' back. But it's scary. It's quite scary to be 10 feet tall on the screen and that everyone knows everything about you, at least physically. You are kind of being watched all the time. Most people are really nice but some stare, like you're some kind of zoo exhibit and not a real person with real feelings."

Fan mail is a regular part of her life now, and some of it is more than just paper or email. "When it was my birthday, someone sent me a massive white cuddly bear, almost as big as me. They sent it in the post! I just thought that was amazing, as they'd never even met me or anything."

Being part of a hugely successful movie has meant earning a lot of money, too, but Watson doesn't pay too much attention to that part of the experience. She lets her parents handle it all and doesn't even know how much she has made. She knows that it is in the bank until she is 21, and then she'll decide what to do with it.

Emma Watson (right) and Daniel Radcliffe (left) pose for photographs with J.K. Rowling at the world premiere of Harry Potter and the Chamber of Secrets, *London, November 2002.*

The amazing changes that have come about from one audition don't seem to phase Watson. Her life still seems normal to her. "You know, I still fall out with my brother, I still have to make my bed, I still see my friends, I try to lead a really normal life. Basically, the only way that it's changed is what I'm doing in everyday life."

HOBBIES AND OTHER INTERESTS

Watson insists that although she likes school and reading, she is not the bookworm that Hermione is. "And I hope I have better fashion sense." She likes to shop; her big reward for completing the first Harry Potter movie was a clothes shopping spree. Some of her favorite makers are DKNY and the Gap. "I wear a uniform at school, but I have these massive bell-bottom flares, and my mom really disapproves of them." Her favorite animals are cats, and she has two. Pop music is another interest, and some of her favorite performers are Bryan Adams, Suzanne Vega, Samantha Mumba, and Dido. Movies, of course, are of great interest to the rising actress. Some of her role models include Julia Roberts, Sandra Bullock, John Cleese, and Goldie Hawn. Watson also plays many different sports, and she hopes to get an art scholarship to college when she is 18.

MOVIES

Harry Potter and the Sorcerer's Stone, 2001
Harry Potter and the Chamber of Secrets, 2002

FURTHER READING

Periodicals

Chicago Sun-Times, Nov. 29, 2002, p.32
Daily Telegraph (London), Oct. 25, 2002, p.23
Entertainment Weekly, Dec. 21, 2001, p.52
Newsday, Nov. 8, 2002, p.D6
Los Angeles Times, Nov. 10, 2002, p.E12
Ottawa Citizen, Nov. 6, 2001, p.D9
People, Nov. 19, 2001, p.64
Toronto Sun, Nov. 10, 2002, p.S14
USA Today, Nov. 20, 2001, p.D10

Online Articles

http://news.bbc.co.uk/cbbcnews/hi/tv_film/newsid_1628000/1628670.stm
(*BBC Newsround*, "Emma Watson: 'I Have the Best Lines,'" Oct. 30, 2001)
http://www.ew.com/ew/report/0,6115,188388~1~0~harrpottershermion
etalks,00.html(*Entertainment Weekly*, "Season of the Witch," no date)

ADDRESS

Emma Watson
Warner Bros.
4000 Warner Boulevard
Burbank, CA 91522

WORLD WIDE WEB SITE

http://harrypotter.warnerbros.com/home.html

Meg Whitman 1956-

American Business Leader
President and Chief Executive Officer of the eBay
Internet Auction Site

BIRTH

Margaret C. (Meg) Whitman was born on August 4, 1956, in
Cold Spring Harbor, New York. Her affluent hometown is located on Long Island, outside of New York City. Her father,
Hendricks, was a "factor" — a person who lends money to
businesses using their accounts receivable (the funds that their
customers owe to them) to secure the loans. Her mother,

———— **"** ————

"When I was growing up on Long Island in the '60s and '70s, my parents raised me largely to become a wife and a mother," Whitman recalled. "A career, they said, was something a woman needed only as a backup. You could get a nursing degree or a teaching certificate or learn secretarial skills because those were jobs you could fall back on if something bad happened, like if your husband left you or was hit by a truck. It wasn't that long ago, but it was a very different time and place."

———— **"** ————

Margaret, was a homemaker who later led delegations and tour groups to China. Meg is the youngest of three children.

YOUTH

Whitman's parents both came from well-established East Coast families. They held conservative political views and social values. In fact, Whitman described her mother as a "rock-ribbed Republican who could wear a Peck & Peck suit," referring to the up-scale department store.

But Whitman credits her mother with teaching her to be adventurous and adaptable. The summer Whitman was six years old, for example, her mother and a friend packed their eight children into a camper for a three-month tour of the United States. When the children got restless and started to squabble, Whitman's mother let them out of the camper to run ahead on the mostly deserted roads. She would trail behind them until they were tired out, then she would pick them up again. Well-meaning truckers occasionally stopped to see if the group needed help. "You could always hear the hiss of the air brakes," Whitman remembered. "We finally put a sign on the back of the camper that said, 'We're OK.'"

Although Whitman's parents taught her to be self-sufficient, they did not always encourage her to pursue a career. "When I was growing up on Long Island in the '60s and '70s, my parents raised me largely to become a wife and mother," Whitman noted. "A career, they said, was something a woman needed only as a backup. You could get a nursing degree or a teaching certificate or learn secretarial skills because those were jobs you could fall back on if something bad happened, like if your husband left you or was hit by a truck. It wasn't that long ago, but it was a very different time and place."

In 1973, when Whitman was a senior in high school, her mother had a life-changing experience that reversed her former attitude about women pursuing careers. She joined a delegation to China organized by Shirley MacLaine, a well-known actress. China had been closed to most outsiders since it adopted a Communist form of government in 1949. (Under a Communist political system, the central government exercises a great deal of control over the lives of citizens. Communism eliminates most private property and gives it to the government to distribute as it sees fit. Communism also places severe restrictions on individual rights and allows the government to control the educations, careers, and cultural experiences of the people.)

MacLaine's delegation to China included several filmmakers who documented the trip. The American visitors learned that Chinese women had much the same level of responsibility as men, whether in factories, farms, or politics. "When Mom came back, she had a whole new point of view on what women could do," Whitman recalled. "She more or less said, 'All that advice I gave you before? Ignore it. You can do anything you want to do. Find a career that you love and that makes you happy, and do that in addition to being a wife and mom.' Here was the most important woman in my life saying basically to just forget what she'd been telling me for the last 15 years."

Her mother's new message really hit home when the delegation's female camera crew came to the Whitman home for dinner. All of the women were accomplished professionals. One was a top documentary filmmaker, and another was the first female technician in her labor union. "From talking to these women, I figured out that the most important thing was to put your head down and do a great job," Whitman said.

Whitman's mother, meanwhile, went on to make a career of leading dele-

"When Mom came back [from China], she had a whole new point of view on what women could do," said Whitman. "She more or less said, 'All that advice I gave you before? Ignore it. You can do anything you want to do. Find a career that you love and that makes you happy, and do that in addition to being a wife and mom.' Here was the most important woman in my life saying basically to just forget what she'd been telling me for the last 15 years."

gations and tour groups to China. In 2002, at age 82, she returned to China with her daughter to mark an eBay business deal. "It was a poignant moment and, in some ways, like coming full circle, for her to see eBay in China," Whitman wrote. "It was just what she taught me: The possibilities were wide open."

EDUCATION

Whitman attended Princeton University, a top American college located in New Jersey. She originally planned to become a doctor, but the pre-med courses turned her off. "I didn't enjoy it," she stated. "Of course, chemistry, calculus, and physics have nothing to do with being a doctor, but if you're 17 years old, you think, 'This is what being a doctor is going to be about.'" She first realized that she enjoyed business when she began to sell advertising for *Business Today*, a magazine published by Princeton undergraduates. She started learning about the business world by ordering the *Wall Street Journal*—the leading U.S. business newspaper—delivered to her dormitory room.

Whitman earned a bachelor's degree in economics in 1977. She continued her education at prestigious Harvard University, earning a master's degree in business administration in 1979. Whitman excelled in her studies at Harvard, but she admitted that she felt intimidated by some of her classmates. In one class, for example, she sat between a manager from Chemical Bank and a 32-year-old Army platoon commander. "It was the first time in my life I worked hard because I was scared [of failing]," Whitman recalled. "Mostly I work hard because I want to achieve, because I love it."

CAREER HIGHLIGHTS

Working Her Way up the Corporate Ladder

Whitman launched her business career at Procter and Gamble, a large U.S. manufacturer of Ivory soap and other consumer products. Working as a brand assistant and brand manager, her responsibilities included finding the best way to sell a particular product. It was during this time that she made what she called one of her biggest mistakes in business. Without conducting customer research, Whitman decided that a new product, Ivory shampoo, should be colored blue so that it would not be mistaken for dishwashing liquid. But customers were shocked, because Ivory soap had always been pure white. Procter & Gamble quickly changed the shampoo's color to white, and Whitman learned the value of market research.

In 1980 Whitman married Griffith R. Harsh IV, a doctor who was training to become a brain surgeon. When her husband entered a medical residency program in California, she went to work for Bain and Company, a consulting firm. One of her first assignments was to help a college food-service company improve its performance. She visited universities and got first-hand feedback from the students and food-service directors. "It was an early introduction in the importance of talking to customers," she said.

During her eight years at Bain, Whitman learned about establishing effective work cultures—work environments that best motivate employees to succeed. She modeled her ideal work culture on her own co-workers, whom she described as "young, smart, aggressive, fun" people who worked toward "a shared vision and values." Whitman used her expertise to help corporate clients determine their focus and develop "vision statements" to help them reach their goals.

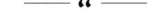

"Meg was willing to mix it up with florists all over the world,"said one colleague about her days working at FTD."She would shake their hands and kiss their babies."

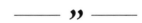

In 1989 Whitman joined the Disney Corporation as a senior vice president of marketing in the consumer products division. In three years at Disney, she helped the company launch a book publishing division and acquire *Discover* magazine. She also oversaw Disney's entry into the world of retail shopping. When she joined the company, there were only three Disney stores in existence. By the time she left, Disney maintained 250 stores, including outlets in Japan.

In 1992 Whitman's husband was named co-director of the brain tumor program at Massachusetts General Hospital. The family subsequently moved to Boston, where Whitman joined Stride Rite Shoes Corporation, a manufacturer of children's shoes, Keds sneakers, and Sperry Topsiders. Whitman rejuvenated the Stride Rite brand and expanded the variety of shoes the company offered. For example, she launched the successful Munchkins line of baby shoes. She also oversaw Stride Rite retail stores and dealers.

During her three years at Stride Rite, Whitman learned that it was critical to involve the entire management team in creating a company strategy. Shortly after joining the company, she wrote down her vision for Stride Rite and passed it out to senior management. "People used to refer to it as

Whitman meets with Pierre Omidyar, founder of eBay.

'Meg's vision,' and that was not a good thing," she said. Whitman later decided to take her team away from the office for a couple of days to develop a vision they could all share in.

In 1995 Whitman accepted a lucrative job offer from Florists' Transworld Delivery (FTD), the flower delivery service. She achieved her dream of leading a major corporation when she was named president and chief executive officer (CEO) shortly after joining FTD. Whitman led the organization's transition from an association owned by florists to a privately owned, for-profit company. Many of the members and managers resisted the plan, but Whitman did her best to convince florists the change was good. "Meg was willing to mix it up with florists all over the world," said a colleague. "She would shake their hands and kiss their babies."

Whitman's reorganization efforts stalled due to infighting among her managers, however. The situation became so frustrating to her that she decided to pursue other career opportunities. In 1997 she left FTD to assume leadership of the Playskool division of Hasbro, one of America's largest toy and game manufacturers. The *New York Times* later described Whitman's FTD experience as one of the biggest disappointments of her career.

Moving to eBay

Whitman remained at Hasbro for only a few months. In November 1997 a corporate recruiter (or "headhunter") asked her to interview for the top job at an Internet start-up company in California. AuctionWeb (as eBay was then called) allowed users to sell goods online to the highest bidder. Whitman told the recruiter that she was not interested. "I had never heard of eBay, and I said, 'I'm not going to move my family 3,000 miles across the country. I'm married to a neurosurgeon, and we have two boys. We aren't going to move our family for this no-name Internet company.' And so I said no, and three weeks later the headhunter called back and said, 'You are perfect for eBay and eBay is perfect for you. I beg you to get on the plane.'" Whitman finally agreed, but only because she thought the recruiter might be able to help her career in the future.

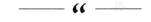

A computer programmer named Pierre Omidyar had launched eBay in September 1995. There's a company legend about how he started the company, although it may or may not be true. Legend says that he originally set up the Internet site to help his girlfriend — a collector of Pez candy dispensers — find a broader network of collectors to trade with. But Omidyar soon found that the appeal of the site went far beyond what he envisioned. It allowed hobbyists and collectors of all sorts of things to share their interests with fellow enthusiasts. The site soon featured Beanie Babies, rare coins, antique glassware, and numerous other items. Sellers posted their items on the site with a description, a minimum bid, and a time period before the sale would be finalized. Buyers then competed for the item until the period of the auction expired. The highest bidder at the deadline claimed the item.

Whitman claims that when she was first asked to head eBay, she said "I'm not going to move my family 3,000 miles across the country. . . . We aren't going to move our family for this no-name Internet company."

At first Omidyar provided his service free of charge. He soon built a foundation of buyers and sellers through word of mouth. Omidyar later introduced a small fee to list an item, as well as a system that automatically charges a small percentage on each item's selling price. The site was so successful that Omidyar quit his day job and incorporated the online venture as a business in May 1996. A year later he sold 22 percent of AuctionWeb to a capital investment firm for $5 million. Around this time, he changed the company name to eBay, in honor of the San Francisco Bay area where it was founded.

During Whitman's initial research into eBay, she was not impressed. "I will never forget, I got on eBay the night before I went to the interview," she recalled. "[The site] was in black and white and there were three components to the site. The first component was the auction business, the second was [Omidyar's] fiancee's web page, and the third was the Ebola virus page, because Pierre was really interested in the Ebola virus [a deadly, highly contagious disease]. And I said, 'I cannot believe I am getting on a plane to go talk about a black-and-white web site called AuctionWeb that has equal billing with the fiancee's web page and the Ebola virus page.' But I had already committed, so I got on the plane."

> **"**
>
> *"[Taking the job at eBay] was a huge risk," admitted Whitman. "But we loved being in California and we thought that tech would continue to play an increasing role in society, and that being in the heartland of tech for us and our two boys would be positive. And we figured, what's the worst that could happen? I get another job."*
>
> **"**

The eBay offices in San Jose, California, were a far cry from Whitman's plush corporate world. The rented offices were dingy, and the company's total work force consisted of only 20 employees. But as Whitman learned more about the company's services and history, she recognized that it had enormous potential. The auction site was able to make a large profit because it had so few expenses. All the merchandise came from users, who also made all the arrangements for payment and shipping. Unlike other Internet retailers, eBay did not need to maintain inventory, warehouses, trucks, or a large staff. As a result, eBay grew by leaps and bounds. "This was a tiny company," Whitman said. "But [it had] a 70 percent compound monthly growth rate. Not compound annual [yearly] growth rate, compound *monthly* growth rate." In other words, each month the auction site operated, it earned 70 percent more revenue than the previous month.

Whitman saw that eBay offered users something that had never before existed — the ability to trade goods in a global marketplace 24 hours a day, seven days a week. It truly was a business that only could be conducted on

The eBay logo is one of the most recognizable logos on the internet.

the Internet. Whitman was even more impressed by the fact that users formed an emotional connection with eBay's service. She heard testimonials from users who would sneak away from business meetings to see how their auction was doing. She also heard about people who had discovered shared interests and become best friends by using the site. In short, people loved it. "For the past 20 years I had thought that great brands were features and functionality—you know, 'whiter whites' or 'cleaner cleans'—and if you can get the emotional connection, then you have a huge winner on your hands," she said. "There's no substitute in the land-based world for eBay. I just had an overwhelming instinct that this thing was going to be huge."

As excited as Whitman was about eBay, the company's founder and investors were even more excited to have her on board. Although she had no significant experience with technology, she did have extensive managerial, marketing, and brand experience. As Robert Kagle, a major eBay investor, explained, "I was looking for a brand-builder to help make eBay a household name."

When nearby Stanford University offered her husband a position as head of its neurosurgery department, Whitman felt as if "the stars aligned." She accepted a job as president and CEO of eBay in March 1998. A few years later, she reflected on her decision. "It was a huge risk. Sometimes my husband and I look back and say, 'What were we thinking?'" she acknowledged. "But we loved living in California and we thought that tech would continue to play an increasing role in society, and that being in the heartland of tech for us and our two boys would be positive. And we figured, what's the worst that could happen? I get another job."

Fitting into the eBay Culture

Even though most of her work experience had been at large corporations, Whitman fit right in at the fast-growing Internet start-up. She had no trouble giving up her fancy office and sharing a personal assistant with another manager. "My cubicle is the same size as the customer service reps'," she said. "You know, I don't actually miss the trappings of the offices I used to have. I love being in a smaller environment, feeling like I'm in a bit of a PT boat [a small, fast, maneuverable boat used to torpedo enemy ships in wartime], as opposed to a battleship."

> **"There is always a lot of laughing in her office," said eBay founder Pierre Omidyar. "You know Meg is in a meeting when you hear her loud laughter."**

In eBay's quick-changing environment, Whitman learned to think and act fast. In fact, she once estimated that in an average day at eBay she made the same number of decisions that would come up in two to three months at a more conventional company. "[It] is in many ways a different company every three months, and that's because the space is changing and the competitors are changing and the technology is changing so rapidly," she said. "In this space, the price of inaction is higher than the price of making a mistake."

Whitman worked closely with Omidyar during her first 18 months to really learn the business. "Side-by-side. Cubicle-by-cubicle," she noted. "I didn't make very many decisions without Pierre's input, and we just had a fabulous working relationship." Omidyar agreed, stating that "It's pretty rare that a founder [of a company] gets along so well with the new 'head of state' like Meg. There is always a lot of laughing in her office. You know Meg is in a meeting when you hear her loud laughter."

Taking eBay Public

One of Whitman's first duties as president and CEO of eBay was to prepare the company for its initial public offering (IPO) in September 1998. An IPO marks the first time that a corporation offers shares of stock for sale to investors on the public stock exchange. Many corporations stage an IPO, or "go public," as they grow in order to get money to pay for further expansion. Investors who purchased stock in eBay would become part-

Whitman poses with Pez candy dispensers during a photo session for a business magazine cover.

owners of the company. They would gain or lose money based on eBay's financial performance.

Prior to the offering, Whitman staged a nationwide eBay "road show." Joined by eBay's other top managers, she met with major investors to convince them that eBay was a good place to put their money. When the IPO finally took place, it was an overwhelming success. By the end of eBay's first day of trading on the stock exchange, its initial price of $18 per share had jumped to $47—an increase of 163 percent. By December 1998 the stock price went as high as $262.25 per share.

The rapid growth in eBay's stock price made Whitman one of the world's wealthiest business women. When she joined eBay in 1998, Whitman received options to buy 14.4 million shares of company stock at only 22 cents per share. A stock option is a common form of compensation that rewards top executives for increasing the price of the company's stock. Executives receive options to purchase shares at a low price, under the assumption that the stock price will go up over time. When they eventually exercise their option to purchase the shares, the executives can pocket the difference between the option price and the stock-market price on the day they are sold. Whitman sold 2.4 million of her shares in 1999 and 1.2 million in 2000. The selling prices ranged from $55 to more than $170 per share. As a result, Whitman's personal fortune has been estimated at between $700 million and $1.2 billion.

Improving eBay

Whitman made a number of improvements within a short time of her arrival at eBay. For example, she moved quickly to upgrade the eBay web site and to improve its look. She also launched a formal marketing plan. Within a year, celebrities were mentioning eBay in public and using the site to sell signed items for charity. As the site gained media attention, its customer base grew rapidly. By 2000 Whitman saw the number of eBay users increase from 750,000 to about 10 million. Two years later the number of registered users had swelled to 42 million, and more than $9 billion worth of merchandise was being traded on the site.

From the beginning, Whitman understood that users were the foundation of eBay's success. With that in mind, she has emphasized that all business decisions should be based on clear customer data. Customer surveys are routinely posted on the site, and many users' ideas have been adopted by the company over the years. The company has also sponsored live seminars around the country to help users make the most of eBay — and to encourage them to share their ideas about the site. Whitman also initiated a monthly "Voice of the Customer" day, when eBay brings a group of up to 20 users from around the world to its San Jose headquarters. The customers meet with eBay employees, including Whitman, to share their opinions, complaints, and ideas for improving eBay.

All of these innovations reflect Whitman's determination to make eBay users feel welcome and valued. "We started with commerce, and what grew out of that was community," Whitman explained. "The stories are myriad of people who really now do full time what they love to do, whether it's sell baseball cards or sell pottery, or whatever, because they can do it on eBay and make a living at what they love."

Whitman claims that eBay's emphasis on service and user satisfaction can be seen in every facet of the company's operations. For example, customers use the site's message boards to comment about fee increases, auction fraud, and other issues. And when Whitman makes a decision users do not like, they bombard her with hundreds of e-mail messages. "The great thing about running this company," she mused, "is that you know immediately what your customers think."

Facing Challenges

Of course, not all of Whitman's strategic decisions have proven successful. The company failed in an effort to establish a presence in the world of traditional auction houses. It also lost out to Yahoo! in a bid to capture the lucrative Japanese online auction market. But Whitman remained unfazed by these setbacks. "We have been careful to remain humble," she said. "We have to be free to say what we did didn't work and we'll try again."

One of the greatest challenges Whitman has faced at eBay occurred in 1999, when the eBay Internet site was shut down for 22 hours because of a system crash. Angry users swamped the site's technical support board with complaints. Whitman then closed the board entirely—a decision that her customers criticized. But Whitman earned back the trust of eBay users through her commitment to solving the technical problems. She worked 100 hours per week for a month—sleeping on a cot at the office—to make sure the outage was fixed. Company founder Pierre Omidyar called the incident "one of her shining moments. . . . Other executives might have said, 'I don't understand what's happening. Fix it.' Meg's response was to learn everything she possibly could learn." Eventually, eBay refunded millions of dollars to users who had listed items during the outage. The company also offered some users free auctions. Finally, Whitman ordered a major overhaul of the entire eBay network to ensure that the company and its users would be protected from future shut downs.

Whitman also moved decisively to address another major issue in eBay's business: auction fraud. Omidyar built the site on the premise that people

> *"The stories are myriad of people who really now do full time what they love to do, whether it's sell baseball cards or sell pottery, or whatever, because they can do it on eBay and make a living at what they love,"* noted Whitman.

441

Whitman stands outside of eBay headquarters in San Jose, California.

are essentially trustworthy. The vast majority of eBay users, he believed, would deliver promised goods and make payments without a hitch. But as a precaution, he also established a message board. Sellers and buyers use the board to provide feedback about their dealings with each other. The site awards one point for a positive comment, zero points for a neutral comment, and minus one point for a negative comment. Users who reach a "minus-four" rating are barred from using eBay. Would-be users can easily access the comments and view the ratings.

In spite of this system, a small percentage of buyers and sellers still failed to deliver. Whitman responded by introducing a "comprehensive trust and safety program" at eBay. Sophisticated software analyzes buying and selling patterns to detect problems. The site offers users free insurance options for purchases up to $200. Customers also have the chance, for a small fee, to verify their identities with a credit-rating company. These measures have kept fraud to a manageable level on eBay.

Expanding eBay

In her five years at eBay, Whitman has won praise for her strategies for expanding the company. Under her leadership, eBay moved well beyond the collectibles, like Beanie Babies, that originally formed the core of the business. Now eBay moves virtually all types of goods — from nails to computer equipment. Different areas of the site are devoted to travel, sports, automobiles, and other types of goods. In addition, eBay has introduced dozens of regional Web sites for items like cars, boats, and other oversized goods that are hard to ship. Whitman also introduced specialty sites under the banner of eBay — much like individual shops housed within a big shopping mall.

In another innovation, Whitman helped move eBay beyond the auction-sale format. Inspired by Half.com — a Web site that offered fixed-price, discounted used merchandise — Whitman decided to offer eBay customers the option to buy goods right away, without an auction. A "Buy Now" button allows users to make a purchase at a set price. The "Buy Now" option proved so popular that it now accounts for about 30 percent of all purchases made on eBay.

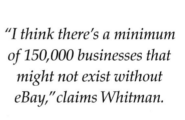

In a further move to stimulate growth, Whitman encouraged companies and retail stores to trade on eBay. Both large corporations and small businesses now use the site to sell surplus goods or trade merchandise. Some of eBay's individual users expressed anger about big business moving onto the site. They feared that the larger companies would crowd them out or claim most of eBay's attention. Indeed, business experts warn that Whitman will have to be careful not to alienate the individual users that have made eBay such a success. Thus far, however, eBay seems to be meeting the needs of all its users. As *Time* noted in 2003, "Mom-and-pop shops peddle their wares alongside IBM, Kodak, and Sears — and many stake their livelihood on the digital marketplace." Indeed, Whitman claims that "I think there's a minimum of 150,000 businesses that might not exist without eBay."

"I think there's a minimum of 150,000 businesses that might not exist without eBay," claims Whitman.

All of these initiatives have helped Whitman transform eBay into a worldwide presence. This expansion into overseas markets started early in her eBay career, when she acquired Europe's largest on-line auction site. She then moved aggressively to make a claim to a global marketplace. By early 2003 eBay either owned businesses or supported trading in about 30 countries. Revenues from this overseas trading grew by 173 percent in the last part of 2002. By mid-2003, eBay was valued at $32 billion, and it was estimated that it was handling transactions worth $59 million a day.

Looking ahead, Whitman acknowledges that eBay faces stiff competition from big Internet players like Yahoo! and Amazon.com, as well as at least 100 other online auction sites. But she claims that her biggest challenge involves attracting people to do business on the Internet. After all, most collectors and hobbyists still operate mainly through antique shops, trading fairs, or newspaper ads. "You know who our real competitor is? It's not the other online auction companies. It's the challenge of getting people to do on eBay what they do in the offline world," she acknowledged. "Our challenge is to get the offline transactions transferred online, because it's more efficient, more fun, and there's a bigger selection. Our real competitor is, in many ways, the old way of doing things."

> "You know who our real competitor is?" said Whitman. "It's not the other online auction companies. It's the challenge of getting people to do on eBay what they do in the offline world. . . . Our real competitor is, in many ways, the old way of doing things."

Success Makes Her a Celebrity

Whitman's management style and strategy won particular acclaim beginning in 2000. At a time when many Internet-based companies lost huge amounts of money or even failed, eBay continued to turn a profit. And its success has continued. In fact, eBay's earnings for the first three months of 2003 grew by 119 percent compared to a year earlier. A record 220 million listings appeared on the site from January through March. Much of the company's growth came from international markets, which provided 30 percent of eBay's revenues. "It seems like every business they touch, whether it be international or payments, they are able to grow it even further," said an industry analyst in 2003.

Whitman's high-profile success has made her a business celebrity and media favorite. She has appeared on magazine covers, television programs, and many lists of top business leaders. Although she does not reveal much about her personal life in interviews, many strangers treat her like a friend. "You know how you watch movies and you follow a star's career? You feel like you know them," she explained. "I think that is a little bit of what is going on now."

In spite of the unexpected burden of celebrity, Whitman loves her job. She particularly enjoys breaking ground in a brand-new marketplace. "It's really an interesting intellectual challenge — to figure out what the right thing to do is because there's really not a lot of 'best practices' to fall back on," she noted. Whitman also appreciates eBay's community of users. "It is incredibly fun to see entrepreneurs take advantage of this marketplace and utilize it in ways that we never would have dreamed of," she noted. Finally, Whitman says that she is happy to "build something that hasn't been done before on a global basis and have the company culture be the kind of company culture I always wanted to work in."

MARRIAGE AND FAMILY

Whitman married Griffith R. Harsh IV, a leading U.S. neurosurgeon, in 1980. They have two teenaged sons, Griff and Will. Whitman reportedly lives a relatively modest lifestyle. For example, she gets her wardrobe at department stores — but claims that she shops for clothes infrequently, because it bores her. Although she could easily afford a full staff at home, she employs only a cleaner. Her oldest son reportedly does most of the family's cooking. One of Whitman's biggest luxuries is avoiding work on the weekends. "Virtually all my time is dedicated to eBay and my family," Whitman said. "It's a wonderful life."

HOBBIES AND OTHER INTERESTS

In her spare time, Whitman enjoys skiing, tennis, and hiking. She and her family also like fly-fishing. "My 16-year-old son was very anxious to learn," Whitman said. "He loved it, and he said, 'Mom, you are going to love this.' We go five or six times a year." The family often spends vacations at her husband's family farm in Sweetwater, Tennessee, or in Colorado.

Whitman has shared her wealth to benefit others. She has given generously to her alma mater, Princeton University, where she sits on the board of trustees. In 2002 she promised $30 million to the university to establish a new residential college. The donation will allow Princeton to expand the number of students it serves and to provide financial help to attract applicants from a wider variety of social and economic backgrounds.

HONORS AND AWARDS

Third Most Powerful Woman in Business (*Fortune* magazine): 2002
Best CEOs (*Worth* Magazine): 2002
Top 25 Most Powerful Business Managers (*Business Week* magazine): 2000, 2001, 2002

FURTHER READING

Books

Bunnell, David, and Richard Luecke. *The eBay Phenomenon: Business Secrets Behind the World's Hottest Internet Company,* 2000
Business Leader Profiles for Students, Vol. 2, 2002
Cohen, Adam. *The Perfect Store: Inside eBay,* 2002

Periodicals

Atlanta Journal Constitution, June 6, 1999, p.H7
Business Week, Mar. 19, 2001, p.98
Current Biography Yearbook, 2002
Detroit Free Press, Apr. 3, 1995, p.F3
Fast Company, May 2001, p.72
Forbes, July 5, 1999, p.81; July 22, 2002, p.68
Fortune, Oct. 25, 1999, p.94; Jan. 21, 2002, p.78
Newsweek International, Oct. 11, 1999, p.50
New York Times, May 10, 1999, p.C1; May 5, 2002, p.L1
Time, Feb. 5, 2001, p.48; July 28, 2003, p.A9

Online Articles

http://business.cisco.com
(*Cisco Systems Online,* "Q & A with eBay's Meg Whitman: The Charlie Rose Interview," July/Aug. 2001)

Online Databases

Biography Resource Center Online, 2003, articles from *Business Leader Profiles for Students,* 2002, and *Newsmakers 2000,* 2000

ADDRESS

Meg Whitman
eBay, Inc.
2125 Hamilton Ave.
San Jose, California 95125

WORLD WIDE WEB SITE

http://www.eBay.com

Reese Witherspoon 1976-

American Actress
Star of the Hit Films *Legally Blonde* and *Sweet Home Alabama*

BIRTH

Reese Witherspoon was born Laura Jean Reese Witherspoon on March 26, 1976, in New Orleans, Louisiana. Her father, John Witherspoon, is a surgeon; her mother, Betty (Reese) Witherspoon, is a nurse with a Ph.D. in pediatric nursing who teaches at the college level. She has a brother, John, Jr., who is three years older.

Witherspoon comes from a very old and distinguished family. One of her father's ancestors, John D. Witherspoon, was a Scottish immigrant who signed the Declaration of Independence and became the first president of Princeton University.

YOUTH

Witherspoon's father was a surgeon in the U.S. Air Force, so Reese spent her first five years living in Germany and traveling throughout Europe. Then her family settled in Nashville, Tennessee, where she and her brother grew up in a very stable and loving home. "I walked to school every day," she says. "My grandmother lived down the street. My grandfather grew all our vegetables in his garden." She idolized her father, who had achieved a perfect score on his S.A.T.s and graduated at the top of his class from Yale. Her mother had a number of college degrees and set high academic standards for her children.

"There was a little girl who lived down the street and her parents owned a flower shop, and they asked me to be in their local commercial," Witherspoon recalls. *"I came home and told my mother I wanted to be an actress."*

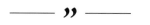

Witherspoon was barely in grade school when she became interested in acting. "There was a little girl who lived down the street and her parents owned a flower shop, and they asked me to be in their local commercial," Witherspoon recalls. "I came home and told my mother I wanted to be an actress." Her parents had hoped their daughter would follow in their footsteps and pursue a medical career, but they didn't try to stand in her way. The enrolled her in acting classes at age seven and let her start modeling for department store ads when she was 10. Within a couple of years she was appearing in TV commercials.

Becoming an Actress

When Witherspoon was 14, she heard that Robert Mulligan, who had directed *To Kill a Mockingbird,* was making a movie in the Nashville area. She auditioned for a role as an extra, but to her surprise, she was given one of the leading roles in *The Man in the Moon,* a story about a young girl growing up in the south in the 1950s. As Dani Trant, she falls in love with a 17-year-old neighbor, only to discover that he is much more interested in her older sister. *The Hollywood Reporter* called Witherspoon's performance "flawless." Although she was barely a teenager, her interest in acting suddenly seemed like more than just a hobby.

After *The Man in the Moon*, Witherspoon was offered a number of smaller television and movie roles. She appeared in "Wildflower," a 1991 HBO movie directed by the well-known actress Diane Keaton. It tells the story of a young woman in the 1930s who is partially deaf and suffers from epileptic seizures, for which her stepfather has locked her in a shed for most of her life. Witherspoon played Ellie, the tomboy who discovers this woman and decides to rescue her. The following year she played Cassie in "Desperate Choices: To

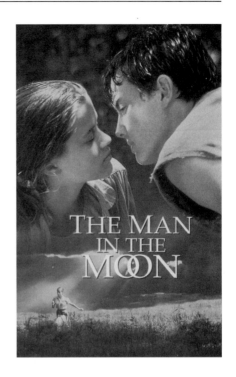

Save My Child," another television drama, about a young girl suffering from leukemia who needs a bone marrow transplant. She also appeared with Danny DeVito in the film *Jack the Bear*. Then she got another starring role, this time in a Disney adventure movie called *A Far Off Place*, which was filmed in Africa's Kalahari Desert. As Nonnie, a teenage girl who has been raised in Africa and whose parents have been killed by elephant poachers, she undertakes a dangerous journey across the desert with a teenage companion named Harry (Ethan Randall), whose parents have also been murdered but who shows little understanding or appreciation of the African way of life.

Many parents would have had reservations about letting their teenage daughter take time away from her studies or travel all the way to Africa to appear in a movie. But Witherspoon gives credit to her parents for their open-mindedness and their willingness to support their daughter's interests. "I have to say that one of the greatest things that my parents did was to encourage my individuality," she told an interviewer some years later. "They just said Okay."

After she returned from filming *A Far Off Place*, Witherspoon had a minor role as the teenage wife of a Scottish land baron in "Return to Lonesome

Dove," a sequel to the Emmy Award-winning television miniseries of the late 1980s. But the sequel was panned by TV critics for its slow pace and mediocre acting.

EDUCATION

While she was already a working actress, Witherspoon attended an elite private all-girls high school in Nashville called Harpeth Hall. She was a top student, a cheerleader, and a debutante who wore a long white gown to her "coming out" ball, a ritual that marks a young woman's introduction to polite society. But she was also what she describes as "the classic nerd who was reading books all the time." She particularly loved doing research in the library and writing papers.

> *"I wore a uniform to school, and I have to say I liked it a lot. It was good not to be so concerned about how I looked. In high school, you are so concerned about your look and your body 'cause you're changing a lot.*
> *I thought it was so cool not to have that pressure, and the comfort to be yourself. And it sucks when you can't afford things or another person doesn't like what you're wearing. That's a terrible feeling."*

When Witherspoon was a teenager, she loved to shop. But except for the Gap, there weren't a lot of good stores near her home. So she ended up buying a lot from catalogs. "I became a catalog shopper growing up and I had to order all my clothes. I would die when I got the new J. Crew catalog 'cause I wanted to have the stuff before my friends." But she couldn't wear those clothes to school at Harpeth Hall. Instead, she wore a uniform. "I wore a uniform to school, and I have to say I liked it a lot," she admits. "It was good not to be so concerned about how I looked. In high school, you are so concerned about your look and your body 'cause you're changing a lot. I thought it was so cool not to have that pressure, and the comfort to be yourself. And it sucks when you can't afford things or another person doesn't like what you're wearing. That's a terrible feeling."

Witherspoon's high school grades were good enough to get her accepted at Stanford University. But after graduating from Harpeth Hall in 1994 she took a year off to appear in a series of films that provided her with more wide-ranging acting experience. In *S.F.W.* she played a hostage trapped in a Los Angeles convenience store. The film received negative reviews, but the "gentle dignity" of Witherspoon's performance attracted notice. She won even higher praise and more public attention for her role in *Fear* as an innocent teenage girl whose relationship with a boy (Mark Wahlberg) she doesn't know very well turns violent when the girl's father tries to keep them apart. *Overnight Delivery* was a more lighthearted film in which she and Paul Rudd travel across the country trying to intercept an overnight delivery letter. Her last film during this period was *Freeway*, a retelling of "Little Red Riding Hood" in which a girl named Vanessa (Witherspoon) is on her way to visit her grandmother when she is picked up on a California highway by a serial killer named Wolverton (Keifer Sutherland). Vanessa, whose mother is a drug addict and whose boyfriend has sexually abused her, turns on her captor and shoots him — quite a change from the innocent young girls Witherspoon had been playing up to this point in her career.

When Witherspoon entered Stanford, she studied English literature and thought about going on to medical school. But after her freshman year she was given an opportunity to star in a film called *Twilight*. "I had to make a choice between Psych 101 and starring in a film opposite Paul Newman, Gene Hackman, Susan Sarandon, and James Garner," she says. "My parents didn't quite understand my decision, but to me it was a no-brainer."

CAREER HIGHLIGHTS

In *Twilight*, Witherspoon plays Mel Ames, the 17-year-old daughter of two movie stars, Jack and Catherine Ames (Gene Hackman and Susan Sarandon). When Mel runs off to be with her boyfriend, Jack and Catherine ask retired private investigator Harry Ross (Paul Newman) to find her and bring her home. Mel ends up accidentally shooting and injuring Harry, who is given a place to live on Jack and Catherine's estate. The plot is complicated by the fact that Jack is dying of cancer and Harry has a long-standing romantic interest in Catherine, whose first husband disappeared 20 years ago and is believed to have committed suicide, although the case has never been solved. It is Harry's involvement in this 20-year-old mystery that becomes the film's focus.

Witherspoon's decision to interrupt her education to appear in a film with Oscar-winning actors Newman, Hackman, and Sarandon turned out to be a smart career move. She was soon receiving so many other movie offers that returning to Stanford was out of the question.

Reese Witherspoon and Tobey Maguire in Pleasantville, *1998.*

Spreading Her Wings

Witherspoon appeared in four more movies during 1998-99, playing very different roles in each and proving herself to be a talented and versatile actress. In *Pleasantville* she plays Jennifer, the teenage sister of David (Tobey Maguire), who is obsessed with a 1950s sitcom that is being re-broadcast on cable television. Jennifer and David have a tough home life, with divorced parents who always seem to be fighting with each other. So for David, the simple and secure life depicted in his favorite TV show is very appealing and comforting. One day, the two siblings get into an argument over the remote control—David wants to watch his re-runs while Jennifer wants to watch a concert on MTV. The remote breaks, and a mysterious TV repairman gives them a new high-tech remote that transports them back to the 1950s in Pleasantville, the location of David's favorite sitcom. They discover that they are now Bud and Mary Sue in a black-and-white world. In Pleasantville, the weather is always sunny and no one ever steps out of line. It's a strange world, with no toilets, no fire, no rain, and no double beds—not even for married couples. It's a completely sanitized life, one in which the other inhabitants don't seem to realize its limitations. Life is predictable, safe, and nonthreatening—but also boring, stifling, repressed, and unimaginative, with enforced conformity. There's no passion, no strong emotions. At first, Bud makes a fairly easy adjustment to his new life, but Mary Sue sets out to change it. Eventually both Bud and Mary Sue begin to affect others, and people begin to experience strange new thoughts and emotions, which are reflected in the bursts of color that begin to appear in Pleasantville's formerly black-and-white world. The movie won praise from critics as a clever, provocative, and complex parable, and Witherspoon won raves for her performance.

Cruel Intentions is a 1990s version of the 1782 French novel, *Les liaisons dangereuses* (*Dangerous Liaisons*), by Pierre Choderlos de Laclos. This novel about the corruption of innocence has been adapted for the big screen several times, including an Oscar-winning version in 1988. Witherspoon plays Annette Hargrove, the very proper and well-behaved daughter of the headmaster of a private school in New York City. Kathryn (Sarah Michele Gellar) and her stepbrother Sebastian (Ryan Phillippe) amuse themselves one summer by making bets with each other. Annette has announced that she intends to stay "pure" until she gets married. So Kathryn bets Sebastian that he won't be able to seduce her before school starts in the fall. *Variety* called Witherspoon's portrayal of Annette "a difficult role" in which she was outshone by her co-star Gellar. But filming *Cruel Intentions* proved to be a turning point in Witherspoon's personal life: not long after the film was released, she and Ryan Phillippe announced that they were expecting a baby and planned to get married.

> *"I had to make a choice between Psych 101 and starring in a film opposite Paul Newman, Gene Hackman, Susan Sarandon, and James Garner.* My parents didn't quite understand my decision, but to me it was a no-brainer."

Witherspoon's third movie during this very busy period in her life was the one that finally brought her the widespread critical acclaim she'd been hoping for. In *Election* she plays Tracy Flick, an ambitious over-achiever in a Nebraska high school who wants desperately to become class president so she can improve her chances of getting into a prestigious college. She's opposed by Mr. McAllister (Matthew Broderick), the teacher who acts as an advisor to the student government. He is so alienated by Tracy's single-minded pursuit of the position that he tries to undermine her plans by finding another student to run against her—and more. His actions cost him his job and his marriage, but Tracy emerges as the movie's most fasci-

Witherspoon as Tracy Flick in a scene from Election, 1999.

nating character. One reviewer called her "Chirpy, clipped, coiled like a rattlesnake . . . The girl with complete homework, perfect hair, and sensible clothes who always thrusts her hand into the air like a Hitler salute when the teacher asks a question." Another described her as "a whole new kind of villain," so dead set on achieving her goal that she won't let anything stand in her way.

Although *Election* was only a modest box office success, it brought Witherspoon her first Golden Globe nomination and a Best Actress award from the National Society of Film Critics. "Witherspoon nails Tracy in a nifty performance that all viewers will recognize as true," commented the reviewer for *Variety*. "There's one of her ilk in every school and office." By this point, Witherspoon was starting to earn a reputation for her varied and nuanced performances in some unexpected films.

The critical success of *Election* was followed by a disappointment: *Best Laid Plans,* in which Witherspoon starred with Alessandro Nivola. Nick (Nivola) is a young man who'd like to escape his job at a recycling plant and run off with his girlfriend, Lissa (Witherspoon). But the only way he can get enough money to finance his dream is to help a friend who is planning a burglary. The friend gets caught, the stolen money disappears, and Nick and Lissa have to find a way to replace it. Critics didn't like the movie and said that even its stars weren't "big enough to power the material." But Witherspoon didn't let the poor reviews bother her as she gave birth to a daughter in September 1999, the same month the movie was released.

Legally Blonde

Witherspoon took some time off in late 1999 to undergo what she calls "a crash course in motherhood." But she was back at work the following year, appearing as Christian Bale's girlfriend in *American Psycho*, as a college girl who is seduced by her roommate's father in *Slow Motion*, and as Adam Sandler's angelic mother in a slapstick film about Hell and Satan called *Little Nicky*. She also appeared as a guest star in two episodes of the television show "Friends," playing Jennifer Aniston's younger sister. But in 2001 her career took another giant leap forward when she appeared as Elle Woods in *Legally Blonde*, her first real box office hit.

—— " ——

Tracy Flick has been described as "Chirpy, clipped, coiled like a rattlesnake . . . The girl with complete homework, perfect hair, and sensible clothes who always thrusts her hand into the air like a Hitler salute when the teacher asks a question."

—— " ——

Elle is a sorority girl and fashion major at a California college who is rich, popular, and determined to marry her boyfriend, Warner Huntington (Matt Davis). He is heading off to Harvard Law School, and she is eagerly anticipating a marriage proposal before he goes. Elle is devastated when instead of proposing Warner dumps her, because he has political ambitions and doesn't think that Elle is smart enough or accomplished enough to be a senator's wife. Rather than admit defeat, she starts cramming for the Harvard Law entrance exam and manages to get accepted there herself. She arrives in Cambridge, among all the serious, snobby, and brilliant students at Harvard Law School, dressed like a California girl and carrying her pet Chihuahua. Determined to get Warner back by proving that she's more than a "dumb blonde," Elle ends up triumphing, winning the respect of her teachers and her fellow law students—and the affection of a large movie audience.

Witherspoon's performance in *Legally Blonde* was compared to Goldie Hawn's in *Private Benjamin* and Melanie Griffith's in *Working Girl*, two

Scenes of Witherspoon as Elle Woods in Legally Blonde.

other movies about blondes who transform themselves into smart, successful women. A critic from *Variety* called her "a comedienne worthy of comparison to such golden era greats as Carole Lombard and Ginger Rogers" and proclaimed her "one of a very small number of screen actors one wants to see in anything she does." More importantly from a career standpoint, *Legally Blonde* was a huge box office hit, earning more than $100 million and catapulting Reese Witherspoon to nationwide fame. While some of her fans were surprised that she would play a "dumb blonde" after her interesting and complex roles in *Pleasantville* and *Election*, Witherspoon defended her choice. "Making *Legally Blonde* was my own private campaign against a lot of prejudices and stereotypes," she said.

Recent Film Roles

In keeping with her determination to avoid being typecast, Witherspoon went from playing a California sorority girl to playing Cecily in *The Importance of Being Earnest*, the new film version of the 1895 Oscar Wilde play. In this classic comedy of errors story, two gents living in England in the 1890s have each bent the truth a bit, inventing a character named Earnest. But things start to go wrong as their lies are discovered. For Witherspoon, it was an enjoyable change of pace. "I haven't done a lot of period [films]," she explained, "and I saw it as a challenge." Even more challenging was learning to speak with an English accent, which took Witherspoon six weeks of study to master. She was the only American in an all-star British cast that included Colin Firth, Judi Dench, and Rupert Everett.

"I had been playing characters that were larger than life, and I decided to do something that was a little more close to my own personality," Witherspoon said about filming **Sweet Home Alabama.** *"[Melanie's] a southern girl who moves away and makes an entirely new life for herself in this urban world, then has to go home again. Eventually, she grows to love what's beautiful about the place she came from and recognizes it as part of herself — maybe the best part of herself."*

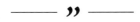

For her most recent film, *Sweet Home Alabama*, Witherspoon had to relearn the southern accent she was born with. Released in September 2002, the romantic comedy *Sweet Home Alabama* tells the story of Melanie Carmichael, a southern girl who moves from Alabama to New York City and becomes a successful fashion designer. She's elated when her new boyfriend Andrew (Patrick Dempsey), who also happens to be the mayor's son and the city's most eligible bachelor, asks her to marry him. But Melanie is forced to return home and confront Jake (Josh Lucas), the man she married as a teenager and never officially divorced. Annoyed that Melanie has re-entered his life, Jake refuses to sign the divorce papers. In the struggle that ensues, Melanie and Jake discover that they are still attracted to one another, and she realizes that she loves both men. Melanie is forced to choose between the man who wants to marry her and the one to whom she has been married all along.

> "
>
> "I'm the classic Type A personality," Witherspoon explains, "because I have a strong tendency towards being compulsive and anxious."
>
> "

"I had been playing characters that were larger than life, and I decided to do something that was a little more close to my own personality," Witherspoon said in an interview. "[Melanie's] a southern girl who moves away and makes an entirely new life for herself in this urban world, then has to go home again. Eventually, she grows to love what's beautiful about the place she came from and recognizes it as part of herself—maybe the best part of herself."

The movie proved to be a bit of a disappointment, earning mixed reviews—some good, but some rather unenthusiastic. *The New Yorker*, for example, panned the movie but praised Witherspoon by saying, "Among the many talents of Reese Witherspoon is the ability to hang around in movies that are unworthy of her, and thus to shine all the brighter." Despite the film's lukewarm reviews, however, it earned $37.5 million the first weekend it opened.

Future Plans and Projects

"I am very ambitious and very focused—that's the kind of character I gravitate toward," Witherspoon explains. "I also feel a responsibility as an actress to represent women in a way that I want to be represented." With this goal in mind, she has recently started her own production company, called Type A Films after her mother's nickname for her. "I'm the classic Type A personality," she explains, "because I have a strong tendency towards being compulsive and anxious." Type A's first film project, which is sched-

Witherspoon with two of her co-stars from Sweet Home Alabama*: Patrick Dempsey, left (Andrew, her fiance), and Josh Lucas, right (Jake, her husband).*

uled to be released in 2003, is a sequel to *Legally Blonde* called *Red, White, and Blonde,* which Witherspoon has directed and stars in. Soon after that, she will appear in the lead role of an independent period film based on the 1848 novel *Vanity Fair* by William Makepeace Thackeray.

Type A Films is currently working on a film adaptation of Melissa Bank's best-selling 1999 novel, *The Girl's Guide to Hunting and Fishing,* which Witherspoon will produce and star in. She is also working on a movie about women's professional tennis—"I'm in awe of female athletes," she says. Other projects include playing Honey West in a film based on the 1960s television series about a woman detective. As both an actress and a producer, Witherspoon remains committed to making small, independent films. If things don't work out for her in Hollywood, she says, "I'll go to medical school."

MARRIAGE AND FAMILY

Witherspoon knew Ryan Phillippe before she worked with him on *Cruel Intentions.* She met him at her own 21st birthday party, to which a friend had invited him. Witherspoon readily admits that her pregnancy was not planned and that, at 23, she was unprepared for motherhood. But Phillippe's mother had run a day care center, and he had a lot of experience handling infants and changing diapers.

———— " ————

"I feel very blessed,"
Witherspoon says.
"Every day of my life I
think God that I found
someone that I'm so in love
with and we have such a
wonderful life. It's really
nice to connect with
someone on pretty
much everything."

———— " ————

Witherspoon and Phillippe were married on June 5, 1999, and their daughter, Ava Elizabeth, was born on September 9. "She really encouraged me to grow up, become more mature," Witherspoon says. She and her husband and daughter now live in Hollywood Hills with their English bulldog. Despite the demands of their busy acting careers, they try to spend no more than a week or two away from Ava or from each other. "We like to cook dinner every night and take our daughter to school every day. We have a pretty normal life outside of the movie stuff," Witherspoon says. Now that Ava is almost four years old, Witherspoon credits her with taking "all the self-obsession out of my life." Her family life is a source of strength for her. "I feel very blessed," she says. "Every day of my life I think God that I found someone that I'm so in love with and we have such a wonderful life. It's really nice to connect with someone on pretty much everything."

MAJOR INFLUENCES

Witherspoon's role models have always been not only actresses, but strong, independent women who have worked hard to make a name for themselves. She calls Jodie Foster, Susan Sarandon, Holly Hunter, and Frances McDormand "actresses who consistently do great work despite ageism and all sorts of other factors working against them." As a comedienne, Witherspoon says that she has been influenced by Lucille Ball, Carol Burnett, and Goldie Hawn.

CREDITS

Films

The Man in the Moon, 1991
Jack the Bear, 1993
A Far Off Place, 1993
S.F.W., 1994
Fear, 1996

Overnight Delivery, 1996
Freeway, 1996
Twilight, 1998
Pleasantville, 1998
Cruel Intentions, 1999
Election, 1999
Best Laid Plans, 1999
American Psycho, 2000
Little Nicky, 2000
Slow Motion, 2000
Legally Blonde, 2001
The Importance of Being Earnest, 2002
Sweet Home Alabama, 2002

Television

Wildflower, 1991
Desperate Choices: To Save My Child, 1992
"Return to Lonesome Dove," 1993
"Friends," 1999

SELECTED HONORS AND AWARDS

Best Actress (National Society of Film Critics): 1999, for *Election*
Best Actress (Kansas City Film Critics Circle): 2000, for *Election*
Blockbuster Entertainment Award: 2000, Favorite Supporting Actress-
    Drama/Romance, for *Cruel Intentions*
MTV Movie Award: 2002, Best Comedic Performance, for *Legally Blonde*
Teen Choice Award for Extraordinary Achievement: 2002

FURTHER READING

Books

Contemporary Theatre, Film, and Television, Vol. 31, 2000

Periodicals

Biography, June 2002, p.38
Cosmopolitan, July 2001, p.170
Entertainment Weekly, Oct. 11, 1996, p.99; Oct. 14, 2002, p.77
In Style, Oct.. 1, 2002, p.458
Interview, Nov. 1994, p.116

Newsweek, Apr. 26, 1999, p.66
People, Oct. 14, 2002, p.77
Premiere, Aug. 2001, p.44
Seventeen, Oct. 2002, p.166
Teen, May 1995, p.90; Sep. 2001, p.50
Time, Aug. 6, 2001, p.58
Times (London), Aug. 25, 2002, Features section, p.6; Dec. 14, 2002,
    Features Section, p.42
Vanity Fair, June. 2000, p.172
W, Sep. 2002, p.416

Online Database

Biography Resource Center Online, 2003, article from *Contemporary Theatre,
    Film, and Television,* 2000

ADDRESS

Reese Witherspoon
Universal Studios
Type A Films
100 Universal City Plaza
Universal City, CA 91608

Yao Ming 1980-

Chinese Professional Basketball Player with the
Houston Rockets
First Overall Pick in the 2002 NBA Draft

BIRTH

Yao Ming was born on September 12, 1980, in Shanghai,
China. In Chinese practice, the family name comes before the
given name, so Yao is his family name (our last name) and
Ming is his given name (our first name). His hometown of
Shanghai is a busy commercial seaport on the East China Sea,
at the mouth of the Yangtze River. Yao's father, Yao Zhi Yuan, is

an engineering manager at the Shanghai harbor. His mother, Fang Feng Di, is an official in China's sports research institute. Both of Yao's parents played basketball for China's national teams in the 1970s. Yao, who is an only child, clearly inherited his height from his parents. His father stands six feet, seven inches tall, while his mother is six feet, three inches tall.

YOUTH AND EDUCATION

Yao grew up in a comfortable middle-class household in Shanghai. He was exceptionally tall even as a child, and his height affected many aspects of his youth. For example, Yao was as tall as his teacher in first grade. He also had to pay the full adult fare to ride public transportation. By the time he was 12 years old he had grown to six feet, six inches—a full foot taller than the average Chinese man. Yao's height eventually reached seven feet, five inches.

Yao's rapid growth left him feeling gawky and uncoordinated. As a boy, he was very thin and weak in the upper body. In fact, his friends jokingly referred to his arms as "chopsticks" because they were so skinny. Yao struggled in sports during this awkward phase. As a result, his first introduction to basketball proved embarrassing to him. When Yao was in the third grade, his teacher asked the class which student could shoot a basket from the free throw line. His classmates immediately suggested him. "This made me very proud at that time," he recalled, "but one of my classmates did better than me, and this remained a sore point for some time. Such was my first close contact with basketball."

When Yao was nine years old, Chinese government authorities selected him to attend the Shanghai Youth Sports School. Yao and his family had no choice but to obey the government's wishes. The People's Republic of China operates under a Communist form of government. Under this type of political system, the central government exercises a great deal of control over the lives of citizens. Communism eliminates most private property and gives it to the government to distribute as it sees fit. It also places severe restrictions on individual rights and allows the government to control the educations, careers, and cultural experiences of the people.

In an effort to build strong national sports teams to compete in the Olympic Games and other international competitions, China identifies potentially promising athletes at an early age. These young people are often taken from their families and sent away to elite sports training schools. Yao was selected for the Shanghai Youth Sports School on the basis of his height and his parents' successful athletic careers. He was initially placed on the water polo team at the school, but he soon switched to basketball. He received intensive training in basketball fundamentals from the school's coaches. He also worked on academics with a tutor for three hours per day and spent two hours each day studying on his own.

In 1994, at the age of 14, Yao was selected to join the Shanghai Youth Basketball Team. His skills improved quickly under the guidance of Coach Wang Qun. "At that time, I trained four times a day—a total of 10 hours," he recalled. "In order to help me master the basic skills, Mr. Wang was very strict. If I slackened my pace, he would punish me. . . . I could not be lazy under my coach's watchful eyes. According to the Chinese Basketball Association standard, I should be able to run 3,200 meters in 18 minutes, but with my coach's rigorous training, I can do it in 14 minutes." In the meantime, Yao continued his academic studies at the Shanghai Physical and Sport Technical Education Institute.

Yao's basketball talents first gained recognition outside of China in 1997, when he attended an elite basketball camp in France sponsored by Nike. During this competition against top young players from around the world, Yao learned new styles of play and improved his confidence. The following year Yao made his first trip to the United States, where he at-

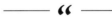

When Yao was in the third grade, his teacher asked the class which student could shoot a basket from the free throw line, and his classmates suggested him. "This made me very proud at the time," he recalled, "but one of my classmates did better than me, and this remained a sore point for some time. Such was my first close contact with basketball."

tended a series of high-profile basketball camps and clinics. He impressed NBA scouts at the Nike Junior Basketball Summer Camp by showing a rare combination of size, agility, intelligence, and outside shooting touch. Yao's excellent performances at these camps and clinics convinced him that he could make a career for himself in the NBA.

Despite his obvious talents, however, Yao still faced challenges in adapting to the American style of basketball. "When I went to America, I didn't like to dunk much," he remembered. "It's not the Chinese way. In America, I'd get the ball near the basket, shoot a layup, and the coach would be saying, 'Dunk the ball!' But I was used to laying it in. Finally,

Yao developed his basketball skills as a member of China's national team.

the coach said, 'If you get the ball in close and don't dunk it, all of your teammates are going to have to run laps.' But I couldn't help it. I was very accustomed to laying the ball in the basket. All of my teammates were running laps, begging me to dunk. Finally after about a week and many laps, I began to dunk it every time."

CAREER HIGHLIGHTS

Chinese Basketball Association: The Shanghai Sharks

Yao's professional basketball career began in 1997, when he joined the Shanghai Sharks of the Chinese Basketball Association (CBA). Basketball is very popular in China. The 12-team CBA attracted 130 million television viewers in China — as many people as typically watch the NFL Super Bowl in the United States — for regular-season games. Yao turned in a solid performance during his rookie CBA season, averaging 10 points and 8.3 rebounds per game. He also won the league's Sportsmanship Award. Unfortunately, the Sharks finished the season ranked eighth in the league.

In 1998 Yao suffered a broken foot and missed much of the CBA season. He came back strong in 1999, however, and improved his averages to 21.2 points and 14.5 rebounds per game.

> "When I went to America, I didn't like to dunk much," Yao remembered. "Finally, the coach said, 'If you get the ball in close and don't dunk it, all of your teammates are going to have to run laps.' But I couldn't help it. I was very accustomed to laying the ball in the basket. All of my teammates were running laps, begging me to dunk. Finally after about a week and many laps, I began to dunk it every time."

By 2000 the 20-year-old Yao had developed into the most dominant player in the league. He averaged an impressive 27.1 points, 19.4 rebounds, and 5.5 blocked shots per game and was named the Most Valuable Player of the regular season. Led by their towering center, the Sharks advanced through the playoffs all the way to the CBA finals. But despite the best efforts of Yao and his teammates, the Sharks were defeated in the finals by the defending champion Bayi Rockets.

Yao posted another outstanding year in 2001. He led the CBA in blocked shots with 4.8 per game, and he ranked second in the league in both scoring (with 32.4 points per game) and rebounding (with 19 rebounds per game). The Sharks advanced to the CBA finals, where they again faced the Bayi Rockets. Yao dominated the championship series, posting 41.3 points, 21 rebounds, and 4.3 blocks per game. His strong performance lifted the Sharks to a 3-1 victory in the series and their first-ever CBA championship.

The Chinese National Team

China has long used its best professional basketball players to represent the country in international competition. Yao was selected to the Chinese National Team in 1998, at the age of 18. He trained with the team while he also continued to compete in the CBA with the Shanghai Sharks. In 2000 Yao played for the Chinese National Team at the Summer Olympic Games in Sydney, Australia.

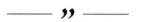

"I don't care if I'm the first Chinese player in the NBA or the second or the third. I just want to try it," Yao said.

The Chinese team's most anticipated game came early in the Olympic tournament, when they faced Team USA. Yao attracted a great deal of attention in the first few minutes of the game, dramatically swatting away shots by NBA stars Vince Carter and Gary Payton. But he eventually fouled out of the game, and the heavily favored American team coasted to a 119-72 victory. After the game, Yao expressed disappointment with his performance against the Americans. "Five minutes of playing well, or ten minutes, do not mean very much," he said afterward. "It's how well you play the entire game. One of American basketball's biggest strengths is understanding that. In the NBA, there are a lot of one-point and two-point games. There is intense competition to the final second."

During the Olympic tournament, Yao led the Chinese National Team in blocks (with 2.17 per game) and rebounds (with 6.0 per game), and he was second on the team in scoring (with 10.5 points per game). But China ended up finishing a disappointing tenth in the men's basketball competition, well out of medal contention. Some analysts claimed that this poor Olympic performance helped convince Chinese government officials to permit the country's star players to join the NBA, where they would gain needed experience against top competition.

In 2001 Yao helped the Chinese National Team capture the Asian Basketball Championship for Men and earn a spot in the World Championships.

He averaged 13.4 points, 10.1 rebounds, and 2.8 blocked shots per game and was named Most Valuable Player of the tournament. He was later named to the All-Tournament Team at the World Championships.

The Long Road to the NBA

Beginning in the late 1990s, NBA scouts kept a close eye on Yao's development as a basketball player. They hoped eventually to lure the young star to play in the NBA, which attracted many of the world's top players during the 1990s. In fact, by the 2001 season there were 45 international players competing on NBA teams. NBA officials also wanted to expand the league's recruiting base into China in order to attract Chinese fans. After all, China was the most populous nation in the world with 1.3 billion people. Around 200 million Chinese played basketball, and NBA games were already seen by 300 million Chinese on television. League officials believed that adding Chinese players to the rosters of NBA teams would dramatically increase the Chinese people's interest in the league.

Yao holds his new team jersey after the Houston Rockets selected him with the first pick of the 2002 NBA draft.

But some Chinese officials were reluctant to allow the country's top athletes to leave the country and play professionally in the United States. Under the Chinese sports system, Yao belonged to the Shanghai Sharks, the CBA, and the Chinese National Team. These entities had invested a great deal of time and money in training, feeding, housing, and educating Yao from the time he was nine years old. As a result, they felt that they should also benefit from his talents.

On the other hand, more progressive Chinese officials felt that the country would gain in the long run by sending its top athletes overseas to play against tougher competition. They wanted to show the world that China could develop basketball talent that could compete against the world's best. These feelings grew stronger following the Chinese National Team's disappointing performance in the 2000 Olympic Games. In 2001 China allowed two players to enter the NBA draft. Wang Zhi-Zhi, the seven-foot center of the Bayi Rockets, was drafted by the Dallas Mavericks, while another seven-footer, Mengke Bateer, went to the Denver Nuggets.

But the Shanghai Sharks refused to release Yao in 2001, so he could only watch as his teammates from the Chinese National Team left for the NBA. "I don't know if I'll be able to go or not, but I want to," he said at the time. "I don't care if I'm the first Chinese player in the NBA or the second or the third. I just want to try it." After the Sharks claimed the CBA title in 2001, team management said they would allow Yao to enter the NBA draft if the Chinese government agreed to let him leave the country.

Chinese officials recognized that Yao had the potential to earn millions of dollars in the NBA. They also realized that Yao's success would bring positive attention to China, which was hoping to host the 2008 Olympic Games in its capital city of Beijing. At the same time, however, they wanted to maintain some control over Yao's career. The Chinese government ultimately agreed to let Yao play in the NBA. But before he was allowed to leave the country, China published new rules that required Chinese athletes who competed professionally overseas to turn over half of their earnings—including income from advertising endorsements—to China for the length of their careers. The Chinese government also emphasized that it could recall its athletes at any time if they ignored the rules or if they were needed to represent China in international competition.

First Overall Pick in the 2002 NBA Draft

Shortly after receiving permission to play in the NBA, Yao was selected with the first overall pick in the 2002 NBA draft by the Houston Rockets. He thus became the third Chinese player in the NBA, and the first top draft pick ever taken from an international league. "I've waited so long for this," he said afterward. "Now I feel a real sense of peace that I've finally made it. But, I know there are many challenges ahead." Yao signed a four-year contract with the Rockets worth an estimated $18 million. He chose uniform number 11, which represents smoothness in Chinese culture.

Although Yao was thrilled to be the top overall pick in the draft, he recognized that this honor would not automatically make him a superstar in the

NBA. "Apart from [Allen] Iverson and [Tim] Duncan, few number one selections in the NBA draft have given an outstanding performance," he noted. "To improve my skills, I must set myself exacting targets. It doesn't matter whether I win the final championship or not. As long as I have tried my best, I will have no regrets."

Many basketball fans had high hopes that Yao would become the next great center in the NBA. The league had seen many of its star centers retire or reach the end of their careers in the late 1990s. By the time Yao was drafted, the only superstar centers playing in the NBA were Shaquille O'Neal of the Los Angeles Lakers and Tim Duncan of the San Antonio Spurs.

Yet some basketball fans doubted whether Yao would be able to make a successful adjustment to the NBA. They pointed out that the Chinese style of basketball—which emphasized teamwork over individual accomplishments—was very different from American basketball. In fact, the Chinese Basketball Association did not begin keeping track of statistics for individual players until 1995. Doubters also noted that Yao would have to deal with an unfamiliar language and culture. Finally, critics predicted that Yao would have trouble handling the pressure and media attention that would follow the first star Chinese player in the NBA.

"To improve my skills, I must set myself exacting targets," declared Yao. "It doesn't matter whether I win the final championship or not. As long as I have tried my best, I will have no regrets."

The Houston Rockets organization took a number of steps to help ease Yao's transition to the United States and the NBA. For example, they brought Yao's mother to Houston several weeks before he arrived. They gave her a tour of the city—including its many Chinese markets and restaurants—and helped her find a comfortable house to share with her son. Yao's father also visited for several weeks early in the season. The Rockets also hired an American, Colin Pine, to live with Yao and act as his translator and guide to American culture. Since Yao did not drive a car in China, the team presented him with a custom-made bicycle featuring an extra-large frame. Finally, the Rockets held a seminar to familiarize all team employees with Chinese cultural traditions.

During Yao's rookie season, he quickly emerged as a force on both the offensive and defensive ends of the court.

NBA: The Houston Rockets

The Rockets had finished the 2001-02 season with a 28-54 won-loss record, which earned the team fifth place in the Midwest Division of the NBA's Western Conference. The team's best player was point guard Steve Francis, nicknamed "The Franchise." The Rockets' starting lineup also included promising young guard Cuttino Mobley and forwards Glen Rice and Maurice Taylor. Many people anticipated that the addition of Yao would eventually help the Rockets become a playoff contender. But others worried that he would struggle to adapt to the NBA and become yet another disappointing high-profile draft pick.

Yao missed the Rockets' training camp and several preseason games because he was playing in the World Championships with the Chinese National Team. When he finally arrived in the United States, it did not take him long to earn the respect of his teammates with his solid fundamentals, hard work, and team-oriented attitude. "He's an incredibly endearing person. He's got this humble demeanor that is refreshing in our sport," said Houston Rockets general manager Carroll Dawson. "I remember the first day he came to practice. He missed all of training camp and most of our preseason because of obligations to his national team. There had been a tremendous amount of hype about him already, so I was curious to see how it went. In the first five minutes, he set three picks, made two terrific passes, and, when he scored, he ran back down the court with his head down. That's all it took. He had won his teammates over."

"I remember the first day [Yao] came to practice," recalled Houston general manager Carroll Dawson. "In the first five minutes, he set three picks, made two terrific passes, and, when he scored, he ran back down the court with his head down. That's all it took. He had won his teammates over."

Yao got off to a slow start once the 2002-03 NBA season began. He scored a total of 13 points in his first five games and sometimes looked a bit lost on the court. After all the attention that had surrounded his entering the league, some people seemed to take satisfaction in his early struggles. For example, the ESPN cable sports network put together a "lowlights" reel of Yao's worst moments on the court during his first week in the NBA. After one particularly poor outing, commentator and former NBA star Charles Barkley bet that Yao would never score 20 points in a game.

But Yao improved so quickly that he amazed many observers. He adapted to the NBA style of play and also adjusted to the constant attention he received from fans and the media. "I feel a lot of pressure on me," he admitted. "But I feel it every day. I am used to it. It is a bit of a burden on me, but I have to realize it's a responsibility I have to shoulder." Yao posted his first 20-point game less than a week after Barkley made his prediction. He scored a season-high 30 points a few weeks later against the Dallas Mavericks and their seven-foot, five-inch center, Shawn Bradley.

"I feel a lot of pressure on me," admitted Yao. "But I feel it every day. I am used to it. It is a bit of a burden on me, but I have to realize it's a responsibility I have to shoulder."

Yao appeared in all 82 games during his rookie season with the Rockets, starting all but 10 games. He averaged a respectable 13.5 points, 8.2 rebounds, and 1.79 blocked shots per game. He achieved a season-high 19 rebounds in a game against Sacramento in March, and he blocked a season-high six shots in two different contests. Finally, Yao shot an impressive 81 percent from the free throw line. He ended up finishing a close second behind Amare Stoudemire of the Phoenix Suns for NBA Rookie of the Year honors.

Rockets fans and management were thrilled with the solid performance of the team's top draft pick. "People ask me all the time if I'm surprised Yao is this good," said Rockets general manager Carroll Dawson. "The answer is no. I knew he'd be this good. We've been following him since he was 15. But I had no idea he'd be this good this fast." For his part, Yao credited Rockets Coach Rudy Tomjanovich and his teammates for his easy transition to the NBA. "I don't know what happened," he stated. "It's a testament to my coaches and teammates. They've helped me very much."

Boosted by Yao's intimidating presence in the middle, the Rockets won 15 more games than they had the season before. He also helped transform Houston into one of the league's most exciting teams. But despite finishing the season with a 43-39 won-loss record, the Rockets failed to qualify for a berth in the NBA playoffs.

At season's end, Yao's mother expressed great pride in her son's accomplishments. "Yao Ming was coming to a completely new environment, an environment completely different from China," she noted. "He never had any NBA experience or much experience in the United States. He had none of the experience of American basketball. And of course, there are differences between basketball in China and the U.S. Before he was playing by international rules, not NBA rules. He's not as big and strong as the American players. I thought there would be a longer period of adjustment for him."

The Start of a Rivalry

As the 2002-03 NBA season progressed and Yao showed rapid improvement, basketball fans eagerly anticipated the first matchup between him and Shaquille O'Neal. The Rockets did not face the defending NBA champion Los Angeles Lakers until January 2003, but O'Neal apparently grew tired of being compared to Yao long before that. When yet another reporter asked the Lakers' star center about the Rockets' rookie center, O'Neal adopted a fake Chinese accent and said, "Tell Yao Ming, 'Ching chong yang wah ah so.'"

NBA observers believe that Yao is one of the few players capable of challenging Los Angeles Lakers center Shaquille O'Neal for recognition as the league's top center.

O'Neal's remark created a controversy. Many people, including members of prominent Asian-American organizations, criticized him for showing a lack of sensitivity toward Chinese culture. But Yao refused to take offense and instead chose to handle the situation diplomatically. When a reporter asked Yao about his rival's remark, Yao joked that Chinese was a difficult language to learn. When the Lakers came to Houston, Yao invited O'Neal to his house for dinner (Shaq had to decline the invitation due to a previous engagement with his daughter). Yao later explained the reason behind his calm reaction to the controversy. "Chinese people don't want other people to lose face," he said. "In Chinese culture, you will be looked down on just for letting someone lose face."

When the two big men finally faced off against each other on the court, O'Neal tested Yao immediately with a series of post-up moves near the basket. Yao responded by swatting away three of O'Neal's shots within the first few minutes of the game. The Lakers' star went on to have an impressive night, with 31 points and 13 rebounds. By contrast, Yao only managed 10 points and 10 rebounds. Nonetheless, many observers felt that a rivalry emerged between the big men during the course of the game. After all, Yao blocked O'Neal's shot five times during the game. Until that time, opponents had only managed to block O'Neal once every other game during the season. Most important of all, Yao's performance helped the Rockets defeat the Lakers 108-104 in overtime.

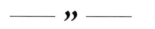

"[Yao's] a really bright guy, and he understands a lot," said his translator. "But he is not fluent [in English] by any means. Imagine if you were dropped into China and had three months to learn the language. Do you think you'd be ready to conduct a press conference?"

A few weeks later, Yao easily beat O'Neal in total fan votes to become the starting center for the Western Conference in the NBA All-Star Game. Yao was excited about appearing in the All-Star Game, but he insisted that he did not deserve to start over O'Neal. "He's the best center in the game," Yao said of Shaq. "Why can't he start and I come off the bench?" In fact, Yao claimed that he needed to improve his upper-body strength, rebounding skills, and reaction time on defense in order to better compete with O'Neal and other NBA stars.

Brings Excitement and an International Audience to the NBA

Throughout his first NBA season, Yao attracted hordes of new fans to the game of basketball. The excitement surrounding his selection in the draft helped the Rockets draw sellout crowds for home games for the first time since 1999. But Yao's appeal was not limited to Houston. People from across the United States also flocked to see Yao play when the Rockets went on road trips. Fans everywhere appreciated his playing skills, humble attitude, solid work ethic, and sense of humor.

*Yao's celebrity status has given him opportunities to meet other
famous athletes, such as tennis star Andre Agassi.*

As the season progressed, Yao also emerged as a particular source of pride for people of Chinese descent. In fact, live broadcasts of Rockets games—which aired early in the morning—attracted 5.5 million viewers in China. Another 11.5 million people tuned in when the games were rebroadcast later in the day. In comparison, an average weeknight telecast of an NBA game drew only 1.1 million viewers in the United States. Some experts have said that if Yao has a successful NBA career, he could become the best-known athlete in the world.

Yao's popularity has already earned him several high-profile endorsement deals. He appeared in television commercials for Visa credit cards and Apple laptop computers, for example, and in a print advertisement for the Got Milk? campaign. In addition, Yao's endorsement opportunities are expected to increase as his English language skills improve. Although he knows enough basketball terms to understand his teammates and converse with them on the court, he still uses an interpreter when speaking with the media. "He is a really bright guy, and he understands a lot," said his translator, Colin Pine. "But he is not fluent by any means. Imagine if you were dropped into China and had three months to learn the language. Do you think you'd be ready to conduct a press conference?" "I still don't understand a lot of things," Yao admitted. "If I did, you would have been fired a while ago," he joked with his translator.

Yao, who has gained such nicknames as "The Little Giant" and "The Great Wall," understands that he represents China in the minds of many basketball fans. "I'm not the only thing that is exciting about China," he noted. "There are a lot of things about China that are exciting. I'm just doing what I always do and doing what I think I should do. I don't think it's a burden. But if people can learn something from that, that's great."

Although he earns millions of dollars and is recognized by fans around the world, Yao claims that he still plays basketball for the love of the game. "Every sound in the gym is so fantastic," he stated. "The screams of the fans, the whistle of the ref, the teammates calling to each other, the sounds of the ball touching the wooden floor, the sneakers touching the floor, and the sounds of the fight, the muscle and the sweat. Oh, and the last one—when the ball goes through the net. Don't laugh at my sensitivity and romanticism, those sounds really attract me."

HOME AND FAMILY

During the NBA season, Yao lives in a four-bedroom house in the Houston suburbs. He shares his home with his interpreter, Colin Pine, and his mother, who stayed in the United States to help ease his adjustment during his rookie year. "I want to give him support," she explained. "I want to be able to provide a place where·he can feel at home, so that when he has worries outside, when he comes back, he has something to rely on. I think a good mother and a good father can do that. I worry about him. I see the pressure." Yao appreciates his parents' support, and especially his mother's home cooking. "The fact that my parents are here has made my adjustment to American life much easier," he acknowledged, "although really there hasn't been anything that difficult to get adjusted to."

Yao is not married, but he does have a long-distance girlfriend, Ye Li. She is a six-foot, three-inch basketball player for the Chinese Women's National Team. Yao always wears a red string bracelet that he received as a gift from her.

"Every sound in the gym is so fantastic," said Yao. "The screams of the fans, the whistle of the ref, the teammates calling to each other, the sounds of the ball touching the wooden floor, the sneakers touching the floor, and the sounds of the fight, the muscle and the sweat. Oh, and the last one—when the ball goes through the net. Don't laugh at my sensitivity and romanticism, those sounds really attract me."

HOBBIES AND OTHER INTERESTS

In his spare time, Yao enjoys playing computer games and fishing. "I like to fish," he said. "But the fish don't pay attention to me." Yao also likes studying Chinese history, especially stories about the ancient leader Zhu Ge-Liang, who was known for his brilliant strategy.

HONORS AND AWARDS

Sportsmanship Award (Chinese Basketball Association): 1997
Most Valuable Player (Chinese Basketball Association): 2000
Chinese Basketball Association Championship: 2001, with Shanghai Sharks
Next Athlete (*ESPN The Magazine*): 2001
Most Valuable Player (Asian Basketball Championship for Men): 2001
First Overall Selection in the NBA Draft: 2002, by Houston Rockets
NBA All-Star Game: 2002-03 (starting center, Western Conference)

FURTHER READING

Periodicals

Boston Globe, Jan. 16, 1999, p.A1; Jan. 13, 2003, p.D1
ESPN The Magazine, Feb. 17, 2003, p.43
Houston Chronicle, Oct. 15, 2002, Sports sec., p.9; Oct. 20, 2002, Sports sec.,
   p.1; Dec. 25, 2002, Sports sec., p.1
Los Angeles Times, Nov. 17, 2002, Sports sec., p.1
New York Times, Apr. 25, 2002, p.A1; Nov. 2, 2002, p.D1; Dec. 15, 2002,
   Sports sec., p.1; Jan. 18, 2003, p.D1; Feb. 8, 2003, p.D4
Newsday, Feb. 9, 2003, p.B14
Newsweek International, Apr. 10, 2000, p.69; Apr. 30, 2001, p.12
Sporting News, Sep. 9, 2002, p.54; Jan. 20, 2003, p.6
Sports Illustrated, Sep. 11, 2000, p.148; May 13, 2002, p.86; Oct. 28, 2002,
   p.66; Jan. 27, 2003, p.58
Sports Illustrated for Kids, May 2003, p.25
Time, Feb. 10, 2003, p.68
USA Today, Oct. 29, 2002, p.A1
Wall Street Journal, Feb. 11, 1999, p.A24
Washington Post, Dec. 13, 2002, p.A1

Online Articles

http://espn.go.com/magazine/vol3no26ming.html
   (*ESPN The Magazine,* "Next Athlete: Yao Ming," Dec. 25, 2000)
http://www.chinatoday.com.cn/English/e20029/yao.htm
   (*China Today,* "Yao Ming: The Chinese NBA Player," Sep. 2002)

ADDRESS

Yao Ming
Houston Rockets
Compaq Center
10 Greenway Plaza East
Houston, TX 77046

WORLD WIDE WEB SITES

http://www.yaoming.net
http://www.nba.com/

Photo and Illustration Credits

Yolanda Adams/Photos: Marc Baptiste; AP/Wide World Photos; copyright © Reuters NewMedia Inc./CORBIS. CD covers: *Believe* copyright © 2001 Elektra Entertainment Group Inc.; *More Than a Melody* (p) & © 1997 Zomba Recording Corporation; *Mountain High . . . Valley Low* copyright ℗ 1999 Elektra Entertainment Group Inc; *Through the Storm* (p) & © 1997 Zomba Recording Corporation.

Mildred Benson/Photos: The *Blade*/Diane Hires; The *Blade*; Book cover from THE SECRET OF THE OLD CLOCK by Carolyn Keene (NANCY DREW MYSTERY SERIES ®). NANCY DREW and all related characters and images are copyright and registered trademarks of Simon & Schuster, Inc. All rights reserved. The classic hardcover editions of these Nancy Drew titles are available from Grosset & Dunlap, an imprint of Penguin Books for Young Readers.; The *Blade*; © ABC Photo Archives; The *Blade*.

Alexis Bledel/Photos: copyright © The WB/Lance Staedler; copyright © The WB/Mitchell Haddad; copyright © The WB/Andrew Eccles; Ron Phillips/ copyright © Disney Enterprises, Inc. All rights reserved; copyright © Disney Enterprises, Inc. All rights reserved.

Barry Bonds/Photos: AP/Wide World Photos; S.F. Giants; Otto Greule, Jr./ Getty Images; Al Bello/Getty Images; AP/Wide World Photos; Jed Jacobsohn/Getty Images; Donald Miralle/Getty Images; Brian Bahr/Getty Images.

Vincent Brooks/Photos: AP/Wide World Photos. Front Cover: copyright © Tim Aubry/Reuters/Landov.

Laura Bush/Photos: George Bush Presidential Library; Greg Mathieson/ MAI/TIMEPIX; White House/TIMEPIX; AP/Wide World Photos. Front Cover: Alex Wong/Getty Images.

Amanda Bynes/Photos: copyright © The WB/James Sorenson; Stephen Osman/Los Angeles Times/Retna; copyright © The WB/Ron Batzdorff; Kevin Winter/Getty Images; What a Girl Wants copyright © 2003 Warner Brothers; DVD cover: courtesy of Universal Studios Home Video.

Kelly Clarkson/Photos: Kevin Winter/FOX; Ray Mickshaw/FOX; Jim Ruymen/Reuters/TIMEPIX. CD covers: RCA Records. Logo: FOX.

Vin Diesel/Photos: AP/Wide World Photos; Bob Marshak/2001 Universal Studios; courtesy Columbia TriStar Home Entertainment; copyright © 2000 New Line Productions, Inc. Courtesy New Line Home Entertainment. DVD covers: *The Fast and the Furious* courtesy Universal Studios Home Video; *Saving Private Ryan* TM & © 1999 DreamWorks LLC and Paramount Pictures and Ambin Entertainment; *The Iron Giant* program content, artwork and photography copyright © 1999. Courtesy Warner Home Video.

Eminem/Photos: AP/Wide World Photos; Eli Reed; AP/Wide World Photos. CD covers: *The Eminem Show* (p) © 2002 Aftermath Records; *The Marshall Mathers LP* (p) © 2000 Aftermath Entertainment/Interscope Records; *The Slim Shady LP* copyright © 1999 Aftermath Entertainment/Interscope Records.

Michele Forman/Photo: AP/WideWorld Photos.

Vicente Fox/Photos: copyright © Reuters NewMedia Inc./CORBIS; AP/Wide World Photos. Cover: copyright © AFP/CORBIS.

Millard Fuller/Photos: Kim MacDonald/Habitat for Humanity International; Robert Baker/Habitat for Humanity International; AP/Wide World Photos; Kim MacDonald/Habitat for Humanity International.

Josh Hartnett/Photos: Ethan Miller/Reuters; Rico Torres; Newscom.com; AP/Wide World Photos; Black Hawk Down © Columbia TriStar Marketing Group, Inc. All rights reserved; Sidney Baldwin; AP/Wide World Photos.

Dolores Huerta/Photos: Walter P. Reuther Library, Wayne State University; Arthur Schatz/Time Life Pictures/Getty Images; Walter P. Reuther Library, Wayne State University; AP/Wide World Photos.

Sarah Hughes/Photos: AP/Wide World Photos; Ezra Shaw/Getty Images; Clive Brunskill/Getty Images; AP/Wide World Photos; Doug Pensinger/Getty Images.

Enrique Iglesias/Photos: Andrea Comas/Reuters/TIMEPIX; copyright © Bettmann/CORBIS; AP/Wide World Photos. CD covers: *Enrique* copyright © 1999 Interscope Records; *Escape* copyright © 2001 Interscope Records.

Jeanette Lee/Photos: Layne Kennedy/TIMEPIX; AP/Wide World Photos; George De Sota/Getty Images;.

John Lewis/Photos: AP/Wide World Photos; copyright © Bettmann/ CORBIS; copyright © Spider Martin Collection (page 142); AP/Wide World

Photos; copyright © Bettmann/CORBIS; copyright © Flip Schulke/COR-BIS; Dirck Halstead/TIMEPIX

Nicklas Lidstrom/Photos: AP/Wide World Photos; Elsa Hasch/Getty Images; AP/Wide World Photos; Elsa Hasch/Getty Images/NHLI. Front Cover: AP/Wide World Photos.

Clint Mathis/Photos: Steve Smith/2002; Aubrey Washington/Getty Images; Stephen Dunn/Getty Images; Steve Smith/2002; copyright © Duomo/CORBIS; AP/Wide World Photos; Michael Stahlschmidt/SSI/TIMEPIX; Jeff Gross/Getty Images.

Donovan McNabb/Photos: Ezra Shaw/Getty Images; Rick Stewart/Getty Images; Ezra Shaw/Getty Images; AP/Wide World Photos.

Nelly/Photos: AP/Wide World Photos; copyright © Paul Smith/Feature flash/Retna; Frank Micelotta/Getty Images; Kevin Winter/Getty Images; copyright © Thorsten Buhe/Vanit/Retna. CD covers: *Country Grammar* (p) © 2000 Universal Records, a division of UMG Recordings, Inc.; *Nellyville* (p) © 2002 Universal Records, a division of UMG Recordings, Inc.

Andy Roddick/Photos: Andrew Wallace/Reuters/TIMEPIX; Eric Gaillard/Reuters/TIMEPIX; Clive Brunskill/Getty Images; Jeff Gross/Getty Images.

Gwen Stefani/Photos: Donald Miralle/Getty Images; copyright © Los Angeles Times/Retna; copyright © Tara Canova/Retna; AP/Wide World Photos; Newscom.com. CD covers: *Rock Steady* (p) © 2001 Interscope Records; *Tragic Kingdom* © 1995 Interscope Records.

Emma Watson/Photos: Lawrence Lucier/Getty Images; Peter Mountain; copyright © Reuters NewMedia Inc./CORBIS; © 2002 Warner Brothers.

Margaret Whitman/Photos: AP/Wide World Photos; Newscom.com.

Reese Witherspoon/Photos: copyright © Rufus F. Folkks/CORBIS; Ralph Nelson/New Line Cinema; copyright © CORBIS Sygma; copyright © 2001 Metro-Golden-Mayer Pictures, Inc.; Timothy White. DVD cover: copyright © 1991 Metro-Golden-Mayer Studios Inc. Front Cover: Sam Emerson.

Yao Ming/Photos: Peter Jones/Reuters/Landov; AP/Wide World Photos; Alex Livesey/Getty Images; AP/Wide World Photos.

How to Use the Cumulative Index

Our indexes have a new look. In an effort to make our indexes easier to use, we've combined the Name and General Index into a new, Cumulative Index. This single ready-reference resource covers all the volumes in *Biography Today*, both the general series and the special subject series. The new Cumulative Index contains complete listings of all individuals who have appeared in *Biography Today* since the series began. Their names appear in bold-faced type, followed by the issue in which they appear. The Cumulative Index also includes references for the occupations, nationalities, and ethnic and minority origins of individuals profiled in *Biography Today*.

We have also made some changes to our specialty indexes, the Places of Birth Index and the Birthday Index. To consolidate and to save space, the Places of Birth Index and the Birthday Index will no longer appear in the January and April issues of the softbound subscription series. But these indexes can still be found in the September issue of the softbound subscription series, in the hardbound Annual Cumulation at the end of each year, and in each volume of the special subject series.

General Series

The General Series of *Biography Today* is denoted in the index with the month and year of the issue in which the individual appeared. Each individual also appears in the Annual Cumulation for that year.

Special Subject Series

The Special Subject Series of *Biography Today* are each denoted in the index with an abbreviated form of the series name, plus the number of the volume in which the individual appears. They are listed as follows.

Adams, Ansel	Artist V.1	(Artists)
GrandPré, Mary	Author V.14	(Authors)
Jackson, Peter	PerfArt V.2	(Performing Artists)
Kapell, Dave	Science V.8	(Scientists & Inventors)
Milbrett, Tiffeny	Sport V.10	(Sports)
Peterson, Roger Tory	WorLdr V.1	(World Leaders: Environmental Leaders)
Sadat, Anwar	WorLdr V.2	(World Leaders: Modern African Leaders)
Wolf, Hazel.	WorLdr V.3	(World Leaders: Environmental Leaders 2)

Updates

Updated information on selected individuals appears in the Appendix at the end of some issues of the *Biography Today* Annual Cumulation. In the index, the original entry is listed first, followed by any updates.

Arafat, Yasir . . . . Sep 94; Update 94;
  Update 95; Update 96; Update 97; Update 98;
  Update 00; Update 01; Update 02

Gates, Bill . . . . Apr 93; Update 98;
  Update 00; Science V.5; Update 01

Griffith Joyner, Florence. . . . . Sport V.1;
  Update 98

Sanders, Barry . . . . Sep 95; Update 99

Spock, Dr. Benjamin . . . . Sep 95; Update 98

Yeltsin, Boris . . . . Apr 92; Update 93;
  Update 95; Update 96; Update 98; Update 00

Cumulative Index

This cumulative index includes names, occupations, nationalities, and ethnic and minority origins that pertain to all individuals profiled in *Biography Today* since the debut of the series in 1992.

491

Places of Birth Index

The following index lists the places of birth for the individuals profiled in *Biography Today*. Places of birth are entered under state, province, and/or country.

George, Jean Craighead . . . . Author V.3
Gore, Al . . . . Jan 93
Jackson, Shirley Ann . . . . Science V.2
Nye, Bill . . . . Science V.2
Pinkney, Andrea Davis . . . . Author V.10
Sampras, Pete . . . . Jan 97
Vasan, Nina . . . . Science V.7
Watterson, Bill . . . . Jan 92

Washington State

Card, Orson Scott – *Richland* . . Author V.14
Cobain, Kurt – *Aberdeen* . . . . Sep 94
Devers, Gail – *Seattle* . . . . Sport V.2
Elway, John – *Port Angeles* . . . . . . Sport V.2
Gates, Bill – *Seattle* . . . . Apr 93; Science V.5
Jones, Chuck – *Spokane* . . . . Author V.12
Larson, Gary – *Tacoma* . . . . Author V.1
Murie, Margaret – *Seattle* . . . . . WorLdr V.1
Ohno, Apolo – *Seattle* . . . . Sport V.8
Stockton, John – *Spokane* . . . . Sport V.3

West Virginia

Gates, Henry Louis, Jr. – *Keyser* . . . . Apr 00
Moss, Randy – *Rand* . . . . Sport V.4
Myers, Walter Dean
  – *Martinsburg* . . . . Jan 93
Nash, John Forbes, Jr.
  – *Bluefield* . . . . Science V.7

Wisconsin

Bardeen, John – *Madison* . . . . . . Science V.1
Cray, Seymour – *Chippewa Falls* . Science V.2
Driscoll, Jean – *Milwaukee* . . . . Sep 97
Henry, Marguerite – *Milwaukee* Author V.4
Jansen, Dan – *Milwaukee* . . . . Apr 94
Nelson, Gaylord – *Clear Lake* . . WorLdr V.3
O'Keeffe, Georgia – *Sun Prairie* . . Artist V.1
Wilder, Laura Ingalls – *Pepin* . . . Author V.3
Wright, Frank Lloyd
  – *Richland Center* . . . . Artist V.1

Wyoming

MacLachlan, Patricia
  – *Cheyenne* . . . . Author V.2

Yugoslavia

Filipovic, Zlata – *Sarajevo,
  Bosnia-Herzogovina* . . . . Sep 94
Milosevic, Slobodan – *Pozarevac,
  Serbia* . . . . Sep 99
Seles, Monica – *Novi Sad, Serbia* . . . . Jan 96

Zaire

Mobutu Sese Seko – *Lisala* . . . . WorLdr V.2

Zambia

Kaunda, Kenneth – *Lubwa* . . . . WorLdr V.2

Zimbabwe

Mugabe, Robert – *Kutama* . . . . . WorLdr V.2

Birthday Index

543

Biography Today

For ages 9 and above

General Series

B iography Today **General Series** includes a unique combination of current biographical profiles that teachers and librarians — and the readers themselves — tell us are most appealing. The **General Series** is available as a 3-issue subscription; hardcover annual cumulation; or subscription plus cumulation.

Within the **General Series**, your readers will find a variety of sketches about:

- Authors
- Musicians
- Political leaders
- Sports figures
- Movie actresses & actors
- Cartoonists
- Scientists
- Astronauts
- TV personalities
- and the movers & shakers in many other fields!

"Biography Today will be useful in elementary and middle school libraries and in public library children's collections where there is a need for biographies of current personalities. High schools serving reluctant readers may also want to consider a subscription."
— *Booklist,* American Library Association

"Highly recommended for the young adult audience. Readers will delight in the accessible, energetic, tell-all style; teachers, librarians, and parents will welcome the clever format, intelligent and informative text. It should prove especially useful in motivating 'reluctant' readers or literate nonreaders."
— *MultiCultural Review*

"Written in a friendly, almost chatty tone, the profiles offer quick, objective information. While coverage of current figures makes Biography Today a useful reference tool, an appealing format and wide scope make it a fun resource to browse." — *School Library Journal*

"The best source for current information at a level kids can understand."
— Kelly Bryant, School Librarian, Carlton, OR

"Easy for kids to read. We love it! Don't want to be without it."
— Lynn McWhirter, School Librarian, Rockford, IL

ONE-YEAR SUBSCRIPTION

- 3 softcover issues, 6" x 9"
- Published in January, April, and September
- 1-year subscription, $60
- 150 pages per issue
- 10 profiles per issue
- Contact sources for additional information
- Cumulative General, Places of Birth, and Birthday Indexes

HARDBOUND ANNUAL CUMULATION

- Sturdy 6" x 9" hardbound volume
- Published in December
- $62 per volume
- 450 pages per volume
- 25-30 profiles — includes all profiles found in softcover issues for that calendar year
- Cumulative General, Places of Birth, and Birthday Indexes
- Special appendix features current updates of previous profiles

SUBSCRIPTION AND CUMULATION COMBINATION

- $99 for 3 softcover issues plus the hardbound volume

1992

Paula Abdul
Andre Agassi
Kirstie Alley
Terry Anderson
Roseanne Arnold
Isaac Asimov
James Baker
Charles Barkley
Larry Bird
Judy Blume
Berke Breathed
Garth Brooks
Barbara Bush
George Bush
Fidel Castro
Bill Clinton
Bill Cosby
Diana, Princess of Wales
Shannen Doherty
Elizabeth Dole
David Duke
Gloria Estefan
Mikhail Gorbachev
Steffi Graf
Wayne Gretzky
Matt Groening
Alex Haley
Hammer
Martin Handford
Stephen Hawking
Hulk Hogan
Saddam Hussein
Lee Iacocca
Bo Jackson
Mae Jemison
Peter Jennings
Steven Jobs
Pope John Paul II
Magic Johnson
Michael Jordan
Jackie Joyner-Kersee
Spike Lee
Mario Lemieux
Madeleine L'Engle
Jay Leno
Yo-Yo Ma
Nelson Mandela
Wynton Marsalis
Thurgood Marshall
Ann Martin
Barbara McClintock
Emily Arnold McCully
Antonia Novello

Sandra Day O'Connor
Rosa Parks
Jane Pauley
H. Ross Perot
Luke Perry
Scottie Pippen
Colin Powell
Jason Priestley
Queen Latifah
Yitzhak Rabin
Sally Ride
Pete Rose
Nolan Ryan
H. Norman
   Schwarzkopf
Jerry Seinfeld
Dr. Seuss
Gloria Steinem
Clarence Thomas
Chris Van Allsburg
Cynthia Voigt
Bill Watterson
Robin Williams
Oprah Winfrey
Kristi Yamaguchi
Boris Yeltsin

1993

Maya Angelou
Arthur Ashe
Avi
Kathleen Battle
Candice Bergen
Boutros Boutros-Ghali
Chris Burke
Dana Carvey
Cesar Chavez
Henry Cisneros
Hillary Rodham Clinton
Jacques Cousteau
Cindy Crawford
Macaulay Culkin
Lois Duncan
Marian Wright Edelman
Cecil Fielder
Bill Gates
Sara Gilbert
Dizzy Gillespie
Al Gore
Cathy Guisewite
Jasmine Guy
Anita Hill
Ice-T
Darci Kistler

k.d. lang
Dan Marino
Rigoberta Menchu
Walter Dean Myers
Martina Navratilova
Phyllis Reynolds Naylor
Rudolf Nureyev
Shaquille O'Neal
Janet Reno
Jerry Rice
Mary Robinson
Winona Ryder
Jerry Spinelli
Denzel Washington
Keenen Ivory Wayans
Dave Winfield

1994

Tim Allen
Marian Anderson
Mario Andretti
Ned Andrews
Yasir Arafat
Bruce Babbitt
Mayim Bialik
Bonnie Blair
Ed Bradley
John Candy
Mary Chapin Carpenter
Benjamin Chavis
Connie Chung
Beverly Cleary
Kurt Cobain
F.W. de Klerk
Rita Dove
Linda Ellerbee
Sergei Fedorov
Zlata Filipovic
Daisy Fuentes
Ruth Bader Ginsburg
Whoopi Goldberg
Tonya Harding
Melissa Joan Hart
Geoff Hooper
Whitney Houston
Dan Jansen
Nancy Kerrigan
Alexi Lalas
Charlotte Lopez
Wilma Mankiller
Shannon Miller
Toni Morrison
Richard Nixon
Greg Norman
Severo Ochoa

River Phoenix
Elizabeth Pine
Jonas Salk
Richard Scarry
Emmitt Smith
Will Smith
Steven Spielberg
Patrick Stewart
R.L. Stine
Lewis Thomas
Barbara Walters
Charlie Ward
Steve Young
Kim Zmeskal

1995

Troy Aikman
Jean-Bertrand Aristide
Oksana Baiul
Halle Berry
Benazir Bhutto
Jonathan Brandis
Warren E. Burger
Ken Burns
Candace Cameron
Jimmy Carter
Agnes de Mille
Placido Domingo
Janet Evans
Patrick Ewing
Newt Gingrich
John Goodman
Amy Grant
Jesse Jackson
James Earl Jones
Julie Krone
David Letterman
Rush Limbaugh
Heather Locklear
Reba McEntire
Joe Montana
Cosmas Ndeti
Hakeem Olajuwon
Ashley Olsen
Mary-Kate Olsen
Jennifer Parkinson
Linus Pauling
Itzhak Perlman
Cokie Roberts
Wilma Rudolph
Salt 'N' Pepa
Barry Sanders
William Shatner
Elizabeth George
   Speare

Dr. Benjamin Spock
Jonathan Taylor
  Thomas
Vicki Van Meter
Heather Whitestone
Pedro Zamora

1996

Aung San Suu Kyi
Boyz II Men
Brandy
Ron Brown
Mariah Carey
Jim Carrey
Larry Champagne III
Christo
Chelsea Clinton
Coolio
Bob Dole
David Duchovny
Debbi Fields
Chris Galeczka
Jerry Garcia
Jennie Garth
Wendy Guey
Tom Hanks
Alison Hargreaves
Sir Edmund Hillary
Judith Jamison
Barbara Jordan
Annie Leibovitz
Carl Lewis
Jim Lovell
Mickey Mantle
Lynn Margulis
Iqbal Masih
Mark Messier
Larisa Oleynik
Christopher Pike
David Robinson
Dennis Rodman
Selena
Monica Seles
Don Shula
Kerri Strug
Tiffani-Amber Thiessen
Dave Thomas
Jaleel White

1997

Madeleine Albright
Marcus Allen
Gillian Anderson
Rachel Blanchard
Zachery Ty Bryan
Adam Ezra Cohen
Claire Danes
Celine Dion
Jean Driscoll
Louis Farrakhan
Ella Fitzgerald
Harrison Ford
Bryant Gumbel
John Johnson
Michael Johnson
Maya Lin
George Lucas
John Madden
Bill Monroe
Alanis Morissette
Sam Morrison
Rosie O'Donnell
Muammar el-Qaddafi
Christopher Reeve
Pete Sampras
Pat Schroeder
Rebecca Sealfon
Tupac Shakur
Tabitha Soren
Herbert Tarvin
Merlin Tuttle
Mara Wilson

1998

Bella Abzug
Kofi Annan
Neve Campbell
Sean Combs (Puff
  Daddy)
Dalai Lama (Tenzin
  Gyatso)
Diana, Princess of Wales
Leonardo DiCaprio
Walter E. Diemer
Ruth Handler
Hanson
Livan Hernandez
Jewel
Jimmy Johnson
Tara Lipinski
Jody-Anne Maxwell
Dominique Moceanu
Alexandra Nechita

Brad Pitt
LeAnn Rimes
Emily Rosa
David Satcher
Betty Shabazz
Kordell Stewart
Shinichi Suzuki
Mother Teresa
Mike Vernon
Reggie White
Kate Winslet

1999

Ben Affleck
Jennifer Aniston
Maurice Ashley
Kobe Bryant
Bessie Delany
Sadie Delany
Sharon Draper
Sarah Michelle Gellar
John Glenn
Savion Glover
Jeff Gordon
David Hampton
Lauryn Hill
King Hussein
Lynn Johnston
Shari Lewis
Oseola McCarty
Mark McGwire
Slobodan Milosevic
Natalie Portman
J. K. Rowling
Frank Sinatra
Gene Siskel
Sammy Sosa
John Stanford
Natalia Toro
Shania Twain
Mitsuko Uchida
Jesse Ventura
Venus Williams

2000

Christina Aguilera
K.A. Applegate
Lance Armstrong
Backstreet Boys
Daisy Bates
Harry Blackmun
George W. Bush
Carson Daly
Ron Dayne
Henry Louis Gates, Jr.
Doris Haddock
  (Granny D)
Jennifer Love Hewitt
Chamique Holdsclaw
Katie Holmes
Charlayne Hunter-Gault
Johanna Johnson
Craig Kielburger
John Lasseter
Peyton Manning
Ricky Martin
John McCain
Walter Payton
Freddie Prinze, Jr.
Viviana Risca
Briana Scurry
George Thampy
CeCe Winans

2001

Jessica Alba
Christiane Amanpour
Drew Barrymore
Jeff Bezos
Destiny's Child
Dale Earnhardt
Carly Fiorina
Aretha Franklin
Cathy Freeman
Tony Hawk
Faith Hill
Kim Dae-jung
Madeleine L'Engle
Mariangela Lisanti
Frankie Muniz
*N Sync
Ellen Ochoa
Jeff Probst
Julia Roberts
Carl T. Rowan
Britney Spears
Chris Tucker
Lloyd D. Ward
Alan Webb
Chris Weinke

2002

Aaliyah
Osama bin Laden
Mary J. Blige
Aubyn Burnside
Aaron Carter
Julz Chavez
Dick Cheney
Hilary Duff
Billy Gilman
Rudolph Giuliani
Brian Griese
Jennifer Lopez
Dave Mirra
Dineh Mohajer
Leanne Nakamura
Daniel Radcliffe
Condoleezza Rice
Marla Runyan
Ruth Simmons
Mattie Stepanek
J.R.R. Tolkien
Barry Watson
Tyrone Willingham
Elijah Wood

2003

Yolanda Adams
Olivia Bennett
Mildred Benson
Alexis Bledel
Barry Bonds
Vincent Brooks
Laura Bush
Amanda Bynes
Kelly Clarkson
Vin Diesel
Eminem
Michele Forman
Vicente Fox
Millard Fuller
Josh Hartnett
Dolores Huerta
Sarah Hughes
Enrique Iglesias
Jeanette Lee
John Lewis
Nicklas Lidstrom
Clint Mathis
Donovan McNabb
Nelly
Andy Roddick
Gwen Stefani
Emma Watson
Meg Whitman
Reese Witherspoon
Yao Ming

Biography Today

For ages 9 and above

Subject Series

Expands and complements the General Series and targets specific subject areas . . .

Our readers asked for it! They wanted more biographies, and the *Biography Today* **Subject Series** is our response to that demand. Now your readers can choose their special areas of interest and go on to read about their favorites in those fields. Priced at just $39 per volume, the following specific volumes are included in the *Biography Today* **Subject Series**:

- **Artists**
- **Authors**
- **Performing Artists**
- **Scientists & Inventors**
- **Sports**
- **World Leaders**
  Environmental Leaders
  Modern African Leaders

AUTHORS

"A useful tool for children's assignment needs." — *School Library Journal*

"The prose is workmanlike: report writers will find enough detail to begin sound investigations, and browsers are likely to find someone of interest." — *School Library Journal*

SCIENTISTS & INVENTORS

"The articles are readable, attractively laid out, and touch on important points that will suit assignment needs. Browsers will note the clear writing and interesting details." — *School Library Journal*

"The book is excellent for demonstrating that scientists are real people with widely diverse backgrounds and personal interests. The biographies are fascinating to read." — *The Science Teacher*

SPORTS

"This series should become a standard resource in libraries that serve intermediate students." — *School Library Journal*

ENVIRONMENTAL LEADERS #1

"A tremendous book that fills a gap in the biographical category of books. This is a great reference book." — *Science Scope*

FEATURES AND FORMAT

- Sturdy 6" x 9" hardbound volumes
- Individual volumes, $39 each
- 200 pages per volume
- 10 profiles per volume — targets individuals within a specific subject area
- Contact sources for additional information
- Cumulative General, Places of Birth, and Birthday Indexes

NOTE: There is *no duplication of entries* between the **General Series** of *Biography Today* and the **Subject Series.**

Artists

VOLUME 1

Ansel Adams
Romare Bearden
Margaret Bourke-White
Alexander Calder
Marc Chagall
Helen Frankenthaler
Jasper Johns
Jacob Lawrence
Henry Moore
Grandma Moses
Louise Nevelson
Georgia O'Keeffe
Gordon Parks
I.M. Pei
Diego Rivera
Norman Rockwell
Andy Warhol
Frank Lloyd Wright

Authors

VOLUME 1

Eric Carle
Alice Childress
Robert Cormier
Roald Dahl
Jim Davis
John Grisham
Virginia Hamilton
James Herriot
S.E. Hinton
M.E. Kerr
Stephen King
Gary Larson
Joan Lowery Nixon
Gary Paulsen
Cynthia Rylant
Mildred D. Taylor
Kurt Vonnegut, Jr.
E.B. White
Paul Zindel

VOLUME 2

James Baldwin
Stan and Jan Berenstain
David Macaulay
Patricia MacLachlan
Scott O'Dell
Jerry Pinkney
Jack Prelutsky

Lynn Reid Banks
Faith Ringgold
J.D. Salinger
Charles Schulz
Maurice Sendak
P.L. Travers
Garth Williams

VOLUME 3

Candy Dawson Boyd
Ray Bradbury
Gwendolyn Brooks
Ralph W. Ellison
Louise Fitzhugh
Jean Craighead George
E.L. Konigsburg
C.S. Lewis
Fredrick L. McKissack
Patricia C. McKissack
Katherine Paterson
Anne Rice
Shel Silverstein
Laura Ingalls Wilder

VOLUME 4

Betsy Byars
Chris Carter
Caroline B. Cooney
Christopher Paul Curtis
Anne Frank
Robert Heinlein
Marguerite Henry
Lois Lowry
Melissa Mathison
Bill Peet
August Wilson

VOLUME 5

Sharon Creech
Michael Crichton
Karen Cushman
Tomie dePaola
Lorraine Hansberry
Karen Hesse
Brian Jacques
Gary Soto
Richard Wright
Laurence Yep

VOLUME 6

Lloyd Alexander
Paula Danziger
Nancy Farmer
Zora Neale Hurston

Shirley Jackson
Angela Johnson
Jon Krakauer
Leo Lionni
Francine Pascal
Louis Sachar
Kevin Williamson

VOLUME 7

William H. Armstrong
Patricia Reilly Giff
Langston Hughes
Stan Lee
Julius Lester
Robert Pinsky
Todd Strasser
Jacqueline Woodson
Patricia C. Wrede
Jane Yolen

VOLUME 8

Amelia Atwater-Rhodes
Barbara Cooney
Paul Laurence Dunbar
Ursula K. Le Guin
Farley Mowat
Naomi Shihab Nye
Daniel Pinkwater
Beatrix Potter
Ann Rinaldi

VOLUME 9

Robb Armstrong
Cherie Bennett
Bruce Coville
Rosa Guy
Harper Lee
Irene Gut Opdyke
Philip Pullman
Jon Scieszka
Amy Tan
Joss Whedon

VOLUME 10

David Almond
Joan Bauer
Kate DiCamillo
Jack Gantos
Aaron McGruder
Richard Peck
Andrea Davis Pinkney
Louise Rennison
David Small
Katie Tarbox

VOLUME 11

Laurie Halse Anderson
Bryan Collier
Margaret Peterson
  Haddix
Milton Meltzer
William Sleator
Sonya Sones
Genndy Tartakovsky
Wendelin Van Draanen
Ruth White

VOLUME 12

An Na
Claude Brown
Meg Cabot
Virginia Hamilton
Chuck Jones
Robert Lipsyte
Lillian Morrison
Linda Sue Park
Pam Muñoz Ryan
Lemony Snicket
  (Daniel Handler)

VOLUME 13

Andrew Clements
Eoin Colfer
Sharon Flake
Edward Gorey
Francisco Jiménez
Astrid Lindgren
Chris Lynch
Marilyn Nelson
Tamora Pierce
Virginia Euwer Wolff

VOLUME 14

Orson Scott Card
Russell Freedman
Mary GrandPré
Dan Greenburg
Nikki Grimes
Laura Hillenbrand
Stephen Hillenburg
Norton Juster
Lurlene McDaniel
Stephanie S. Tolan

Performing Artists

VOLUME 1

Jackie Chan
Dixie Chicks
Kirsten Dunst
Suzanne Farrell
Bernie Mac
Shakira
Isaac Stern
Julie Taymor
Usher
Christina Vidal

VOLUME 2

Ashanti
Tyra Banks
Peter Jackson
Norah Jones
Quincy Jones
Avril Lavigne
George López
Marcel Marceau
Eddie Murphy
Julia Stiles

Scientists & Inventors

VOLUME 1

John Bardeen
Sylvia Earle
Dian Fossey
Jane Goodall
Bernadine Healy
Jack Horner
Mathilde Krim
Edwin Land
Louise & Mary Leakey
Rita Levi-Montalcini
J. Robert Oppenheimer
Albert Sabin
Carl Sagan
James D. Watson

VOLUME 2

Jane Brody
Seymour Cray
Paul Erdös
Walter Gilbert
Stephen Jay Gould
Shirley Ann Jackson
Raymond Kurzweil
Shannon Lucid
Margaret Mead
Garrett Morgan
Bill Nye
Eloy Rodriguez
An Wang

VOLUME 3

Luis W. Alvarez
Hans A. Bethe
Gro Harlem Brundtland
Mary S. Calderone
Ioana Dumitriu
Temple Grandin
John Langston
  Gwaltney
Bernard Harris
Jerome Lemelson
Susan Love
Ruth Patrick
Oliver Sacks
Richie Stachowski

VOLUME 4

David Attenborough
Robert Ballard
Ben Carson
Eileen Collins
Biruté Galdikas
Lonnie Johnson
Meg Lowman
Forrest Mars Sr.
Akio Morita
Janese Swanson

VOLUME 5

Steve Case
Douglas Engelbart
Shawn Fanning
Sarah Flannery
Bill Gates
Laura Groppe
Grace Murray Hopper
Steven Jobs
Rand and Robyn Miller
Shigeru Miyamoto
Steve Wozniak

VOLUME 6

Hazel Barton
Alexa Canady
Arthur Caplan
Francis Collins
Gertrude Elion
Henry Heimlich
David Ho
Kenneth Kamler
Lucy Spelman
Lydia Villa-Komaroff

VOLUME 7

Tim Berners-Lee
France Córdova
Anthony S. Fauci
Sue Hendrickson
Steve Irwin
John Forbes Nash, Jr.
Jerri Nielsen
Ryan Patterson
Nina Vasan
Gloria WilderBrathwaite

VOLUME 8

Deborah Blum
Richard Carmona
Helene Gayle
Dave Kapell
Adriana C. Ocampo
John Romero
Jamie Rubin
Jill Tarter
Earl Warrick
Edward O. Wilson

Sports

VOLUME 1

Hank Aaron
Kareem Abdul-Jabbar
Hassiba Boulmerka
Susan Butcher
Beth Daniel
Chris Evert
Ken Griffey, Jr.
Florence Griffith Joyner
Grant Hill
Greg LeMond
Pelé
Uta Pippig
Cal Ripken, Jr.
Arantxa Sanchez Vicario
Deion Sanders
Tiger Woods

VOLUME 2

Muhammad Ali
Donovan Bailey
Gail Devers
John Elway
Brett Favre
Mia Hamm
Anfernee "Penny"
  Hardaway
Martina Hingis
Gordie Howe
Jack Nicklaus
Richard Petty
Dot Richardson
Sheryl Swoopes
Steve Yzerman

VOLUME 3

Joe Dumars
Jim Harbaugh
Dominik Hasek
Michelle Kwan
Rebecca Lobo
Greg Maddux
Fatuma Roba
Jackie Robinson
John Stockton
Picabo Street
Pat Summitt
Amy Van Dyken

VOLUME 4

Wilt Chamberlain
Brandi Chastain
Derek Jeter
Karch Kiraly
Alex Lowe
Randy Moss
Se Ri Pak
Dawn Riley
Karen Smyers
Kurt Warner
Serena Williams

VOLUME 5

Vince Carter
Lindsay Davenport
Lisa Fernandez
Fu Mingxia
Jaromir Jagr
Marion Jones
Pedro Martinez
Warren Sapp
Jenny Thompson
Karrie Webb

VOLUME 6

Jennifer Capriati
Stacy Dragila
Kevin Garnett
Eddie George
Alex Rodriguez
Joe Sakic
Annika Sorenstam
Jackie Stiles
Tiger Woods
Aliy Zirkle

VOLUME 7

Tom Brady
Tara Dakides
Alison Dunlap
Sergio Garcia
Allen Iverson
Shirley Muldowney
Ty Murray
Patrick Roy
Tasha Schwiker

VOLUME 8

Simon Ammann
Shannon Bahrke
Kelly Clark
Vonetta Flowers
Cammi Granato
Chris Klug
Jonny Moseley
Apolo Ohno
Sylke Otto
Ryne Sanborn
Jim Shea, Jr.

VOLUME 9

Tori Allen
Layne Beachley
Sue Bird
Fabiola da Silva
Randy Johnson
Jason Kidd
Tony Stewart
Michael Vick
Ted Williams
Jay Yelas

VOLUME 10

Ryan Boyle
Natalie Coughlin
Allyson Felix
Dallas Friday
Jean-Sébastien Giguère
Phil Jackson
Keyshawn Johnson
Tiffeny Milbrett
Alfonso Soriano
Diana Taurasi

World Leaders

VOLUME 1: Environmental Leaders 1

Edward Abbey
Renee Askins
David Brower
Rachel Carson
Marjory Stoneman
  Douglas
Dave Foreman
Lois Gibbs
Wangari Maathai
Chico Mendes
Russell A. Mittermeier
Margaret and Olaus J.
  Murie
Patsy Ruth Oliver
Roger Tory Peterson
Ken Saro-Wiwa
Paul Watson
Adam Werbach

VOLUME 2: Modern African Leaders

Mohammed Farah
  Aidid
Idi Amin
Hastings Kamuzu Banda
Haile Selassie
Hassan II
Kenneth Kaunda
Jomo Kenyatta
Winnie Mandela
Mobutu Sese Seko
Robert Mugabe
Kwame Nkrumah
Julius Kambarage
  Nyerere
Anwar Sadat
Jonas Savimbi
Léopold Sédar Senghor
William V. S. Tubman

VOLUME 3: Environmental Leaders 2

John Cronin
Dai Qing
Ka Hsaw Wa
Winona LaDuke
Aldo Leopold
Bernard Martin
Cynthia Moss
John Muir
Gaylord Nelson
Douglas Tompkins
Hazel Wolf